The Mainst

The MAINSTAY

A Commentary on Qaṣīda al-Burda

Shaykh Aḥmad Ibn ʿAjība al-Ḥasanī

TRANSLATED BY

Abdul Aziz Suraqah

FOREWORD BY ABDAL HAKIM MURAD

ABU ZAHRA PRESS

Published by

ABU ZAHRA PRESS
DEVONSHIRE STREET
KEIGHLEY
WEST YORKSHIRE BD21 2BL

www.abuzahra.org

info@abuzahra.org

Managing Editor: Khalid Hussain
Proofreading: Rashid Hussain, Mohammed Majid
Cover Design and Typesetting: Abdallateef Whiteman
British Library Cataloguing in Publication Data available
Printed and bound by TJ International, Cornwall, UK.

ISBN 978-0-9928065-1-4

Contents

Abu Zahra Foundation is raising funds to fully refurbish a converted Victorian church built in 1890, which serves as a madrasa and zawiya in the town of Keighley, West Yorkshire, U.K. All the proceeds from the sale of this book will go to the refurbishment fund.

To donate and for further information, please visit www.abuzahra.org.

Foreword

IT IS AN honour to be able to introduce the first full English commentary on Islam's great poem, the *Burda*. As one would expect from a civilisation so passionate about its founder, Islam has historically produced a copious outpouring of panegyrics about the Best of Creation, accompanied by a no less prolific mass of commentaries. Many glosses to the *Burda* have achieved a just renown, but it is pleasing and appropriate that the first to appear in translation should be Ibn ʿAjība's *al-ʿUmda fī Sharḥ al-Burda* (The Mainstay: a Commentary on *Qaṣīda al-Burda*). As well as drawing on the long and distinguished line of its predecessors, the *ʿUmda* is redolent with a distinctively Muhammadan fragrance, deriving from the profound soul of this great North African whose discernment was applied to the most subtle aspects of the Qur'an, the Ḥikam of Ibn ʿAṭāʾ Allāh, the *Mabāḥith* of Ibn al-Bannā, and other spiritual monuments which, being products of the spirit rather than ordinary texts, can only disclose their depths to the eyes of true lovers. In our time of glittering but mean horizontality, when religion is in danger of being reduced to little more than a set of beliefs, practices and laws, it is urgently necessary to open the heart to this perspective, which, despite the centuries which separate us from its blessed author, reminds us that religion's foundation and focus rests squarely on self-knowledge, passion, and beauty.

ABDAL HAKIM MURAD
Muharram 1437 [October 2015 CE]

Preface

EVER SINCE ITS composition in the seventh Islamic century, by the poet, scholar and spiritual master Muhammad b. Saᶜīd al-Būṣīrī, *al-Kawākib al-durriyya fī madḥ Khayr al-Bariyya* ('The Celestial Lights in Praise of the Best of Creation'), more commonly known as the *Burda,* has been a mainstay of the Muslim choral tradition from East to West. It is the quintessence of devotional praise and expression of passionate love for the Prophet (Allah bless him and give peace), for both the expert and layman. It adorns architecture throughout the Muslim lands and also found a place on the walls of the Prophet's Mosque in Medina.

The tradition of panegyrics on the Prophet (Allah bless him and give him peace) has its roots in the Prophetic era; hence, to understand the power and beauty of the *Burda* of al-Būṣīrī, one must look to its predecessor, the *Burda* ode of the Companion Kaᶜb b. Zuhayr (Allah be pleased with him), also called *Bānat Suᶜād* ('Suᶜād has gone').

Kaᶜb's father, Zuhayr b. Abī Sulmā, was a revered poet of the Age of Ignorance (*Jāhiliyya*), whose poetry was included amongst the famous *Muᶜallaqāt* (Suspended Odes) hung upon the walls of the Kaᶜba in Mecca. Zuhayr passed away before the Prophet Muḥammad (Allah bless him and give him peace) was tasked with the divine message, but he left behind two sons, Bujayr and Kaᶜb.

Bujayr embraced Islam and supported the Prophet (Allah bless him and give him peace), but Kaᶜb remained a disbeliever. Having inherited much of his father's lyrical skill, Kaᶜb began to lampoon the Prophet (Allah bless him and give him peace) and use his poetry to instigate people to rise against him. Kaᶜb's brother Bujayr accompanied the Prophet (Allah bless him and give him peace) during the conquest of Mecca and the subsequent siege of Ṭā'if, and observed that he did not give a guarantee of safety to other poets who had lampooned him, slandered his wives and used their poetry to incite war against the nascent Muslim community. Bujayr wrote a letter to Kaʿb informing him of the situation and advised him to come to the Prophet (Allah bless him and give him peace) and express remorse for his invective poetry.

With the seed of faith in his heart, Kaʿb made his way to Medina to present himself before the Prophet (Allah bless him and give him peace) and seek forgiveness. He arrived shortly before dawn, as the Prophet (Allah bless him and give him peace) was about to lead the Fajr prayer, and so he offered his very first prayer behind him. After the prayer, Kaʿb approached the Prophet (Allah bless him and give him peace), sat down in front of him, placed his hands in the Prophet's hands and spoke about himself in the third person: 'Kaʿb b. Zuhayr has come as a Muslim and to repent and seek a guarantee of protection. Will you accept that from him if he comes to you?' The Prophet (Allah bless him and give him peace), ever ready to forgive those who transgressed against him, said, 'Yes.' Elated, Kaʿb said, 'I am Kaʿb b. Zuhayr!'

On the way to Medina, Kaʿb had composed an eloquent panegyric to read before the Prophet (Allah bless him and give him peace) as an expression of remorse over his past calumnies. So he stood and recited his poem, in the presence of the Prophet (Allah bless him and give him peace). Here is a translation of its opening lines:

Suʿād has departed, and as a result
my heart has grown sickly and weak today;
enslaved to her in her wake, and shackled
[as though in chains], with no [means of] escape.

Following traditional Arab poetic tradition, Kaʿb began his poem by soliloquising amid the traces of his beloved's camp and recalling her beauty. Later in his panegyric, speaking of his repentance for past slanders, he said:

I was told that Allah's Emissary had threatened me,
Though when in his presence one hopes for pardon.

As a conclusion to the poem he said:

Verily the Emissary of Allah is a light from whom illumination is sought,
An unsheathed Indian sabre, one of the swords of Allah.

Al-Ḥāfiẓ Ibn ʿAbd al-Barr says in *al-Istiʿāb* that when Kaʿb read the couplet above, the Prophet (Allah bless him and give him peace) signalled to his Companions to listen carefully to what Kaʿb had recited. Other narrations say that the Prophet (Allah bless him and give him peace) tossed him his *Burda*—his cloak. Later on, Muʿāwiya offered Kaʿb ten thousand dirhams for it, but Kaʿb replied, 'I shall not prefer anyone over the Emissary of Allah (Allah bless him and give him peace)!' When Kaʿb died, Muʿāwiya sent twenty thousand dirhams to Kaʿb's heirs and acquired the blessed *Burda* from them.

Some 650 years later, al-Būṣīrī too had the Prophet's blessed *Burda* wrapped around him, though in a miraculous dream. Many commentators on the *Burda*, including Shaykh Aḥmad Ibn 'Ajība in the introduction to this work, have mentioned that al-Būṣīrī was stricken with a debilitating sickness that paralysed one side of his body. One day some of his colleagues paid him a visit, and after he had complained of his incapacitating illness, one of them said, 'You are a scholar of Arabic and poetry. Why not compose an ode in praise of the Emissary of Allah (Allah bless him and give him peace) as a means of intercession through his exalted person?' Al-Būṣīrī asked his colleague, 'Do you think it will help cure my illness?' He replied, 'No one who draws near the exalted Prophet and beloved intercessor (Allah bless him and give him peace) is ever disappointed; and no one seeks his intercession without attaining what he seeks!'

That very night al-Būṣīrī composed his *Burda* ode, and after he went to sleep he saw in a dream the Prophet Muḥammad (Allah bless him and give him peace), who covered him in his mantle (*Burda*); and he was immediately cured of his ailment.

* * *

The earliest English translation of the Burda appears to be the one published in India in 1893 by Shaykh Faizullah-Bhái, entitled *The Poem of the Scarf*. More recent and notable translations include Shaykh Hamza Yusuf's *The Burda of al-Busiri: The Poem of the Cloak* (London: Sandala, 2002) and Shaykh Abdal Hakim Murad's *The Mantle Adorned: Imam Bûsîrî's Burda* (London: Quilliam Press, 2009).

Dozens of commentaries and glosses on the poem have been written, by such luminaries as Ibn Ḥajar al-Haytamī, ʿAlī al-Qārī, al-Bājūrī and

Shaykh-Zādah. This indicates its widespread acceptance within the mainstream Muslim scholarly tradition and unquestionably dispels the doubts that some have raised about the poem's content. While a plethora of material exists in Arabic, Urdu and Persian, no complete commentary on the *Burda* has hitherto been written in or translated into English.

People's hearts can be moved and stirred by poetry without their being able to understand the high Arabic of the poem. However, delving deeper into the meanings can really take one to the heart of the author; and a poem of this stature deserves to have its essence and interpretations explained to English readers. It was with this aim that Abu Zahra Press commissioned a translation of a commentary on this monument of Arabic literature.

Choosing an appropriate commentary on the *Burda* for translation must take into consideration the needs of the average English reader who desires to understand the background and essence of the ode and does not necessarily want to get bogged down in discussions on linguistic analysis and prosody and academic minutia, all of which are commonplace in most commentaries—including Shaykh Ibn ᶜAjība's *al-'Umda fi sharḥ al-Burda* ('The Mainstay: a Commentary on *Qaṣīda al-Burda*'). This is, however, perhaps the most suitable commentary to render into English, as it comprehensively explains the meanings of each couplet and gleans beneficial spiritual lessons from it. For every reference in the *Burda* to events in the Prophet's life, Shaykh Ibn ᶜAjība cites the primary texts that mention them and offers valuable details and enlightening clarifications of areas of possible confusion. It further offers the reader beautiful imagery and aesthetic refinement that perfectly complement al-Būṣīrī's ode.

For the above reasons, the translation presented here omits the sections discussing linguistics and declension (*iᶜrāb*). For *ḥadīth* referencing, I have relied upon Shaykh ᶜAbd Allāh al-Talīdī's critical edition of Shaykh Ibn ᶜAjība's commentary. Additional explanatory comments from myself have been marked with a lowercase (t), or from the publisher with a lowercase (p).

Finally, I would like to offer my deep appreciation to the Board of Abu Zahra Foundation for giving me the opportunity to work on this tremendous and edifying text. Many thanks also to the editor, who has asked for anonymity, for his outstanding editing and improvement upon the ode's translation. It is said that poetry is what gets lost in translation, but thanks to his careful eye and aesthetic taste, it was found.

Thanks are also due to Shaykh Idris Watts for typing out the entire text of the *Burda* and for offering several insightful comments on the placement and translation of certain lines that differ in the variants of the poem; to Shaykh Abdul-Rahim Reasat and Shaykh Muhammad ibn Yahya al-Ninowy for providing the biographies of Shaykh Ibn ʿAjība and Imam al-Būṣīrī; to Rashid Hussain for proofreading the text; and finally to Abdallateef Whiteman for beautifully designing and typesetting the book.

ABDUL AZIZ SURAQAH
Muharram 1437 [October 2015 CE]

Biography of Shaykh Aḥmad Ibn ᶜAjība al-Ḥasanī d. 1224 AH [1809 CE]

HE WAS THE Imam, the perfected saint, the Gnostic, and master scholar Abū al-ᶜAbbās Aḥmad b. Muḥammad b. al-Mahdī b. al-Ḥusayn b. Muḥammad al-Ḥasanī al-Shādhilī al-Darqāwī, generally known as Shaykh Aḥmad ibn ᶜAjība. Of Prophetic descent, he was born in the year 1162 AH [1768 CE] in the village of Aᶜjībish, between Tangier and Tetouan in Morocco.

Shaykh Ibn ᶜAjība's family was well known for their moral rectitude and sainthood and the signs of righteousness appeared in him from a very early age. He recalled in later years that he never missed an obligatory prayer, and even in early childhood he spent half the night in worship. As a child, he was not disposed to fun and games but was inspired with the love of sacred knowledge. Consequently, he memorised the Qur'an and various didactic poems before going on to study the Islamic sciences and then moving to Tetouan at the age of twenty. There, he devoted himself to his studies completely until he surpassed all his contemporaries. He continued to seek knowledge earnestly, receiving licences to teach texts and taking up teaching positions in the mosques and schools of Tetouan.

At the age of forty, Shaykh Ibn ᶜAjība moved to Fez to pursue advanced studies with the most erudite scholars of his time. After two years, he returned home and dedicated himself to the remembrance of Allah, reciting the Qur'an and invoking blessings on the Prophet (Allah bless him and give him peace). He then decided to sell all his books and devote himself completely to worship but divine fate would have him teaching for another fifteen years. By this time a great many people had benefited from him – indeed, most of Tetouan's scholars were his students. During these years of teaching, he maintained his intensive worship, and many miracles were seen at his hands.

Subsequently, Shaykh Ibn ʿAjība returned to Fez with the intention of visiting his teachers and those known for righteousness. On the way, he travelled via Banī Zarwāl in order to visit the great and famed gnostic Mawlāy al-ʿArabī al-Darqāwī and his foremost student, the gnostic Muḥammad al-Būzīdī to gain blessings from them and ask for their prayers. Both rejoiced over him, the latter predicting a tremendous future for him. Mawlāy al-ʿArabī al-Darqāwī asked Allah to make him like Imām al-Junayd, and Shaykh al-Būzīdī prayed for him to be comparable to Shaykh ʿAbd al-Qādir al-Jīlānī. Shortly after this, Shaykh Ibn ʿAjība was initiated into the spiritual path at the hands of Shaykh al-Būzīdī, and after a period of rigorous training he was blessed with a tremendous spiritual illumination.

Shaykh Ibn ʿAjība was then instructed by Shaykh al-Būzīdī to roam through the land as a spiritual guide, instructing people in the path and authorising them to recite the litanies of the Shādhilī Darqāwī Order. He passed through many areas of Morocco, and throngs of people entered the spiritual path at his hands. His fame spread far and wide, and this caused those who envied him, and those who disliked the Sufis in general, to spread lies about him amongst the public and among rulers.

Before long, the Shaykh was imprisoned in Tetouan with his brother and disciples. Such was the effect of his presence and teachings that the entire prison was transformed into a makeshift *zāwiya* after all the inmates repented of their past ways and took the spiritual path. The authorities forced the inmates to abandon the way of their teacher, and, after allowing Shaykh Ibn ʿAjība to leave the prison, shut down his *zāwiya,* thereby forcing him to leave the city that had derived such tremendous benefit from him. He attempted to move to other towns, but there too he was faced with similar difficulties. He remained patient throughout these trials, expecting a release and a great reward from Allah. Eventually, the governor of Tangier was replaced and matters improved significantly.

Shaykh Ibn ʿAjība wrote several works on a number of Islamic sciences including Sufism, the best known being his commentary on the aphorisms of Shaykh Aḥmad Ibn ʿAṭāʾ Allāh, *Īqāẓ al-himam*, and his exegesis of the Holy Qur'an, *al-Baḥr al-madīd*; the latter was composed at the behest of his Shaykh with the purpose of combining linguistic exegesis and spiritual allusion. He performed many miraculous acts both before and after he took to the spiritual path; many of them are described in his autobiography [*al-Fahrasa*. Cairo: Dār al-Ghad al-ʿArabī, 1411/1990.]

The masters of the path who came after him all praised him and his works, and he is regarded by some authorities as the greatest of all Sufi scholars.

Shaykh Aḥmad ibn ʿAjība returned to his Lord in the year 1224 AH [1809 CE], during the lifetime of his Shaykh and Grand-Shaykh. He was buried in the village where he died, Bū Salāma, but his remains were moved shortly afterwards to a permanent grave at Zammīj. May Allah Most High be well pleased him and benefit us through this work.

Biography of Imam Abū ᶜAbd Allāh Muḥammad b. Saᶜīd al-Būṣīrī d.694 AH [1294 CE]

HE WAS THE poet, the truthful and sincere lover of our Master the Emissary of Allah (Allah bless him and give him peace), Muḥammad b. Saᶜīd b. Ḥammād b. Muḥsin b. ᶜAbd Allāh b. Ṣanhāj b. Hilāl b. al-Ṣanhājī al-Būṣīrī. In the year 608 AH al-Būṣīrī was born in the village of Dallāṣ, in the region of Banū Yūsuf b. Ṣaᶜīd, Egypt, where his mother had grown up. He spent his youth in Būṣīr, his father's village, an ancient hamlet resting between Fayyūm and Banī Suwayf.

While still young, al-Būṣīrī emigrated to Cairo and, in one of the small mosques there, he memorised the Holy Qur'an and learned the elementary sciences of the Sharīᶜa and the Arabic language. Allah Most High endowed al-Būṣīrī with the gift of beautiful handwriting, so he earned his living through writing calligraphic inscriptions on tombstones. When his penmanship became well known, many people sought him out to learn the art of calligraphy.

Al-Būṣīrī went on to assume several public offices within Cairo and its surrounding areas, and after a while he started working for the Egyptian state as a clerk in the town of Balīs in the eastern province, where he was to reside for some years. However, he soon clashed with the civil servants around him and felt disgruntlement and annoyance at their character after witnessing their faults. As a result, al-Būṣīrī compiled a number of invective poems against them, exposing their infamies.

This soon earned al-Būṣīrī the ire and enmity of Egypt's political élite. They began to spread rumors and gossip about him until he grew weary of public office and removed himself from all government work. Returning to Cairo, he opened a primary school for children. Yet he was to suffer in his primary school as well. Soon afterwards he set out for Alexandria, where he finally found the repose he had longed for, and there he lived out the rest of his years, may Allah Most High have mercy upon him.

In those days Alexandria was a centre of sacred knowledge and Sufism, and there lived its Shaykh and scholar, the illustrious Imam Abū al-ʿAbbās Aḥmad b. ʿUmar al-Mursī al-Anṣārī (Allah have mercy upon him), student and successor of the great Imam Abū al-Ḥasan al-Shādhilī al-Ḥasanī (Allah have mercy upon him). Al-Būṣīrī eagerly sought out Imam Abū al-ʿAbbās al-Mursī and adopted his path in Sufism.

He abandoned his early career of composing poetry that was no different from that of worldly poets: verses of praise and blame, insult and complaint. Allah granted him an opening to compose praise-poetry in honour of our Master the Emissary of Allah (Allah bless him and give him peace). He then produced odes whose beauty surpassed the works of other master poets, and so his popularity and prestige spread far and wide.

Al-Būṣīrī's poems in praise of the Prophet (Allah bless him and give him peace) are distinguished by their fresh and sweet spirit and sincere expression of emotions. They are marked by splendid meanings, beautiful imagery, precise word choice, aesthetic refinement, and overall sound structure and organisation. He focused his efforts on reading the prophetic biographical literature and learning about our Master the Emissary of Allah (Allah bless him and give him peace). He expended enormous efforts and dedicated all of his poetry and craft to praising the Prophet, may the benedictions and salutations of Allah be upon him!

His famous ode, *al-Kawākib al-durriya fī madḥ Khayr al-Bariyya* (The Celestial Lights in Praise of the Best of Creation), better known as the *Burda*, is one of the quintessential pieces of Arabic poetry, and one of the most splendid panegyrics ever written in praise of the Prophet (Allah bless him and give him peace). The veritable jewel of the *dīwān* of praise-poetry in Islam, this ode has remained a source of inspiration for poets, who have for many generations striven to follow in al-Būṣīrī's footsteps.

Al-Būṣīrī passed away in Alexandria in 694 AH [1294 CE] at the age of eighty-seven, may Allah Most High have mercy upon him. He was buried there, in a small *zāwiya* that was later transformed into a mosque and named after him. This mosque is close to the seashore, in the Maydān al-Masājid area of Ḥayy al-Anfūshī. Allah Most High so willed that the mosque housing al-Būṣīrī's grave be directly facing, and very similar in design to the mosque of his teacher, Abū al-ʿAbbās al-Mursī—may Allah have mercy upon them both!

As well as the *Burda*, al-Būṣīrī left behind a number of other odes and poems, such as *al-Qaṣīda al-Muḍariyya fī madḥ Khayr al-Bariyya* (The *Muḍariyya* Ode in Praise of the Best of Creation); *al-Qaṣīda al-Muḥammadiyya* (The Muḥammadan Ode); and the *Hamziyya*.

May Allah have mercy upon al-Būṣīrī and grant him a goodly abode, and may He benefit us by the fragrant breezes of love whose redolent scent comes from his praises of the Beloved and Chosen One (Allah bless him and give him peace).

Introduction

In the name of Allah, the Compassionate, the Merciful.
May Allah send blessings and salutations upon our Master Muḥammad, and upon his Family and Companions.

SAYS THE POOR servant in dire need of his Lord's mercy, Aḥmad b. Muḥammad Ibn ʿAjība, the Sharifan of Ḥasanī pedigree, may Allah assist him: All praises are due to Allah, who blessed us with innumerable graces and preferred us over all other nations by bestowing us with the noblest of creation and the Master of the Emissaries, our Master and liege lord Muḥammad, who was sent to the red and to the black [races] and the Arabs and the non-Arabs alike. May Allah send blessings and salutations upon him, his Family, his Companions, his wives and his progeny for as long as rain falls in torrents and flows in streams!

The most essential task with which minds should be engaged, and the most important subject that should be recorded in books and ledgers, is praise for this most esteemed Prophet (Allah bless him and give him peace) and eminent Emissary. Verily it is one of the shortest of paths that lead to guidance and rectitude, and one of the greatest means of approaching the King of Kings and Lord of Lords [Allah].

Among those who have attained this loftiest of stations and gained the greatest success in this regard is Sharaf al-Dīn Abū ʿAbd Allāh Muḥammad b. Saʿīd al-Būṣīrī—the unrivalled master of his age, the consummate knower, the erudite and eloquent man of letters, the leader of the poets and the most gifted of scholars in its craft, the most articulate of the jurists and the most skilful of the rhetoricians. One of his parents (it is said that it was his father) hailed from [the village of] Būṣīr in Upper Egypt, the other from [the village of] Dallāṣ [also in Upper Egypt], and so his name was a combined ascription and he was known as al-Dallāṣīrī, and later as al-Būṣīrī.

He, Allah have mercy upon him, was born in the year 608 AH [1212 CE]. He studied under Imam Abū Ḥayyān, Ibn Sayyid al-Nās, Ibn Jamāʿa, and others. He passed away in or around the year 694 AH [1294 CE]. He is indeed one of Allah's marvels in poetry and prose, and would have been so even if he had only authored his famous ode known as the *Burda*.

His reason for writing this ode was that paralysis struck one side of his body as the result of a stroke. Doctors were confounded and unable to treat his condition, so he thought to compose an ode by which to seek the Prophet's intercession. After he had done so he saw the Prophet (Allah bless him and give him peace) in a dream and the Prophet touched him with his blessed hand. When he awoke he had completely recovered from his ailment. When he left his house afterwards he met a righteous man who asked him to recite the ode. Al-Būṣīrī was astonished since he had not told anyone about his poem. The man said to him, 'I heard it last night in the presence of the Prophet (Allah bless him and give him peace), and he was swaying to and fro just as the branches of a tree do.' Al-Būṣīrī gave the man [a copy of] the ode and later said, 'After I had given him the ode I realised that it had immense value.'

The man in question soon took the poem to others and relayed what had transpired between him and al-Būṣīrī. News of it reached the king's vizier, Bahāʾ al-Dīn. The *Burda* made a great impression on the vizier – so great, in fact, that he took a vow that he would only hear it while standing up barefoot and bareheaded. He would recite it frequently and listen to it attentively, and he and his household made it their constant companion, and as a result of its blessings they began to witness tremendous effects taking place in their religious and worldly affairs.

Saʿd al-Dīn al-Fārūqī, who would attend these gatherings of the vizier, was afflicted by trachoma, an eye disease, that left him on the verge of blindness. During that time he saw a dream in which someone said to him, 'Go to the vizier Bahāʾ al-Dīn, and take the *Burda* from him and place it over your eyes. You will be healed.' Saʿd al-Dīn went to the vizier and relayed to him the dream, but the vizier, who did not know the ode as the Ode of the *Burda*, said, 'I don't have anything called the *Burda*; all I have is an ode praising al-Muṣṭafā (Allah bless him and give him peace) composed by al-Būṣīrī. We seek healing through it and use it to treat our sick.' The vizier then handed him the ode, and Saʿd al-Dīn placed it over his eyes and was healed on the spot.

It is also said that the Shaykh [al-Būṣīrī] was afflicted with a severe case of trachoma soon after composing the *Burda*, whereupon he saw the Prophet (Allah bless him and give him peace) in a dream and recited some of it in his presence, and the Prophet blew spittle into his eyes and he was immediately healed. In sum, this ode is famous for its many blessings and is used as a means of having supplications answered, averting calamities and fulfilling needs.

This, with Allah's help, is a concise commentary upon the words [of the *Burda*], which will succinctly manifest its lights to the extent required. May Allah make it a triumphant means of meeting with its object of praise [the Prophet (Allah bless him and give him peace)] and remaining eternally with him in the Garden of Refuge. Amen!

CHAPTER I

Nostalgic Rhapsody and Love Complaint

THE SHAYKH (Allah be pleased with him) adhered to the way of the poets of old by prefacing his ode with a nostalgic rhapsody, also called a *nasīb*. A *nasīb* is where the eulogist mentions love and passion and the resultant blame that is incurred as a result, and speaks about the tears, the sadness, the sleepless nights and the emaciation that stem from ardent love. The wisdom behind mentioning these things is that they stir the listener and evoke yearning in the heart for the object of praise. The Shaykh sets up for himself in the first section an imaginary person whom he addresses and questions as to the cause of his ardent love and intense passion. This section is dedicated to expressing lyrical yearning and complaining about his love.

أَمِنْ تَذَكُّرِ جِيرَانٍ بِذِي سَلَمِ مَزَجْتَ دَمْعًا جَرَىٰ مِنْ مُقْلَةٍ بِدَمِ
أَمْ هَبَّتِ الرِّيحُ مِنْ تِلْقَاءِ كَاظِمَةٍ وَأَوْمَضَ الْبَرْقُ فِي الظَّلْمَاءِ مِنْ إِضَمِ

Is it from remembering neighbours at Dhū Salam
That you shed tears admixed with blood from your eyes?
Or because wind has blown from the direction of Kāẓima
And lightning has flashed in the dark of Iḍam?

The Shaykh, after setting up an imaginary individual for himself, begins to question him about the reason for his sadness and crying that have become so intense that his tears have mixed with blood. Is it, he asks, the memory of neighbours and loved ones at Dhū Salam whom he left behind which has caused him to yearn for meeting them and keeping company with them once more? Or is it because of a wind that has blown from their direction, or flashes of lightning that have appeared from their region? It is as if the author were asking himself 'What is it that causes your pain to be so intense and your tears to flow so profusely, leaving you in such an extreme state of passion and sadness that you have mixed tears with blood, contrary to the manner of sad people and what is deemed normal among those who weep? Is it because of remembering your neighbours at Dhū Salam and recalling the bygone days spent with them, a remembering which has increased your yearning and intensified your passion, and has caused your tears to flow [down your cheek] mixed with blood? Or is it because of the winds that blow from the direction of your beloveds, and the flashes of lightning that appear over their homeland, all of which remind you of the nights of intimacy and the days of union and togetherness and the familiar places of your beloved ones? Are these the reasons why your longing and passion has stirred so, resulting in your tears being mixed with blood?'

The reason why the author does not say 'Is it from remembering beloved ones... ?', although the poetic metre would support it, is to avoid using a word that is commonplace, because only inept poets use ordinary, common words. Capable poets do not make that error; in fact, they consciously avoid them and steer clear of everyday words used by common folk. What is more, the fact that they are his beloveds is understood from the context of the verses, so had he used the word 'beloved ones' instead of *neighbours* he would have been unable to employ a simile. Between the words 'beloved ones' and neighbours there are generalities and particularities that they share with each other; nevertheless, the Shaykh used these terms as figures of speech connoting places of his love-union and gathering with his beloved ones, using them as similes and expressions of his lyrical yearning.

It is common for poets to give the homeland of their beloved a different name from its own, and to give their beloved a different name from his or her own. They are not wont to change the actual name of their beloved or the name of the tribe or neighbourhood, so instead they use other names like Laylā and Salmā to allude to their beloved, and name the places of love-union and gathering Salaʿ or al-Naqā or Dhū Salam. Some say that lovers invariably use terms of endearment in place of the actual names of their beloved and his or her neighbourhood and tribe. Yet for a variety of reasons, they avoid changing [the names] directly, either because they wish to conceal the beloved, or because of protective jealousy for them, or for fear of onlookers.

By mentioning the remembrance of the beloved as a means of stirring desire and evoking love, the Shaykh employs a time-honoured poetic device used by love poets. For example, there is the statement of the poet:

I recalled a time [with the beloved] sweeter than sleep
And shorter than [the beloved's] familiar apparition.

And there are the lines of [the famous poetess] al-Khansāʾ:

The rising of the sun reminds me of Ṣakhr
And I weep at every sunset!

Lightning is mentioned [in love poetry] because the beloved is typically looked upon when lightning flashes, which reassures the lover that his gaze and the gaze of his beloved meet. It is narrated that Qays al-Majnūn would often stare unflinchingly at the crescent moon. When asked about this he said, 'Perhaps Laylā is looking at it now, and so our gazes can meet.' This was a consolation to him.

As for what the author mentions regarding tears mixing with blood when they are shed in abundance, this is true. In the *Ṣaḥīḥ* of al-Bukhārī there is a description of the denizens of the Hellfire, and it says they will weep tears till their tears are no more, whereupon they will weep blood. (But alas, *poets do not do as they say*.)

Know that tears of sadness are warm and that tears of joy are cool. This is why people say in supplication 'May Allah cool your eye' [*aqarr Allāh ʿaynak*], because the word *qurr* means coolness, and so the supplication means 'May Allah cool your eye with cool tears of joy.'

You might remark: 'The author's intention in this ode is to praise the Prophet (Allah bless him and give him peace). But erotic love-lyricism contradicts such a noble pursuit, so how can he mention these things at the start of his ode?' To this I reply: He mentions these things in conformity to the way of the poets who compose nostalgic rhapsodies before their panegyrics; this practice is extremely common among poets, and one will be hard-pressed to find a single panegyric that does not open with a nostalgic rhapsody of this sort. This style was presented by Kaʿb b. Zuhayr in his *Lāmiyya* panegyric poem which he read before the Prophet (Allah bless him and give him peace). The nostalgic rhapsody evokes feelings in the soul and softens the heart when heard. It provides extra energy for listening, and no sooner does the poet finish it and continue to the panegyric that souls are collected, hearts softened and bodies stilled. When this is achieved, the praise leaves a deep impression and powerful impact. It is akin to the plucking of lute strings and the striking of drums that take place before a song is sung. And Allah Most High knows best.

فَمَا لِعَيْنَيْكَ إِنْ قُلْتَ اكْفُفَا هَمَتَا   وَمَا لِقَلْبِكَ إِنْ قُلْتَ اسْتَفِقْ يَهِمِ

So what ails your eyes that when you tell them 'stop', they continue to weep still more?
And what ails your heart that when you bid it awake, it wanders further in distraction?

Here the author (Allah have mercy upon him) sets up an imaginary individual (as mentioned earlier) and addresses him, saying: 'What is wrong with your eyes, and what ails them and causes them to weep, that when you tell them to stop weeping they do not obey you and respond to your demand but instead overcome you with yet more weeping? And what ails your heart, that when you tell it to arise and awaken from its stupors and drunkenness and turn back from its wayward state, and when you guide it to what is in its best interest, it refuses to obey you and instead turns away and persists in its condition?' Such a state can only result from a burdensome longing and love that has completely overtaken the heart and the limbs.

It is possible that this expression is literal, in which case it is like the statement of the poet:

I said to my heart when love burdened it:
'You have burdened me with more love than I can bear!
O heart led by love, awake from your slumber;
may Allah not cool your eye with another heart!'

It is also possible that he has used the phrase *tell them* to express the implication, and that he tried to stop his eyes from crying and tried to lift his heart, but they did not obey him. The connection between this couplet and the previous couplet is through his question *So what ails your eyes…?*, which is based on an imagined denial (*inkār mutawahham*). Essentially, after setting up this abstract person, the author asks him why he is crying; however, because this person denies anything of the sort, the author establishes proof against him by asking: Why are your eyes filled with tears, and what is the matter with your heart that when you bid it come to its senses and awaken from its slumber, it turns away and continues in its state unabated?

أَيَحْسِبُ الصَّبُّ أَنَّ الْحُبَّ مُنْكَتِمٌ   مَا بَيْنَ مُنْسَجِمٍ مِنْهُ وَمُضْطَرِمِ

Does the lovelorn man think that love can be hidden
Behind a torrent from his [eyes], or a heart's raging fire?

Here the author (Allah be pleased with him) asks: Does this person, described as having such extreme yearning, ardent love, weeping eyes and raging fire in his heart, think that he can hide his secret or conceal his condition from others? How could that be, when he is beset with two things: weeping eyes that flow with tears and a heart with a raging fire? Just one of these two is enough to expose him and show the intensity of his love and the zeal of his passion, let alone when both are combined within him? The author links the question to the *lovelorn man* and not just 'the man' in order to allude to his intense love and yearning; had he phrased it instead as 'does this man think', or 'does this person think', he would not be able to convey this meaning. Do you not consider the words of the Most High: '*Whoever is an enemy to Allah and His angels and emissaries, and Jibrīl and Mīkāl, indeed Allah is an enemy to the disbelievers*' (Qur'an 2:98)? Notice that Allah did not say 'indeed Allah is an enemy to him', for had He done so the verse would have missed the opportunity to mention the quality that merited the enmity of the angels, and they would not have been denounced for disbelief because of their enmity towards the angels.

Having said this, poets disagree about the object of blame in these couplets: is it the eye or is it the heart? Some ascribe the sin to the eye and consider it the reason for passion. Others, however, ascribe the sin to the heart, because it is possible that one's passion can be stirred by the mere act of hearing. This is why the Prophet (Allah bless him and give him peace) has made it forbidden for a woman to describe another woman's features in detail to her husband[1] (so that it is as if he could see them), since that would be likely to create in his heart an emotional attachment to the other woman even though he has not seen her. In most cases, however, it is the eye that brings passion into the heart, and that is why the Lawgiver (Allah bless him and give him peace) has forbidden all but the first, unintentional glance. He said, 'An [unrestrained] glance is an arrow from the arrows of the Devil. Whoever refrains from it out of fear of Allah, Allah shall confer upon him a faith whose sweetness he can taste within his heart.'[2]

لَوْلَا الْهَوَىٰ لَمْ تُرِقْ دَمْعًا عَلَىٰ طَلَلٍ وَلَا أَرِقْتَ لِذِكْرِ الْبَانِ وَالْعَلَمِ

§ وَلَا أَعَارَتْكَ ثَوْبَيْ عَبْرَةٍ وَضَنًى ذِكْرَى الْخِيَامِ وَذِكْرَىٰ سَاكِنِ الْخِيَمِ

Shaykh Ibn ʿAjiba uses the western transmission of the Burda text for his commentary. Therefore, there are a number of extra lines that do not appear in the eastern versions. These have been marked with a § in the margin, next to the Arabic text.

But for passion, you would not shed tears at an abandoned camp,
Or lie awake at night recalling the fragrant willow or the mountain;
Nor would you be clad in the twin garments of tears and gauntness
At the mere memory of the tents and those who dwelt in them.

Here the author (Allah have mercy upon him) says to the imaginary person, as he establishes the proof against him and details the evidence of his intense love and heartfelt connection: 'Were it not for your passion and your heartfelt connection and ardent love, you would not weep at the traces of an abandoned camp; nor would your yearning stir upon mention of the house or the willow fragrance or the mountain; nor would you weep so and be denied the sweetness of sleep.'

By saying *clad in the twin garments of tears and gauntness*, the author speaks of the man's yellowish complexion [from gauntness] and the redness caused by tears mixed with blood. [It is as if he were saying:] 'Memory of the tents and those who dwelled in them has brought you to tears and altered your state, to such an extent that your tears are mixed with blood. Such a state can only be the result of a lovelorn passion that has taken you

1 Aḥmad, Bukhārī and Abū Dāwūd.

2 Ṭabarānī in *al-Muʿjam al-kabīr*.

in its powerful grip, whence the frequent bouts of weeping and your intense longing.'

The indefinite noun *tears* can indicate that there are many tears (because indefinite nouns can be used to describe a thing as much or few). So it is as if the author were to saying: 'Were it not for passion you would not see so many tears upon arriving at the traces of an abandoned camp.' Some rhetoricians interpret as 'few' the indefinite noun in the words of Allah about the Prophet Ibrāhīm's address to his father[3] [Āzar] '*Dear father I fear lest you be touched by a punishment from the All-Merciful and so become a close ally of Satan!*' (Qur'an 19:45) One of the rhetoricians said:

> Ibrahim (upon whom be peace) upheld good manners with his father in four places [in the Qur'an]. In the first place he said '*I fear.*' Out of mercy and concern, he expressed himself using the word 'fear'. He did not say to him, 'Divine punishment will most surely descend upon you!' This is the essence of gentleness and propriety. In the second place he said '*lest you be touched.*' He did not say 'lest you be afflicted,' because in the word *touch* there is a gentleness and propriety not found in the word 'afflicted'. In the third place he said '*a punishment.*' He put it in the indefinite form to imply that it would be light—as if to say it was a light punishment. In the fourth place he said '*from the All-Merciful.*' That is to say: 'from Him whose qualities are mercy, compassion and gentleness.'

In some places an indefinite noun is used to imply great extent, such as the words of the Most High: '*For you in retribution there is life.*' (Qur'an 2:179).

The mention of standing at the traces of abandoned campsites, recalling the tents and those who dwelled in them, the memories of love-pacts, and other things that stir passion and increase longing, are all well-known devices used by poets…

The author's line *Nor would you be clad in the twin garments of tears and gauntness* is like a repetition of the line that precedes it, for someone who sheds tears at the traces of an abandoned camp and weeps so much that he cannot sleep will take on a sallow, yellowish complexion, since that is

3 There is a difference of opinion amongst the scholars of Qur'anic exegesis whether this address is to Prophet Ibrahim's father or uncle. The author has mentioned father so we have remained loyal to his text. (p)

one of the effects of sleeplessness. The word *tears* in the same line is also like a repetition of the line *But for passion you would not shed tears at an abandoned camp*.

فَكَيْفَ تُنْكِرُ حُبًّا بَعْدَ مَا شَهِدَتْ   بِهِ عَلَيْكَ عُدُولُ الدَّمْعِ وَالسَّقَمِ

So how can you deny this love when tears and sickness,
truthful witnesses, have testified to it against you?

After setting up an imaginary person and responding to him on the basis of an imagined denial, and after showing ample proofs and establishing evidence against him at length, the author explains that he is lying and fallacious in his denial. So he asks him: 'Does a lovelorn man whose heart is subdued by passion think that his secret can be hidden and that his love can be concealed, even when the proofs of his love are so obvious and plain—from the torrent of tears and a heart raging with fire, to the weeping at the traces of an abandoned camp when seeing it, and agitation when remembering the trysts of intimacy and union with the beloved?' These signs and proofs leave no room for concealment; and tears and sickness are sufficient as just and acceptable witnesses. As the poet said:

> He tries to conceal it, but tears divulge his secrets;
> And his breaths disclose his lovesickness within.

And as another poet said:

> What is the state of the person who is with another?
> And how can one whose secret is in his eyes keep it concealed?

After establishing these proofs against the lovelorn denier, the author asks him the reason for his denial, and reproaches him by saying: 'Just proofs have been established against you, and corroborating evidence has disclosed your condition, so how can you hide your reality when they have exposed you?' It is only feasible to conceal [one's love] before these signs manifest, as disclosing the secret of one's love for another and expressing it openly are considered blameworthy; and indeed, divulging a secret is considered a form of recklessness and weakness that entails abandonment and separation, as is the chatter of detractors and gossips.

If you say, 'This goes against the *ḥadīth* in which the Prophet (Allah bless him and give him peace) said, "When one of you loves his brother, let him inform him,"'[4] I respond: Such love is limited to that which is for the sake of Allah and free of corrupt motives, and it is the love mentioned in the [other] *ḥadīth*, 'Those who love one another for Allah's sake shall be upon pulpits of light on the Day of Resurrection, and people shall be jealous of them.'[5] This form of love is one of the [means] of divine proximity, and is a noble merit for anyone who adopts it as a quality. As for love that is mixed with pleasures that are usually dependent on beautiful forms, if a lover adorns it with concealment and strives against his lower self to exercise chastity (*ʿiffa*), seeking thereby divine reward and desirous of recompense, he will join the ranks of those to whom this *ḥadīth* applies: 'Whoever loves passionately yet keeps chaste and conceals [his passionate love] and then dies, dies the death of a martyr.'[6] Some [scholars] have in fact counted such a person among the ranks of the martyrs. But as for the one whose inclination is to carnal desires and pleasures, and who divulges and announces that [to others], he is disobedient to Allah and His Emissary (Allah bless him and give him peace).

وَأَثْبَتَ الْوَجْدُ خَطَّيْ عَبْرَةٍ وَضَنًى   مِثْلَ الْبَهَارِ عَلَى خَدَّيْكَ وَالْعَنَمِ

Lovesickness has etched two lines, of tears and gauntness,
Upon your cheeks, like yellow spice[7] and red *ʿanam*[8]

Here the author (Allah have mercy upon him) says, completing what he was saying above: 'How can you deny your love when lovesickness has etched two lines upon your cheeks—two lines of tears from so much weeping, to the extent that they appear red like *ʿanam*—and made you skinny and gaunt, to the extent that your complexion is yellow like *bahār*?' This couplet contains a form of semantic embellishment known as epanodos (*laff wa nashr*), whereby the two etched lines are likened to *ʿanam* in their redness, and *gauntness* is likened to *bahār* in its yellowness.

4 Aḥmad, Abū Dāwūd.

5 Tirmidhī, *Sunan* and Ibn Ḥibbān.

6 Al-Khaṭīb al-Baghdādī, *Tārīkh Baghdād*.

7 *Bahār* is a yellow flower from which a powdered spice is made. [t]

8 ʿAnam is explained as either an Arabian tree with reddish branches from which a dye is made, or a red worm that is found in water. [t]

نَعَمْ سَرَىٰ طَيْفُ مَنْ أَهْوَىٰ فَأَرَّقَنِي ۝ وَالْحُبُّ يَعْتَرِضُ اللَّذَّاتِ بِالْأَلَمِ

Yes, my beloved's apparition came to me and denied me sleep,
For love always opposes pleasures with pain!

After the proof was established against the lovelorn denier and the evidence was made clear, and it was shown that he was not truthful in his denial (since the witnessing against him left no room for denial or rejection), he admitted the charge against him and submitted, and he agreed and returned to the truth. He acknowledged what he previously denied, disclosed what he previously tried to keep hidden, and saw that the truth had more right to be followed. So he said *Yes!* to his interlocutor and then explained the cause and reason for his weeping and his resultant gauntness and sleeplessness, explaining what exposed him and laid his condition bare. He said: 'My beloved's apparition had come to me at night and I was delighting in our union, when suddenly my beloved vanished and I woke up and found nothing there. So I suffered immense grief and kept thinking about my beloved. That is the reason for my weeping and sleeplessness, and why my life is so disturbed that it has earned me a gaunt body, a sallow, pallid complexion and tears mixed with blood!'

Then he completed his expression of this sentiment with an analogy: *For love always opposes pleasure with pain!* It is an undeniable fact that pleasures are confronted with things that spoil and disturb them. Such are the vicissitudes of time; no one enjoys a pleasure save that it is soon followed with pain, and no one enjoys recreation save that it is soon followed by toil.

What confront the lover and spoil his life and dampen his pleasure are distance, yearning, abandonment and the efforts of detractors and gossips, among other negative factors and loathsome conditions, such as taking pleasure in [mere] apparitions only for the dreamer to wake up and find nothing there.

There is indeed no pleasure without disturbances ensuing shortly thereafter. All of the pleasures of the lower world (*dunyā*) suffer spoilage. Its moments of happiness are fleeting and its enjoyments momentary; that is why every nation praises the practice of worldly renunciation [*zuhd*] and non-attachment, as [this life] is short-lived, ephemeral and transitory. There is no abiding enjoyment for anyone in this world, and no one can live in it forever. It abases those who are exalted and exalts those who are abased. It often resists the intelligent stubbornly yet yields willingly to the ignorant. It is ever fading and does not endure. If it gives itself over [to someone] it becomes a preoccupation, and if it turns away [from them] it becomes a source of regret. How excellent are the words of the one who said:

> Suppose that the world was given to you freely,
> Does it not end up in evanescence?
> Your world is nothing more than a shadow
> That provides you with shade and then departs!

It is related in a tradition that a man was attending a funeral when he noticed an old man and heard him say, 'I have never seen any ruin like that suffered by these people!'—pointing to the deceased [in the cemetery]—and 'I have never seen any heedlessness like that of these people!'—pointing to the living. Then he said, 'O Allah, free me up for the purpose for which You have created me, do not deny me while I beg of You, and do not torment me so long as I seek Your forgiveness!' The man said, 'I approached him and said, "O Shaykh, teach me that supplication!" And so he taught me the supplication, and then I asked him 'Who are you?' He replied, 'I am al-Khiḍr.

يَا لَائِمِي فِي الْهَوَى الْعُذْرِيِّ مَعْذِرَةً مِنِّي إِلَيْكَ وَلَوْ أَنْصَفْتَ لَمْ تَلُمِ

O you who blame me for this chaste love[9], pardon me!
But had you judged fairly, you would not have blamed me.

Having acknowledged the blamer, the addressee turns to him and seeks his sympathy and pardon. It is also possible that the addressee, with the intention of giving sincere advice and counsel, addresses all who might be expected to blame him or reproach or pity him, and hence he turns to the blamer and presents his excuse and says that his emotional state is too overwhelming, his heart too possessed, so he repudiates any claim to power or force and presents his excuse so as not to be blamed or upbraided.

9 The phrase 'chaste love' comes from *ʿudhrī*, which is ascribed to the tribe of Banū ʿUdhra, who were known for their tenderheartedness and sincere love, and whose womenfolk were famous for their chastity. [t]

He says: 'O you who blame me for this chaste love that is against the norm and which entails certain ruin and death, pardon me! For had you judged fairly you would have excused me, and had you known what has come of me you would not have blamed or rebuked me!' It is as if he considers his predicament outside of his control and something that he cannot remove from himself. A person can [only] be blamed and rebuked for that which is in his power of acquisition; to blame someone for something that he has not acquired on his own and which is not in his power to control is oppression and unfairness, since it is tantamount to 'being charged with an unbearable burden' (*taklīf mā lā yuṭāq*).

'The blamer' (*al-lāʾim*) is someone who forbids and rebukes the lover, either because of the infatuation of the lover's heart and his mind's preoccupation [with the beloved] which distracts him from his religious and worldly concerns (though without involving himself in either praise or condemnation of the beloved, his intention being only to offer sincere advice and show pity and protective concern for the lover); or else he is an envier, a *wāshī* or a *raqīb*. And Allah Most High knows best.

The words 'blame' (*lawm*) and 'rebuke' (*ʿadhl*) have the same meaning [here]. The *wāshī*, however, is worse than the blamer or rebuke, since he works to spread gossip between lovers and sow enmity and discord between them. This word *wāshī* is derived from *washshā*, which means 'to embellish' (because the gossiper embellishes and adorns his speech and presents truth in the image of falsehood and makes the ugly appear beautiful and the beautiful ugly). The *raqīb* is a person who sets himself against two lovers and strives to split them apart with his actions, and who is keen that there be no love between them. The *raqīb* attempts to disrupt their intimate moments and spoil their pleasure. He does not tire or slacken from his efforts [to cause a rift between them]. Thus the *wāshī* is worse than the one who rebukes, but milder than the *raqīb*. The *raqīb* is worse than both.

By describing the [abstract] person's love as *chaste* (*ʿudhrī*), the author follows the custom of the poets who, when they describe someone as having attained the pinnacle of love and passion, say his love is ʿudhrī, [named after] the tribe of Banū ʿUdhra, who surpassed all limits when it came to chastity, temperance, loyalty, fidelity and tender-heartedness. They were known to lament over the homes [of their loved ones], and would compose [love] poetry, even though their love was platonic in nature.[10] Love would enchant them from an early age and take the reins of their hearts at the onset of their youth; they were raised with the qualities of chastity, fidelity and soft-heartedness, and there are numerous stories and astonishing anecdotes about them in this regard.

Al-Aṣmaʿī said, 'Jamīl b. ʿAbd al-Raḥmān went to see ʿAbd al-Malik b. Marwān and the latter said, "Jamīl, relate to me some of the stories of Banū ʿUdhra, for I have learned that they are a people of dalliance and soft-heartedness." Jamīl said, "O Leader of the Believers, know that the Arabs are the softest of people in temperament, the most beautiful of them in loyalty and the best of them in fidelity. Each tribe among them possesses certain traits and qualities that they are known for and in which they surpass others. Banū ʿUdhra are famous for their passion and love; we may see a man among them who outwardly looks very rough; but the moment he falls in love we see that he is softer than water and lighter than air. Yazīd b. Muʿāwiya had a confidant from the tribe of Banū ʿUdhra. One day he said to him, 'I have heard that your folk are very soft-natured.' The confidant replied, 'Leader of the Believers, my family in Thanīma moved to a distant land, and I came along with them. After we arrived, I went out and happened upon a shepherd at the base of a mountain who had herded his sheep into a cave. I greeted him and he replied, then he said to me 'That's enough; you have lost your way!' I replied, 'You're right, so please show me the way.' He said, 'Stay here with me and take a rest.' I stayed with him and he welcomed and honoured me; he went and slaughtered a sheep, lit a fire, roasted the sheep and placed it before me to eat. After the meal he went and prepared a corner [for me to sleep in]. In the middle of the night I could hear him crying and lamenting to someone there, so I spent the night awake looking over at him in that state. When the morning came I sought permission to leave and told him, 'I must leave;' but he refused, saying 'Don't you know that a guest is to be entertained for three days?' And so I acquiesced and remained with him. Upon asking his name and lineage I discovered that he was from one of the notable families of Banū ʿUdhra. I asked him, 'So what brings you here, and what has caused you to tend to sheep?' He informed me that he was in love with his cousin from his

10 The literal phrase used by the author is 'They were chaste from what lies under the loin-wrap.' That is to say, their love was platonic and not of a sexual nature. [t]

father's side, and that she was in love with him, too; he had gone to her father and sought her hand in marriage, but the father had declined because of his poverty and paucity of material wealth. Soon after that, he told me, the father had married off the girl to another man from Banū Kilāb, who took her away from her neighbourhood and had her settle with him in another area. [The man said] 'I could not endure losing her, so I went and got myself employed as a shepherd in order that my cousin could come to me so I could see her and she could see me.' He went on to complain of his lovelorn passion and love for her, and told me that she paid him a visit every night. When nightfall came and the time for her arrival approached, he was on the lookout for her, going here and there, sitting and standing, like someone waiting and looking anxiously. When he sensed that she was late he stood up in agitation and sang the following verses:

What can one say of a love who does not arrive as usual?
Was she stymied by something, or held up by some task?
May my soul be your ransom! You have spurred my yearning –
A yearning so hot that it well-nigh sets my limbs on fire!

"He said to me, 'Stay put, O brother in care of Banū ʿUdhra, until I return, for I sense that things are not well with my cousin.' Then he left and I followed him with my eyes till he was out of sight. He was gone for about an hour, and when he returned he was carrying something in his arms; and I could hear him sobbing and wailing. I asked him, 'What is wrong? What misfortune has struck you?' He replied, 'O brother in care of Banū ʿUdhra, this is my cousin's body. She wanted to come to see me, but was met by a lion on the way and it killed her!' Then he placed her body on the ground and told me, 'Wait here till I return.' He then set off, and was gone for so long that I began to worry; but eventually he came back, this time carrying a lion's head. 'O brother in the care of Banū ʿUdhra' he said, 'you will soon find me dead, so take my cousin and me, wrap us in a single burial shroud, and bury us in a single grave; and write upon the gravestone the following verses:

'We were on earth's surface but for a short while.
We were united by passion, time and homeland;

But fate soon separated us from our intimacy,
So we are now united in a shroud beneath the earth!'

Also take these sheep and return them to their owner', he added. Then he went and tied a noose around his neck. I swore a solemn oath that he should not kill himself, but he refused and hanged himself and died. I did everything he instructed me to do; I wrote the two couplets on his gravestone, and returned the sheep to their owner and told him all that had happened. Upon hearing the story, the owner of the sheep became quite saddened and felt great pity for the man and his lover."""' Al-ʿUtbī said, 'No one among the lovers has reached the level of love that Qays al-Majnūn felt for Laylā. So powerful was his love that he could neither understand nor comprehend [without her], and he could not put on a stitched garment without tearing it [out of lovelorn passion]. He fled from the people and did not find intimacy with anyone, and would not sit with anyone, unless that person reminded him about Laylā, in which case he would speak of his intense love for her and become happy and take solace in her mention. He would sing odes in her praise in the most eloquent language, but when anyone would bring up another topic besides Laylā or change the topic of conversation, he would mix up and muddle his words and soon leave.'

One of the *Salaf* (Early Muslims) said, 'I saw Qays al-Majnūn in a dream [after his death] and asked him, "What did Allah do with you?" He replied, "He forgave me and made me a proof against the lovers."'

It is related that on the Day of Resurrection a divine call will be made, asking 'Where is the madman of Laylā?' and he shall be brought before [Allah] with dishevelled hair and will be covered in dust, as if he were a ghoul or limpid creature, as he was in the life of this world. Allah will take him to account and then forgive him and say 'Where are those who claim to love Me? Is there any amongst you whose obedience has reached the level of Qays's obedience to Laylā, and whose love has reached his level of love for her?'

It is related that a man from Banū Tamīm said, 'In one of my journeys I passed by an oasis belonging to the people of Ṭayʾ. Erected there in the front of the campground was a tent in which a marriage celebration was going on. I got down from my camel, and the people were fed and the bride was mounted [on the howdah] and carried off in a procession to her husband. She rode off until she arrived at her [new] home. Soon after she had entered and settled in, a young man appeared atop a hill in front of the house and called out:

Though your form may be absent from me
I swear that my heart remains in love with you,
For as long as I live with this pact;
And it remains in this state that you know—
Of yearning, remembrance, love and affection!

When she heard him recite these lines she hastened towards him, and he towards her, and the women folk tried to take hold of her; but she broke free from their grip, and she and the young man embraced one another and wept till both of them collapsed in death as the womenfolk looked on. One of the elders then came out and stood over their bodies. He wept and said, "To Allah we belong and to Him we shall return!" Then he said, "I did not join the two of you in union in your lifetimes, so by Allah I will join you after death." Then he instructed some of the people to wash their bodies and wrap them in a single shroud. When I asked about the couple, he told me: "This young man is my nephew from my brother's side, and she is my daughter; and as you can see, they were deeply in love with one another."'

It is reported that a young man from Baṣra fell deeply in love with a young cousin of his from his father's side. He went to her father and asked for her hand in marriage but the father refused, and instead turned him down because of his poverty and refused to allow him to marry her. The young man was extremely distraught and had nearly lost his mind, and when news of his state reached the young girl she sent for him and said, 'I've been apprised of your intense love for me, and I've come to know your condition. But know that my love for you exceeds your love for me, so if you like I can come out to see you without my family knowing, and if you like I can facilitate your visit to me in secret.' The young man sent back the message, 'I have no need for any of that; I fear a blazing fire and everlasting torment [Hell].' When the messengers went back to her with his message, she wept and said, 'By Allah, no one has more right to that than me, and verily all of creation are equal when it comes to the divine threat and promise!' Immediately thereafter, the girl began a life of spiritual devotion and worship. Her change weighed heavily upon her family, but she continued in her devotions till she died. The young man would visit her grave every day and pray for her and seek forgiveness for her and then leave. She later came to him in a dream and he said to her, 'Are you the girl so-and-so?' She replied, 'Yes.' He said to her, 'Tell me what became of you [after death].' She then stood up and sung the following lines:

> Unto delight and never-ending life
> In gardens eternal, never-fading!

The young man asked her, 'Do you remember me?' She replied, 'By Allah, I shall never forget you; indeed, I ask my Lord to reunite us.' He asked, 'So when shall we meet?' She replied, 'Very soon, Allah willing.' After this dream, the young man strove in pious devotions and worship for a few days and then died and joined her. May Allah have mercy upon both of them!

Sulaymān b. ʿAbd al-Malik had a personal muezzin who would give the call to prayer inside his palace and let him know of the times of prayer. Sulaymān also had a young slave girl in his palace and the muezzin would often stare at her. The girl informed her master Sulaymān of the muezzin's stares—Sulaymān was an intensely jealous man—and he thought to kill the muezzin. Instead, however, he said to the girl, 'Adorn yourself and apply fine scent, and walk over to him and say that you are not oblivious to his stares. Tell him that the passion in your heart for him is far greater than his passion for you, and say to him, "If you have a [sexual] need then fulfil it through me, as the Leader of the Believers is sleeping right now."' She did as she was told and offered herself to the muezzin. He replied to her advances, 'If you mean what you say, go now and come back tomorrow.' She went back and told Sulaymān his response. Sulaymān said, 'Go back to him and say "I find no other time better than now."' The girl went back to the muezzin and said as she was told, and the muezzin raised his gaze towards the sky and said, 'O Majestic One, where is Your beautiful concealment?' Then he said to the slave girl, 'Go away and never come back, for soon there shall be a meeting before the One who will not disappoint!' The slave girl returned to Sulaymān crying and in a state of anguish, and told him about what transpired. Upon hearing what happened, Sulaymān went to see the muezzin. When he got there one of his retinue said, 'The Leader of the Believers gives you the slave girl and orders that you be given fifty thousand dirhams to ready her for betrothal.' The muezzin replied, 'By Allah, O Leader of the Believers, I have slaughtered my desire for the girl upon my very first glance at her and have given her up [so as to have the reward for doing so] as a treasure with Allah [for the Hereafter]. I would be ashamed to take back what I have left in His care!' Sulaymān insisted that he accept the girl as a gift, but he refused her as well as the wealth. Sulaymān was marvelled at the muezzin and would repeat his story [to others] out of astonishment.

It is related that a young man from Banū ʿUdhra married a girl from his tribe and had intense love for her. One day she looked at him and as a result he began to weep. This caused her to weep, too, so he asked her, 'Why do you weep?' She replied, 'First you tell me why you are weeping, and then I will tell you why I am weeping.' 'Will you believe me?' he asked. 'Yes', she replied. 'I recalled your goodness and beauty and my love for you, and then I said to myself "I will die and she will marry someone else"—so I was unable to control my weeping.' She said, 'By Allah, I was saying the same thing to myself as you were, and I was unable to control my weeping.' He said to her, 'After your death I shall consider all women forbidden to me!' And she said to him, 'And I likewise, after your death, shall consider all men forbidden to me!' They lived on for as long as Allah willed, and then the man died. His wife was extremely saddened and grieved at his death – so much that her family feared for her sanity. They agreed among themselves to marry her off to another man, and so they did, though against her will, in the hope that by marrying someone else she would be too preoccupied to grieve for her late husband. When the wedding night arrived and she was being prepared to go with her new husband, slumber overtook her, and in a dream she saw her late husband. He had come in to see her and said, 'You have broken our pact. May you find no enjoyment in life after me!' She woke up in a terrible fright, left her quarters and began to wander [in the wilderness]. Her family went out looking for her but found no trace of her—until a few days had passed and she returned and refused the [new] marriage, slamming the door in the would-be-groom's face.

ʿIkrima said: 'Once, when we were with Ibn ʿAbbās, a group of young men from Banū ʿUdhra came carrying a young man whose body had withered and wasted away. They said, "Nephew of Allah's Emissary (Allah bless him and give him peace), seek a healing for us [for this young man]!" Ibn ʿAbbās asked, "What is his condition, and what has afflicted him?" Just then, the young man sung in a low, solemn voice:

We suffer lovesickness from intense longing and loneliness.
The lover's soul nearly melts from its intensity.
It is no wonder that lovers should die of passion;
The wonder is that ardent lovers should survive!

Then he let out a shriek and died on the spot, may Allah have mercy upon him. Ibn ʿAbbās said, "Have you ever seen anyone like him? Verily he is a martyr of love, for which there is no blood wit or indemnity. We ask Allah for well-being!"'

Yūnus b. ʿAbd Allāh said, 'I kept company with al-Ḥasan al-Baṣrī for over twenty years, and not once did I ever hear him say [anything mundane, like] "Prices have gone up" or "Prices have gone down", or "The Emir has set out on a journey" or "The Emir has returned." His conversations were nothing but talk of death. One day, however, a girl came to see him; she was the pinnacle of beauty and attractiveness, and of fine bodily proportion. She sat before him and said, "O Shaykh, is it permitted for a man to marry a second wife even though the first wife is young, fertile and beautiful?" Al-Ḥasan replied "Yes, he is permitted to marry up to four wives." She said, "Even if his first wife is like me?"—and then she uncovered her face. Al-Ḥasan replied "Yes." She said, "Peerlessly Glorified is Allah (*subḥān Allāh*)! By your life, please don't give people this fatwa!" and then she got up to leave. Al-Ḥasan's eyes followed her as she made her way out, after which he said, "What harm shall come to a man in this life if his wife is like her?"'

Abū Nawfal al-Hudhalī was asked, 'Is there anyone who is safe from passion?' He replied, 'Only a boorish and brutish person devoid of all virtue and forbearance!'

One of the wise observed that 'Passion is a delightful companion, an intimate confidant and domineering king that takes possession of bodies and their souls, hearts and their passing thoughts, eyes and their glances and egos and their opinions. Its entry point is concealed from visions, and its passageway is hidden from eyes.'

The difference between love (*ḥubb*) and passion (*ʿishq*) is that the latter is usually coupled with carnal desire while the former is not. All that has been mentioned here concerns love between created beings, so the question here is: Does the Creator love His creation? The answer is 'Yes', and there are many signs of divine love. Among these signs is that acts of obedience are made easy and the servant is blessed with the enabling grace to perform them, and that the servant is tested and is patient. As is stated in a *ḥadīth*: 'When Allah loves a servant He tests him, and if he is patient He selects him for Himself, and if he is satisfied He chooses him.'[11] In addition, 'When Allah loves a servant He appoints the servant's own self as an exhorter over him.'[12] When Allah loves a servant He causes him to see his personal faults.[13] And—as is recorded in the *Ṣaḥīḥ* of al-Bukhārī—when Allah loves someone, He calls out to Jibrīl and says, 'Truly I love so-and-so, so love him.' Then Jibrīl calls out to those [angels] in the heavens, 'Truly Allah loves so-and-so, so love him'; and then the inhabitants of the heavens love that person, and acceptance is placed for that person in the earth.

As for the signs of the servant's love for Allah, understand that people are careless and indulgent in their expressions regarding them—and how easy it is to make a claim, and how difficult it is to attain its reality! There are, however, signs which show that one's claim to love is true. Among them is being immune from sin and love of [acts of] obedience [to Allah]. How can one [truly] love One whom he disobeys? As has been said:

You disobey God yet claim to love Him.
That is untenable and repugnant to reason!
Were you sincere in your claim to love you would obey Him,
For the lover is ever obedient to the one he loves!

Another sign of a servant's love for Allah is that he loves to meet Him. The lover does not dislike meeting his beloved; however, it is possible that he may dislike death because of his scant provisions [for the

11 Daylamī in *Musnad al-Firdaws* without a direct chain of transmission.

12 Ibid., with a weak chain of transmission.

13 Ibid., with a weak chain of transmission.

Hereafter], and because he hopes to live longer so he can increase in righteous deeds and make up for what was lost.

Other signs are that the servant prefers Allah's good pleasure over the desires of his ego; that he is infatuated with Allah's remembrance, his tongue never slacking from invocation and his heart never empty of Him; and that his solace is in seclusion and intimate prayers to Allah and recitation of His Book, isolated from creation, as was related about Ibrāhīm b. Adham. It is said that he once came out of his cell[14], when a man saw him and asked, 'Where have you come from?' Ibrāhīm b. Adham replied, 'From intimacy with Allah!' Allah revealed to the Prophet Mūsā (upon whom be peace), 'How wonderful a servant is Barkhā, although he likes the early morning breeze! Whosoever loves Me [truly] does not incline to anything [besides Me]!' It is reported that an avid worshipper (*ᶜābid*) who had devoted himself to Allah's worship for years on end once looked at a bird as it was building its nest in a tree and chirping. The worshipper said, 'Would that this bird would move to this [nearer] tree so I could enjoy its sound!' Allah revealed to the Prophet of that time, 'Tell so-and-so the worshipper, "You have sought intimacy with a created being. I have therefore lowered you one degree—a degree that you cannot attain with your pious works!"'

Among the signs that a servant loves Allah is that he is merciful towards Allah's servants and compassionate with them, yet stern against the people of sin, this being out of reverence and esteem for his Beloved. Also, out of protective jealousy over his secret, he conceals his love and avoids pretentious claims, such as public displays of love. For love is one of the secrets of the lover, and it is conceivable that one make tall claims and be beset, as a result, with afflictions and severe punishment—and we seek refuge in Allah from being stripped [of love] after receiving it!

عَدَتْكَ حَالِيَ لَا سِرِّي بِمُسْتَتِرٍ عَنِ الْوُشَاةِ وَلَا دَائِي بِمُنْحَسِمِ

May you be spared my condition! My secret cannot be concealed
From detractors, nor is there any cure for my ailment!

Here the author (Allah have mercy upon him) says: *May you be spared my condition*, this being a form of affection and sympathy for the blamer, just as

14 His *khalwa*: a room or isolated place where he would stay for long periods and engage in private devotions and invocation. [t]

you might say to a doctor while describing your sickness 'May Allah grant you well-being! I am suffering from such-and-such ailment.' So here the author is being tender and submitting his plea. He is making a confession in the hope that the blamer will limit his reproach and censure and show mercy and pardon, realising his lovelorn state after receiving a prayer that Allah spare him the malady and not afflict him with something similar. For the ailment that afflicts him is love, which is incurable, irrepressible and hopelessly persistent, and which exposes one's secrets and lays bare one's condition. Had [the poet's] secret been divulged to others who were not detractors (*wushāt*) it would have been easier to bear, but its disclosure to detractors is likely to result in alienation and abandonment. For detractors spread gossip about the lover and try to frustrate his desires and come between him and his beloved by circulating misinformation and abhorrent words. So the lover, expressing the dreadfulness of this condition, prays for his detractor and asks that he not suffer such a disastrous affliction or be tested with the like of it.

In similar situations where a reprimand is given out of kindness and affection, post-classical Arab poets and lyricists would often preface their address with a prayer. In addition, a prayer can be made before a [light] reprimand in order to allay fear and show care and concern for the addressee, such as Allah's words, '*May Allah pardon you! Why did you grant them leave?*' (Qur'an 9:43) Pardon was mentioned before the reprimand, and had it not been mentioned, the Prophet's heart would have split apart out of fear of the reprimand and awe for the position [of the One addressing him]. Another example of this [though not a prayer], in which a statement is prefaced with gentleness and sympathy appropriate to the situation and the required etiquette and shyness, is the statement of Umm Sulaym, who said 'O Emissary of Allah, "*Verily, Allah is not shy to speak the truth*" (Qur'an 33:53). Is a woman required to take a full ablution (*ghusl*) when she has a wet dream?' The Emissary of Allah (Allah bless him and give him peace) replied, 'Yes, if she sees water (secretion).'[15] By saying '*Verily, Allah is not shy to speak the truth*', Umm Sulaym removed any objections that could have been raised to her asking about something shameful in the presence of men. On the other hand, one could say that questions on such obligatory matters do not need to be prefaced with statements

15 Bukhārī and Muslim.

such as these, and that the verse '*Verily, Allah is not shy to speak the truth*' means He does not command others to be shy of speaking the truth, and is not pleased with anyone being too shy to speak it. So Umm Sulaym prefaced her question with this verse as a way of seeking pardon for asking about an issue that women are shy to bring up.

Just as Umm Sulaym sought pardon for asking about something women are shy to bring up, likewise men are usually shy to bring up certain things before women, as Abū Mūsā al-Ashʿarī did with ʿĀʾisha (Allah be pleased with both of them). Abū Mūsa said to her, 'O Mother of the Believers, the difference of opinion amongst the Companions of Allah's Emissary over a particular matter disturbs me, but I am reluctant to raise it with you!' ʿĀʾisha said, 'Whatever you would ask your mother about, ask me.' He said, 'A man penetrates his wife but becomes tired and does not ejaculate.' She said, 'When the circumcised part meets the other circumcised part [penetration], the ritual bath (*ghusl*) is obligatory.'[16]

All of what is said above is based on the premise that the phrase in the first line is a supplication ('May you be spared…'). Al-Azharī[17], however, considered it a predicate. He said:

> The meaning of the couplet is as follows: 'O you who blame and reproach me for my chaste love—ascribed to Banū ʿUdhra—had you any fairness, no blame would come from you, since I have conveyed to you the condition I suffer from, and the reality of my passion and lovesickness; for my secret is not hidden from the gossipers, nor is my ailment alleviated that I may take rest.' This phrase, then, is an explanation of his condition, and Allah Most High knows best.

مَحَّضْتَنِي النُّصْحَ لَكِنْ لَسْتُ أَسْمَعُهُ   إِنَّ الْمُحِبَّ عَنِ الْعُذَّالِ فِي صَمَمِ

You have given me sincere advice, but I cannot hear it;
A lover's ears are deaf to the reproaches of critics.

Having understood that his critic only blamed him for the sake of rendering sincere advice, and out of protective concern and eagerness to comfort him after the loss of his beloved, and for the sake of consoling

16 Imam Mālik, *al-Muwaṭṭā'*.

17 Shaykh Khālid b. ʿAbd Allāh al-Azharī (d. 903 AH), in his commentary *Sharḥ al-Burda*. [t]

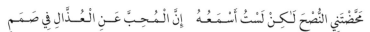

him and desiring to stabilise his condition—the author acknowledges the advice given and admits to the truth, and concedes that his critic has done his best and given sincere advice. He says: 'You, O blamer, are sincere in your advice. You have given me generous counsel and discouraged me from passion (wanting to put me at ease); and you have encouraged me to follow right guidance and what is in my best interest. However, my ears are deaf to your advice and unable to accept your exhortation; I am satisfied with the circumstances in which I find myself!'

If you ask 'But how can he describe himself as deaf when he has clearly heard [the critic's] statement?' the response is: Even though he heard it, he has negated hearing because it did not leave an impression on him; it was as if he did not hear it at all and was on an equal footing with a deaf person insomuch as he gained no benefit from what was said. This is comparable to the words of the Most High [about the disbelievers] '[*They are*] *deaf, dumb and blind*' (Qur'an 2:18), even though they do not have these qualities literally, but are so described because they did not benefit from what they heard and they failed to acknowledge the statement of divine unity (*Lā ilāha illā Allāh*) and the testimony of faith regarding the divine message of Allah's Emissary (Allah bless him and give him peace). So because they did not benefit from the clear and inimitable miracles that they had witnessed—even though they were able to see, hear and speak—they were considered deaf, dumb and blind; and since they were on an equal footing with those who are physically deaf, dumb and blind they were described in the same terms. The common quality [between them and those who are physically deaf, dumb and blind] is inability to benefit [from what is said]. This is similar to Allah's words '*How wretched is that for which they sold themselves, if only they knew!*' (Qur'an 2:102) This verse means: If only they knew with a knowledge that was of benefit! It is also similar to the couplet by the author [further on], '*Blind and deaf, they heard not the glad tidings*...': even though in reality they did hear the glad tidings and see the radiant lights [that shone during the Prophet's birth], none of that profited them.

Should you ask 'Why did he fail to heed the advice and accept the counsel despite acknowledging that doing so would rectify his condition and put him at ease?' I would reply: 'Because it is not within his power or ability to divert himself from it [his passion].' We mentioned earlier how passion is not just a fleeting opinion that can be taken hold of, nor is it based in the rational mind and thus subject to management. Rather, its power is overwhelming and its force is too great to effect through guile. We ask Allah (Glorified is He) to make our portion of love be for Him, Exalted is He, and for His Pure Prophet (Allah bless him and give him peace)! Some people who were withered and worn from their love of created beings were granted solace and blessed to ascend higher and experience love for the Lord, and their hearts were occupied with that lofty station. As a result, their heartfelt attachment to the divine became a ladder and rope by which Allah made the path easy for them, and by which He guided them to success. This most often happens when people reach old age and the warner of grey hairs appears [on their heads] and they feel fear and shame. The love they have for someone gives rise to soft-heartedness and eagerness for union with their beloved, and rouses in them a desire to be close with that person. These feelings then transcend [the ephemeral] and rise above to the divine, and love for creatures is replaced with love for the Creator. This idea was alluded to in the couplet:

May Allah reward on my behalf the scolding grey hairs
With the best that is awarded to an adviser, whose good I've grasped
I was well acquainted with the path of love, until it came to an end
And then I replaced my love for another with love for Allah!

إِنِّي اتَّهَمْتُ نَصِيحَ الشَّيْبِ فِي عَذَلٍ   وَالشَّيْبُ أَبْعَدُ فِي نُصْحٍ عَنِ التُّهَمِ

I hold suspect even the advice of my own grey hairs,
Even though their advice is far from deception.

Here the author (Allah have mercy upon him), after mentioning in the previous couplet that he did not accept the advice of the adviser or heed the exhortation of the exhorter or comply with the blamer, emphasises his reasoning and essentially says: 'I have been warned before you by one whose advice and exhortation is not considered suspect, and whose advice and counsel must be heeded and received: by grey hairs which announce an impending demise and a passing life; scouts of death and couriers of the final journey, and warners of imminent transfer from this abode to the presence of the One and the Overpowering (*al-Wāḥid al-Qahhār*).' 'However', he says, 'I have not listened to their exhortation or accepted their advice, even though they are free of ulterior motives and far from deception.'

This couplet gives the impression that the blamer is considered suspect (even though he is exonerated when the author says, *You have given me sincere advice…*) while the warner of grey hair is not, since its exhortation and advice is via the mute tongue of expression (*lisān al-ḥāl*), and it is inconceivable that it could lie or utter insincere words that go against what it truly intends, or whose outward contradicts its inward.

If you ask: 'How can the author ascribe deception to grey hair when such an ascription is absurd?' I reply: Since the grey hairs of warning appeared on [his head] yet he persisted in his passions and did not forsake his ways and repent of his errors, and there was no sign of them making an impression upon him, he considered them equivalent to one whose exhortations and advice go unheard and who is deemed suspect. The shared quality between them is his failure to accept their advice and change his bad condition to a good one. Thus, his grey hairs assume the role of a person who is considered suspect inasmuch as their advice and exhortation go unheeded. Allah Most High knows best.

CHAPTER 2

Warnings about the Caprices of the Ego

فَإِنَّ أَمَّارَتِي بِالسُّوءِ مَا اتَّعَظَتْ مِنْ جَهْلِهَا بِنَذِيرِ الشَّيْبِ وَالْهَرَمِ

وَلَا أَعَدَّتْ مِنَ الْفِعْلِ الْجَمِيلِ قِرَىٰ ضَيْفٍ أَلَمَّ بِرَأْسِي غَيْرَ مُحْتَشِمِ

Because of its ignorance, my ill-commanding ego has paid no heed
To the warner of grey hair and approaching old age;
Nor has it prepared good deeds in welcome
For an unannounced guest who has settled on my head.

THESE TWO COUPLETS are proof for what was mentioned earlier, and show that the warner of grey hair has assumed the position of one who is deemed suspect. That is because the warner of grey hair appeared on his ill-commanding self and announced the imminent journey and informed it—with its mute tongue of expression—that naught remains but a few short years. So the grey hairs exhorted, reminded and delivered warnings and cautions, but this idle and ill-commanding self was not frightened by them, and did not desist from its sinfulness. Instead it continued unabated in its wanton ways and travelled on no path other than the path it was already on; nor did it prepare good deeds and righteous works to welcome an impending guest coming to see it—these being the grey hairs. [It is as if he says] 'Had you honoured them as they truly deserved you would have found them on the Day of Poverty and Need [the Day of Judgment], but since you failed to do that, they have assumed the position of one who is deemed suspect, since you have not benefited from their exhortation or acted in accordance with their promise. Had you listened to them you would have renounced folly and wantonness.'

The author's statement, *Because of its ignorance*, is a notice that a sinful person's disobedience only stems from his ignorance. This is attested to in the words of the Most High: '*Whosoever amongst you did evil out of ignorance and thereafter repented and made amends...*' (Qur'an 6:54) Had the sinful person been described with beneficial knowledge when he thought to commit sin he would not have gone forward with it. If you contend: 'But everyone knows that disobedience is unlawful and that it comes with the threat of punishment, so in what sense can a sinful person be described as ignorant?' I respond: What is meant by ignorance here is ignorance brought on by the sin when it is committed, and neglecting to bring to mind the sin's punishment at the time of its commission, when passion and caprice cloud one's intellect, as the poet said:

When facing a test, a man becomes clouded over
Until he sees as good that what is not!

When in that state, it is as if that person's knowledge is stripped from him. It states in a *ḥadīth*, 'The fornicator does not fornicate while he is a believer (*mu'min*), and he does not drink alcohol while he is a believer.'[18] It is related that such a person has a dark cloud hovering over his head[19]—may Allah, out of His generosity and largesse, and by the rank of our Master Muḥammad His Noble Prophet, protect us from losing [our faith] after it has been given!

Know that there are three types of selves: the irascible, ill-commanding self (*al-nafs al-ammāra*), the reproachful self (*al-nafs al-lawwāma*) and the tranquil self (*al-nafs al-muṭma'inna*). The ill-commanding self is the self that the author intends; the tranquil self is the highest of the three, and the reproachful self is between the two of them.

The ill-commanding self is the self that commands and incites evil. It is the most intractable of your foes. As for the reproachful self, it is the self that retreats when it stumbles [i.e., sins], and turns back when it transgresses and seeks forgiveness when it sins. It is always in a state of shakiness. As for the tranquil self, it is the self that treads the path of earnestness and takes up residence in the abodes of obedience, and is given

18 Bukhārī

19 Abū Dāwūd.

enabling grace to do righteous works. Between the tranquil self and the ill-commanding self lie numerous trials and misfortunes, so no one can be delivered from the latter to the former except with pre-eternal divine grace. The tranquil self is addressed in the words of the Most High, '*O tranquil self, return to your Lord, well-pleased and pleasing.*' (Qur'an 89:27–28) Allah praised it by describing it with serenity, submission and trust in Him. Linguistically, the word '*muṭma'in*' means a low ground. When the self lowers itself through its humility and brokenness, its Master praises it by saying '*Return to your Lord, well pleased and pleasing.*' This is an indication that the reproachful self and the ill-commanding self are not given leave to return to Allah in a state of honour, as that is reserved for the tranquil self. Essentially, the Divine says to it: 'Return, for We have permitted you to enter our Divine Presence and to dwell eternally in Our Garden!' The word 'well pleased' [in the verse] means well pleased with Allah's rulings and injunctions in this world, and well pleased with Allah's generosity and graces in the Hereafter. The word 'pleasing' [in the verse] means pleasing in Allah's sight. This is a tremendous compliment. We ask Allah that He not forbid us to join the people of tranquillity and certitude. Amen, Amen!

Know also that mankind has three foes: his world (*dunyā*), his satanic consort (*Shayṭān*) and his own self (*nafs*). See to it, therefore, that you keep guard against the world by practising non-attachment (*zuhd*); guard against Satan by seeking refuge in Allah from him; and guard against your own self by forsaking [its] passions. One of the wise has said, 'Whoever is overcome by his ego will become a prisoner to its passions and locked up in the jail of its desires, and it will prevent his heart from receiving benefit.' Others have said that for the one who exercises self-control and keeps it from desiring the unlawful, the unlawful will not occur to his mind; and for the one who assists his own self in acting upon its passions, it will cause him to fall into the unlawful. That is because desire for what is unlawful is a type of border, and 'the one who grazes near the border is likely to cross that border.'[20] The remedy for this disease is repentance and purification of the self from filth. This is why the Prophet (Allah bless him and give him peace) would often say, 'O

20 Bukhārī and Muslim.

Allah, grant my soul its godfearingness (*taqwā*), and purify it, for You are the best to purify it. You are its Master and Guarantor.'[21]

People have spoken at length about grey hair, both in poetry and in prose, dramatically expressing their distress and lamenting the passing of their youth. An example of this is the statement of the poet:

As a branch, I was stripped of my youth
As leaves are stripped away from a twig.
I wept tears from my eyes over my lost youth
But weeping and wailing are of no avail.
Would that [my] youth return to me some day
So I might tell it what grey hairs have done!

And one virtuous person stated:

Before grey hairs, have you ever seen a guest who,
When he appears, forces you to travel?
Before it, I've never seen a rose that, when it blossoms
Causes the branch to wither away!

In another line, a poet sang a line in which he consoled someone who experienced the fear that comes with grey hairs:

Servant of Allah, let not grey hairs scare you when they appear,
For grey hairs are adornment and a mark of dignity.
A garden is only beautiful when
The flowers are laughing (blooming) therein.

Another consolation for those who receive grey hair are the prophetic *ḥadīth* reports that speak of its virtue. In one of these narrations, the Prophet (Allah bless him and give him peace) said, 'Whosoever has his hair turned grey in Islam, it shall be a light for him on the Day of Resurrection.'[22] When Prophet Ibrāhīm (upon whom be peace) first saw grey hair on his beard he said, 'O Lord, what is this?' Allah (Glorified is He) said, 'It is dignity.'

The upshot is that grey hair occasions dignity and induces remorse over what has been missed in a life wasted in idleness (which cannot be

21 Muslim and Aḥmad.
22 Tirmidhī, *Sunan*.

returned). Muḥammad b. Aslam al-Khawwāṣ related, 'I saw al-Qāḍī Yaḥyā b. Aktham in a dream and I said to him, "What has Allah done with you?" He replied, "He caused me to stand before Him and said to me, 'O evil old man, were it not for your grey hair I would have burnt you in Hellfire!' He then took me to task as a slave is taken to task before his master, and I passed out. When I came to He repeated [the interrogation] a second time, and I said, 'Lord, this is not what has reached me concerning You!' He asked, 'And what has reached you concerning Me?' I replied, "ᶜAbd al-Razzāq narrated to me on the authority of Maᶜmar, on the authority of al-Zuhrī, on the authority of Anas b. Mālik, who related on the authority of Your Prophet, who related on the authority of Jibrīl, who related from You, O Generous One, that You said, "There is no one whose hair turns grey in Islam but that I am shy to punish him with Hellfire."[23] Allah Most High said, "ᶜAbd al-Razzāq has spoken the truth; Maᶜmar has spoken the truth; al-Zuhrī has spoken the truth; Anas has spoken the truth; My Prophet has spoken the truth; and Jibrīl has spoken the truth—I said that, so usher him [He said to the angels] to Paradise!"'

It is also related that a young man from the Children of Israel had worshipped Allah devoutly for twenty years and then spent twenty years disobeying Him, flinging himself headlong into sin and vain passions. Then one day he looked at himself in the mirror and saw grey hairs on his beard. This disturbed him and caused him to pity himself. Then he said, 'O God, I have obeyed You for twenty years and disobeyed You for twenty years; if I return to You will You accept me?' Just then a caller (*hātif*) called out, whose voice he could hear but whose form he could not see. The voice said, 'You loved Us, so We loved you; and you left Us, so We left you; and you disobeyed Us, and then We granted you respite. So if you return to Us We will accept you!' (O Allah, turn to us with Your tenderness and care, O Most Merciful of those who show mercy!)

لَوْ كُنْتُ أَعْلَمُ أَنِّي مَا أُوَقِّرُهُ   كَتَمْتُ سِرًّا بَدَا لِي مِنْهُ بِالْكَتَمِ

Had I realised, I would not have honoured it;
I would have used [black] *katam*-dye to hide what it showed

23 Related by Abū Yaᶜlā with a weak chain with the wording: 'I am too shy, when My bondsman's beard turns grey and My bondswoman's hair turns grey in Islam to punish them after that.'

In this couplet the author (Allah be pleased with him) admits his neglect and remissness, and expresses regret over the good deeds that passed him by and his failure to honour the rights owed to his grey hairs, and his failure to prepare [for death] with beautiful actions and righteous works, and to renounce, upon their arrival, his wayward ways of youth. Essentially he is saying: 'I thought that my grey hairs would garner respect, and I thought that with their arrival I would find myself repentant, and that their appearance would deter me from the lowly pleasures of [my] ill-commanding self. So with their arrival I held out hope that I would become righteous (since grey hair is a mark of the righteous and a raiment of the penitent), but when the legions of grey hairs spread across my head and took to the pulpit of exhortation, my ego continued in its enjoyment of forbidden pleasures and persisted in its vain desires to which it was accustomed, and the grey hairs were unable to pry my ego away from its bad habits and passions. Had I the chance to go back and change things, and had I known from my ego what I know now, and had I realised beforehand that it would not change its ways after the appearance of grey hairs, I would have felt shame before Allah and before people, and I would have hastened to dye my grey hairs and do my best to conceal them so as to avoid humiliation. I would have concealed them with dye and hidden them with *katam*. I thought things would be different, but alas they are not; my resolve has weakened and my success is only by Allah!'

There are scholarly disagreements over the ruling on dying grey hairs and what type of dye should be used. Some authorities maintain that it is better to avoid using dye altogether, while others maintain that it is better to use it. Others differentiate between using black dye and using henna (and other types of dye), disliking the former and approving of the latter. A number of the *Salaf* from the Companions and Followers (*Tābiʿūn*) dyed their hair, and as proof for their action they cited the Prophet's command to use dye. It is reported in the *Ṣaḥīḥ* [of al-Bukhārī] that the Emissary of Allah (Allah bless him and give him peace) said, 'Verily the Jews and the Christians do not use [hair] dye, so be different from them.'[24] On the day of the Conquest of Mecca, Abū Quḥāfa was brought forth and his hair was completely white, so the Prophet (Allah

24 Bukhārī and Aḥmad.

bless him and give him peace) instructed, 'Change [the colour of] these grey hairs, and avoid using black [dye].'[25]

The command to avoid using black dye is understood to be a recommendation [and not obligatory]. Al-Māzirī quoted [Qāḍī] ʿAbd al-Wahhāb as saying, 'Because of the deception to women that it entails, and since it gives the impression that one is young, it is offensive to use black dye.' Most of the *Salaf* would dye their hair with yellow dye. Those who permitted the use of black dye include ʿAlī, ʿUthmān, al-Ḥasan and al-Ḥusayn. It is reported that Ibn ʿUmar would say, 'It is better for eliciting the appreciation of one's spouse, and is more likely to terrify one's enemy.' Some scholars opined that when it comes to either using or not using dye, two factors should be considered. The first factor one must consider is the customs of his land. If it is the custom of a people to dye their hair (or not to), then for him to go against local custom is tantamount to seeking notoriety (*shuhra*). The second factor one must consider is how different people look with grey hair, for how many a grey head would look handsomer if it were dyed! Then there are some who look unsightly with grey hair, and for such people it is better to use dye.

Dye is said to have two benefits: it cleanses the hair of what dirties it, such as dust and grime, and it is a way of being different from the People of the Scripture, and it frightens one's enemies.

مَنْ لِي بِرَدِّ جِمَاحٍ مِنْ غَوَايَتِهَا كَمَا تُرَدُّ جِمَاحُ الْخَيْلِ بِاللُّجُمِ

Who will help me restrain my bolting ego from its wilfulness
As a rebellious horse may be restrained with reins?

Here the author (Allah have mercy upon him) says: Who will take it upon himself to help me restrain this lower self from its errors and vain desires? For it has bolted and transgressed and taken delight in sinfulness, and has grown accustomed to forbidden and loathsome pleasures. It has become nigh impossible to rectify it and remedy its illness. But for strength provided by the King and the All-Powerful, diverting it from its bad habits will be an arduous task, and preventing it from bolting will be incredibly difficult.

It is therefore necessary to struggle against the lower self and forcibly prevent it from its bad habits, just as a horse is restrained after bolting.

25 Muslim and Aḥmad.

When a horse bolts and goes outside its boundaries, it will only be brought back after great effort and fatigue. Likewise with the lower self: when it bolts from its owner it is harder to bring back than a bolting horse, since a horse can be persuaded to return with ruses and guile and kind words, but there is no stratagem to bring back a bolting ego. It can only be brought back by Lordly providence (*jūd rabbānī*) and divine grace (*tawfīq ilāhī*).

It is also possible that the author's statement here is in response to an imagined question. So after he said *Had I realised, I would not have honoured it*, he produced an imaginary questioner who asked him, 'What prevents you from honouring your grey hairs when they are yours and you are their owner and it is fully within your power to honour them?' He responds by saying that he rode the mount of his lower self but it bolted and he was overcome and unable to rein it in. It is as if he is saying: 'Though the rein of acquisition (*kasb*) is in my hands, I have been overcome by my bolting ego that has gone with the winds of pre-eternal decree and destiny. Who will help me restrain it, and how can I ever hope of turning it back when I am the most feeble and incapable of all—unless it be returned by Him in Whose Hand is the kingdom of the heavens and the earth?'

Shaykh Abū al-Ḥasan al-Shādhilī (Allah be pleased with him and benefit us by him) has said, 'For him who clings heavily to the ground of vain passions and caprice, and whose soul does not help him remove what is bad, and who is prevented from adorning himself with [beautiful qualities]—his servitude will take on one of two forms. In the first form he will know Allah's bounty in the faith and belief in divine oneness He has given him. As a result, Allah will engender love for Him in his heart, and will adorn it for him and make detestable to him disbelief, sinfulness and disobedience, and the servant will say, "O Lord, You have bestowed these favours upon me and decreed that I be rightly guided, so how could I ever despair of You when You confer upon me Your grace? If I have been wayward, please accept me." In the second form he will turn constantly to Allah and express his utter poverty and need before Him, saying: "O Lord, grant me safety, grant me safety!" For anyone whom divine decrees overwhelm and cut off from pure servanthood there is no way but between these two forms.' If the servant fails in these two forms, damnation is his lot and remoteness from the divine is inescapable—and we seek refuge in Allah Most High! (This is quoted from Shaykh Aḥmad Zarrūq's ʿ*Umdat al-murīd al-ṣādiq*.)

فَلَا تَرُمْ بِالْمَعَاصِي كَسْرَ شَهْوَتِهَا إِنَّ الطَّعَامَ يُقَوِّي شَهْوَةَ النَّهِمِ

Do not try to thwart unlawful desires by satisfying them,
For food only increases a glutton's desires.

Here the author (Allah have mercy upon him) says: Do not allow your lower self to fool you and say 'Allow me just this one unlawful desire and grant my wish just this one time, for once I have gotten what I want and sated myself of this desire I will settle down and will not hanker after another!' This is the essence of trickery and deceit, since enabling the lower self to engage in unlawful desires only increases it in cravings and wants, and creates in it even more desires for similar unlawful wants. That is because the lower self, once it has enjoyed its sinful pleasure which it craved, experiences it first-hand and thus develops a taste for its sweetness. That experience stirs its desire and intensifies its covetousness, causing it to become like a glutton who, when he tastes a delicious meal, grows ever hungrier and more desirous of food. That is because by tasting the food he has experienced it first-hand, while before tasting it his craving was not as strong. The same may be said with regard to the lower self: Once it has become accustomed to the pleasure of a sin and tasted its sweetness, it is difficult to thwart it and turn it away from desiring it again. However, when the door [to sin] is shut in its face and its hands are struck and firm resolve is summoned to overpower it and prevent it [from sin], it will relinquish its desire and lose hope and no longer hanker after sin or grow accustomed to what it once coveted.

وَالنَّفْسُ كَالطِّفْلِ إِنْ تُهْمِلْهُ شَبَّ عَلَىٰ حُبِّ الرَّضَاعِ وَإِنْ تَفْطِمْهُ يَنْفَطِمِ

The ego is like a child: neglect it and it will grow up loving
To suckle; but if you wean it, it will be weaned.

Here the author (Allah have mercy upon him) says that the self is like a child. What makes the two alike is that both are feeble of mind, both prefer their desires [over all else], both are overcome by their passions and neither of them is responsible with money. A young child is receptive to everything and therefore does not know the difference between what is good and what is evil, and does not discriminate between benefits and harms. This is likewise the nature of the ill-commanding self that overpowers the intellect: it prefers desires and passions and does not consider the outcome of its actions or look after its best interests. Its ambition is limited to the enjoyment of its desires or the passions of sin that assail it, for which it shows no concern. The lower self thus becomes like a child who is without sound mind.

If you contend 'How can the lower self be made to resemble a child when a child does not know what is good and evil and cannot distinguish between harms and benefits, while the lower self of a legally responsible person (*mukallaf*) does know what is unlawful and what is permitted, and can distinguish between harms and benefits?' The answer is as follows: Since the lower self knows what is evil yet still falls into it, and knows what is harmful and forbidden yet still engages in it, it has become like an unmindful, undisciplined child left to its desires, which grows up accustomed to suckling and the habits of youth and unwilling to leave behind its desires and cravings.

The author only used the phrase *it will grow up loving to suckle* as an example. What he means is that the child will grow up retaining all of his youthful habits if he is not weaned gradually and trained and redirected away from them and prevented from his desires. If these do not occur, it will be difficult to treat him and dislodge from him the habits to which he has grown accustomed and the desires that he has grown to enjoy. But if you wean him when he is young and prevent him from the breast and at the same time occupy him with something else, then he will become busy with that thing and you will be at ease with him. This is why it is important that a child be forbidden from keeping company with immoral people or bad peers. Indeed, human natures steal from one another and character traits are acquired, so it is incredibly hard to turn a child around later if at the very beginning he is neglected and left to freely indulge in his lower desires, prefer the comfort of his lower self [over all else], keep company with immoral people and bad peers and is not restrained from his corrupt wants.

Keeping righteous company leaves a tremendously [positive] influence and is a great honour. How excellent is the statement of the poet:

Keep company with the best of people and know
That he who associates with the noble will one day be noble.
Do you not see the honour received by the once paltry hide
After they used it to bind the written pages of the Qur'an?

It is the same with the lower self: if you overpower it and curb its desires when it is in the throes of youth and in the heat of passion you will take control over it, master it and preside over it. But if you neglect it and follow its desires and allow it to enjoy its passion, it will take control over you and exercise its authority over you as it sees fit. It will become the ruler and you will become the ruled, and you will go along with its wants and spend your possessions in its service. When your lower self takes control over you Satan gains the upper hand and fulfils his promise, as he said, '*By Your honour, I will surely beguile them entirely...*' (Qur'an 38:82) That is because Satan and the lower self are brothers; their path is one and their aim is one. Both of them encourage vain passions and embellish the unlawful and detestable. Both of them showcase the ugly in garments of beauty.

It is not possible for one to be delivered from Satan and the lower self except by turning to the One and the Overpowering (*al-Wāḥid al-Qahhār*) who will assist him in his struggle. This is the supreme jihad (*al-Jihād al-Akbar*). Some of the sages have said, 'The noblest of people is the one who disobeys his unlawful desires and refuses to hand over the reins to his lower self.' Another sage said, 'With the lower self, only the hand of the intellect can hold its bridle, so the one whose intellect is overcome will be controlled by it.' It is stated in the Ḥikam [of Ibn ʿAṭāʾ Allāh], 'When two matters seem confusing to you, consider which one is heavier on the lower self, for nothing weighs heavily on the lower self except that it is true.' Shaykh Abū al-Ḥasan al-Shādhilī (Allah be pleased with him) said, 'When Allah honours a servant in his movements and in his stillness, He places in front of him [true] servitude to Himself, and conceals from him his selfish interests, and causes him to move about in servitude while [his] selfish interests are hidden from him. All the while he receives what was decreed for him, yet he does not glance towards it; it is as if he is removed from it all. And when Allah debases a servant in his movements and in his stillness, He places his selfish interests in front of him and conceals [true] servitude, and causes him to move about in his vain passions while [true] servitude to Allah is removed from him. Yet, if there appears from him any servitude outwardly, he says, "This is a door of sainthood and debasement." As for the [station] of supreme veracity and supreme sainthood, then all selfish interests and rights are equal in the sight of those who possess spiritual insight, since everything he takes and leaves is by Allah.'

فَاصْرِفْ هَوَاهَا وَحَاذِرْ أَنْ تُوَلِّيَهُ إِنَّ الْهَوَىٰ مَا تَوَلَّىٰ يُصْمِ أَوْ يَصِمِ

Divert its vain desires and beware of giving it power,
For vain desires pollute or destroy whatever they control.

Here the author (Allah have mercy upon him) advises his interlocutor by saying: 'Divert the vain desires of your lower self and prevent them from reaching your heart; do not help it attain its pleasures and do not consent to its aims. If you fail to heed my command then beware lest your lower self turns against you and rules over you as it wishes, in which case you will have ceded authority to it and allowed it rule over you, making you the servant of your lower self and not the servant of your Lord.'

It is stated in the Ḥikam, 'Never do you love something without you being a slave to it; but He does not want you to become a slave to any other besides Him.' And the Prophet (Allah bless him and give him peace) said, 'May he perish—the slave of the dinar and the dirham, and the slave of fine clothing! Let him perish and relapse, and if he is pricked by a thorn let him not find anyone to remove it for him!'[26]

So if you follow the desires of your lower self or cede authority to it, it will destroy you or cause you to become cut off, which will lead you to fall from the station of perfection and plunge into the abysses of the heedless and misguided. Abū al-ʿAbbās Ibn ʿAṭāʾ (Allah have mercy upon him) said, 'The lower self is predisposed to ill manners, while the servant is commanded to uphold good manners. Hence the lower self, by its very nature, meanders in the arenas of contravention,[27] while the servant exerts himself in turning it away from evil pursuits. So whosoever gives it free rein shares in the sin it incurs.' Some of the Gnostics have said, 'It is the loftiest degree of the believer and his highest rank and most righteous

26 Bukhārī.
27 That is to say, the lower self is predisposed to engage in the unlawful. [t]

state of scrupulousness [*waraʿ*] that he die whilst striving against his lower self and overcoming his vain passions. For taking possession of the lower self and subduing desires and reining in passions is an exalted station reserved for none except a saint.'

One of the *Salaf* said, 'Shayṭān has several traps that he sets for man. If he finds someone suffering from weak faith, he will remove his faith all together and destroy him, and if he finds someone with strong faith whom he is unable to ensnare or trap, he will content him with doing actions that are offensive (*makrūh*), make vain passions beloved to him and urge him to commit lewd acts in private that degrade his moral standing.' Perhaps the author alludes to this when he says *For vain desires pollute or destroy whatever they control*. So beware of giving unlawful desires authority over you lest you suffer destruction, or lest you suffer a loss of your manly comportment (*murūʾa*), or your station falls from perfection—or both at the same time. The word for desires, *hawā*, is an abbreviated form of the word *hawān* (abasement), with the letter *nūn* omitted. For more on this, read Ibn ʿAbbād [al-Rundī's] commentary on the aphorism in [Ibn ʿAṭāʾ Allāh's] *Ḥikam*: 'It is from the ignorance of the spiritual novice that he acts with impropriety and then, with his punishment being delayed, says, "Had this [truly] been an impropriety, He [Allah] would have cut off divine aid and imposed remoteness."' May Allah grant us enabling grace to do what He loves and is pleased with!

وَرَاعِهَا وَهْيَ فِي الْأَعْمَالِ سَائِمَةٌ   وَإِنْ هِيَ اسْتَحْلَتِ الْمَرْعَىٰ فَلَا تُسِمِ

Guard it as it grazes in the field of actions;
And should it find the grazing sweet, do not let it roam.

Here the author (Allah have mercy upon him) says: Guard your lower self and be vigilant over it so it is within earshot and eyeshot. Look after it carefully when it performs an action and grazes in its field. If you sense that your lower self finds an action sweet and inclines strongly towards it (even if that thing is permissible or recommended), then consider it suspect and know that your lower self only takes delight in the action and loves to graze in it and hasten to perform it because of a stealthy aim or ulterior motive that is realised through, or by means of it; such as having a good reputation, fulfilling a hidden desire, or because of self-admiration, enjoying the praise of others, delighting in hearing his name mentioned or having an increase in energy when others see his works. These are amongst the qualities that take away sincerity and bring about diminishment and ruination. A person is responsible for his flock, and the direst thing under his care is his own self, for it only inclines to what will destroy him, even if it is outwardly an act of obedience and goodness. It is stated in the Ḥikam, 'The ego's share in disobedience is obvious and clear, while its share in obedience is inward and hidden. Curing what is hidden is a difficult course!'

Sayyidī Muḥammad Ibn ᶜAbbād [al-Rundī] (Allah be pleased with him) said, 'It is in the nature of the lower self to always seek after its share and flee from fulfilling rights [owed to others]. It strives only in pursuit of its own interests, even when in acts of obedience, not to mention acts of disobedience. Anyone who takes his lower self to account and carefully observes his passing thoughts will confirm this. It is possible that you experience energy and enjoyment from one type of worship that you do not find in another, even though the other type is more virtuous than the one in which you find energy and enjoyment. This is only because the share of the ego in the former is greater than what is found in the latter. And because of their awareness of the ego's machinations and plots, the people of experience and spiritual insight reproach themselves when they find their egos getting accustomed to a particular area of worship, so they confound their egos and move on to other [acts of worship].

It is reported that Abū Muḥammad al-Murtaᶜish (Allah be pleased with him) said, 'I performed the Ḥajj one year in a state of divestment, and it later occurred to me that it was tainted with my own selfish interests. That is because my mother had asked me one day to give her a drink of water, but her request weighed heavily against me, so I knew that my soul's desire to perform the Ḥajj was tainted with selfish interests; had my soul truly been annihilated it wouldn't have been difficult for it to fulfil what is considered a legal right in the Sharīᶜa [obeying his mother].'

So it is clear that the ego has a vested interest in obtaining its share from acts of obedience. But because this fact is hidden to the one performing an action, it is difficult for him to treat the problem, since it requires from him exactitude and a deep understanding by which he can search for the faults of his ego and its subtle deceptions and hidden interests, and then work to purify his works from them.

Shaykh Abū Bakr al-Khaffāf (Allah be pleased with him) said, 'I heard our teacher relate that Aḥmad b. Arqam al-Balkhī (Allah be pleased with him) said, "My ego once spoke to me about going out for battle, so I said 'Glory be to Allah! Allah Most High says "*Verily, the ego ever commands to evil...*" (Qur'an 12:53), but here my ego is commanding me to do something good! That can never be!' The fact of the matter is that it felt lonely and wanted to meet with other people and repose with them, and wanted people to hear about it so they could receive it with honour, largesse and kindness. So I said to it, 'Rather I bid you stay put.' It accepted my demand, but then I held it in suspicion [again] and said, 'Allah is the most truthful in statement!' Then I said to it, 'I shall go and fight the enemy and you will be the first to be slain!' It accepted my decision, so I prayed, 'Lord, tell me what I should do, for I hold my ego in suspicion and believe in Your words!' I later intuited that it was telling me 'Each day you kill me by going against my wants and preventing me from my desires and no one notices it in the least. So if you go and fight and are killed it will be a single killing and I will be saved from you, and people will hear about you and say that Aḥmad has been martyred. Then I shall have honour and goodly mention among people!' So that year I stayed back and did not go out to battle."'

So when the ego finds an action sweet do not leave it there but move it on to another action, as the author indicates when he says *And should it find the grazing sweet, do not let it roam.*

كَمْ حَسَّنَتْ لَذَّةً لِلْمَرْءِ قَاتِلَةً   مِنْ حَيْثُ لَمْ يَدْرِ أَنَّ السُّمَّ فِي الدَّسَمِ

How often it has found delight in something fatal,
For [one] cannot tell that there is poison in the fat!

Here the author (Allah have mercy upon him) says: Do not leave the lower self to engage in what it finds sweet and pleasurable, for it often finds delight in things that are outwardly good but inwardly bad. It is the nature of the lower self always to consider pleasurable things lovely and to crave for things that bring blameworthy consequences. It presents the loathsome in the guise of the beautiful and beautifies unlawful pleasures that are infused with deadly poison, all the while the person is heedless, ignorant of the fact that poison can be hidden in delicious and tasty fat. It is possible that an ignorant person is beguiled and overcome by his ego and its cravings and goaded to consume the poisonous fat and thereby unknowingly succumb to destruction. The same may be said with regard to sins and acts of disobedience. You have come to know that the primary causes of sin are those things which are pleasurable to human nature and desirable to the lower self, whose taste is as sweet as honey but whose effects and ill consequences are that of poison. Therefore, the intelligent person who is granted enabling grace is he who, when presented with honey infused with poison, is not fooled and deluded by its sweetness, and who instead turns away from it and does not pay attention to it—since he is intelligent and understands that the honey will destroy him because it will produce intense pain and agony. On the other hand, the ignorant dolt who is overcome by fleeting passion will not consider the ill consequences of his sins or think of the outcome [of his acts], so he will be deluded by the honey and its sweetness and will partake of it and drag himself into destruction and fatigue. It is stated in a *ḥadīth* from the Prophet (Allah bless him and give him peace), 'Paradise is surrounded by distasteful things, while Hellfire is surrounded by desires.'[28] And in another *ḥadīth*, 'On the Day of Resurrection, a man who was the most affluent of the people of the world will be brought forth and dipped into Hellfire for only a single moment. Then he will be asked, "Did you ever experience any pleasure?" He will say, "No, by Allah! I never experienced it!" Then a man who was the most downtrodden person in the world will be brought forth and dipped into Paradise for only a single moment. Then he will be asked, "Did you ever experience any hardship?" He will say "No, by Allah, I never experienced [any]!"' This was recorded by al-Bukhārī in his *Ṣaḥīḥ* collection. So, if a person of intelligence and success reflects on the pleasure of disobedience, he will realise that its delight is fleeting while its ignominy and sin remain, and he will say to himself, 'Perhaps the wrath of Allah lies in this particular act of disobedience, due to which I will lose out on the eternal delight [of Paradise].' Such a person will pull his lower self away from sinful acts and Allah will safeguard him from his lower self and protect him from falling

28 Muslim and Aḥmad.

into sin. May Allah, out of His generosity and largesse, protect us by the rank of our Master, His Prophet Muhammad (Allah bless him and his Family and give them peace)!

وَاخْشَ الدَّسَائِسَ مِنْ جُوعٍ وَمِنْ شِبَعٍ   فَرُبَّ مَخْمَصَةٍ شَرٌّ مِنَ التُّخَمِ

Beware of the snares of hunger and of satiety,
being hungry at times can be worse than gorging oneself!

Here the author (Allah have mercy upon him) warns against both the snares of hunger and satiety and calls for a balance between them, with neither excess on the one hand or negligence on the other. This is because frequent hunger is harmful to humans and has with it many dangers. It diminishes strength, spoils one's temperament, and weakens the body, making it difficult to carry out tasks. It harms the limbs, causes an increase in hallucinations, and leads to several intractable illnesses. And so perhaps the hunger which leads to these maladies is, for the one suffering them, worse than having gorged one's self.

Satiety also has several pitfalls and its ill effects are severe. It diminishes intelligence, hardens the heart, increases desire for sleep, corrupts the humours and brings on intractable illnesses. Through satiety, Satan is able to make headway against man and strengthen his authority over him. Satiety causes one to be lethargic and lazy, disinclined to acts of goodness and obedience.

It is related that the Prophet Yaḥyā son of Zakariyyā᾿ (upon them be peace) was confronted by Satan, who had with him several iron hooks. Yaḥyā asked him, 'What are those iron hooks?' Satan replied, 'They are the vain passions that I set as traps for the children of Ādam.' Yaḥyā asked, 'Is there among them an iron hook for me?' Satan replied, 'No, however some days past you ate till you were sated and became too slothful for worship.' Yaḥyā said to him, 'I hereby take a solemn covenant with Allah that I will never eat to satiety!' Satan said, 'And I hereby take a solemn covenant—that I refrain henceforth from giving advice to a Muslim!'

Luqmān advised his son, 'When the stomach is full, the intellect sleeps, wisdom is silenced and the members of the body are too slothful to perform worship.'

[Sufyān] al-Thawrī would say, 'O assembly of aspirants! Do not eat too much lest you drink much, sleep much and then lose much.'

One of the ill effects of satiety is that it causes one to forget what it is like to be hungry. One cannot realise the value of something unless he is tested [with its opposite]. Someone said to Yūsuf (upon whom be peace), 'Do you endure hunger even though you are in charge over the treasure stores of the earth?' He replied, 'I fear lest I eat to satiety and forget the hungry as a result.'

In sum, both extremes are blameworthy, and the best of all affairs are those in the middle, so one third should be for food, one third should be for drink, and one third should be for air. Satiety is neither unlawful nor forbidden, as there are reports from the *Salaf* which show that it is permissible. There is the *ḥadīth* of Anas that mentions the bowls of Umm Sulaym, which relates that the Companions ate till they were sated. Another example of this is the *ḥadīth* of Abū Hurayra in the story about the milk. It relates that he said [to the Prophet (Allah bless him and give him peace)], 'By Allah, I cannot find any more room [to drink]!' This report is well known, found in al-Bukhārī's collection and elsewhere. Nevertheless, it is said that satiety was a rare occurrence among the *Salaf*. Most often they did not eat to satiety, as ʿĀʾisha (Allah be pleased with her) said 'The first innovation (*bidʿa*) that was inaugurated after the passing of the Emissary of Allah was satiety.' Whoever would like a more detailed discussion on the virtue of hunger and eating less should refer to the *Iḥyā*ʾ (*ʿUlūm al-Dīn*)[29]. I cited a number of quotations from it in my commentary on the *Hamziyya*, under the couplet where the author says 'He bound his stomach…' Allah Most High knows best.

It is possible that the author is alluding to complete denial of the lower self, where it is prevented from enjoying permissible pleasures. He warns against that out of fear that it will bring on malaise, ennui and despair. Indeed, if the ego is deprived all at once of the pleasures it is accustomed to, it will become exasperated and discontent. Instead, one should deal gently with it and train it gradually until it develops the strength to be content with less. One *ḥadīth* mentions, 'Make things easy and do not make things difficult; give glad tidings and do not push others away…'"[30]

29 Imam al-Ghazali's *Ihya*ʾ *ʿulum al-din*. [t]
30 Bukhārī.

Another *ḥadīth* states, 'Do the good works that you are able to bear…'[31]; another states, 'Verily Allah does not become bored when you become bored…'[32], and another says, 'A broken saddle neither covers distance in travel nor preserves a back.'[33] And from Allah comes all enabling grace.

وَاسْتَفْرِغِ الدَّمْعَ مِنْ عَيْنٍ قَدِ امْتَلَأَتْ   مِنَ الْمَحَارِمِ وَالْزَمْ حِمْيَةَ النَّدَمِ

Empty out the tears from an eye that has filled itself up with forbidden sights. Maintain a strict diet of remorse.

Here the author (Allah have mercy upon him) says: Purify your eyes with the water of tears and frequent weeping, and strive to force tears from your eyes—eyes that have stuffed themselves with forbidden sights. Forbidden sights are everything deemed unlawful to look at. The Prophet (Allah bless him and give him peace) said, 'The fornication of the eye is in looking…'[34] And he said (Allah bless him and give him peace), 'The unrestrained glance is a poisoned arrow from the arrows of Satan. Whosoever forsakes unlawful glances out of fear of Allah, Allah will grant him faith whose sweetness he will taste in his heart.'[35] The eye is the scout of sins, the courier of base desires and passions and the primary cause of the heart's attachment [to others]. How excellent is the saying of the poet:

> If, for a single day, you send your eye as a scout
> For your lower self, then the images will soon fatigue you;
> You will have seen what you cannot obtain in their entirety
> Nor a portion of which you can endure patiently without!

When the servant's repentance is actualised, he will feel remorse over what he has done in the past, and he will weep over what he has lost, until ultimately—with his tears—he purifies his eyes from the filth of sin that had polluted them. The purification of the eyes through tears augurs the purification of the heart, since crying indicates remorse and regret, the soul's drive to repentance, penitence and forsaking of sin. [On the

31 Bukhārī.
32 Tirmidhī, *Shamā'il*.
33 Bazzār.
34 Bukhārī
35 Aḥmad.

other hand] the lack of tears from the eye and their remaining inside [the body] are a proof that the heart has not been purified and that repentance has not taken place, and that instead one continues [in sin] unabated, and that his soul has yet to experience remorse or regret, and has yet to desist from its error—for no sign of repentance has appeared from him, of sadness, weeping or regret over past sins. When a person is sick and he takes a laxative to remove excess humour from his body, a sign of healing is that he able to purge his body of it. In a similar manner, emptying out tears from the eyes is a sign that one's state is rectified and that there is a true repentance and liberation from the ill effects of his sins and transgressions. This, however, is only when the sins in question do not involve the rights of creation; if they involve others then it is obligatory to make amends, whether the sin involved is a person's honour or his wealth. It is recorded in the *Ṣaḥīḥ* [of al-Bukhārī] that the Prophet (Allah bless him and give him peace) said, 'Whoever has wronged his brother, let him make amends now, for in the Hereafter there shall be neither dirhams nor dinars. [Let him seek his forgiveness] before some of his good deeds are taken away and given to his brother, and if he has no good deeds, the sins of his brother are taken and cast upon him, and he is cast into the Hellfire. Let none of you say, "But what about being exposed in this world?" Truly, being exposed in the Hereafter is more grave than being exposed in this life!'

Regarding the author's words *Maintain a strict diet of remorse* it is said that just as a sick person is instructed to avoid certain harmful foods when he takes medicine, likewise anyone who is sick with sins and who takes the medicine of repentance must maintain a strict diet of fear and beware of the things that will spoil his repentance. You might say, 'But keeping to a strict diet of remorse will cause a person to always remain in a state of fear, and that will induce a state of severe regret which might lead him to despondency and feelings of hopelessness, which are blameworthy.' To that I respond: When a servant is remorseful for his remissness and neglect of obedience, and saddened and fearful over his sins, it does not necessarily mean he will be led to despondency and hopelessness. Rather, he should in fact show remorse over the pious and voluntary good deeds he neglected and the sins he committed, while not suffering from despondency or fearing [Allah] to such a degree that he despairs [of His mercy]. He should instead maintain a state between fear and hope. Some scholars have said, 'When a person is healthy the state of fear should predominate, and when a person is sick the state of hope should predominate, and he should remember the clemency of the Most High, Glorified is He, as well as His mercy, benevolence and kindness to the believers.' Allah Most High said upon the tongue of His Prophet (Allah bless him and give him peace), 'I am as My servant thinks of Me...'[36] And the Prophet (Allah bless him and give him peace) said, 'There are two good qualities that are unsurpassed by any other goodness: having a good opinion of Allah and having a good opinion of Allah's servants.'[37] And the Prophet (Allah bless him and give him peace) also said, 'Let none of you die save that he holds a good opinion about Allah Most High.'[38] May Allah grant us such by His bounty and largesse!

وَخَالِفِ النَّفْسَ وَالشَّيْطَانَ وَاعْصِهِمَا   وَإِنْ هُمَا مَحَّضَاكَ النُّصْحَ فَاتَّهِمِ
وَلَا تُطِعْ مِنْهُمَا خَصْمًا وَلَا حَكَمًا   فَأَنْتَ تَعْرِفُ كَيْدَ الْخَصْمِ وَالْحَكَمِ

Oppose the self and Satan and disobey them;
If they offer you advice, be suspicious of them.
Obey neither of them, whether they oppose or give judgment,
For you know the wiles of opponent and judge.

Here the author (Allah have mercy upon him) says, addressing all who will lend an ear to his advice and accept his counsel: Oppose the lower self in everything it commands or forbids, for it is your fiercest foe; it wears the attire of a loved one and makes what is good look bad and what is bad look good. It covets selfish gains and desires and is keen to accomplish its goals. Despite the fact that it is the closest and most inseparable thing to you, you must remedy it with struggle (*mujāhada*) and self-reckoning (*muḥāsaba*).

As for Satan, his enmity towards you is long-standing. Allah Most High says, '*Verily Satan is an enemy to you, so take him as an enemy.*' (Qur'an 35:6). Moreover, Satan flows through the veins of man like his blood, and he is the brother of the lower self and keen to see that nothing but

36 Bukhārī.

37 Shaykh ʿAbdullāh al-Talīdī notes that the *ḥadīth* could not be traced.

38 Muslim.

evil is done by man. To realise Satan's enmity and envy it is enough for you [to hear] the Prophet's words, 'When the son of Ādam prostrates, Satan withdraws and weeps, saying "Woe is me! The son of Ādam was commanded to prostrate and he prostrated, so for him is Paradise, but when I was commanded to prostrate I refused, so for me is Hellfire!"'[39] Likewise, when a servant [of Allah] is sleeping, Satan ties knots at the back of his head to discourage him from praying in the night. He also flees when he hears the call to prayer. All of these actions are because of his envy and rage. If you were to ask 'How is it that he flees during the call to prayer but does not flee during the prayer itself, even though the prayer is greater?' I would respond: This is unique to him and does not entail that the call to prayer is somehow superior [to the prayer]. We find something similar in the narration about Satan fleeing from ʿUmar (Allah be pleased with him), though there is no report of him fleeing from Abū Bakr (Allah be pleased with him), even though it is a point of consensus that he is superior in rank to ʿUmar. What is more, it is authentically recorded that the Prophet (Allah bless him and give him peace) said, 'Satan came upon me last night while I was offering prayer, and I wanted to tie him up to one of the pillars of the mosque… '[40] Satan flees during the call to prayer because he is afraid of being called to bear witness on the Day of Resurrection that his enemy uttered the testimony of faith. So keen is he to harm his foe that he does not want to testify and bring him any benefit at all. He is predisposed to cause harm to the son of Ādam and keep benefit from him. It is also said that Satan flees from the call to prayer out of anger and envy when hearing the general invitation [to prayer] and the utterance of the testimony of faith, especially when also seeing people hasten and get ready for the prayer and respond to its call. During the call to prayer, all he sees are those busy in invocation or repeating the words of the muezzin, or those busy in purification or walking to the mosque—all of which increase him in envy and cause him to flee. But once he knows that people have responded to the call to prayer he returns once more, this time to spoil the prayer that they had prepared for and to deny them the sweetness of that to which they had hastened. May Allah protect us from him!

39 Muslim.
40 Aḥmad.

Because of all this, the Shaykh (the author) orders you to oppose the lower self and Satan and to disobey them, and he cautions you from being duped by their display of sincere advice. He says: *If they offer you advice, be suspicious of them*—in other words, hold them in suspicion in what they command you, and oppose them in what they invite you to, for they are lying in wait to ambush you and take advantage of you.

Furthermore, do not obey them when they oppose and object to you when you wish to do a righteous action—as it says in the *ḥadīth* report found in *al-Targhīb* [*wa al-Tarhīb* of al-Mundhirī], 'The son of Ādam cannot spend in charity until he pulls it from the clutches of seventy devils'[41]—and do not obey them when they level judgement on you to do something or abstain from something, for their judgment is predicated on their hatred and envy, for you know the plots and machinations and schemes of the opponent, and you know the plots of the enemy judge. It is inconceivable that he could be just with you.

If you say 'It is clear how an opponent can be described as plotting, but it is problematic to describe a judge as such,' I reply: If the opponent and judge are the lower self and Satan then it is easy to see how they can be described as plotting. It is as if the author were saying: For you know their wiles, whether they are two opponents or two judges. What the author intends to say here is that the lower self and Satan can be either opponents or judges. If a person is in control of his lower self and overpowers its appetites and desires, it will be his opponent, opposing his commands and prohibitions. But if a person is overcome by his lower self, his lower self will be a ruler over him and order him to do as it wills. So, he says, if the lower self or Satan make their commands or encouragements seem beneficial, you must oppose them and not feel secure from their plotting, even if no harm seems apparent to you. And if they overcome you and get the upper hand and assume the role of a judge who executes his judgements with force, then disobey them and meet them head on with intensity and violent force.

If you feel weak, seek recourse with the All-Powerful, the Mighty (al-Qawī al-Matīn), in whose Hands is the dominion of all existence, and place your trust in Him to repel their aggression. The Most High says, '*Truly Satan has no authority over those who believe and place their trust in their*

41 Ṭabarānī, *al-Muʿjam al-kabir*.

Lord.' (Qur'an 16:99). It is said in the *Ḥikam*, 'If you know that Satan does not forget you, do not forget Him in whose Hand is your forelock.' I say: Satan's forelock is also in Allah's Hand, so though He has given Satan leave to entice and seduce, He has not given him the ability to forsake and lead astray. So turn to the One in whose Hand are [all] hearts and forelocks, and do not look at the one who brings on enticement and sin. The One whom you fear may give Satan free rein over you is the same One whom you hope will repel Satan's evil from you.

It is said that Satan is like a dog: if you try to fight him, he will tear at your garments, but if you go to his master, the master will kindly keep him away from you. Dhū al-Nūn [al-Miṣrī] (Allah be pleased with him) said, 'If [Satan] sees you while you cannot see him, know that Allah sees him while he cannot see Allah. So seek Allah's aid against him!' (This was quoted by Shaykh Aḥmad Zarrūq, may Allah benefit us by him, Amen.)

This, then, is the wisdom behind Satan and the lower self assailing mankind: so they can express their utter neediness for Allah and their gatheredness unto Him, Most High. It states in the Ḥikam, 'Allah appointed [Satan] as your foe so that through him He might drive you towards Himself, and He stirred your ego against you so that your turning to Him might be constant.' Shaykh Aḥmad Zarrūq (Allah be pleased with him) said [in his commentary on this aphorism]:

> That is because the one who fears his enemy will seek refuge with his beloved, and when there is no enemy then the refuge sought with the beloved is incomplete. This is one of the wisdoms behind the creation of Satan and his imposition. Secondly, Satan was created in this [worldly] abode to be a rag on which the filth of mankind is wiped. Thirdly, Satan was created so that Allah might distinguish the vile from the pure, to set apart those who follow the Emissaries (*Rusul*) from those who follow Satan, so as to establish the proof and make matters clear (since there should be no confusion after matters have been explained). Abū Saʿīd al-Khudrī (Allah be pleased with him) related, 'I heard the Emissary of Allah say, "Iblīs said to his Lord, 'By Your Might and Majesty, so long as their souls remain in them, I will persist in leading astray the sons of Ādam!' His Lord said to him, 'By My Might and

> Majesty, so long as they continue seeking My forgiveness, I will persist in forgiving them!'""[42]

In addition to this, there is wisdom behind the imposition of creation (who cause injury), and the imposition of the lower world and caprice—namely for the servant to express his weakness and poverty, and to turn to his Lord and flee from everything else besides Him. It states in the *Ḥikam*, 'He only made injury come at the hands of other [people] so that you do not repose in them. He wanted to stir you out of everything so that nothing would occupy you from Him.' Therefore Allah has subjected you to the injury and affliction of creation, the stresses and spiritual grime of the lower world, the whispering and harm of Satan and the fluctuations and vicissitudes of the lower self. These are the four hurdles that encompass all of creation. They have destroyed those for whom destruction was decreed, and only those protected by Allah are saved from them. One of the poets spoke well when he said about them:

> I have been tested through four things
> That shoot at me with a taut bow:
> Iblīs, the world, my ego and creation.
> O Lord, You alone can deliver me!

The lower self (*nafs*) is in fact the soul (*rūḥ*); in its genesis it is called a soul. The soul is a subtle entity through which life is possible (conventionally). When the soul inclines towards lower appetites it is called a lower self. So as long as a foetus is in the womb of its mother it possesses a soul, and when it is born and develops and acquires blameworthy character traits it is called a lower self. It may be likened to the water that nourishes a tree: it is originally water, then it transforms into grapes, and those grapes then transform into wine and then transform into vinegar and so on. Allah Most High knows best.

أَسْتَغْفِرُ اللَّهَ مِنْ قَوْلٍ بِلَا عَمَلٍ   لَقَدْ نَسَبْتُ بِهِ نَسْلًا لِذِي عُقُمِ

I seek Allah's forgiveness for words bereft of deeds,
As by them I attributed progeny to a sterile man.

42 Tirmidhī, *Sunan*.

Here the author (Allah have mercy upon him) expresses his humility and lack of reliance upon his works, essentially saying: 'I seek Allah's forgiveness for my words of advice and counsel, and for my encouragement and exhortation to follow the path of guidance, since everyone who hears these counsels and warnings thinks that I, as the speaker and guide to them and based on my state of being, only make the effort to exhort others because I practice what I preach and follow the same straight path and upright way that I urge others to follow—but that is not the case! No, rather I have deluded myself and fallen for illusion and failed to do as I say. I have encouraged others to do good works but I have not done them myself. I have sated myself with what is not truly in my possession. To the one I speak with it appears that I have self-control and that I have overcome my personal demon, but in reality my condition is quite the opposite. And in giving listeners the impression that I also act on the advice I give them—even though I am utterly bereft of good deeds—I am akin to someone who attributes progeny to a barren and childless man; for I have encouraged good deeds but have not done any myself, and I have given counsel to others but have not accepted it myself. So anyone who believes that I act upon my own words of advice is like a person who believes that an impotent man can have offspring. Because of the misleading impression given by my advice I have, in a sense, attributed progeny to an impotent man.'

This couplet is the author's way of expressing humility and self-depreciation. What he has said here is not a falsehood, for two reasons. The first reason is that he felt that his actions were tainted and not fit for divine acceptance, so he did not rely upon them. The second reason is that, with the exception of the Prophets, it is almost impossible to be completely safe from obeying the dictates of the ego or Satan. So it is as if he were saying: 'I have enjoined you to oppose the ego and Satan in all that they tell you to do, yet I was unable to comply with the same command; so how can I say *Oppose the self and Satan and disobey them*? I enjoined you to do righteous works but forgot myself; I neither acted upon what I enjoined, nor did I abstain from what I had forbidden others to do. So it is only right that I seek forgiveness for this.'

ʿAlī (Allah be pleased with him) believed that seeking forgiveness was the remedy for every stressful matter. It is related that a man came to him and said, 'O Leader of the Believers, for years now we have been suffering drought and shortages!' ʿAlī replied, 'Seek Allah's forgiveness and He will remove the affliction that is upon you.' Shortly thereafter another man complained to ʿAlī of weakness and poverty, to which ʿAlī replied, 'Seek Allah's forgiveness.' Then came another man who complained to him that he desired children but was infertile, so ʿAlī said to him, 'Seek abundant forgiveness from Allah and He will bless you with many offspring.' Then came a man who complained to ʿAlī that his orchard was ruined, so ʿAlī said to him, 'Seek Allah's forgiveness.' Someone then said, 'Abū al-Ḥasan [ʿAlī], you enjoined all of those men to seek forgiveness despite the fact that their requests were varied.' ʿAlī replied, 'I enjoined upon them what the Prophet Nūḥ enjoined upon his people when he said, "*Seek the forgiveness of your Lord. Verily He is Oft-Forgiving*" (Qur'an 71:10)—and Nūḥ knew that by [nothing less than] divine revelation.'

أَمَرْتُكَ الْخَيْرَ لٰكِنْ مَا ائْتَمَرْتُ بِهِ   وَمَا اسْتَقَمْتُ فَمَا قَوْلِي لَكَ اسْتَقِمِ

I enjoined goodness upon you while failing to heed the same.
I was not upright, so what use is my enjoining uprightness?

Here the author (Allah have mercy upon him) says: I enjoined goodness upon you while failing to heed the same. I enjoined you to be upright while I am not upright myself, but how can one who does not tread the path of rectitude and uprightness advise others to tread it? How can one who beguiles himself exhort others? And in the event that he exhorts others, his words will leave no effect and his counsel will not be accepted, for seldom does an exhorter's counsel and advice benefit others if he is bereft of the very qualities he encourages others to adopt. Had those qualities taken root in his heart then his exhortation would have taken root in the hearts of others. How excellent is the statement of the poet:

O you who teach others
Why don't you teach yourself?
You prescribe medicine for the sick and emaciated –
Yet you too are sick and suffering gauntness!
I see you pollinating our minds with guidance and advice
Even though you are bereft of guidance yourself.

Begin with your self, forbid it its errant ways,
When you do so, you will truly be a sage;
Then others will accept your exhortations
And follow your words, so your lessons will benefit.
Do not forbid others something you do yourself.
If you do, what an enormity and shame!

In a *ḥadīth* recorded in the *Ṣaḥīḥ* [of al-Bukhārī] and other collections it is related that the Emissary of Allah (Allah bless him and give him peace) said, 'A man will be brought on the Day of Resurrection and thrown into the Hellfire. His intestines will be hanging out, spilling onto the ground, and he will go around Hell as a donkey goes around a millstone. The denizens of Hell will gather around him and say, "O so-and-so, what is the matter with you? Used you not to enjoin us to do good deeds and forbid us from doing evil deeds?" He will reply, "Yes. I used to enjoin you to do good deeds, but I did not do them; and I used to forbid you from doing evil deeds yet I would do them myself!"'

The words of the Most High '*Do you enjoin people to righteousness yet forget [it] yourselves, whilst you recite the Scripture?*' (Qur'an 2:44) seem to censure those who do not act on their knowledge. Indeed, a scholar's slip is punished more severely than the slip of an ignorant person, and his burden is greater because he disobeys and transgresses knowing full well the gravity of his sin. Disobedience when near is more severe than disobedience when distant. And though an ignorant person is not excused for his sin, still one who disobeys Allah while ignorant of Allah's ruling concerning that act (and who is not wilfully transgressing) is not comparable to one who disobeys Allah while knowing the ruling of his sin but who still does it wilfully and flagrantly. We ask Him, the Most High, for protection by His grace and generosity!

وَلَا تَـزَوَّدْتُ قَبْـلَ الْـمَـوْتِ نَـافِلَـةً   وَلَـمْ أُصَـلِّ سِـوَىٰ فَـرْضٍ وَلَـمْ أَصُـمِ

I have not gathered provisions of voluntary prayers before death, or prayed and fasted beyond what is obligatory.

Here the author (Allah have mercy upon him) expresses remorse over himself and what has passed of a life bereft of voluntary good deeds, and laments the fact that he has failed to gather provision of voluntary prayers and fasts before his death. Because he has limited himself to the [five] obligatory prayers and the obligatory fasting [in Ramaḍān] he has missed the opportunity to reach the levels of those brought near (*al-muqarrabīn*). Indeed, people will have stations and ranks in Paradise according to their pious works. Consider the narration in the *Ṣaḥīḥ* [of al-Bukhārī] in which it is related that the Prophet (Allah bless him and give him peace) said, 'Verily, a man from the inhabitants of Paradise will gaze up at a man above him just as one of you gazes up at distant planet in the heavens.' That is because the man above will have a high rank and lofty station [in Paradise]. If, despite the divine care shown to him and his lofty station and nobility in the sight of Allah, the Prophet (Allah bless him and give him peace) wished to be killed in the path of Allah as a martyr and then resurrected so to be killed again, and then resurrected and to be killed again, seeking divine largesse and exalted rank in the Hereafter (even though he had complete certainty that he was going to enter Paradise and receive the utmost special favours)—if that was the Prophet (Allah bless him and give him peace), what can be said of someone who has not offered voluntary prayers or fasting, and has not smelled even a whiff of the station of Prophethood!

This couplet is an acknowledgement of the previous one in which the author says he is not upright. You may ask, 'How can he claim that neglecting voluntary acts voids uprightness (*istiqāma*) when we have the *ḥadīth* of Ḍamām b. Thaʿlaba who, when the Prophet (Allah bless him and give him peace) explained to him the obligatory acts of the prayer and zakāt and fasting, said "By Allah, I will neither do more or less than that" and the Prophet replied, "He has attained success—if he is truthful," or he said 'He will enter Paradise if what he says is true"?[43] Were it not that uprightness is attainable by merely performing the obligatory acts, the Prophet (Allah bless him and give him peace) would not have testified that [Ḍamām] would enter Paradise.'

To this I reply: The uprightness that the author denies possessing is complete uprightness (*al-istiqāma al-kāmila*), which is usually only attainable by one who completes his obligatory acts by offering voluntary acts as well. Voluntary acts mend and make good the defects and shortcomings of the obligatory acts. As for Ḍamām b. Thaʿlaba, all of his obliga-

43 Bukhārī and Muslim.

tory acts were perfect by virtue of the fact that he acquired them from the radiant lights of the Prophet's countenance. [The Prophet (Allah bless him and give him peace) said] 'Were you to spend gold equal to the weight of Mount Uḥud you would still not reach the measure of a handful (*mudd*) of one of them, or even half of that.'[44]

If you ask 'How can he swear an oath that he will not do anything more than the obligatory acts when neglect of the *witr* prayer, the Eid prayers, and the prayer for rain is cause to have one's testimony in court rejected, and anyone who persistently neglects them is to be disciplined?' There are two possible answers to this. First, it is probable that the incident with Ḍamām took place before the *witr* prayer and the Eid and other Sunna prayers were legislated. That is because only the obligatory prayers were legislated during the Night Journey (*Isrāʾ*). (al-Alyūrī mentioned this point, but it is questionable.) Second, it is probable that the Prophet (Allah bless him and give him peace) understood from the words of the Bedouin [Ḍamām] that his intention was that he would not alter Allah's legal rulings by adding or subtracting from them, and would not contravene Allah's commands or innovate anything himself outside the Sunna acts. As such, he did not intend the Sunna acts, and in fact they did not cross his mind. This is a good response.

[Regarding the couplet] it is possible that the author's denial is literal, and it is also possible that he is merely expressing his lack of reliance upon his deeds, even if he did in fact offer voluntary prayers and fasts. So it is as if he were saying, 'I have not gathered provisions of much voluntary prayer or fasting.' This is the ostensive meaning of the couplet and is more fitting, given the station of the Shaykh.

44 Bukhārī and Muslim.

CHAPTER 3

Praise of the Prophet ﷺ

ظَلَمْتُ سُنَّةَ مَنْ أَحْيَا الظَّلَامَ إِلَى   أَنِ اشْتَكَتْ قَدَمَاهُ الضُّرَّ مِنْ وَرَمِ

I have wronged the Sunna of him who enlivened the dark nights
By praying till his feet complained of painful swelling.

THE AUTHOR (Allah have mercy upon him) means to say: I have wronged the Sunna of Allah's Emissary (Allah bless him and give him peace), whose practice was to maintain the night vigil prayer, arising at night to endure the rigours of keeping awake and strive and stand at length. The Prophet (Allah bless him and give him peace) continued like this until his two blessed feet would swell owing to the immense fatigue and effort they bore.

[It is as if he says:] 'I have short-changed myself by not adopting the Prophet's Sunna, and have not given it its proper place.' Notice that he did not say: 'I have wronged the Sunna of Allah's Emissary (Allah bless him and give him peace),' for his intention here is to encourage and engender a longing for following the Prophet (Allah bless him and give him peace) in this particular action, and to bring to attention the trait that deserves to be emulated. So it is as if he is saying: [I have wronged the Sunna of] the one who was like this in his worship, and who was like this in his devotions.

In this couplet the author says that the Prophet (Allah bless him and give him peace) *enlivened the dark nights*. This is metaphorical, for the dark nights are not [literally] characterised by life; however, since the Prophet (Allah bless him and give him peace) would spend his entire nights awake in nocturnal devotions standing before his Master, the author described him as having enlivened the dark nights.

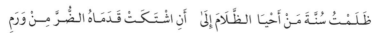

There are reports that have been transmitted concerning the night vigils and prayers of Allah's Emissary (Allah bless him and give him peace). It is reported that ʿAwf b. Mālik said, 'One night I was with the Emissary of Allah. He cleaned his teeth with a tooth-stick, performed ablutions and stood up to pray, so I stood up with him. He began by reciting Sūrat al-Baqara. He did not recite a single verse of glorification without glorifying [Allah]; and he did not recite a single verse of refuge without seeking refuge [with Allah]; and he did not recite a single verse of mercy without pausing and asking for mercy. After that he bowed and then raised his head and said, "Exalted and Transcendent is Allah, Master of the material and spiritual realms, and Possessor of Magnificence." Then he prostrated and said the same thing. Then [after standing again] he recited Sūrat Āl ʿImrān, and then another Sūra and then another, doing the same in his bowing and prostration [as he did in the first unit of prayer].'[45]

Al-Nasāʾī related from Ḥudhayfa b. al-Yamān who said: 'I once prayed behind the Emissary of Allah and he began by reciting Sūrat al-Baqara. I said to myself, "He will bow after he recites one hundred verses," but he continued. I then said to myself, "He will bow after reciting two hundred verses," but he continued. I then said to myself, "He will recite the entire chapter in the first unit," but he continued. He then began reciting Sūrat al-Nisāʾ, followed by Sūrat Āl ʿImrān. He did not recite a single verse of glorification without glorifying [Allah], and he did not recite a single verse of refuge without seeking refuge [with Allah]. He would say in his bowing, "Exalted and transcendent is my Lord, the Magnificent" and in his prostration he would say, "Exalted and transcendent is my Lord, the Most Exalted."'

When the Prophet (Allah bless him and give him peace) recited these chapters in his prayer, he would do so with a slow melody and with deep contemplation, and would invoke [Allah] and humbly entreat Him. It is inconceivable that these chapters could be recited in this manner unless the entire night, or a greater portion of it, were spent in prayer. A report found in al-Bukhārī's collection and others states that the Emissary of Allah (Allah bless him and give him peace) would spend the night in prayer until his feet swelled. He was asked, 'Why do you do this, O

45 Tirmidhī, *Shamāʾil*.

Emissary of Allah, when Allah has forgiven your past and future sins?' He replied, 'Shall I not then be a grateful servant?'

There is a difference of opinion regarding the ruling of the night vigil prayer for the Emissary of Allah (Allah bless him and give him peace): was it recommended for him or was it compulsory? And if it is said that it was compulsory for him, was it later abrogated or not? The position of the majority of scholars is that it was always compulsory for him and that it was at one time compulsory for others, but later abrogated. Ibn al-Ḥabīb stated:

> It [the night vigil prayer] was compulsory before the [five prayers] were prescribed, and after they were prescribed the [compulsory status of] night vigil prayer was abrogated; similarly, fasting on the day of ʿĀshūrāʾ was once compulsory but abrogated (while remaining recommended) after fasting in the month of Ramaḍān was made compulsory.

The Emissary of Allah (Allah bless him and give him peace) used to enjoin and encourage the night vigil prayer. In one *ḥadīth* the Emissary of Allah (Allah bless him and give him peace) stated, 'Abū Hurayra, do you wish to have Allah's mercy upon you in life and death and in the grave and after resurrection?' 'Yes,' said Abū Hurayra. He said, 'Then stand in the night, Abū Hurayra, and pray while desiring the good pleasure of your Lord. If you pray in the inner confines of your home, the light of your home [seen] in the heavens will be like the light of the celestial bodies.'[46] It is also related that if a person who prays the night vigil prayer, his place of prayer on the ground weeps for him, as does the area in the heavens to which his deeds are raised.

When the Emissary of Allah (Allah bless him and give him peace) arose to perform the night vigil prayer he would look out upon the horizon and recite the final verses of Sūrat Āl ʿImrān: '*Indeed, in the creation of the heavens and the earth…*' (Qur'an 3:190–193) The Prophet (Allah bless him and give him peace) should be emulated [in this].

The night vigil prayer has several benefits. Firstly, it is an emulation of the Emissary of Allah (Allah bless him and give him peace).

46 Shaykh ʿAbdullāh al-Talīdī notes that there is no basis for this narration.

Secondly, it contains an immense reward and mighty honour. It is stated in a *ḥadīth*, 'After the prescribed prayers, there is none more meritorious than the night vigil prayer.' Some of the early *Salaf* used to say, 'Were it not for the night vigil prayer, I would not have liked to remain in the world.' Others would say, 'The delight of the night vigil prayer is not of this world; it is but of the bounties of the Hereafter that Allah has advanced to His saints [in this life].' On one occasion Junayd was seen in a dream vision after his death and he was asked, 'What has Allah done with you?' He replied, 'Perished are those spiritual allusions (*ishārāt*), and passed are those expressions; I have benefited from nothing save those few cycles of prayer that I used to perform in the darkness of night.'

Thirdly, Allah has extolled those who are frequent in their night vigil prayers: '*It was but little of the night that they would sleep*' (Qur'an 51:17), and: '*And those who spend the night for their Lord, prostrating and standing.*' (Qur'an 25:64)

Fourthly, someone who prays the night vigil prayer is likely to encounter the hour during which prayers are answered.

Fifthly, the time of the night vigil prayer is one wherein mercies descend and fragrant breezes fall. The Emissary of Allah (Allah bless him and give him peace) said, 'During the last third of each night, our Lord descends to the lower heaven and says, "Who calls upon Me, that I may respond to him? Who asks of Me, that I may give to him? Who seeks My forgiveness, that I may forgive him? Is there anyone supplicating?" And this is until the appearance of dawn.'[47] This *ḥadīth* entails that the caller's prayer will be answered and the supplicant's request will be granted.

Sixthly, the night vigil prayer is a genuine expression of sincerity and is free of ostentation or noticing creation, for no one makes the effort to stand in the night and gives preference to it over sleep unless his faith is complete and his certainty true.

Seventhly, the night vigil prayer adds blessing and increase to one's life: sleep is death and wakefulness is life, so when someone rises in the night he has essentially added to his lifespan, and when he goes to sleep he has decreased it. That is because sleep accounts for half of one's time, so the one who sleeps the entire night away has lost half of his lifespan,

47 Bukhārī and Muslim.

and whoever stands during the night stands for half of his lifespan. May Allah aid the one who said:

> If a young man lives for sixty years,
> Half of his life is effaced in the nights.
> And for one quarter he tarries heedlessly,
> Not knowing his left from his right;
> And one third of it is but hopes and cravings,
> Preoccupation with earnings and kin.
> And the remainder of life is illness and grey hair
> And ailments that portend relocation.

Another benefit is that the night vigil prayer takes a portion of the Praiseworthy Station, even if that station is exclusively for the Emissary of Allah (Allah bless him and give him peace). Because the Emissary of Allah made it a result of the night vigil prayer, and everyone who is in conformity with his practice will obtain of the Praiseworthy Station as is commensurate with his rank and station. In addition, praying in the night confers on one a beautiful countenance, since the Prophet (Allah bless him and give him peace) said, 'He who has many prayers at night will have a beautiful face in the day.'[48] Furthermore, praying in the night expels illness from the body and protects one from Satan's urine, for it states in a *ḥadīth*, 'When a servant goes to sleep, the angels bid him awake three times. If the servant awakens and rises to perform his night vigil prayer [he is protected]; otherwise, Satan urinates in his ear.'[49]

Another benefit of the night vigil prayer is that the angels, as well as the jinn who inhabit the heavens, listen and are gladdened by the recitation of the one who arises at night to pray. And we have already cited the *ḥadīth* describing how the light of one's home can be seen like the light of the celestial bodies. May Allah Most High, out of His grace and largesse, and by the rank of our Master Muḥammad (Allah bless him and give him peace), grant us the ability to stand in prayer during the night!

48 Shaykh ʿAbd Allāh al-Talīdī notes that this is not a *ḥadīth* but a statement of Shurayk, as narrated in the *Sunan* of Ibn Mājah.

49 Ṭabarānī, *al-Muʿjam al-awsaṭ*.

وَشَدَّ مِنْ سَغَبٍ أَحْشَاءَهُ وَطَوَىٰ   تَحْتَ الْحِجَارَةِ كَشْحًا مُتْرَفَ الْأَدَمِ

He placed a stone over his belly and soft skin,
Tightening a belt over it to diminish the hunger pangs.

The author (Allah have mercy upon him) says: Such were the Prophet's renunciation (*zuhd*), frugality and lack of concern for the world that he used to place a stone over his belly out of hunger—and this was after Allah gave him the choice to either be a Prophet-king or a Prophet-servant, and he chose servitude. This was also after Allah offered the Prophet (Allah bless him and give him peace) to turn the mountains of Tihāma into gold and silver for him, and he turned away from it.

This is the lead-in to the praise intended in this ode. The recipient of praise may be praised for several qualities that exist within him: traits that he acquires; innate qualities or gifts that Allah favours him with; and those which are not within the grasp of human effort, such as the inimitable miracles of the Prophet (Allah bless him and give him peace) or the charismatic gifts of a saint. Here the author begins by praising the Prophet (Allah bless him and give him peace) for the first type: the acquired traits. He deems it better to start with this type since it shows how the Prophet (Allah bless him and give him peace) adopted the character traits of servanthood (*ʿubūdiyya*) and manifested the might of Lordship (*rubūbiyya*). For someone who overpowers his self, orders it to follow his bidding and is severe with it in pursuit of its Master's pleasure—by standing before Him during the night in intimate conversation and recitation of His Book—has manifested the humility of servitude and the might of Lordship.

In the second half of the couplet the author mentions the Prophet's patience with the pangs of hunger and his bearing its difficulties for the sake of the benefits and advantages that it entailed. The wisdom behind placing a stone over one's belly during hunger is that stones, by nature, are cooler than other things, and when one suffers extreme hunger he is susceptible to imbalances in his temperament and aches in his liver, as well as an excess of yellow bile. However, when a hungry person places a stone over his belly, tightening a belt over it, its coolness dispels the excess heat of the liver and removes imbalances in the body's constitution, preventing instability in the humours. This practice is better at keeping away pain and more likely to preserve the [strength of the] limbs.

Despite the Prophet's practice of limiting his intake of food and avoiding satiety, his body was delicate (though he did not pursue luxury), and his skin was soft without opulence. The reason why Allah condemned the people of opulence is that their enjoyment came through means of luxury and varieties of food and drink, and they aspired to that which went into their stomachs and made themselves slaves to their appetites and carnal passions. As for the Prophet's *taraf*[50] and the delicacy of his pure body, they were not the result of gluttonous eating or enjoying a wide variety of foodstuffs; rather, they were a result of divine largesse and pre-eternal lordly favour and divine concern. Days would pass without the Prophet (Allah bless him and give him peace) tasting food. This is known from the *ḥadīth* collections that describe his form and traits (Allah bless him and give him peace), and is alluded to in the author's statement, *tightening a belt over it*—that is, his belly and soft skin—*to diminish the hunger pangs*.

The Prophet's skin was soft, and that was a break with natural phenomena, because those who limit their intake of food usually have dry skin and appear emaciated, but the Prophet's hunger only increased him in delicacy and suppleness.

The author's reference to the Prophet (Allah bless him and give him peace) placing a stone over his belly is well known. Once during the Battle of the Trench, some of the Companions went and complained to the Prophet (Allah bless him and give him peace) about their severe hunger, and uncovered their stomachs to show a stone tied to each of them. Upon seeing this, the Prophet (Allah bless him and give him peace) uncovered his stomach to show not one stone but two.

ʿĀʾisha (Allah be pleased with her) said, 'The Emissary of Allah never ate barley bread three nights in a row until he met Allah, the Exalted and Sublime. He never complained to anyone, and poverty was dearer to him than wealth. He would spend an entire night writhing in hunger, but that would not prevent him from fasting the following day.'[51] ʿĀʾisha

50 Elsewhere in his commentary, Shaykh Aḥmad Ibn ʿAjība defines *taraf* as delicacy and beauty, although an alternative translation—the Qur'anic usage, in fact—renders *taraf* as 'opulence' or 'luxury'. [t]

51 Tirmidhī, *Shamāʾil*.

also reported, 'The Emissary of Allah never ate his fill. Sometimes, seeing his hunger, I would weep out of pity for him and rub his belly with my hand, saying, "May I be your ransom! If only you would partake of the world, just enough would strengthen you!" But he would only say, "ʿĀʾisha, what have I to do with the world? My brethren from the Emissaries of High Resolve (*Ulū al-ʿAzm*) were patient with circumstances much harsher, but they persevered and continued as they were until they met their Lord and He granted them an honoured place of repose. I find myself ashamed to enjoy any comforts in this life of mine, lest I do not attain to their degree. There is nothing dearer to me than catching up with my brethren and intimate friends." It was no more than a month thereafter that he met Allah, the Exalted and Sublime.'[52]

Despite the Prophet's way [of hunger], he was granted such strength of body and limbs as no other man had ever attained. He was the strongest and most robust of people. He wrestled with [the master wrestler] Rukāna and defeated him time and time again, and would walk faster than everyone else; his stride, although tranquil and composed, was so swift that it seemed as if the earth was folded for him.

Anas (Allah be pleased with him) said, 'The Prophet was given the sexual stamina of forty men. In the span of a few hours, he would visit each of his eleven wives [and have intimate relations with each of them] and take a bath after seeing each one.'[53] And when the Prophet (Allah bless him and give him peace) woke up in the morning, his eyes would be fresh as if with antimony, and his hair would be oiled. He was more beautiful than the full moon on a clear night.

The reports concerning the Prophet's frugality and contentment with little are well known, and the narrations concerning them are mass-transmitted and famous. The author of *al-Shifā'* [Qāḍī ʿIyāḍ] has supplied the healing in this regard.[54]

The lawgiver (Allah bless him and give him peace) has condemned satiety and praised hunger and the one who practices it. The Prophet (Allah bless him and give him peace) said, 'The most exalted of you in rank in the sight of Allah shall be those who hungered, thirsted and

52 Qāḍī ʿIyāḍ, *al-Shifā'*.

53 Ibid.

54 This refers to Qāḍī ʿIyāḍ's work *al-Shifā' bi taʿrīf ḥuqūq al-Muṣṭafā*. [t]

contemplated the most, while the most despised of you in the sight of Allah shall be those given to excessive sleep and gluttony.'[55] The Prophet (Allah bless him and give him peace) also said, 'Slay not your hearts with excessive food and drink, for the heart is like farmland that will perish if watered excessively.'[56] The Prophet (Allah bless him and give him peace) told Usāma (Allah be pleased with him), 'If you are able to be in such a state that death comes to you while your stomach is hungry and your mouth is parched with thirst, do so; for by that you shall attain the stations of nobility or abide with the Prophets, the angels will rejoice at the appearance of your soul, and the Compeller (al-Jabbār) will exalt your mention.'[57]

The Prophet (Allah bless him and give him peace) said, 'Indeed, Satan courses with the blood in the son of Ādam, so straiten his courses with hunger and thirst.' The Pious *Salaf* used to consider it a divine gift if they were tried with hunger. It is related that no one will be tried with hunger save the best of people, followed by those who are the most like them, and those for whom Allah shows care and divine concern. Fuḍayl b. al-ʿIyāḍ once said (in intimate conversation with his Lord): 'You have made my family and me hungry; by what means have I obtained this blessing from You? This is how You treat Your friends; would that I knew I was among them, that I might rejoice!' ʿAbd al-Raḥmān b. Yazīd would often swear an oath by Allah that no one has attained spiritual purity save with hunger, that no one has ever walked upon water save with hunger and that no one has had the earth fold up for him save with hunger.

Earlier we discussed how extreme hunger is blameworthy, and how the best of all matters are those in the middle course: a third for food, a third for drink, and a third for air. With Allah is all success. Anyone who would like to learn about the benefits of eating less should look into the *Iḥyāʾ*. I have also cited it extensively in my commentary on the *Hamziyya*, so anyone who would like more detail may refer to that. And with Allah is all providential grace, and there is no might or power save with Allah.

55 Shaykh ʿAbd Allāh al-Talīdī observes that this narration is baseless (*lā aṣl lah*).

56 Al-Ghazālī, *Iḥyāʾ ʿulūm al-dīn* (this *ḥadīth* is without basis).

57 Ibn al-Jawzī says that this *ḥadīth* is a forgery (*al-Mawḍūʿāt*, 3:148).

وَرَاوَدَتْهُ الْجِبَالُ الشُّمُّ مِنْ ذَهَبٍ عَنْ نَفْسِهِ فَأَرَاهَا أَيَّمَا شَمَمِ

Lofty mountains tried, to tempt him with turning to gold,
But he showed them the height of his own loftiness!

We mentioned earlier how praise can be given for acquired traits, such as standing in prayer during the night and renouncing the world, or for instinctual and innate qualities, such as generosity and bravery, or for things that amount to breaks with natural phenomena, in which the servant has no share, such as inimitable miracles or charismatic gifts—as in our case here, when the lofty mountains sought to tempt the Emissary of Allah. Essentially this couplet means: The Emissary of Allah (Allah bless him and give him peace) reached such pinnacles of worldly renunciation and detachment from it that he turned his nose up to it and showed it lofty height. In other words, he did not turn his attention to it or incline in its direction, nor was he fooled by its ornaments or deluded by its temptations. The temptation by the mountains is metaphorical, for in reality it was the angel who offered them to the Prophet, by the command of Allah Most Exalted.

The author (Allah have mercy upon him), alludes here to the *ḥadīth* in which the Angel Jibrīl (upon whom be peace) descended upon the Emissary of Allah (Allah bless him and give him peace) and said to him, "Allah relays His salutations to you and says: 'Would you like Me to turn these mountains into gold and silver for you, being with you wherever you go?' The Emissary of Allah lowered his head for some time and then said, "O Jibrīl, this world is the abode of him who has no abode, and it is the wealth of him who has no wealth; only a person lacking intellect seeks to amass it." Jibrīl said, "May Allah make you firm, O Muḥammad, with the firm statement!"[58]

ʿĀʾisha (Allah be pleased with her) reported in another *ḥadīth*: 'The Emissary of Allah said, "Truly, Allah presented the mountains of Mecca to me and offered to turn them into gold and silver, but I said, 'Lord, I prefer to go hungry one day and eat to my fill the next: for the day in which I go hungry I turn fervently to You and call upon you, and on the day in which I eat my fill I praise and extol You.'"'[59] When the Prophet

58 Bayhaqī, *Sunan* al-kubra.

59 Aḥmad.

(Allah bless him and give him peace) said "eat my fill," he meant it as the converse of hunger, for his satiety was in that which maintained his life and health. ʿĀʾisha (Allah be pleased with her) said, "Never was the Prophet's belly filled with food."[60] ʿAbd al-Raḥmān b. ʿAwf (Allah be pleased with him) said, "The Prophet passed away while neither he nor his family had eaten their fill of barley bread."[61]

It behoves the Prophet's heirs among the scholars and saints to emulate him (by whom they received the honour of their inheritance) and eschew the world and avoid casting furtive glances at it, busying themselves instead with the obligations of servitude that are incumbent upon them, such as disseminating sacred knowledge, actualising it in themselves, and performing and perfecting righteous works. Likewise, it behoves the saints to avoid inclining to or longing for miracles and breaks with natural phenomena or anything of the sort; for according to the realised masters, the most tremendous miracle is upright rectitude (*istiqāma*) in the inward and outward.

Shaykh Abū al-Ḥasan al-Shādhilī (Allah be pleased with him) said:

> They are the two comprehensive and encompassing miracles: actualising the miracle of faith (īmān) with an increase in certitude and direct witnessing, and actualising the miracle of works that are through emulation and following [the Prophet (Allah bless him and give him peace)] and avoiding false, pretentious claims and self-delusion. If someone is granted these two miracles and yet still longs for something else besides them, he is a gross liar and slanderer, or he is badly mistaken in knowledge and action. He may be likened to a person who is honoured to witness a king who is well pleased with him, yet longs to go out and tend the beasts and refuses the king's good pleasure. Every 'miracle' that is not accompanied by good pleasure from Allah and through Allah, its recipient is deluded and lured to destruction (*mustadraj*), or is deficient or destroyed.

May Allah benefit us by him and grant us—out of His grace and favour, and by the rank of His Prophet, our Master and liege lord Muḥammad

60 Tirmidhī, *Shamāʾil*.
61 Ibid.

(Allah bless him and give him peace)—the goodliest portion of the miracle of upright rectitude.

وَأَكَّدَتْ زُهْدَهُ فِيهَا ضَرُورَتُهُ   إِنَّ الضَّرُورَةَ لَا تَعْدُو عَلَى الْعِصَمِ

وَكَيْفَ تَدْعُو إِلَى الدُّنْيَا ضَرُورَةُ مَنْ   لَوْلَاهُ لَمْ تَخْرُجِ الدُّنْيَا مِنَ الْعَدَمِ

His dire neediness only strengthened his detachment;
neediness like his never leads to transgression.
How could need tempt him with worldliness, when but for him
The world would not have emerged from non-existence?

The author (Allah have mercy upon him) says: One of the things that will confirm for you the Prophet's renunciation and exalted aspiration is the fact that outwardly he was in need of taking from the world yet he did not turn to it or allow his lofty aspiration to become attached to it, despite the fact that having a need for something typically gives rise to avidness and longing for that thing. This shows that the Prophet's renunciation (Allah bless him and give him peace) was from choice, for the world was brought to him lock, stock and barrel, and kings, out of their awe for him, lavished him with gifts, and war-spoils were brought to him—yet despite all of that he would spend the night in hunger and passed away with his armour mortgaged to him.[62] There are a great many reports on this subject that cannot be fully enumerated here; all of them prove that the Prophet (Allah bless him and give him peace) was fully capable of taking from the world; yet he turned away from it, desirous instead of what is with Allah, and in conformity with what Allah Most High loves. For the world is contemptible in the sight of Allah Most High, and so whoever's attitude towards the world corresponds to how it is considered in Allah's sight, Allah will love and prefer that person. The Prophet (Allah bless him and give him peace) said, 'If, in the sight of Allah, the world equalled the weight of a gnat's wing, He would not have given a disbeliever a single sip of water.'[63] Shaykh Aḥmad Zarrūq (Allah be pleased with him) mentions a report in one of his books: 'Since Allah created the world He has not looked upon it. After creating it He said to the gnat, "Purchase it from me." The gnat said, "For how much,

62 Bukhārī and Aḥmad.

63 Tirmidhī, *Sunan*.

O Lord?" Allah said, "For one of your wings." The gnat asked, "Then what shall we do with the rest?" Allah said, "Descend to it [i.e., the world] and take repose in it." The gnat said, "I have no need of anything that will hold my life back."'

The Prophet (Allah bless him and give him peace) knew the reality of the world and its meanness in the sight of Allah, because Allah Most High said, '*The life of the world is but play and jest*' [Qur'an 47:36] and, '*The example of the life of this world is but like rain that We send down from the sky...*' [Qur'an 10:24]. [Qāḍī] Ibn al-ʿArabī (Allah have mercy upon him) said:

> There are several benefits found in likening the world to rain. The first benefit is that rain does not come down through stratagem: and likewise with the world, for it is only gained through apportioning. Allah Most High says, '*We apportioned for them their livelihood.*' [Qur'an 43:32] The second benefit lies in the fact that rain comes down on account of begging, longing and fervent prayer: likewise the world and its provisions are obtained through longing and supplication. The third benefit is that in one place rain is a cause of life, and in another place it is a cause of destruction: likewise with wealth; for the one who deserves it, wealth is a cause of obedience, and he spends it for the sake of good, but for the one who does not deserve it, wealth is a cause of destruction and transgression, and he spends it on different types of disobedience. The fourth benefit is that rain is beneficial when it comes down in a measure that is needed, but harmful when it comes down more than needed: likewise with wealth; if it is enough for one's needs it is beneficial and pleasurable for him, but if it exceeds that, it harms him and he transgresses the limits with it, and may neglect its rights that are due upon him, or spend extravagantly on his desires... .

The author then explains how the need that causes man to crave the world and amass it does not affect or harm one who is infallible; nor does it cause him to do anything offensive, for truly he is protected with the Eye of Divine Care and guarded with pre-eternal concern. The greatest and most exalted of them in this regard is he by whom all of existence became manifest, and by whose light the cosmos received support: the Master of the first and the last, the Seal of the Prophets and Emissaries (Allah bless him and give him peace). For this reason, the author expresses his amazement by saying, *How could need tempt him with worldliness...?* In other words, 'How could the poverty of this magnificent creation tempt him to worldliness, when but for him it would not have come into existence? How could that be, when he was the cause for the creation of the world? How can he have any need of it, when it was only created for his sake?' Certainly, 'there is nothing that is not conditioned by him, since if not for the means, the end—as has been said—would have gone' [a quotation from *al-Ṣalāt al-Mashīshiyya*, The Prayer on the Prophet by Mūlāy ʿAbd al-Salām ibn Mashīsh]. How excellent are the words of the one who said:

O best of those whose bones are buried in the deep earth
And from whose fragrance depth and height became sweet,
You are the Emissary whose intercession is hoped for
Upon the Traverse when feet shall slip.
But for you, neither sun nor moon would be created
Nor stars, nor the Tablet or the Pen.
May I be the ransom for a grave you inhabit
In which are found purity, bounty and munificence!

This was said by a virtuous person as he visited the noble grave. One of the people from the latter ages sang an excellent ode:

O Chosen One, Your light shone on everything created by means of you.
Were it not for you there would be no existence
And its manifestations would not be adorned by sun or star.
You came close to creation bearing subtle kindness,
And it is to the celestial realm that you are ascribed
Like the sun that orbits the lofty heavens
But whose light is close to the eyesight [of all]!

Our master ʿAlī b. Abī Ṭālib (Allah be pleased with him) said: 'When Allah Most High willed to create the cosmos, spread humanity and originate the marvels of existence, He arranged the creation into images like fine dust particles (*habāʾ*) before outstretching the earth and erecting the heavens—and He was Singular in His sovereignty and One in His dominion. Then He prepared a light from His Light and a portion of it shone and radiated, and that light gathered in the midst of the subtle images (*ṣuwar*) and joined with the image of our Prophet Muḥammad (Allah bless him and give him peace). Allah said, Exalted and Sublime is He: "You are the chosen and elect; you are the repository of My light and the treasure of My guidance; it is for your sake that I shall spread out the earth, mix the waters, erect the heavens and create reward and punishment and the Paradise and Hellfire." Then Allah concealed His creation in His Unseen and withdrew it in His hidden knowledge. Then He erected the worlds, spread out time, mixed the waters, set into motion the ocean's foam and drove the winds. Next He set His Throne upon the water and outstretched the earth upon the water's surface. Then He called it to obedience and it responded with submission. Then He created the angels from light that He formed, and connected His Unicity with the Prophethood of Muḥammad (Allah bless him and give him peace). Thus his Prophethood was attested to in the heavens before he was sent to the earth. When Allah created Ādam, Ādam's virtue was made clear to the angels, and Allah had shown them the unique favours granted to him from His pre-eternal knowledge, instructing him in the names of things after He made him a Prophet. Allah made Ādam a niche (*miḥrāb*), a Kaᶜba, a door and a *qibla* to which the pious and the spiritual beings (*rūḥāniyyūn*) and lights all prostrated. Then Allah informed Ādam of what was deposited in him, and disclosed the immensity of the trust he was made to bear, after having named him an Imam in the presence of His angels. The Prophet Muḥammad (Allah bless him and give him peace) had a portion of this good, half of which was deposited light. Allah continued to conceal this light under the vicissitudes of time until Allah made Muḥammad (Allah bless him and give him peace) distinct in his own physical form, after which he invited mankind outwardly and inwardly and encouraged them secretly and publicly, and brought to man's attention the pre-eternal covenant that was made in the spiritual realm before the creation of the physical forms. Whoever acknowledges him will have grasped a portion of his primordial light that was prepared, and been guided to his secret and gained clarity as to his manifest stature. But whoever is confounded by heedlessness will be humiliated by [Allah's] wrath.'

May Allah be pleased with him and pour out to us from the ocean of his sciences and knowledge. Amen. It should come as no surprise that ᶜAlī says this, for he was the gateway to the city of the Prophet's knowledge.

مُحَمَّدٌ سَيِّدُ الْكَوْنَيْنِ وَالثَّقَلَيْـ ـنِ وَالْفَرِيقَيْنِ مِنْ عُرْبٍ وَمِنْ عَجَمِ

Muḥammad is the Master of both abodes, of both kinds,
And both classes [of people]: Arabs and non-Arabs

After having mentioned the qualities of praise, the author (Allah have mercy upon him) mentions the recipient of praise: our Master and liege lord Muḥammad (Allah bless him and give him peace). Here he states that the Prophet (Allah bless him and give him peace) is the Master of the two abodes, meaning this life and the Hereafter; the Master of the two kinds, meaning human kind and jinn; and the Master of the two categories, meaning the Arabs and non-Arabs. There is no doubt about what the author mentions here (Allah be pleased with him).

As for the Prophet (Allah bless him and give him peace) being the *Master of both abodes*, it has already been mentioned that the creation of this world, the Hereafter, Paradise, and Hell was only for the sake of the Prophet (Allah bless him and give him peace)—as was eloquently expressed in the words of our master ᶜAlī (Allah be pleased with him) that we quoted earlier… . If the author means the two abodes in and of themselves, then this is the meaning of the couplet; and if he means the inhabitants of the two abodes, then again there is no doubt that the Prophet (Allah bless him and give him peace) is the Master of them all.

In the life of this world the believers would seek refuge with the Prophet (Allah bless him and give him peace) in times of adversity and tribulation, and when facing pressing matters, and they would go to him to seek help in their religious concerns and receive counsel and guidance from him (Allah bless him and give him peace). They followed his upright path and traversed upon his straight way until he enabled them to reach permanent and everlasting bliss.

The Prophet (Allah bless him and give him peace) also has a rank of mastery (*siyāda*) over the disbelievers, for it is because of him that their punishment in this life is averted and they are granted respite until the Hereafter. Before them, however, the previous nations that disbelieved would receive their punishments swiftly. Allah Most High said, '*We have not sent you but as a mercy unto the worlds.*' (Qur'an 21:107). The Prophet (Allah bless him and give him peace) was given the choice to have the Akhshabān—two mountains near Mecca—crush the disbelievers, but he felt pity and mercy for them, as was his noble character. Instead, the Prophet (Allah bless him and give him peace) said, 'It is my hope that Allah will take from their progeny a people who will worship Allah and declare His unicity.'

Allah also said to His Prophet, '*But Allah was not going to punish them while you were in their midst.*' (Qur'an 8:33) The pronoun in this verse, *them*, refers to the disbelievers. Allah Most High informs that He averted the torment from them—though they deserved it—due to the presence of the Prophet (Allah bless him and give him peace) in their midst.

As for the Prophet's rank of mastery over the angels, it is substantiated by the fact that Allah Most High commanded the angels to send blessings upon him, exalt him and help him in his battles, and because the Prophet (Allah bless him and give him peace) led them in prayer during the miraculous Night Journey. In fact, some of the investigating scholars said that 'the reason why Allah took His Prophet (Allah bless him and give him peace) on the miraculous Night Journey was so the inhabitants of the celestial realms could take from his effulgent lights as the inhabitants of the earthly realm had taken.'

As for the Prophet's rank of mastery over the jinn, it is because he is undoubtedly sent to them, and they are legally responsible (*mukallafūn*) to have faith in him and act in accordance to what he has brought. This is expressed in sound *ḥadīth* reports and is explicitly mentioned in the Magnificent Qur'an, in the story of the jinn who listened to the Prophet's recitation of the Qur'an. The scholars disagree over their exact number: some say they were seven and other say they were nine. It is reported in *Ṣaḥīḥ* Muslim that the Prophet (Allah bless him and give him peace) spent the night in company of the jinn and instructed them and recited to them the Qur'an. It is related that he recited to them Sūrat al-Raḥmān and after he recited the verse '*Which of the favours of your Lord will you two* [men and jinn] *deny?*' they replied, 'O Lord, we will not deny any of Your favours; all praise belongs to You!" After that group of jinn left, they travelled about the lands warning their fellow jinn, imparting guidance to them and explaining what they understood and learned from the

Prophet (Allah bless him and give him peace). They said, as Allah informed about them, '*People of ours, we have heard a Book...*' [Qur'an 46:30] There are no doubts as to the devotional worship of the believing jinn and their recitation of the Qur'an. Some of the shaykhs endowed with knowledge have transmitted the jinns' recitation of the Qur'an. Shaykh Abū ʿAbd Allāh al-Alyūrī related from his teacher, Shaykh Abū Saʿīd, who said:

> It has been transmitted from one of the scholars among the pious *Salaf* and saints that he would sit down to listen to the students rehearsing the Qur'an, and that one of the believing jinn would rehearse it with him. That jinn came to the Shaykh one day to greet him and bid him farewell, and said, 'Master, we have a firm resolve to march out today and wage battle against a group of disbelieving jinn and kill them in pursuit of a reward from Allah; so if Allah decrees that I remain safe and triumph I must return to sit with you, and if He decrees martyrdom for me there shall descend a reed pen in the area where you sit during rehearsal. If you see that reed pen you will know that I have been slain in battle, and so I adjure you to invoke Allah's mercy upon me and request my classmates and those in attendance to invoke Allah's mercy and pray for me.'
>
> After some days had passed, while the Shaykh was sitting in his circle with the students busy rehearsing the Qur'an before him, a thought about the jinn's promise occurred to him, and as suddenly as he thought it a reed pen fell in the middle of the circle. The Shaykh remembered the jinn's promise and began to weep and invoke Allah's mercy upon him, and he requested the students to pray for his mercy and forgiveness.

[Shaykh Abū ʿAbd Allāh al-Alyūrī] also said:

> Many people who are unable to recite even one verse of the Qur'an correctly have been seen while in a state of possession with the inhabiting jinn reciting the Qur'an upon their tongues in the most beautiful and melodious of recitals.... My teacher, Shaykh Abū Saʿīd, related to me that he dealt with an elderly woman who had raised her children but was unable to read well. He recounted how he went to great lengths and tired himself out trying to help her memorise Sūrat

> al-Fātiḥa and another Sūra for her to recite in her prayers. After much effort she was finally able to memorise Sūrat al-Fātiḥa. One day, after returning from a journey, the Shaykh saw the elderly woman and she greeted him and sat down to speak. Shortly afterwards, he glanced at the woman and noticed that her complexion had changed and that she had suddenly been possessed by a jinn. He said, 'Her appearance frightened me, so I told myself that I should recite some Qur'an over her; perchance its blessings would ease its effects. As I sat near her and explained what I wanted to do, she uttered with a hideous voice that was not her own, "Do you reckon yourself more skilful in reciting the Qur'an than me? That cannot be!" "Since when," I asked, "have you been a reciter? In my experience you cannot even recite al-Fātiḥa well!" "What would you like me to recite?" she asked. Now at the time, no portion (*ḥizb*) was more difficult for me then the *ḥizb* starting with "*And do not dispute…*" (from Sūrat al-ᶜAnkabūt: 46), so I said to her, "Recite the *ḥizb* starting with '*And dispute not…*'" I opened up the *ḥizb* and she continued to recite it well until she had finished the entire Sūrat al-ᶜAnkabūt. Then she began to recite Sūrat Rūm till the end and then began to recite Sūrat Luqmān till the end of the *ḥizb*. She recited all of these with eloquence, melody and beauty as I sat before here in utter astonishment.' I [al-Alyūrī] said to him, 'Surely you were astonished at something that merits astonishment!'

All of this shows that the Prophet's mastery extends over jinn, humankind and angels. As for when the Prophet (Allah bless him and give him peace) said, 'I am the Master of humankind on the Day of Judgment,' that Day is mentioned in particular because it is unique in the sense that his leadership and intercession shall be singularly manifest for him above all others, when humanity will seek refuge in him in that place and find no one but him. On that Day, all of creation shall be assembled—the first and last of them, mankind and jinn, including all of the Prophets and Emissaries. That abode is the Abode of Permanence and Subsistence, and it is the Day that counts.

The Prophet's mastery, be it in his lineage, nature, physical form, character and manners, was known both before and after he was tasked with the prophetic mission. These things are acknowledged by those who are knowledgeable about the prophetic biography. Further, the

Prophet's many states are known from the time he was young to the time he was old.

The Prophet's statement in another *ḥadīth*, 'I am the Master of the children of Ādam... ,'[64] refers to the human species, which means that Ādam (upon whom be peace) is also included within it. This is supported by the aforementioned *ḥadīth* where the Prophet (Allah bless him and give him peace) used the word 'humankind' (*nās*). And the Prophet's mastery over Ādam is attested to in the *ḥadīth*, 'Ādam and those after him shall all be under my Banner on the Day of Resurrection,'[65] as well as the famous *ḥadīth* on the intercession in which the Prophet (Allah bless him and give him peace) is put forward above the elect among the Emissaries and his mastery over them is manifest without any opposition, as well as his statement (Allah bless him and give him peace), 'I am the first intercessor and the first whose intercession shall be accepted, and I am the first person for whom the earth shall be cleft (on the Day of Judgment);'[66] and the *ḥadīth*, 'I was a Prophet when Ādam was between clay and water.'[67] May Allah send prayers upon him and honour, ennoble, exalt, and magnify him!

نَبِيُّنَا الْآمِرُ النَّاهِي فَلَا أَحَدٌ   أَبَرَّ فِي قَوْلِ لَا مِنْهُ وَلَا نَعَمِ

Our Prophet, who commands and who forbids;
None is more true than him in saying "yes" or "no".

The author (Allah have mercy upon him), after having mentioned the noble name [Muḥammad] (Allah bless him and give him peace), says that our Prophet is of lofty rank and magnificent status in the sight of his Lord. Allah tasked him with prophecy and invested him with revelation, and sent him as a warner and giver of glad tidings, and as one who commands and forbids. The Prophet (Allah bless him and give him peace) is the commander who conveys from Allah, and he is the forbidder: he commands every beautiful deed and forbids every odious statement or action. The odious is what the Sacred Law declares odious, and the good

64 Muslim.

65 Ibid.

66 Ibid.

67 This wording is without basis. The sound narration from Tirmidhī and Ḥākim reads, 'I was a Prophet when Ādam was between spirit and body.'

is what the Sacred Law declares good. So when the Prophet (Allah bless him and give him peace) says "no" or "yes" about anything, nothing in existence occurs that contradicts what is indicated in his words. That is the essence of veracity (*ṣidq*).

With these words, the author wishes to emphasise the veracity of Allah's Emissary (Allah bless him and give him peace) with melody and hyperbolic form. The truthfulness of Allah's Emissary (Allah bless him and give him peace) is considered rationally necessary, since infallibility is also necessary and his veracity is established. Everything that the Prophet (Allah bless him and give him peace) manifested from his purity and dignity to his holiness and lofty aspirations, and from his tremendous character and noble disposition to his intense modesty and sound intellect and judgment—all are nothing less than necessary corollaries of his veracity.

The Prophet (Allah bless him and give him peace) was recognised as possessing these character traits during his youth and after he was tasked with the prophetic message, and he was even called the Veracious and Trustworthy (al-Ṣādiq al-Amīn). He promoted and encouraged truthfulness with his statement, 'Be truthful, for verily truthfulness leads to goodness, and goodness leads to Paradise. A man will continue to speak the truth and be intent on truthfulness until he is written as a truthful person with Allah... .'[68] And in another report someone asked, 'O Emissary of Allah, can a believer be miserly?' The Prophet replied, 'Yes.' The man asked, 'Can he be a coward?' and the Prophet said, 'Yes.' The man asked, 'Can he be a liar?' and the Prophet said, 'No.'[69]

Due to the immense difficulties and hardships that come with truthfulness, some have said that 'there is no group among the believers fewer in number than the truthful.'

You may retort: 'But the implication of the author's words is that when the Prophet (Allah bless him and give him peace) says "yes" or "no" he does not break his promise, and this includes his threatening [others] with divine punishment; however, it is considered praiseworthy to forgo a threat, as a poet said:

68 Muslim.

69 Mālik, *al-Muwaṭṭa*ʾ.

Indeed, when I threaten or promise him
I forgo my threat and fulfil my promise.

And the eloquent Arabs and poets were always wont to compete in their praises of the one who forgoes punishment and harm and returns to forbearance, pardon and control of his rage.' To this contention I say: The author does not intend it in that fashion; what he means is that when the Emissary of Allah (Allah bless him and give him peace) commands or forbids something, he does not contradict it or retract it. For the Prophet (Allah bless him and give him peace) only commands what is legislated and only forbids what is odious, so how could he possibly contravene what he has commanded? How can he retract what he forbade?

Alternatively, the author's words could be interpreted as a description of the Prophet's truthfulness in his spoken words, as if to say that everything he utters is veracious and true. He does not say 'no' except where 'no' is fitting, and he does not say 'yes' except where 'yes' is fitting—regardless of the issue of divine promises and threats, which had not crossed the author's mind. The meaning of this line is comparable to the rigorously authentic *ḥadīth* in which the Prophet (Allah bless him and give him peace) stated, 'I wish that I could fight in the path of Allah so I can be slain and then brought back to life, and then killed again and brought back to life, and then killed and brought back to life.'[70] It may be said that the Prophet's wish to be killed in the path of Allah entails a wish for the disbelief of a disbeliever, for the one who fights the Emissary of Allah (Allah bless him and give him peace) is undoubtedly a disbeliever. The response to this is the same as what we have just mentioned: the Prophet's intention was for martyrdom due to its lofty rank, regardless of the perceived implication that anyone who fights against him is a disbeliever. Likewise is the case for the author here: his intention is simply to express the fact that the Emissary of Allah (Allah bless him and give him peace) is the most truthful of creation.

This line can be interpreted in another way, too. It may be that when the author says *None is more true…* , he is alluding to the fact that when the Prophet (Allah bless him and give him peace) gave an order he would be the first to adhere to it, and when he forbade anything he would be the first to abstain from it. So by this interpretation, compliance is expressed

70 Bukhārī and Aḥmad.

as 'yes' and abstinence is expressed as 'no.' And Allah Most High knows best. This was stated by al-Alyūrī.

هُوَ الْحَبِيبُ الَّذِي تُرْجَىٰ شَفَاعَتُهُ لِكُلِّ هَوْلٍ مِنَ الْأَهْوَالِ مُقْتَحَمِ

He is the Beloved whose intercession is hoped for,
Victorious over every terror and disaster.

Here the author (Allah have mercy upon him) says that our Prophet (Allah bless him and give him peace) is the Beloved (al-Ḥabīb), to the exclusion of others who have attained the station of intimate friendship (*khulla*). The station of the Beloved is higher than the station of the Intimate Friend (*Khalīl*, i.e., Ibrāhīm), and proof for this can be inferred in different ways. Firstly, the Intimate Friend arrived unto the Divine through the intermediary of his rational deduction: '*And thus did We show Ibrāhīm the kingdom of the heavens.*' (Qur'an 6:75). The Beloved (Allah bless him and give him peace), on the other hand, attained to the Divine without an intermediary: '*and* [he] *was at a distance of two bows' length or nearer.*' (Qur'an 53:9)

Secondly, the Intimate Friend's forgiveness was expressed in terms of aspiration, as proven by Allah's words, '*And I aspire that He forgive my error*' (Qur'an 26:82), but the Beloved's forgiveness was expressed in terms of certainty, as proven by Allah's words, '*...that Allah may forgive you your past and future sins.*' (Qur'an 48:2)

Thirdly, the Intimate Friend said, '*And disgrace me not upon the Day they are resurrected.*' (Qur'an 26:87), but Allah Must High said [about the Beloved (Allah bless him and give him peace)], "*On the day when Allah will not disgrace the Prophet and those who believe with him... .*' (Qur'an 66:8) So the Intimate Friend asked that he not be disgraced, whereas the Beloved (Allah bless him and give him peace) was given without asking. In fact, our Prophet (Allah bless him and give him peace) was given the glad tidings before asking: '*We have given you Kawthar* [abundance]... .' (Qur'an 108:1).

Fourthly, during his trial, the Intimate Friend said, '*Allah is sufficient for me...*' (Qur'an 9:129), the Beloved (Allah bless him and give him peace) was told, '*O Prophet, Allah is sufficient for you... .*' (Qur'an 8:64).

Fifthly, the Intimate Friend said, '*And grant me a reputation of honour among later generations*' (Qur'an 26:84), the Beloved (Allah bless him and give him peace) was told, '*And* [did We not] *exalt your mention?*' (Qur'an 94:4).

Sixthly, the Intimate Friend said, '*And keep me and my children from the worship of idols*' (Qur'an 14:35), but the Beloved (Allah bless him and give him peace) was told, '*Allah intends only to remove from you impurity* (rijs), *O People of the Household*' [Qur'an 33:33].

Since the rank of the Beloved (Allah bless him and give him peace) is tremendous and his station is lofty, it is *his* intercession that is hoped for. That is because the Beloved's word is listened to, his speech heard and his intercession accepted. The love that the recipient of intercession has for the intercessor is the most likely cause for the intercession to be accepted and for his needs to be fulfilled.

The Prophet's intercession is hoped for during the onset of the ghastly terrors, momentous events and panic-inducing calamities that are burdensome and difficult to bear with patience. When the author says *Victorious over every terror and disaster*, it is as if he is saying 'the Prophet (Allah bless him and give him peace) will assume awesome and momentous stations, such as his ascending to the Praiseworthy Station (*al-Maqām al-Maḥmūd*) which none have attained besides him and to which no one else will aspire.' The *ḥadīth* about the Greatest Intercession is well known and in the rigorously authentic collections of al-Bukhārī, Muslim and others, so we need not draw things out and cite it here. Al-Ghazālī says, 'Those who seek refuge with the Prophets [on the Day of Resurrection] are not from this *Umma*, since [this] *Umma* knows that the [right of] intercession belongs to their Prophet (Allah bless him and give him peace). And Allah Most High knows best.

Qāḍī ᶜIyāḍ states in *Ikmāl al-muᶜlim*:

> The Prophet (Allah bless him and give him peace) shall have five forms of major intercession. The first form will be for granting people respite from standing [before Allah for Judgment]. The second form will cause people to enter Paradise without reckoning. The third form will be reserved for those who deserve the Hellfire. The fourth form will be for those believers who are subjected to the divine threat, and he will take them out [of Hell]. And the fifth form will be for an increase in rank in Paradise...

May Allah make us among [those who benefit from] the last, by the rank of this noble Prophet!

The Prophet (Allah bless him and give him peace) is compassionate towards his *Umma*, has great mercy for them, and is eager to intercede for them. He was granted a supplication which Allah told him would be accepted. He was given the choice to use it for himself, but chose instead to use it for his *Umma*. This is the pinnacle of generosity and preference to others. It is stated in *Ṣaḥīḥ* al-Bukhārī that the Emissary of Allah (Allah bless him and give him peace) said, 'Each Prophet is granted a supplication that is answered and by which he supplicates, but I have saved my supplication for my *Umma* in the Hereafter.' So the Prophet (Allah bless him and give him peace) has delayed his supplication and stored it up for his *Umma* on the Day of Resurrection. May Allah reward him with the best reward given to a Prophet on behalf of his nation!

دَعَا إِلَى اللَّهِ فَالْمُسْتَمْسِكُونَ بِهِ   مُسْتَمْسِكُونَ بِحَبْلٍ غَيْرِ مُنْفَصِمِ

He called [people] to Allah, so those who hold fast to him
Are holding fast to a rope that never shall break.

There is no doubt that our Master (Allah bless him and give him peace) called [all of] creation unto Allah. His invitation was inclusive of all, both the red and the black [i.e., all races]. Allah sent him to all of creation, as a mercy for them, keen for their felicity and desirous of their good. He did not seek any reward or compensation, nor did he hope for any reward from other than Allah—as Allah Most High commanded him. Whosoever responds to his invitation, hears his words and clings fast to his firm rope has traversed upon the path of the saved, and has grasped the firm handhold that shall never break. But those who deviate from his way and are not guided to travel upon his path have lost the way and have fallen into a bottomless abyss. We ask Allah Most High for protection and enabling grace by His bounty and generosity!

The perfected Pole-Saint, my master Abū al-ʿAbbās al-Mursī (Allah be pleased with him) said:

> 'The Prophets were created from mercy, and our Prophet (Allah bless him and give him peace) is the essence of mercy (*ʿayn al-raḥma*); as the

Most High said, "*And We have not sent you save as a mercy unto the worlds.*"' [Qur'an 21:107]

The Prophet (Allah bless him and give him peace) called unto Allah with clear insight, firm proofs and with the nearest of reaches and ways. He urged others to travel the path of right guidance and to shun lowly paths. He did not leave anything that draws near to Allah without calling people to it, and he did not leave a single point of etiquette that a servant should adopt with Allah without enjoining it. He did not leave anything that takes one away from Allah without warning against it, and he did not leave a single deed that alienates one from Allah without urging people to abstain from it. He was unceasing, indefatigable in his sincere counsel to deliver the servants from the mires of alienation and loci of destruction, until the dark night of polytheism faded and its alterities were cut off, and the daylight of faith shone and its lights dawned.

The Prophet (Allah bless him and give him peace) raised the banner of the religion, completed its order, established its obligations and rulings and explained its lawful and unlawful. Just as he explained legal rulings to the servants, he also expanded their horizons of understanding—without a doubt such that one narrator even said, 'The Emissary of Allah passed away and we would gain some knowledge from the very birds flying in the sky. Allah Most High said, "*There is no compulsion in the religion; right guidance has been made clear from error*" (Qur'an 2:256) and, "*Today I have completed for you your religion.*"' (Qur'an 5:3) And the Prophet (Allah bless him and give him peace) said, 'I have left [the religion] white [and] clear.'[71] May Allah reward him with the best reward given to a Prophet on behalf of his nation!

Once the Prophet (Allah bless him and give him peace) had fully explained the path of right guidance and made clear the ways that cause [His] servants to reach Allah, Allah took him to an abode that is better and more fitting for him. That was after Allah gave him a choice, and he chose the companionship of the Highest Assembly (*al-Rafīq al-Aʿlā*). After that, Allah placed within his *Umma* callers (*duʿāt*) who shall remain and continue forever with what they inherited and took from him (Allah bless him and give him peace). Allah Most High has testified

71 The author has paraphrased a lenghty *ḥadīth* narrated by Aḥmad.

to their existence and made them deserving of that. He said, '*Say, "This is my path: I call to Allah with insight, I and those who follow me...*"' (Qur'an 13:108) Thus end [Abū al-ʿAbbās al-Mursī's] words, may Allah allow us to benefit by him. Amen!

فَاقَ النَّبِيِّينَ فِي خَلْقٍ وَفِي خُلُقٍ   وَلَمْ يُدَانُوهُ فِي عِلْمٍ وَلَا كَرَمِ

He excelled the other Prophets in form and qualities;
Their knowledge and nobility did not come near his.

After having mentioned the qualities of the Emissary of Allah (Allah bless him and give him peace) such as being a Master, a commander and forbidder and the Beloved and caller to Allah, the author (Allah have mercy upon him) laments the fact that he cannot encompass the Prophet's qualities, even if he attempts to enumerate them and go to great lengths in lauding and praising him. For that reason, the author gives an exhaustive description indicating the unattainable nature of the Prophet's numerous qualities, and that no human has any hope of encompassing them. No one among the [previous] Prophets attained these qualities, much less those who are not Prophets. And even though the Prophets have obtained the qualities of perfection, they have not obtained or drawn them from any source other than the Emissary of Allah himself (Allah bless him and give him peace), for he is the source of these qualities and the treasure-store of their perfection. The Prophet (Allah bless him and give him peace) has therefore excelled and surpassed them in his material form and well-pleasing physical creation.

Regarding the goodness and beauty of his form and the exquisite balance of his bodily limbs, there are many rigorously authenticated reports and mass-transmitted narrations that speak of them. It is not undisclosed that the Prophet (Allah bless him and give him peace) was the most perfected of people in good qualities and the most striking of them in beauty. ʿAlī, Abū Hurayra, al-Barāʾ [b. ʿĀzib] and others all described him as having a fair red complexion, with a slightly rounded face and with a broad forehead and a thick beard that reached his chest. They described him as having a broad chest and shoulders and as being of medium stature—neither excessively tall nor short, yet when walking with anyone he would always seem taller. When he laughed it was mostly smiles, revealing [teeth as white] as hailstones; and when he spoke, a light would be seen emanating from between his teeth.

Al-Barāʾ said, 'I saw him wearing a red shawl, and I have never seen a more beautiful sight than him.'[72] Abū Hurayra said, 'I never saw anyone more beautiful than the Emissary of Allah. It was as if the sun shone upon his face, and when he smiled, his light would shine upon the walls…'[73] Umm Maʿbad described him (Allah bless him and give him peace) thus: 'I met a man of visible radiance whose appearance was beautiful, his face bright, with neither protruding ribs nor a small head. He was handsome and fair. His eyes were a deep black colour and his eyelashes were lush. His voice was soft and smooth. The whiteness of his eyes was bright, and his pupils were very black. His eyebrows were fine at the corners, and connected. His neck was long and his beard was full. When he was silent, he appeared dignified, and when he spoke, he was eminent and crowned with magnificence. His speech was sweet, his words were precise, neither too little nor too much, like a string of pearls flowing down… ."[74]

ʿAlī (Allah be pleased with him) said, 'Whoever saw him unexpectedly would be filled with awe. Whoever came to know him would love him. Whoever would describe him would say, "Neither before him nor after him have I seen anybody like him."'[75]

As for the Prophet's bodily cleanliness and his fine scent and fragrant odour, Allah, the Exalted and Sublime, granted him many unique qualities in that regard that are not found in others. Anas (Allah be pleased with him) said, 'I have never smelled ambergris or musk or anything sweeter than the Emissary of Allah'[76] Jābir (Allah be pleased with him) mentioned how the Prophet once touched his cheek. He said, 'I experienced a coolness and fragrance from his hand; his hand smelled as if he had dipped it in a perfumer's bottle, whether he was wearing scent or not. When he shook someone's hand, a pleasant fragrance would stay with that person for the rest of the day. He would pat the heads of children, and any child who received a pat from him would stand out from

72 Tirmidhī, *Shamāʾil.*

73 Ibid.

74 Bayhaqī, *Dalāʾil al-nubuwwa.*

75 Tirmidhī, *Shamāʾil.*

76 Muslim.

the other children [due to his blessed fragrance].'[77] Because of his fine scent, when the Prophet (Allah bless him and give him peace) walked down a path, anyone who later walked that path would know that the Prophet had been there.'[78] This topic is vast and could fill volumes.

As regards his inner character traits, Allah Most High preferred him with lofty character traits, high qualities and inward, Sharī'a-based etiquettes, such as knowledge, religion, forbearance, patience, gratitude, justice, renunciation, humility, pardon, temperance, generosity, bravery, shyness, respectability, amiability, silent reflection, dignity, mercy and filial piety, among others. He embodied and personified all of these traits. It should be enough for you that Allah, the Exalted and Sublime, praised his character by saying, '*And truly you are of a most immense character.*' (Qur'an 68:4) To detail all of the elements of his character would prove extremely lengthy; so whoever would like [to gain] 'healing' in this , let them refer to the *Shifā'*.

As regards the Prophet's knowledge and his vast sciences, he was the most knowledgeable of people concerning Allah Most High. Allah acquainted him with the contents of the Torah and Gospel and the other revealed scriptures, as well as the wisdom of the sages and the narratives of the past nations. He taught him to strike of parables and how to manage the affairs of creation and establish sacred laws. He vouchsafed to him knowledge of the myriad disciplines of sacred knowledge, such as exegesis, mathematics, genealogy—all of which he obtained and embraced without prior learning or perusal of the books of those before him, and without sitting in the company of their scholars. Rather, he was an unlettered Prophet without prior knowledge of any of that until Allah expanded his breast and made clear His divine command, teaching him and instructing him to recite what He disclosed to him by way of past and future marvels of Allah's omnipotence and magnificent visible and spiritual worlds. Allah Most High says, '*And He taught you what you knew not; and the bounty of Allah towards you is immense.*' (Qur'an 4:113). Al-Būṣīrī says in his *Hamziyya*:

He surpasses [all] creation in knowledge and forbearance;
He is an ocean unencumbered by difficulties.

77 Ibid.
78 Qāḍī 'Iyāḍ, *al-Shifā'*.

As for the Prophet's munificence and generosity, he was without rival or parallel. The kings of the world are incapable of offering even the most miniscule of his gifts and offerings. Jābir (Allah be pleased with him) reported, 'Never did the Emissary of Allah refuse anything he was asked for.'[79] Ibn ᶜAbbās (Allah be pleased with him) said, 'The Emissary of Allah was the best and most generous of mankind. He was most generous during the month of Ramaḍān, when Jibrīl would meet with him and review the Qur'an.'[80] Indeed, the Emissary of Allah (Allah bless him and give him peace) was more generous with doing good than a swift breeze. The reason why the Emissary of Allah (Allah bless him and give him peace) was more generous in Ramaḍān than in the other months is that Ramaḍān is the marketplace of spiritual capital and the arena of competition in good works. In addition, plenteous good works in that time result in an increase in rewards, for one good deed is rewarded a thousandfold. Ibn Shihāb said in a *marfūᶜ* report i.e. a report ascribed to the Prophet (Allah bless him and give him peace), 'One utterance of Allah's transcendence (i.e., saying *subḥān Allāh*) in the month of Ramaḍān is better than one thousand such utterances said in other months.' In addition, the Prophet (Allah bless him and give him peace) would see Jibrīl in Ramaḍān and increase in generosity out of gratitude for these bounties.

It is reported that a man once asked the Prophet (Allah bless him and give him peace) for something and he gave him an immense number of sheep that were between two mountains. That man returned to his people and said, 'Embrace Islam, for Muḥammad gives like a man who does not fear poverty!'[81] This was the Prophet's character before and after he was tasked with the prophetic mission. When the Prophet (Allah bless him and give him peace) first received divine revelation and said to Khadīja 'I fear for myself,' she replied, 'No, by Allah! Allah will never forsake you; you maintain ties with your kinsfolk, you are kind to your neighbours, you are charitable to the poor, you are hospitable to guests and you defend the truth!'[82]

A man once asked the Prophet (Allah bless him and give him peace) for something, to which he said, 'I have nothing, but go and buy some-

79 Bukhārī and Muslim.

80 Bukhārī.

81 Bukhārī and Muslim.

82 Bukhārī.

thing with a deferred payment and I will take care of the debt.' ᶜUmar (Allah be pleased with him) said to the Prophet (Allah bless him and give him peace), 'O Emissary of Allah, Allah has not ordered you to do this!' but a man from the Helpers (Anṣār) said, 'Spend, O Emissary of Allah, and fear not poverty from the Possessor of the Throne!' Upon hearing this, the Prophet smiled and said, 'That is what I have been ordered to do.'[83]

Abū ᶜAlī al-Daqqāq, one of the early shaykhs and erudite scholars of the Sufis, spoke about the spiritual chivalry (*futuwwa*) of the Sufis and the terms used in Sufi nomenclature, and described the Prophet's immense generosity and selflessness: 'These character traits are not realised in their full plenitude except in the Emissary of Allah (Allah bless him and give him peace), for on the Day of Resurrection everyone will say, "Myself, myself!" but he will say, "My nation, my nation!"'

In short, it is not possible to examine fully the Prophet's qualities, especially his generosity and munificence. We shall soon examine the author's couplet:

> For this world and the Next are from your bounty;
> And knowledge of Tablet and Pen are of what you know.

This couplet is similar to the one we are discussing here, where he says *He excelled the other Prophets*: that is, he surpassed them *in form and qualities*, and *their knowledge and nobility did not come near his*, meaning they did not come close. So glorified and exalted is the One Who favoured him and made him its due recipient; and may Allah confer upon us a portion of his sciences and secrets, by the rank of his lofty status and position. Amen!

وَكُلُّهُمْ مِنْ رَسُولِ اللَّهِ مُلْتَمِسٌ غَرْفًا مِنَ الْبَحْرِ أَوْ رَشْفًا مِنَ الدِّيَمِ

They all seek something from Allah's Emissary –
handfuls from the sea, or small sips of drizzle.

Here the author (Allah have mercy upon him) is saying that since Allah Most High conferred upon our Master (Allah bless him and give him peace) perfect knowledge and blessed him with the secrets of gnosis, the sciences of the previous Prophets are minuscule in comparison. Hence they seek something of his knowledge and wish they could obtain a por-

83 Ṭabarānī, *al-Muᶜjam al-awsaṭ*.

tion from it that is comparable to a handful taken from the sea or a single sip of drizzle.

Many theologians have taken umbrage at the author's words here and said that this assertion requires proof from revelation. One may respond, however, by saying that the intellect (*ᶜaql*) is the basis for the sciences and branches of knowledge. It is the well-spring of knowledge and gnosis. Wahb b. Munabbih said, 'I have perused seventy-one of the sacred books [of old] and found stated in all of them that the intellect that Allah Most High gave mankind—from the beginning of the world till its end—when compared to the intellect of Muḥammad (Allah bless him and give him peace) is like a grain of sand compared to the world.' So if knowledge springs from the intellect, and if the comparison between humanity's intellect and the Prophet's intellect is like that of a grain of sand to the world, it is not farfetched to conclude that the knowledge of the Prophets and others is comparable to the Prophet's knowledge in a similar manner, and thus the problematic ambiguity is resolved.

If you retort, 'But how is it possible for the Prophets to seek something from him when they came before him?' the response is that each Prophet recognised him and knew him, and took a covenant to believe in him and support him. Allah Most High says, '*And [remember] when Allah took the covenant from the Prophets… to believe in him and support him.*' (Qur'an 3:81) So all of the Prophets have clear knowledge concerning him (Allah bless him and give him peace); they acknowledge his rank and long to behold him. Many of them in fact wished to belong to his *Umma*. And as we mentioned earlier, Allah Most High created the cosmos only for the Prophet's sake, and the other Prophets and the callers unto Allah are his representatives. So it is not farfetched to say that their knowledge is but an outpouring of the Prophet's knowledge—and Allah grants His mercy to whom He wills, and Allah is the possessor of immense bounty!

The vast knowledge of the other Prophets is to the knowledge of the Prophet Muḥammad (Allah bless him and give him peace) as the prosperous are to the master of alchemy. The fact that they are wealthy does not entail that they stand as equals to the alchemist who is the master of his craft. Even though they are looked upon as wealthy, they are deemed poor in the eyes of the alchemist, even if their treasure-stores are filled with wealth. For the alchemist possesses more munificence and generosity, gives more freely and fears poverty less than someone whose wealth is acquired through conventional means (*māl muktasab*). This was stated by al-Alyūrī, and Allah Most High knows best.

وَوَاقِفُونَ لَدَيْهِ عِنْدَ حَدِّهِمُ   مِنْ نُقْطَةِ الْعِلْمِ أَوْ مِنْ شَكْلَةِ الْحِكَمِ

They all stand before him, observing their limits;
Dots to his knowledge, or vowel-marks to his wisdom.

The author, Allah have mercy upon him, observes that the Prophets stand before the Emissary of Allah (Allah bless him and give him peace) seeking a portion from the sea of his knowledge and wisdoms; each of them stands within the limits of the knowledge and wisdom conferred upon him. Their knowledge in comparison to the Prophet's knowledge is like a dot compared to a letter, and their wisdom in comparison to his is like a vowel-mark compared to a letter. The letter is the primary means of indication, but what it stands for is made clear with a dot or vowel mark. The Prophet's knowledge and wisdom are likened to letters used for writing, with their dots and vowel marks, because they are a conventional means of gaining knowledge, and the portion of that knowledge and wisdom taken by the other Prophets is made to resemble the dots and vowel marks on those letters. Since knowledge is that which draws distinctions between things and makes them clear, it is likened to the dots on letters, since they also draw distinctions. And since vowel-marks increase the clarity of letters they are likened to wisdom, because wisdom increases knowledge in clarity and disclosure. Wisdom is knowledge with an added mastery, and on that account it is said that every sage is a scholar, but not vice versa. The reason for this, it is said, is that a dot has one shape, just as knowledge is a single reality, which is to have knowledge of that which is known as it truly is. On the other hand, vowel-marks have four shapes: *ḍamma* (u), *fatḥa* (a), *kasra* (i), and *sukūn* (no vowel); and likewise wisdom can be verbal (*qawliyya*), physical (*fiʿliyya*), or mental (*ʿaqliyya*).

Verbal wisdom is in exhortation, the Qur'an, and explication of the lawful and unlawful. It is not possible to take every statement that indicates a correct meaning and call it verbal wisdom; verbal wisdom is a statement which has within it an added subtlety and finesse that is only discerned by the elect, and which includes either an immediate or future benefit, even if through reminder and increased knowledge and acumen. An example of this is found in the statement of our master ʿAlī (may Allah ennoble his countenance), 'What cause has the son of Ādam to boast? In the beginning he was but a scattered sperm-drop, in the end he will be a rotten corpse, and between those two stages he carries within him putridity (i.e. faecal matter).'

When it came to verbal wisdom, the Prophet (Allah bless him and give him peace) was an unfathomable ocean and inexhaustible, all-engulfing flood. How could it be otherwise when he is the Well-spring of Wisdom, the Illuminating Lamp of Guidance, the City of Knowledge, the Imam of the Godfearing and the Exemplar of the Gnostics? Several books and volumes have been dedicated to compiling and expositing the Prophet's wisdoms.

Physical wisdom includes crafts of marvel and wondrous deeds, and mental wisdom includes the extrapolation of logical proofs and rational analysis. It is said that wisdom was conferred upon three: the hearts of the Greeks, the tongues of the Arabs, and the hands of the Chinese. The Greeks were gifted in rational thought, the Arabs were granted wisdom in poetry and speeches, and the Chinese were skilled in the manufacture of quality crafts and awe-inspiring handiwork. And Allah Most High knows best and is the Most Just, and in His keeping is all providence.

فَهْوَ الَّذِي تَمَّ مَعْنَاهُ وَصُورَتُهُ ثُمَّ اصْطَفَاهُ حَبِيبًا بَارِئُ النَّسَمِ

It is he whose meaning and form attained perfection
Then the Maker of Souls chose him for His beloved.

Having established that the Emissary of Allah (Allah bless him and give him peace) possesses attributes of perfection, the author (Allah have mercy upon him) draws the conclusion that Allah Most High has perfected the Prophet's inner and outer traits of excellence. Allah has gathered for him a beautiful appearance, and noble and virtuous character; and that is the meaning of the author's statement, *whose meaning and form attained perfection*. Then he says that Allah increased the Prophet (Allah bless him and give him peace) in honour and nobility by drawing him close and choosing him as His beloved. So Allah has elevated his station, ennobled his rank, drawn him near and bestowed upon him the greatest portion of His good pleasure.

Allah Most High made the Prophet (Allah bless him and give him peace) naturally disposed to goodness during his youth and safeguarded him from the impurities of the pre-Islamic period of ignorance (*jāhiliyya*). He is the most honoured of creation in the sight of Allah and the noblest of humanity. The Prophet (Allah bless him and give him peace) stated, 'When I was young, the idols were made detestable to me.'[84] [He also said], 'I never thought to do any of the acts done in *jāhiliyya* save twice, but then Allah safeguarded me and I did not do them.'[85]

The Prophet's status continued to grow; the divine aid conferred upon him became more and more munificent; Allah's divine concern for him continued to increase and gain firmness; the fragrant breezes of mercy blew upon him in succession; and the lights of mystical sciences dawned upon his heart, until he reached the utmost rank and attained the foremost honour of prophethood and beyond (Allah bless him and give him peace).

He was raised in his early years in the best of conditions. He was the most temperate and truthful of people, and Allah gathered within him the traits of goodness, so much that he was given the title al-Amīn (the Trustworthy) during his youth, and he was readied for the immense honour that Allah desired of him. It is related from Ibn Masʿūd (Allah be pleased with him) that the Prophet (Allah bless him and give him peace) said, 'Indeed Allah, the Exalted and Majestic, looked upon the hearts of the servants and chose from them the heart of Muḥammad and selected him for Himself, sent him with His Message, and took him as a beloved. He is written in the Torah as Muḥammad, the Beloved of the Merciful (*Ḥabīb al-Raḥmān*).'[86]

The author's placement of the subject's pronoun in the beginning of the couplet indicates restriction (*ḥaṣr*), and it communicates that no one has obtained the qualities of perfection found with the Prophet (Allah bless him and give him peace), such as his beautiful form and august character. The reports that speak of the beautiful forms and good character of

84 Abū Nuʿaym, *Dalāʾil al-Nubuwwa*.

85 Bazzār.

86 Aḥmad.

the Prophets are famous and well known, but it is our Prophet (Allah bless him and give him peace) who is at their forefront and who carries this banner. Not a single one among them attained his rank or reached the quintessential perfection of his status.

You may object and say, 'But there is a narration prohibiting us from giving preference to some Prophets over others, so how are we to reconcile that with the author's statement? Also, the Prophet (Allah bless him and give him peace) stated, "Do not show preference between the Prophets."'[87] The reply to that is that the Prophet (Allah bless him and give him peace) said this before he knew that he was the Master of the children of Ādam and the Master of humanity on the Day of Resurrection. Alternatively, it can be said that the Prophet (Allah bless him and give him peace) only proscribed the type of preference that leads to diminishing the rank of, or showing aversion to, the one less preferred. It is also possible that the Prophet (Allah bless him and give him peace) said this statement out of humility, or that he forbade showing preference with regard to Prophethood or Messengership as such, since Prophethood is the receiving of revelation, in which all Prophets are equal. This means essentially that the only difference between the Prophets is in relative superiority in spiritual states, unique charismatic gifts and abundant inimitable miracles. It is on this account that some of them are Emissaries, while others are called the 'Possessors of Resolve' (*Ulū al-ᶜAzm*) and others are spoken to by Allah. The Most High says, '*Those Emissaries, We preferred some of them over others…*' (Qur'an 2:253) This verse is a proof of relative superiority, and Allah Most High knows best.

مُنَزَّهٌ عَنْ شَرِيكٍ فِي مَحَاسِنِهِ   فَجَوْهَرُ الْحُسْنِ فِيهِ غَيْرُ مُنْقَسِمِ

Exalted above having a rival in his perfections;
In him is the undivided essence of beauty.

The author (Allah have mercy upon him) states that Allah exalted His Emissary (Allah bless him and give him peace) and elevated him above having a co-sharer in any of his inward and outward traits of perfection. No one in creation has any hope of obtaining a portion thereof. This couplet is a continuation and explanation of the previous couplet. In other words, it is he and he alone whose meaning and form attained

87 Bukhārī.

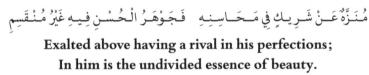

perfection, and consequently Allah has exalted him above having any co-sharer. By saying *In him is the undivided essence of beauty*, the author informs us that the essence of beauty is confined to the Prophet (Allah bless him and give him peace) alone. The word *essence* (*jawhar*) means that which is undivided and does not accept division. Likewise, the essence of the Prophet's beauty is exclusive and undivided, so no one in creation has any hope of obtaining a portion of it.

If you were to behold the Prophet (Allah bless him and give him peace) among people, you would say he is a man, just as he said of himself (Allah bless him and give him peace) and as Allah said, "'*I am but a man like you...*'" (Qur'an 19:110). But if you were to consider the unique traits and exemplary qualities with which Allah favoured him, and the favours Allah granted him, such as his beautiful form and character, you would say he is not human. The upshot of this is that the Prophet (Allah bless him and give him peace) is human, but not like other humans; he is like a ruby among ordinary stones. The wisdom behind Allah sending the Prophet (Allah bless him and give him peace) in a human form—though his soul is dissimilar to the souls of the rest of humanity—lies in the fact that had he been other than human, such as an angel, no human would be able to interact with the angels or receive revealed laws from them. However, Allah Most High has strengthened the souls of the Prophets, enabling them to behold the angels, and has ordered mankind to follow them in their statements, actions, and inward and outward states: the outward emulating their outward, and the inward emulating their inward. May Allah bless us to follow them and love them till death. Amen!

دَعْ مَا ادَّعَتْهُ النَّصَارَىٰ فِي نَبِيِّهِمُ وَاحْكُمْ بِمَا شِئْتَ مَدْحًا فِيهِ وَاحْتَكِمِ

Eschew the claim Christians have made for their Prophet.
Then say in his praise what you will, but wisely!

Here the author (Allah have mercy upon him) addresses those to whom an address can be directed, and does not intend anyone in particular. It is as if he is saying, 'O you who lend an ear to my address and listen to my words, set aside the description the Christians have claimed for their Prophet—that description of misguidance and abomination that led them to disbelief and affirmation of a co-sharer with divinity—and take care lest you say similar things about your Prophet, and be led astray as they were led astray, and disbelieve as they disbelieved. Once you have taken care to avoid the expressions used by the Christians for their Prophet, laud and praise the Prophet Muḥammad (Allah bless him and give him peace) by mentioning his noble qualities, his beautiful way, his stunningly clear miracles, his many dazzling signs that fill the horizon and that are as clear as day, as well as the gifts of Prophethood, Messengership, and comprehensive goodness which Allah gave him. State what you like and be ambitious in your praise and lauding of him, for it is all good and the scope is vast.'

How excellent is the one who said:

You have found the space for words wide in scope;
So speak if you find a tongue with which to speak.

Nonetheless, even if a speaker of immense skill and sagacity expressed the Prophet's praise with unparalleled eloquence and rhetoric, and reached its utmost limit, he would still be incapable of fully expressing his qualities (Allah bless him and give him peace), and he would have no choice but to admit his inability and inadequacy in conveying his praise—as the author himself says immediately following this couplet. [Imam al-Būṣīrī] also says, in his *Hamziyya*:

I spoke not at length enumerating your praises
Intending thoroughness with my words.
I am but thirsty, in a state of longing for you,
And without copious water I'm not quenched.

The content of this couplet is taken directly from the statement of the Prophet (Allah bless him and give him peace): 'Do not exaggerate about me as the Christians exaggerated concerning the Son of Maryam; say instead, "the servant and Emissary of Allah."'[88] The Christians were deluded to the point where they claimed what they claimed concerning the Prophet ʿĪsā, and that was because of the acts which had been manifested at his hands, such as reviving the dead, healing the lepers and giving sight to those born blind, and because he was born without a father. Consequently, the Christians split up into three distinct forms of disbelief. The first group said that he is the son of Allah—far exalted is Allah above what they say! The second group said that the *Lāhūt* (Divine) connected with the *Nāsūt* (human), meaning that the quality of divinity

88 Bukhārī.

inhered in the essence of ʿĪsā. And the third group said that Allah is the third of three: Allah, Maryam, and ʿĪsā. Allah refuted all three of these doctrines and declared their foundation false, and He explained the utter feebleness of their minds, the flimsiness of their belief, and the horridness of their way: '*The Messiah, son of Maryam, was nought but an Emissary; other Emissaries have passed on before him. And his mother was utterly veracious. They both used to eat food.*' (Qur'an 5:75)

Allah made the path clear and explained the proof. His statement '*They both used to eat food*' demonstrates Prophet ʿĪsā's and Maryam's absolute poverty and utter need for food and drink; it follows that if someone stands in need of something (without which he will perish), he can in no way be described as divine. No one who stands in such need will claim divinity for himself, unless he is of lowly aim, weak-minded, and dim-witted. Allah Most High says, '*Say, "Shall I take other than Allah as a protector, the Creator of the heavens and the earth, while it is He who feeds and is not fed?"*' (Qur'an 6:14)

It was because of this specious argument, which gained credence among the Christians, that the Prophet (Allah bless him and give him peace) warned his Companions, 'Do not exaggerate about me as the Christians exaggerated concerning the Son of Maryam. Say instead, "the servant and Emissary of Allah."' The Prophet (Allah bless him and give him peace) also said, 'May Allah curse the Jews and the Christians! They took the graves of their Prophets as places of prostration.'[89] He cautioned against what they did and took both groups to task, and cursed them explicitly so as to show the repugnance of their state and to safeguard his nation out of concern for their felicity. May Allah reward him with the best reward given to a Prophet on behalf of his nation!

With respect to the Prophet ʿĪsā's acts of quickening the dead, healing the lepers and giving sight to the blind, the Mighty Qur'an explicitly states that these were miracles vouchsafed to him. The same applies to his speaking to the people and exonerating his mother [of charges of fornication] while still in the cradle. Consider the words of Allah Most High: '*with My permission*' (Qur'an 5:110): Allah repeated this phrase to dispel the false imaginings of the Christians that these acts came from him [independently].

89 Aḥmad.

The reason why the Prophet ʿĪsā's miracles took these forms is that the sciences of medicine and anatomy were dominant in his time, and so his miracles of quickening the dead (entirely impossible for anyone), bringing sight to those who were born blind and healing lepers (a disease that is extremely difficult to treat and almost impossible to cure) were all breaks with the conventions of medicine.

And because the dominant practice in the Prophet Mūsā's time (upon whom be peace) was sorcery, Allah granted him the ability to transform a staff into a serpent, and it consumed all of the serpents produced by the sorcerers' magic and sought to enter Firʿawn's palace. When the sorcerers witnessed that, they admitted that this was not a form of magic and that it was not within human capacity to produce it. Their knowledge of sorcery benefited them ultimately, for they realised that what the Prophet Mūsā (upon whom be peace) brought could not be magic craft.

And because the dominant feature of society in our Prophet Muḥammad's time was eloquence in speech and rhetorical prowess, Allah gave him the Mighty Qur'an, and people were incapable of producing even a single chapter like it. They listened dutifully to its rhetorical strength and submitted to its eloquence, and not a single one among them was able to counter it or object to it in the least. The upshot is that every Prophet brought with him inimitable miracles that corresponded to the dominant practice of his time; and Allah Most High knows best.

Al-Ghazālī said:

> It is related that the Prophet ʿĪsā (upon whom be peace) was in the company of his disciples when he passed by a village and found its inhabitants dead in the street, unburied and strewn about on the side roads. The Prophet ʿĪsā (upon whom be peace) said, 'These people died because of tremors and punishment that descended upon them; had they died in any other way they would have been buried.' One of the disciples said, 'Pray to Allah to bring them back to life, that we may ask them about their condition', and so the Prophet ʿĪsā prayed to Allah. When nightfall came, Allah revealed to the Prophet ʿĪsā, saying 'Call them when the darkness of night falls, and they will respond to you.' When the darkness of night fell he called out to them, 'O inhabitants of this village!' and one of them responded, 'At your service, O Spirit of Allah!' ʿĪsā (upon whom be peace) asked, 'What happened to you all

and what is your story?" The man said, 'Prophet of Allah, we spent the night in well-being and woke up to an abyss!' 'Why is that?' ᶜĪsā asked. 'Because', the man replied, 'we loved the material world and obeyed the disobedient folk.' The Prophet ᶜĪsā said, 'How was your love for the world?' The man replied, 'It was like a child's love for its mother: when it came to us we would show delight, and when it turned away from us we would weep and feel sadness.' The Prophet ᶜĪsā then asked, 'Why do your fellow villagers not respond to me, while you do?' 'Because', the man said, 'they are bridled by a rein of fire held in the hands of angels, stern and severe.' 'But why do you respond to me when you are among them?' ᶜĪsā asked. 'Because', he said, 'I was among them but I was not *from* them. When the punishment descended I was caught with them, and so I am fettered at the precipice of Hell; and I know not whether I shall be saved or if I shall be cast headlong into it.' Upon hearing this, the Prophet ᶜĪsā (upon whom be peace) turned to his disciples and said, 'O disciples, truly eating barley bread, sleeping in rubbish heaps and donning coarse woollen garments are to be considered much if accompanied with well-being in this life and the Hereafter!'

وَانْسُبْ إِلَىٰ ذَاتِهِ مَا شِئْتَ مِنْ شَرَفٍ　　وَانْسُبْ إِلَىٰ قَدْرِهِ مَا شِئْتَ مِنْ عِظَمِ
فَإِنَّ فَضْلَ رَسُولِ اللَّهِ لَيْسَ لَهُ　　حَدٌّ فَيُعْرِبَ عَنْهُ نَاطِقٌ بِفَمِ

Ascribe whatever honour you will to his essence,
And ascribe what greatness you will to his worth;
For the worth of Allah's Emissary has no limit
That could be expressed by a human mouth.

Explaining the previous couplets that praised the Prophet's noble essence and lofty rank, the author says that you may ascribe to his honourable and holy essence whatever you will of perfections, meaning qualities of praise and exaltations befitting his essence, and detail his perfections which proclaim his sublime eminence and lordly station. You may ascribe to his immense rank whatever you will of beautiful qualities whose immensity prove his august rank and magnificent station. For the Prophet (Allah bless him and give him peace) fully merits whatever beautiful traits you ascribe to his essence, and is worthy of whatever perfections and marvels you ascribe to his rank. Indeed, the merit and perfect nobility of the Emissary of Allah (Allah bless him and give him peace) has no limit that can be reached, that it might be fully expressed on the tongue. That is because the grandeur and immensity of his essence and rank that Allah bestowed him with are limitless and endless, so it is not possible to elucidate them fully. If all of the rhetoricians and eloquent speakers came together and endeavoured to use their eloquent tongues to describe the Prophet's virtues and qualities of perfection, their descriptions would only amount to a drop of water from an ocean. Not one speaker is capable of fully expressing his perfections. How excellent is what Abū al-Qāsim Ibn Juzayy al-Kalbī said:

I attempt to praise the Chosen One but am prevented
By my inadequacy in comprehending his merits.
How can I possibly contain the brimming ocean?
How can I possibly count all the grains of sand and stars?
Had my every muscle turned into a tongue
I would still be unable to attain a portion of his praise.
Had the creation entire assembled together in his honour
They would not fulfil what is truly incumbent.
So our tongue has held us back out of awe and courteousness
And out of fear and exaltation for the one of loftiest rank.
How often eloquence is found in silence,
And how often does speech reprove the speaker!

The Gnostic Ibn al-Fāriḍ was once seen in a dream and was asked, 'Why don't you praise the Prophet (Allah bless him and give him peace)?'—meaning, 'Why don't you praise him in prose or poetry, in either the Divine Presence or in the Prophet's presence?' Ibn al-Fāriḍ replied:

I consider all praise of the Prophet inadequate
Even if his praises are extensive and far-reaching.
When Allah praises him with what he merits,
What worth is praise given to him by man?

May Allah be pleased with him and allow us to benefit from him!

لَوْ نَاسَبَتْ قَدْرَهُ آيَاتُهُ عِظَمًا   أَحْيَا اسْمُهُ حِينَ يُدْعَى دَارِسَ الرِّمَمِ

If his miracles were commensurate with his greatness,
The mere mention of his name would give life to dry bones.

This is a completion to the previous couplet where the author (Allah have mercy upon him) said, *And ascribe what greatness you will to his worth*. He informs us that the status of Allah's Emissary (Allah bless him and give him peace) is exalted in the sight of Allah, and that his rank is firmly established; so if the Prophet's miracles and the breaks with natural phenomena that Allah caused at his hands were in proportion to his tremendous rank, the mere mention of his name upon dry bones would instantaneously bring them to life by Allah's leave, and the enlivened person would stand up straight. That happened even if the Prophet (Allah bless him and give him peace) did not call the person himself, and the person would be brought to life without the Prophet needing to stand over his grave as the Prophet ʿĪsā used to do [when bringing the dead back to life by Allah's leave]. For his immense rank and Allah's divine concern for him are too great to require any of that; however, it was Allah's will that the only miracles and breaks with normal phenomena that appeared at his hands were those that were manifested. And although the Prophet ʿĪsā was granted the unique ability to quicken the dead, that uniqueness does not prove superiority, for the Emissary of Allah (Allah bless him and give him peace) was vouchsafed signs and miracles that match the quickening of the dead, such as the moaning of the date-palm tree, the gushing of water from flesh and blood [from his blessed fingers], and innumerable other miracles.

It is reported that al-Ḥasan said, 'A man came to the Emissary of Allah and told him about an infant daughter of his that he had buried in a certain valley. Then the Emissary of Allah headed to that valley and called out to the girl, saying, "So-and-so, respond to me by Allah's permission." Suddenly, the girl came out of the valley and said, "I answer your call and am at your service, O Emissary of Allah!" The Prophet said to her, "Your parents have embraced Islam. Would you like me to return you to them?" The girl replied, "I have no need of them! I found Allah better than them."'[90]

90 Qāḍī ʿIyāḍ, *al-Shifā'*.

It was also reported from Anas b. Mālik (Allah be pleased with him) that a young man from the Anṣār died leaving behind a blind and elderly mother. Anas said, 'We buried him and sent our condolences to his mother and she asked, "Has my son died?" "Yes", we replied. She then supplicated, "O Allah, if You know that I migrated to You and Your Prophet in the hope that You would help me in every adversity, I ask that You not make me bear this tribulation." No later than the next day, her son removed the burial covering from his face and we were eating with him!'[91]

As for the Prophet (Allah bless him and give him peace) being addressed by young children, suckling babes, and assorted animals, trees, and inanimate objects, the reports concerning those are mass-transmitted (*mutawātir*); whoever would like healing in this, let him refer to *al-Shifā'*.

Some people have objected to the Shaykh's statement that the Prophet's miracles are not in proportion to his rank, and they said that it is a dreadful and horrendous statement. To that the response is: 'A miracle is Allah's creation, so what is wrong with comparing two created things?' Hence it is permissible to say that the rank of the Emissary of Allah (Allah bless him and give him peace) is greater than the miracles Allah created for his sake and caused to appear at his blessed hands; and that had Allah vouchsafed to him such miracles and breaks with natural phenomenon as were commensurate with his rank and position in His sight and His divine concern for him, his miracles would have been greater and clearer than the miracles that appeared in the cosmos at his hands. However, Allah only willed to manifest what He did: '*And He will not be asked about what He does, but they shall be asked [about what they did].*' (Qur'an 21:23)

Now, none of what we have said here applies to the Qur'an, for it is Allah's uncreated speech, and it is transcendent above being subject to comparison with anything—and it is for this reason that some people have objected to the above words of the author. In reply, it is said that the author's statement is general in its wording but specific in its application. That is similar to Allah's statement: '*Destroying everything by the command of its Lord.*' (Qur'an 46:25) This is widespread in the language of the Arabs, and Allah knows best.

91 Bayhaqī, *Dalā'il al-nubuwwa*.

لَمْ يَمْتَحِنَّا بِمَا تَعْيَا الْعُقُولُ بِهِ حِرْصًا عَلَيْنَا فَلَمْ نَرْتَبْ وَلَمْ نَهِمِ

He did not try us with things that confound the mind
Out of concern for us, so we neither doubted nor strayed.

Here the author (Allah have mercy upon him) says that out of his great concern and mercy and pity for us, the Emissary of Allah (Allah bless him and give him peace) did not inform us of anything our minds would be unable to comprehend, and he did not try us with anything that would confound our minds, nor did he leave us to our own personal understandings or burden us with things that would result in us suffering doubt or bewilderment. He did not burden us with having to know the reality of the spirit or the soul, nor did he order us to know the reality of the spiritual real (*Malakūt*), or what is above the heavens or below the earths. He did not try us with contemplation on Allah's Divine Entity; rather, he forbade us to do so because of the intellect's inability in that regard. In fact, the Emissary of Allah (Allah bless him and give him peace) provided us an example in our own selves, namely the soul between our two sides, by which we live, eat, drink, and come and go: if the soul, which is a creation between our two sides, is unknown to us, how can anyone hope to comprehend and contemplate the Pre-eternal Divine Entity? Intellects are utterly incapable of comprehending Him. Anybody who attempts such a task should be told: 'First come to know what is in you and from you, and the cause of your life and what enables you to sit and stand. You do not know that, so how, pray tell, will you come to know the Exalted Divine Entity?' How excellent is the one who said:

Where is the spirit's essence in relation to you?
Do you see it and how it moves about?
Where is your heart in relation to your body?
Indeed, as he said, it is the Lord's House.
Tell me, O dolt, where is the light of intellect
And the light of cognition when sleep overcomes?
You know not these breaths that you take
Yet despite your ignorance they continue to come;
You know not the qualities of your own form;
The mysteries of your self confound the minds.
So if you are at a loss as to the mysteries

Contained between your two sides,
How can you know Him who rose above the Throne?
And how can you ask how He rose, how is the descent?
How can you know when you know not how you see?
By my life, this is nothing but frivolity!
To say 'how' is to make a likeness of Him;
To say 'where' is affirm indwelling;
There is no 'where' or 'how' for Him.
He is the Lord of 'how', and 'how' undergoes change;
He is above 'above': no above for Him.
He is unchanging in every direction.[92]
Exalted are His Entity, Attributes, and Splendour
And transcendent His description above what I say!

The upshot is that the Emissary of Allah (Allah bless him and give him peace) did not address us in a manner that our intellects cannot bear; he only ordered us to know what our minds can handle. He said, 'Speak to people in proportion to what they can understand; do you want them to belie Allah and His Emissary?'[93] Such was the Prophet's concern for our felicity, lest we fall into that which bygone nations fell into before us. We have no doubt about what the Prophet (Allah bless him and give him peace) brought to us from our Lord, and we have no misgivings in accepting and practicing it. Indeed, the Prophet (Allah bless him and give him peace) brought to us that which intellects can comprehend, and which sound human dispositions can immediately follow; so to Allah belongs all praise and bounty.

أَعْيَا الْوَرَىٰ فَهْمُ مَعْنَاهُ فَلَيْسَ يُرَىٰ   لِلْقُرْبِ وَالْبُعْدِ فِيهِ غَيْرُ مُنْفَحِمِ

Man's mind is exhausted trying to understand his meaning;
All of them, near or far, appear as if dumbstruck.

Here the author (Allah have mercy upon him) says that all of creation are incapable of understanding the meaning and secret that Allah preferred for His Prophet (Allah bless him and give him peace), and unable to grasp

92 This is in reference to Allah's perfect, pre-eternal knowledge and not an affirmation of a place for Him. [t].

93 This is not a Prophetic *ḥadīth* but a statement of ʿAli recorded by Muslim.

his lofty rank and exalted pre-eminence not attained by the previous Prophets—such as his reaching the level wherein he heard the scratching of the [recording angels'] pens; when he was at the distance of two bow's lengths or nearer to his Lord (according to one interpretation); when he led the Prophets and angels in prayer during the miraculous Night Journey; his intercession when assuming the Praiseworthy Station (*al-Maqām al-Maḥmūd*), in which no other has stood and which has been prepared for none but him; his surpassing the station of the Angel Jibrīl on the night of the miraculous journey; and his being a Mercy unto the Worlds, and other favoured positions of grace and honour and miraculous signs that Allah vouchsafed to him alone.

Because of these unique favours that Allah conferred upon the Prophet (Allah bless him and give him peace), the human mind is exhausted and rendered incapable of comprehending the full scope of what Allah has blessed him with; unable to grasp the full extent of the mystical sciences and secrets encompassed in his noble self. This point was alluded to by the perfected Pole (*Quṭb*), the Gnostic of his time and unrivalled of his era, my master ʿAbd al-Salām b. Mashīsh, who said in his prayer, '*and before whom all understandings dwindled; thus none of us before has ever realised his true essence and none of us ever will.*' ... So those near to him and those far from him are all seen to be dumbstruck, incapable. That is to say, those who keep his company and stick closely to him are like those who neither met him nor kept his company, in that they all share in their unfamiliarity with this secret and meaning. It is sufficient for us to say that Allah grants His favour to whom He wills of His servants, so Allah's bounties and gifts to the Prophets, and what He conferred upon them to the exclusion of [the rest of] humanity, cannot be attained through acquisition or works, or through conventional means: they are attainable only through Lordly munificence and Divine favour. Allah favours whomever He wills with His mercy; and Allah is the Possessor of immense bounty.

كَالشَّمْسِ تَظْهَرُ لِلْعَيْنَيْنِ مِنْ بُعُدٍ صَغِيرَةً وَتُكِلُّ الطَّرْفَ مِنْ أَمَمِ

He is like the sun: small to the eye when seen from afar,
But dazzling to the sight when seen close up.

The author (Allah have mercy upon him) tells us that the human mind becomes exhausted when trying to understand the ultimate reality of the secret with which Allah favoured His Emissary (Allah bless him and give him peace), and when attempting to comprehend the unrivalled status that He conferred upon him. And so in that regard the author says that those near and far—in other words, those who lived during his time and those who did not see him—both share in their lack of full understanding.

The Prophet (Allah bless him and give him peace) is likened to the sun in order to convey this meaning, since anyone who looks at it directly is overwhelmed, and its rays confound his sight; and those both near and far are equally unable to arrive at an understanding of its reality. Its true extent is unknown to those near it and to those far from it. Such a person cannot arrive at a judgment about the sun due to its supposed smallness or largeness, for he has not discovered the true knowledge of its reality. To him who looks at it from afar it appears small, although it is not, and he who looks at it from up close is blinded by it and overwhelmed, unable to look upon it; so ultimately neither party, whether near or far, has discovered the true knowledge of the sun's reality.

The same may be said regarding the secret of the favoured position of grace and honour that our Prophet (Allah bless him and give him peace) attained to the exclusion of all others: those near to him, who lived during his time, and those far from him, who did not meet him, share in their lack of full knowledge of him. You might object, 'But how is it conceivable to see the sun up close, since conventionally speaking that is impossible?' The reply would be: The assumption is absurd, for if it were assumed that the one looking was close to the sun, he would be unable to describe it or understand its reality owing to the immense heat of its rays. You might also object, 'But the object that is likened (i.e., the Prophet's rank and secret) is not quantified by smallness or largeness, so how can a simile be applied between it and the thing it is likened to (i.e., the sun), when the "likened to" has a quality not found in the object that is likened?' In answer to that it is said: The intention behind the simile is to explain the equivalence and correspondence in a shared quality, namely inability to realise the object likened and what it is likened to; the details regarding smallness and largeness are simply details added to the object that is likened. And Allah knows best.

وَكَيْفَ يُدْرِكُ فِي الدُّنْيَا حَقِيقَتَهُ قَوْمٌ نِيَامٌ تَسَلَّوْا عَنْهُ بِالْحُلُمِ

How can his reality be grasped in this world
By sleeping folk, distracted from him by dreams?

Here the author (Allah have mercy upon him) asks how this marvellous secret can be realised, and how the reality of this meaning granted by Allah—the favoured position of grace and being chosen to surpass all of the other Prophets, the lordly sciences, the divinely vouchsafed secrets (*asrār ladunīyya*) and the realities of gnosis—can be grasped by people who have been preoccupied by their sleep and distracted from him by dreams. Essentially this means that the Companions and others only grasped the Prophet's human form, and none of them grasped the true reality of his inward self and the mystical secrets it contained. The Prophet (Allah bless him and give him peace) told Abū Bakr (Allah be pleased with him), 'By Him who sent me with the truth, no one knows me truly save my Lord.'[94] And Uways al-Qaranī (Allah be pleased with him) said to the Companions of the Emissary of Allah (Allah bless him and give him peace), 'None of you have seen anything of the Emissary of Allah but his shadow.' The Companions asked, 'Not even [Abū Bakr] Ibn Abī Quḥāfa?' He said, 'No. Not even Ibn Abī Quḥāfa.' Once, when this was mentioned in the presence of Shaykh Abū al-Ḥasan al-Shādhilī (Allah be pleased with him), he said, 'Uways spoke truthfully, may Allah be pleased with him. It was by ʿAlī's rank that he understood the self of Allah's Emissary; it was by ʿUthmān's rank that he understood his heart; it was by ʿUmar's rank that he understood his intellect; and it was by Abū Bakr's rank that he understood his spirit; but the ultimate reality of Allah's Emissary is the hidden secret unknown to all but Allah Most High.'

After citing this quotation, Imam al-Jazūlī (Allah be pleased with him) said:

> His Aḥmadan reality, then, is part of the hidden secret and one of the safeguarded matters known only to Allah Most High; of him the believers have only comprehended the Muḥammadan form, which Uways spoke of as his shadow. Moreover, the believers are of varying ranks when it comes to their grasp [of him], and it is commensurate with their closeness. The greatest of mankind in comprehension of the

94 Shaykh ʿAbd Allāh al-Talīdī notes that this *ḥadīth* is without basis.

Prophet (Allah bless him and give him peace) are the four Caliphs, for they were the closest of mankind to him (Allah bless him and give him peace). However, since their stations were varied their grasp of his reality also varied. Each comprehended the realities of the Prophet (Allah bless him and give him peace) that corresponded to the station he himself was in, and this was alluded to in the above statement of Shaykh [Abū al-Ḥasan] al-Shādhilī.

Since the predominant trait of ʿAlī (Allah be pleased with him) was his knowledge of laws, and his state of expansiveness was found therein, it follows that he grasped the 'self' of the one from whom he inherited his knowledge: our Master Muḥammad (Allah bless him and give him peace). For expansiveness is a trait of the self, which is why it is said that no matter how hard you try to silence the self, it will not remain silent.

Since the predominant state of ʿUthmān (Allah be pleased with him) was deep meditation upon the sciences, it follows that he grasped the Prophet's heart, since deep meditation is a trait of the heart. And since ʿUmar's trait was contemplation of the sciences, it follows that he understood the intellect of the Emissary of Allah (Allah bless him and give him peace), contemplation being a trait of the intellect. And since the predominant state of Abū Bakr (Allah be pleased with him) was the comprehension of realities, and his state of contraction was found therein, it follows that he understood the Prophet's spirit. That is because contraction with the sciences of spiritual realities is a state of the spirit. The dominant trait of the spirit is silence, which is why it is said that no matter how hard you try to make the spirit express itself, it will not speak. Now, despite the fact that the four [first] Caliphs—Allah be pleased with them all—have a predominant knowledge or spiritual state, or a known station among the spiritual stations, they are still leaders in the braches of knowledge and the states and stations that do not predominate over them, and they surpass those for whom these states and stations predominate; but each of them became known for what was predominant in him.

Thus ends the quotation from Imam al-Jazūlī. What he said is good. When you contemplate the states of the four Caliphs (Allah be pleased with them all), Imam al-Jazūlī's comments will be clear. Our master ʿAlī

(Allah be pleased with him) was the gate of the City of Knowledge, and to him the sciences were self-evident (*ḍarūriyya*): he would provide intuitive and spontaneous answers to complex and abstruse questions that would perplex [others'] minds. Consider, for example, the story of al-ʿAnbariyya, and the story of the seven who fell into a well, whom he killed. These incidents are recorded in the books of jurisprudence, such as [the work of] Ibn ʿArafa and others. It is reported from Zirr b. Ḥubaysh that he said: 'Once two people sat down to take a meal. One of them had five loaves of bread, and the other had three. A third person approached and sought permission to eat with them; they allowed him to, and they all ate an equal amount of food. After the meal was finished, the third man (the guest) gave the two men eight dirhams and said, "This is in return for what I ate of your food." Soon thereafter the two men disputed with one another over this money and how it should be divided. The man with five loaves of bread said, "I should have five [dirhams] and you should have three!" The man with three loaves said, "No, we should instead divide the money equally between the two of us!" They soon brought their dispute to ʿAlī, who said to the man with three loaves, "Accept what your companion has offered you." "I will not!" the man protested, "I only want what is my full right." ʿAlī said, "In that case you receive one dirham, while your companion receives seven." "How can that be, O Leader of the Believers?" the man asked. "Because", said ʿAlī, "you had eight loaves between you, and each loaf was broken in three parts. Therefore you had twenty-four equal parts. Your three loaves made nine parts, out of which you have eaten eight portions, leaving just one to the third man. Your friend had five loaves, which divided into three and made fifteen pieces. He ate eight pieces and gave seven pieces to the guest. So the guest shared one part from your loaves and seven from those of your friend, so you should get one dirham and your friend should receive seven dirhams."'

There are many other examples of ʿAlī's judiciousness. In fact, our master ʿUmar (Allah be pleased with him) used to seek refuge from a judgment that was not presided over by Abū al-Ḥasan [ʿAlī]. He would say, 'Were it not for ʿAlī, ʿUmar would have perished!'

Consider the state of our master ʿUthmān (Allah be pleased with him). He was the scribe of the Prophet's secret, and the locus of secrets is the heart, whose function is meditation. This is why ʿUthmān was chosen to write down the revelation as it came down, and so revelation descended upon his heart. And during his final illness before his passing, the Emissary of Allah (Allah bless him and give him peace) entrusted ʿUthmān with secrets that no one had any knowledge of prior to that.

Also consider the state of our master ʿUmar (Allah be pleased with him): his opinions corresponded with the rulings of his Lord in several verses of the Qur'an, to the point that ʿAlī (Allah be pleased with him) said, 'We would notice speech in the Qur'an that corresponded with ʿUmar's speech, and we would notice rulings in it that corresponded with ʿUmar's views.' ʿUmar's adeptness at extrapolating legal rulings and his penetrating insight in management are the effects of deep contemplation and thoughtfulness that stem from the intellect.

The state of our master Abū Bakr (Allah be pleased with him), who grasped the mysterious secrets and hidden subtleties of Divine Unity, stemmed from the soul, to the point that our master ʿUmar (Allah be pleased with him) said, 'I used to visit the Emissary of Allah as he and Abū Bakr were conversing about Divine Unity. I would sit in their company as if I were a non-Arab slave, and I could not understand what they were saying.' May Allah benefit us with love for them. Amen!

فَمَبْلَغُ الْعِلْمِ فِيهِ أَنَّهُ بَشَرٌ ۞ وَأَنَّهُ خَيْرُ خَلْقِ اللَّهِ كُلِّهِمِ

The extent of our knowledge is that he is a mortal –
And that he is the best of Allah's creation!

The author (Allah have mercy upon him) says that the most we can arrive at concerning this noble Prophet (Allah bless him and give him peace), and the fullest extent of our knowledge about him, is that he is a mortal man among men and that he is the best of Allah's creation. The Prophet's humanity is articulated in the Qur'an and Sunna in several places. Allah Most High said about him, '*Say, "I am but a man like you."*' (Qur'an 19:110) And the Prophet (Allah bless him and give him peace) said about himself, 'I am but a man like you, and you take your disputes to me… .'[95]

The Prophet (Allah bless him and give him peace) is also the best of Allah's creation, as proven in rigorously authentic *ḥadīth* reports, such as

95 Bukhārī and Aḥmad.

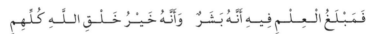

his saying, ‘I am the noblest of the first and the last in the sight of my Lord, and that is no boast; I am the master of the children of Ādam on the Day of Resurrection; I am the first person for whom the earth shall be cleft open; and I am the first intercessor and the first person whose intercession shall be accepted.’ The Prophet (Allah bless him and give him peace) also said, “I am the Master of the first and the last, and the Master of humanity on the Day of Resurrection.’

Indeed, it is the Prophet (Allah bless him and give him peace) who taught us about himself, and it is through true reports from him that we have attained realisation of him and come to know him. It is in him we have faith and believe, and it is at his limits set for us that we stop. As for the secret by which he was preferred over the other Prophets, and the divine grace and care that distinguish him from the rest of creation, there is no hope of us—including the generality of humanity and the angels—attaining knowledge of this in this life. The Prophet’s superiority over the other Prophets is a matter of consensus, excluding those whose disagreements are not relied upon, such as al-Zamakhsharī. We have already discussed the difference of opinion regarding the relative superiority between the angels and the Prophets when we discussed the author’s couplet, *Muḥammad is the Master of both abodes*… And Allah Most High knows best.

وَكُلُّ آيٍ أَتَى الرُّسْلُ الْكِرَامُ بِهَا   فَإِنَّمَا اتَّصَلَتْ مِنْ نُورِهِ بِهِمِ

Every miracle produced by the noble Emissaries
Came to them by virtue of his light alone

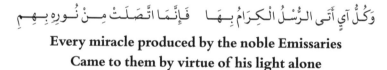

The author (Allah have mercy upon him) says that the miracles conferred upon the Prophets and Emissaries—from Ādam all the way to our Prophet (Allah bless him and give him peace)—were only connected to them and obtained through the Prophet Muḥammad’s light and because of him. For it is from his light that all things were created, and it is because of him that all existent things have come to be. This meaning was expressed earlier in the author’s couplet, *but for him, The world would not have emerged from non-existence*. However, since the Prophet Muḥammad (Allah bless him and give him peace) challenged [his opponents] with clear signs and inimitable miracles that proved the truth of his prophethood, and the other Prophets also challenged [their opponents] with clear signs and inimitable miracles that proved the veracity of their prophethood, someone might imagine that the Prophet Muḥammad (Allah bless him and give him peace) and the other Prophets are equal in rank, status and favour, and might surmise that they are all the same since they were all granted miracles and signs.

The author said in the previous line, *And that he is the best of Allah's creation*, and with this line here he clarifies that the previous Prophets only obtained their miracles and breaks with natural phenomena thanks to the Prophet Muḥammad (Allah bless him and give him peace) and his light. Since the Prophet (Allah bless him and give him peace) is the basis for all that exists and the integral link in the cosmos and cause of every mercy, there should be no objection to the fact that the miracles of the Prophets came to them due to the Prophet Muḥammad and his light. He said, 'I was a Prophet while Ādam was between clay and water.'[96] And in another *ḥadīth* he said, 'I was a Prophet while Ādam was between spirit and body.'[97] In this couplet the author expresses this meaning in a restrictive form (*ḥaṣr*) so as to impart to it a meaning that goes beyond mere statement of fact. And we quoted earlier the statement of one of the learned scholars who determined this meaning in the Qur'an through induction (though, truth be told, the induction of this from the verse is farfetched).

فَإِنَّهُ شَمْسُ فَضْلٍ هُمْ كَوَاكِبُهَا   يُظْهِرْنَ أَنْوَارَهَا لِلنَّاسِ فِي الظُّلَمِ

§ حَتَّىٰ إِذَا طَلَعَتْ فِي الْأُفْقِ عَمَّ هُدَاهَا الْعَالَمِينَ وَأَحْيَتْ سَائِرَ الْأُمَمِ

For he is the sun of virtue, and they are its planets;
They display its lights to mankind in the darkness.
Until finally his light rose on the horizon, and his radiant guidance
dawned upon the world, bringing life to the other nations

In the first couplet the pronoun 'he' refers to the Prophet (Allah bless him and give him peace), and means that he is the sun of virtues, the treasure-store of perfections, the source of lights and the well-spring of secrets. Every holder of perfection has only drawn his perfections from the perfect Prophet (Allah bless him and give him peace); every caller

96 This wording is without basis.
97 Tirmidhī, *Sunan* [t]

unto Allah Most High only invites others on his behalf; and the lights of the Prophets are all acquired from his light (Allah bless him and give him peace).

So when the sun of his virtues rose and the lights of his guidance dawned, the lights of guidance with the other Prophets dimmed, and the rulings of their sacred laws were abrogated on account of the appearance of their ultimate source. The lights of the Prophets are to the Prophet Muḥammad's light as the stars are to the sun: so long as the sun has not appeared, people acquire their light from the light of the stars, but once the sun appears—with its complete light and suffusion—it is sufficient for them. In this couplet the Prophet's lights are likened to the rays of light emitted by the sun, and the lights of the other Prophets are likened to the light emitted by the stars. The 'lights' that are drawn from the Prophet (Allah bless him and give him peace) are used as a metonym for the guidance that mankind receives at their hands, and for the sciences and branches of knowledge that are acquired by the blessings of following them. And there is no doubt whatsoever that he is the greatest of the Prophets in guidance, whose followers outnumber [the others'], and whose nation is the greatest of all nations. Allah guided people at the Prophet's hands in much greater numbers and in a much shorter time than occurred with the other Prophets before him. In fact, creation was guided through the Prophet (Allah bless him and give him peace) *before* his physical appearance in the world. Shaykh ʿUthmān al-Farghānī (Allah be pleased with him) said:

> There has been no actual caller, from the beginning till the end, but this Muḥammadan Reality (*al-Ḥaqīqat al-Muḥammadiyya*) that is the source of all the Prophets, who are as its constituent parts and the details of its reality. As for the individual Prophets, their call was representative of some of its particulars, but the Prophet Muḥammad's call was a universal one that included all of the particulars of his universal. This is alluded to in Allah's words, '*And We have not sent you save to all of mankind.*' (Qur'an 34:28) Now, the Emissaries and their nations, and all of humanity from the first to the last, are subsumed under the phrase '*all of mankind*', and the Prophet Muḥammad's role as a caller is foundational (*bi-al-aṣāla*), whereas the invitation to the truth carried out by

the other Prophets and Emissaries was subordinated to him, and they were his representatives and delegates in the call.

The meaning of al-Farghānī's statement is implied within the author's couplet, and Allah knows best. In actual fact, stars do not draw their light from the sun, but that is not the intended meaning of the author's couplet: it is intended as a simile comparing light to representation. And Allah knows best.

أَكْرِمْ بِخَلْقِ نَبِيٍّ زَانَهُ خُلُقٌ   بِالْحُسْنِ مُشْتَمِلٍ بِالْبِشْرِ مُتَّسِمِ

How noble the qualities of a Prophet beautified by such traits: Full of beauty, and marked by smiles and good cheer!

Here the author (Allah have mercy upon him) says: How noble are the qualities of this esteemed Prophet (Allah bless him and give him peace), and how beautiful is his form adorned by Allah with august character, pure disposition, and well-pleasing traits. It is sufficient for you that Allah Most High has lauded the Prophet (Allah bless him and give him peace) in His book, saying, '*And indeed you are of an immense character.*' (Qur'an 68:4)

The Prophet (Allah bless him and give him peace) was unparalleled in the perfections of his outward attributes (his physical form), and his inward perfections (his character); he donned the raiment of goodness and was cloaked in it. In other words, he was adorned by such traits and they embraced his noble body and outward limbs.

The Prophet (Allah bless him and give him peace) was also gifted with a smiling face, and one of his signs and distinguishing marks was the smiling, happy countenance that he displayed to others. Whenever meeting anyone he would do so with a smiling, shining face. So how noble are the perfect qualities that Allah favoured him with, both in his inward and outward! And how deserving he is of this description by his uncle Abū Ṭālib:

A fair one, by virtue of whose face the rain is sought:
a carer for orphans, a guardian of widows.

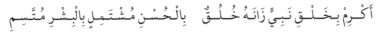

All of the Prophets are of beautiful form and character, but our Prophet (Allah bless him and give him peace) is at the absolute pinnacle of perfection in character and form. May Allah send prayers and salutations upon him, and glorify, honour, and exalt him!

كَالزَّهْرِ فِي تَرَفٍ وَالْبَدْرِ فِي شَرَفٍ وَالْبَحْرِ فِي كَرَمٍ وَالدَّهْرِ فِي هِمَمِ

Like flowers in delicate beauty, like the full moon in honour;
like the sea in generosity, like time in persistence.

After offering in the previous couplet a general description of the Prophet's perfections in character and physical form, the author (Allah have mercy upon him) proceeds to give descriptions in detail, expanding on what he said. He informs us that the Emissary of Allah (Allah bless him and give him peace) resembles a flower in his stunning beauty and delicacy, this being the meaning of the word *taraf* [used in the Arabic]. You might object, 'But Allah condemned people of *taraf* in the Mighty Qur'an, so how can he be praised for it?' I reply: *Taraf* does not merit condemnation in and of itself, and it is not intrinsically blameworthy. The reprehensible *taraf* is the acquired *taraf* of the disbelievers; for they partook of its means, such as preferring the material world [over the Hereafter], enjoying its base desires with reckless abandon, and inclining towards its passing enjoyment and deceptive delight. As for one whose *taraf*, enjoyment and beautiful form are without cause, being solely from divine generosity and pre-eternal concern without preceding cause or self-acquisition, in his case they are not blameworthy but are in fact a miracle and an honour.

We have already mentioned the Prophet's asceticism and renunciation of the world, be it in food or drink or clothing … In the couplet above, the author likens the Prophet's august rank and lofty station and mention to a full moon, complete with the qualities of exaltedness, honour, and spiritual light through which guidance is obtained. He also likens him to the sea in his generosity, largesse and tremendous giving. Indeed, the Prophet (Allah bless him and give him peace) was the most generous and benevolent of mankind. He grew up with these qualities during his formative years, and after the angel descended upon him with revelation and gripped him, Khadīja recounted his generous traits for which he was known before prophecy. After the revelation descended upon him, he was overtaken by fear and knew not what was wanted of him. He said, 'I fear for myself'; but Khadīja sought to alleviate his worry and console him, and said, 'No, by Allah! Allah will never forsake you. You maintain ties with your kinsfolk, you are kind to your neighbours, you are charitable to the poor, you are hospitable to guests and you defend the truth!'[98] She mentioned the means that lead to safety and protection, and she acknowledged the good end that he would enjoy on account of his natural disposition towards good works. And so it is Allah's wont that a person who is naturally disposed to good works will not fear harm or be afraid of creation. We have already spoken in detail about the Prophet's generosity in our commentary on the couplet *He excelled the other Prophets in form and qualities …*

The author continues, and likens the Prophet's lofty persistence to time itself, for according to the Arabs, time is described as persistent, this being personified in its swift and violent impact and steadfast indifference to vicissitudes. The Arabs say, 'Time has taken its toll on me and afflicted me with such-and-such.' So time is described as the source of all manner of events, tribulations and momentous happenings that occur within it. Being described as persistent, time is unwavering and firm, without flattering or complaining to anyone or anything. It is likewise with our Prophet (Allah bless him and give him peace): due to his lofty aspiration and persistence, he proclaims the truth, as he was commanded by Allah's words, '*So proclaim what you are commanded and turn away from the idol-worshippers.*' (Qur'an 15:94)

The Prophet (Allah bless him and give him peace) feared no one when it came to truth; he never engaged in fawning flattery or yielded to a disbeliever in a docile manner; and in his call to Allah he never shied away because of the blame of a blamer. A rigorously authenticated *ḥadīth* records that the Prophet (Allah bless him and give him peace) said, 'When one of their noblemen committed theft the Children of Israel would leave him be, but when a weak person amongst them stole they would cut off his hand. I swear by Allah that had Fāṭima the daughter of Muḥammad stolen, I would have cut off her hand!'[99]

98 Bukhārī.
99 Bukhārī.

Another example of the Prophet's high persistence is the incident in which Quraysh offered him wealth so he could be the richest of them, and they proposed to make him king to reign over them in return for leaving them to their religion unimpeded. However, the Prophet (Allah bless him and give him peace), due to his exalted persistence, refused their offer and was determined to fulfil Allah's command and make His religion and law reign supreme over them. For that reason, he spoiled their dreams, found fault with their gods and was unperturbed by their large numbers or insolence, until finally Allah made him victorious against them and he ruled over them, ultimately showing them his largesse and freeing them.

The upshot of all this is that the author likens the Prophet's *taraf*—that is, the delicate beauty of his body—to a flower, comprising goodness, handsomeness and resplendence; he likens the Prophet (Allah bless him and give him peace) to a moon, comprising good repute, light, exaltedness and guidance; he likens the Prophet's generosity to a sea, comprising munificence and giving, and the goodness and benefits found in a sea, as well as the valuable jewels of knowledge and marvellous wisdoms contained within him; and he likens the Prophet's lofty persistence to time itself, comprising dignity, indifference [to opposition] and frankness and unwaveringness when speaking the truth to others.

CONCLUDING REMARKS IN PRAISE OF GENEROSITY, AND MENTION OF VARIOUS STORIES ABOUT THE BENEVOLENT

The Prophet (Allah bless him and give him peace) said, 'The generous person is close to Allah, close to people, close to Paradise, and distant from Hell; and the miser is far from Allah, far from people, far from Paradise, and close to Hell.'[100] There is no doubt that generosity is one of the greatest qualities of good and one of the best traits of piety; indeed, it is one of the qualities of the Lord, exalted is He, and the qualities of His elect Prophets and Saints. Generosity has remained a praiseworthy trait from the pre-Islamic period of ignorance until now, and it is deemed commendable by the elect and common folk alike.

100 Tirmidhī, *Sunan*.

Al-Madāʾinī (Allah have mercy upon him) said:

Al-Ḥasan, al-Ḥusayn and ʿAbdullāh b. Jaʿfar embarked on a journey for Hajj, but lost track of their supplies and suffered hunger and thirst on the way. They soon passed by the tent of an elderly lady and asked, 'Is there any drink?' The elderly lady replied, 'Yes', and they disembarked and hobbled their camels. As they approached, they noticed that the lady only had a single sheep at the side of her tent. She said to them, 'Milk it for yourselves and chew its curd', and so they did. Afterwards they asked, 'Is there any food?' The elderly lady replied, 'At the moment I have nothing to offer but this sheep; let one of you slaughter it so I may prepare a meal of it for you.' So one of them went forward and slaughtered and skinned the sheep, and she prepared a meal for them of it. They ate their meal and remained with the elderly lady for some time, after which they cooled off and prepared to resume their journey. As they were leaving they said to the elderly lady, 'We are a group from Quraysh; when we return safe and sound by Allah's leave, see to it that you find us, for we shall return the favour.' When the lady's husband came and she informed him of what transpired, he asked her incredulously, 'Did you slaughter the only sheep we own, and for absolute strangers?' Not long after, this elderly lady and her husband were in dire straits and settled in Medina, where they made their living selling unripe dates. One day, as the lady was passing through one of the alleyways of Medina, she walked by al-Ḥasan b. ʿAlī as he was sitting by the front door of his home. He immediately recognised her but she did not remember him. He called out, 'O Bondswoman of Allah, don't you recognise me?' 'No', she said, 'by Allah, I do not recognise you.' He reminded her, 'I was your guest on such-and-such day.' Remembering him, she cried out, 'May my mother and father be sacrificed for you! You are the one!' 'Yes', Ḥasan said, and he ordered that she be given one thousand sheep, and sent her to his brother al-Ḥusayn. Upon seeing her, al-Ḥusayn asked, 'How many sheep did my brother give you?' 'One thousand', she said. And so al-Ḥusayn gave her a like number of sheep and sent her to ʿAbd Allāh b. Jaʿfar b. Abī Ṭālib. ʿAbd Allāh b. Jaʿfar asked, 'How many sheep did al-Ḥasan and al-Ḥusayn give you?' 'Two thousand in total', she said. ʿAbd Allāh b. Jaʿfar said to her, 'Had you come to me first I would have made things challenging for them!' And so ʿAbd Allāh b. Jaʿfar went to his farm [to give her sheep] and on his way stopped near a wall surrounding date palm trees that belonged to some people. There was a young black boy working the land and ʿAbd Allāh b. Jaʿfar looked on as the boy was given his daily bread. Suddenly, a dog trespassed inside the grove and stood menacingly near the boy. The boy threw a round loaf at the dog, who ate it, and then the boy threw a second and a third round loaf at the dog, who ate them. Looking on, ʿAbd Allāh asked the young boy, 'What is your daily wage?' The boy answered, 'My wage is in these loaves you see here before you.' 'If that is so', ʿAbd Allāh said, 'why do you prefer this dog over yourself?' The boy replied, 'O master, this is not a land populated by dogs. This dog comes hungry from a distant land, and I am loathe to refuse him.' ʿAbd Allāh asked, 'What do you do?' The boy replied, 'I stack bricks all day long.' ʿAbd Allāh said, 'I am called generous and giving, but this boy is more giving and generous than I am!" ʿAbd Allāh then asked about the owner of the grove and the boy, and he purchased both together, after which he emancipated the boy and gave him the grove.

It is also reported that there were three men debating in the courtyard of the Kaʿba as to who was the noblest and most generous person. The first man said, 'The noblest and most generous person is ʿAbd Allāh b. Jaʿfar.' The second man said, 'The noblest and most generous person is Qays b. Saʿd b. ʿUbāda.' And the third person said, 'The noblest and most generous person is ʿArāba al-Awsī.' They went back and forth between themselves, debating about who was the most generous, until one of them said, 'Let us go to them and pretend to be beggars, and let each of us ask the one whom he deems most generous. That way we can see what each of them gives, and judge them individually.'

The man who preferred ʿAbd Allāh b. Jaʿfar walked over to him as the latter was inserting his foot in his camel's stirrup to ride off. The man called out, 'O cousin of Allah's Emissary!' 'Speak', said ʿAbd Allāh. The man said, 'I am a passer-by who has fallen into difficulty.' ʿAbd Allāh removed his foot from the camel's stirrup and said, 'Here, take this camel and the contents of its load; but take not the sword, for it is the sword of ʿAlī.'

The man who preferred Qays b. Saʿd b. ʿUbāda al-Awsī approached him but found him asleep. Qays' servant said, 'He is asleep; what do you need?' The man said, 'I am a stranger and passer-by a long way from home, and I have fallen upon hard times.' The servant said, 'Fulfilling your needs is easier than wakening him. Take this bag; it contains seven hundred dinars. Go to the resting-area of the camels and convey a message to the person there. He will give you a camel and a slave, and then you can be on your way.' Finally, when Qays woke up, his slave told him what he had done, and Qays set him free.

The man who preferred ᶜArāba al-Awsī approached him as the latter was leaving his home on the way to offer his prayer, leaning between two servants and lowering his gaze. The man called out, 'O ᶜArāba!" 'Speak', said ᶜArāba. The man said, "I am a passer-by, a stranger who is stranded alone and in need." Suddenly, ᶜArāba dismissed the two slaves and clapped his hands, saying, 'Ah! The rights of others have not left with ᶜArāba any wealth; however, you may take these two slaves if you wish.' The man said, 'I shall not clip your wings.' 'In any case', ᶜArāba replied, 'if you refuse to take them they are considered free; so if you like you may take them, and if you like they will be emancipated.' The man decided to leave them.

The third man then made his way to the courtyard of the Kaᶜba, and he and his companions all concurred that ᶜArāba was the most generous of the three because he gave despite his lack of means, whereas the former two gave only of their excess wealth.

It is reported that a man stood in front of ᶜAbd Allāh b. ᶜAbbās and said, 'Ibn ᶜAbbās, I have a right over you and I need it fulfilled!" Ibn ᶜAbbās asked, 'What is your right over me?' The man replied, 'I once saw you standing at the well of Zamzam as your servant boy collected water from it for you; and you were suffering from the extreme heat of the sun and took shade under one of my coverings as you drank.' 'You are right,' Ibn ᶜAbbās said, 'I remember that day and it continues to trouble my conscience.' Ibn ᶜAbbās then asked his servant boy, 'What do you have with you now?' The boy replied, 'I have ten thousand dirhams and one hundred dinars.' Ibn ᶜAbbās said, 'Give them to this man; but, I do not think they can compensate for this man's right.' 'By Allah!' the man proclaimed, 'had Ismāᶜīl no son but you it would have been sufficient to establish his honour and virtue; so what can be said when his progeny includes the Master of the first and the last, Muḥammad (Allah bless him and give him peace). May he intercede for you and your father!' ʿAbdullāh b. ʿAbbās was the first person to set out table spreads of food beside the roads.

Know that the highest grade of generosity and loftiest degree of munificence is contained in altruism, or selflessly preferring others over oneself despite need. Allah Most High says, '*They prefer others over themselves even though they be in privation.*' (Qur'an 59:9) This verse was revealed concerning a man from the Anṣār who took on a guest who had come to the Emissary of Allah (Allah bless him and give him peace). The Anṣārī did not find any provision in his possession, so after putting his hungry children to sleep he instructed his wife to dim the lantern, whereupon she got up and pretended to fix it and then extinguished it. The Anṣārī then placed the only remaining portion of food he had before the guest and sat with him in the dark, moving his hand as if he was eating with the guest—only he was letting the guest eat to his fill. When the morning came, the Emissary of Allah (Allah bless him and give him peace) said, 'Allah is amazed [i.e., well pleased] with what you did with your guest,' and then the verse was revealed, '*They prefer others over themselves even though they be in privation.*' (Qur'an 59:9)

This is how the Prophet (Allah bless him and give him peace) would prefer others over himself. The most amazing and awe inspiring example of altruism and selflessness is found in the story of Ḥudhayfa al-ʿAdawī. He said, 'During the Battle of Yarmūk, I set out looking for one of my cousins among the wounded fighters. I was carrying a container of water and said to myself that I could drink it when thirsty, or wipe my face with it. When I finally found my cousin I decided to give him drink instead, and he indicated with his facial expression as if to say "Yes." When I got to him and prepared to give him drink, suddenly a man shouted "Ah!" out of severe thirst, and my cousin indicated that I should instead give him drink. When I went to that man I discovered that he was none other than Hishām b. al-ʿĀṣī, and as I prepared to give him drink, suddenly another man shouted "Ah!" out of severe thirst, and Hishām indicated that I should instead give him drink. When I went to that man to give him drink I discovered that he had perished, so I went back to Hishām, but he had perished too, and then I returned to my cousin, but he had perished as well." What is greater than this selflessness and preference for others? What patience is greater than this patience? This was related by al-Alyūrī.

كَأَنَّهُ وَهْوَ فَرْدٌ فِي جَلَالَتِهِ   فِي عَسْكَرٍ حِينَ تَلْقَاهُ وَفِي حَشَمِ

So majestic was his presence that even when alone
he appeared surrounded by a large army and retinue.

The author (Allah have mercy upon him) says that because of the Prophet's splendour and sublime majesty, and the awe felt for him in [people's] hearts, when he was met while alone he would appear as if he stood in the midst of a vast and powerful army, even though he was by himself without retinue or servants. Normally a person will only be feared if he wields force and authority and maintains an aura of inapproachability; however, the Prophet (Allah bless him and give him peace) would visit the sick, follow funeral processions, and sit with the weak and indigent among his Companions, such as ᶜAmmār, Ṣuhayb, Bilāl and Khabbāb, and would not leave their presence until they got up to leave. He would say to them, 'Your life is our life, and your death is our death.'[101] He would never interrupt a person in mid-sentence. Slave men and women would meet him in the street and speak with him about their concerns and problems, and they would walk and stand with him and address him as if he were one of them. But despite that, the believers' hearts were filled with unparalleled awe for the Prophet's splendour and sublime majesty, and because of the immensity of their awe and respect for him, those sitting in his presence would sit as if birds were perched above their heads, and his Companions would avoid laughter in his gathering—smiling instead—and would not raise their voices. This same etiquette is required of us now in front of the Prophet's holy Sanctuary (*Rawḍa*) and Sacred Mosque, for his sanctity after his passing is the same as his sanctity during his worldly life.

It is reported that Abū Jaᶜfar al-Manṣūr once debated a legal issue with [Imam] Mālik in the Mosque of the Emissary of Allah (Allah bless him and give him peace) and raised his voice above Mālik's, whereupon Mālik said, 'Leader of the Believers, do not raise your voice in this Mosque, for

101 Muslim.

Allah said, "*And do not raise your voices above the voice of the Emissary*" (Qur'an 49:2); and He praised others when He said, "*Those who lower their voices in the presence of the Emissary of Allah. they are the ones whose hearts Allah has tested for righteousness*" (Qur'an 49:3); and indeed, the Prophet's sanctity in after his passing is just like his sanctity in life.' Abū Ja'far conceded his point and asked, 'O Abū Abd Allāh, should I face the *qibla* when I supplicate or should I face the Emissary of Allah (Allah bless him and give him peace)?' Mālik replied, 'Why would you turn your face from the one who shall be your intermediary (*wasīla*) and that of your father Ādam (upon whom be peace) before Allah Most High on the Day of Judgment? Indeed, you should face him and seek intercession through him unto Allah, for Allah Most High said, "*And if only, after wronging themselves, they had come to you and sought Allah's forgiveness, and the Emissary had sought forgiveness for them, they would have found Allah Oft-Relenting, Merciful.*"' (Qur'an 4:64)

Let it be known that every single mosque shares a portion of the sanctity held by the Mosque of Allah's Emissary (Allah bless him and give him peace), for Allah Most High says, '*In houses built by the permission of Allah…*' (Qur'an 24:36): voices should not be raised in them, nor should lost items be announced, and buying and selling should not take place in them, as is explicated in the books of jurisprudence; and Allah knows best.

كَأَنَّمَا اللُّؤْلُؤُ الْمَكْنُونُ فِي صَدَفٍ   مِنْ مَعْدِنَيْ مَنْطِقٍ مِنْهُ وَمُبْتَسِمِ

It is as if precious hidden pearls, sparkling from their shells, came from the treasure-mine of his speech and smile.

Here the author (Allah have mercy upon him) completes the meaning of the preceding couplet. In other words, if you were to meet this magnificent Prophet and noble Emissary (Allah bless him and give him peace), your mind would be bewildered and dazzled on account of his tremendousness and awe; and if you were to encounter him by himself it would seem to you that he was standing in the midst of a vast and powerful army, and if you were to keep his company and sit with him, you would find his speech the sweetest, his expressions the most eloquent, his words the most expressive. In sum, he was the most eloquent of humanity. He would produce jewel-laden words of wisdom, and would extract rare pearls of beauty. When the Prophet (Allah bless him and give him peace) smiled it seemed that precious hidden pearls were sparkling—nay, hidden pearls in their shells are drawn and extracted from the mine of his mouth and smile. The meaning of this couplet is that when the Prophet (Allah bless him and give him peace) spoke, he would utter jewel-laden words of wisdom, and when he smiled [his teeth] would appear as shining, hidden pearls, something akin to hailstones.

In this couplet the author has reversed the simile for the sake of hyperbolic embellishment and described the pearls as precious and hidden in their shell, unmolested and untouched by man, for that is purer and clearer, loftier and more unique. This couplet expresses the perfect beauty of the Prophet's speech and his complete eloquence; and if the precious pearls hidden in their shells are drawn and extracted from the treasure-mine of the Prophet's mouth and smile, what can one say of his mouth and smile, the source from which they are drawn?

Besides describing the pearls as hidden, the author also says they are contained in their shell. Pearls may be hidden in something other than their shells, but when they are taken out and change hands in transactions they lose the purity, sheen and beauty they would maintain in their shells. Pearls can only resemble the Prophet's speech and be extracted from the mine of his smile if they are in their shells. Abū Hurayra (Allah be pleased with him) said, in a *ḥadīth* recorded by al-Tirmidhī, 'I never saw anyone more beautiful than the Emissary of Allah. It was as if the sun shone upon his face, and when he laughed, his light would shine upon the walls.'[102] [al-Tirmidhī also recorded], 'When he spoke, it appeared as though light was emanating from between his teeth.'[103] And there is also the statement of Ibn Abī Hāla mentioned at the end of his *ḥadīth*: 'His laughter was mostly smiles, revealing something akin to hailstones...'

لَا طِيبَ يَعْدِلُ تُرْبًا ضَمَّ أَعْظُمَهُ   طُوبَىٰ لِمُنْتَشِقٍ مِنْهُ وَمُلْتَثِمِ

No perfume can match the ground that holds his bones.
Blessed are those who breathe in its fragrance or kiss it!

102 Tirmidhī, *Sunan*.
103 Tirmidhī, *Shamāʾil*.

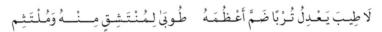

The author (Allah have mercy upon him) says that there is no fragrance in existence as sweet as the ground that holds the blessed bones of Allah's Emissary (Allah bless him and give him peace) and covers his pure body and noble and holy person. No fragrance of any kind comes close to matching or rivalling the earth around him. It is possible that the author (Allah have mercy upon him) intends by his couplet a physical fragrance, and that is the apparent meaning. Many people of established probity who have performed Hajj and come into physical contact with the blessed grave have reported that they smelled supranormally fine scents there.

Fine scent is linked to that earth because of the one located within it; and if fine scents are smelled near the graves of the righteous who had inherited from the Prophet (Allah bless him and give him peace) thanks to their frequent prayers upon him, how can there not be found sweet scent near the grave of the one whose fragrance has filled the entire cosmos?

During the Prophet's worldly life he would emit a fine fragrance whether he applied perfume or not. His sweat was finer than the finest scent; those who came into contact with it would mix his sweat in their perfume, and those who wiped it on themselves would smell like him, and the inhabitants of Medina would smell it and recognise its source. They found no scent sweeter or better smelling than his, and whenever he passed down any of Medina's streets, people would notice the fragrant scent and know that he walked by. Isḥāq b. Rāhawayh observed that this was his [natural] scent without perfume.

It is reported from Jābir (Allah be pleased with him) that he said, 'The Emissary of Allah placed me behind him on a riding animal, and I placed my mouth over the Seal of Prophecy and it smelled like musk.'[104]

The palms of his hands were more fragrant than fine musk and ambergris; it was as if his hands were those of a perfumer. Whenever anyone shook his hand, his fragrance would remain with them for the remainder of the day. If he patted a child's head, that child would be distinguishable from other children. When the Prophet (Allah bless him and give him peace) went to answer the call of nature, the earth would split open and swallow up what came out of him and a fine scent would emerge from that place. No man has ever seen what came out of him.

104 Qāḍī ʿIyāḍ, *al-Shifāʾ*.

Umm Ayman once drank the Prophet's urine mistakenly and did not smell in it the normal smell of urine; ʿAbdullāh b. al-Zubayr (Allah be pleased with him) once drank the Prophet's blood and his mouth was filled with the scent of musk — and its fragrance remained in his mouth until he was killed.

When the Prophet (Allah bless him and give him peace) passed away there was nothing unpleasant that appeared from him as typically appears from the deceased; he was fragrant in his worldly life and after his passing. In sum, Allah scented the cosmos with his gentle breeze and everything was perfumed by him; hearts drew sustenance from him and were made agreeable; and souls inhaled his sweet aroma and were expanded. Certainly there is no match or rival to the scent of the earth that contains the Prophet's blessed bones. That is a unique favour granted by Allah.

It is also possible that the author intends by his couplet a metaphorical fragrance: an expression of fine praise for the one contained in that earth, lauding his blessing body, noble soul and fine character. This is similar to the words of the poet who said:

It is not the aroma of musk that you find;
It is the fine praise that is left behind.

—but the former view [the non-figurative] is the more obvious one, and Allah knows best.

CHAPTER 4

The Prophet's Birth ﷺ

أَبَانَ مَوْلِدُهُ عَنْ طِيبِ عُنْصُرِهِ يَا طِيبَ مُبْتَدَإٍ مِنْهُ وَمُخْتَتَمِ

His birth made the purity of his pedigree evident;
O how pure were his beginning and his end!

THE AUTHOR (Allah have mercy upon him) says that all that manifested during the Prophet's birth of palpable signs, clear portents and wondrous breaks with normal phenomena (*khawāriq lil-ʿādāt*) point to his lofty rank, his noble station and his advent. The miraculous events and extraordinary happenings that appeared during his birth made clear his pure origin, lofty rank and the divine concern of Allah (the Exalted and Sublime) for him.

The miraculous and extraordinary signs that manifested during the Prophet's birth are amazingly numerous and are as familiar as the sun over the horizon. People are in unanimous agreement about the authenticity of those signs.

Among these signs is that when Āmina b. Wahb [the Prophet's mother] received the good news that she was pregnant with the Prophet (Allah bless him and give him peace) she was told, 'You are carrying the Master of this nation, so when he is born you must supplicate, "I seek refuge for him in The One [*al-Wāḥid*] from the evil of every envier," and then you must name him Muḥammad…'

When she was pregnant with him [Allah bless him and give him peace] she saw a light emitted from her that lit up the palaces of Bostra in the Levant. Al-Suhaylī (Allah have mercy upon him) said, 'That was because Allah granted him victory over the lands, and the servants in that region sought illumination from his light and received through him guidance and mercy…'

Among these signs is that when he was born, the Prophet (Allah bless him and give him peace) raised his head and looked towards the heavens.

Among these signs is that Umm ʿUthmān b. Abī al-ʿĀṣ saw the stars drawing near and light manifested during the Prophet's birth, until all that she could see was light.[105]

Among these signs was the collapse of Khusraw's arch [*īwān*]—meaning his palace—and the drying up of Lake Taberias and the receding of its water.

Among these signs is that the sacred fire of the Zoroastrians was extinguished, and the devils were assailed with flaming meteors that thwarted their ability to spy news [in the celestial realm].

Among these signs is that a group of people from Quraysh had an idol that they venerated and to which they would sacrifice animal offerings, but on the day of the Prophet's birth they saw the idol fall over and land upon its face. This disturbed them, so they pulled it back up – only to see it fall once again. They pulled it back up a third time, but when it fell again they became distraught and asked themselves, 'Why does it keep falling over? This can only be the result of some [extraordinary] event that has taken place!' They looked to see what significant event had happened that day, and found that it was the day of the Prophet's birth.

Among these signs is that when he was born, the Prophet's mother sent a message to his grandfather ʿAbd al-Muṭṭalib informing him of the birth of his grandson and requesting that he visit her to see him. He arrived and looked at the Prophet (Allah bless him and give him peace), and his mother related to him what she had seen during her pregnancy with the Prophet and the astounding things that had been said to her on the night of his birth. ʿAbd al-Muṭṭalib then took him, entered the precincts of the Kaʿba and supplicated and thanked Allah for the blessing He had given him. Then he returned the Prophet (Allah bless him and give him peace) to his mother and set out to find wet-nurses for him. He found Ḥalīma bint Abī Dhuʾayb, who was to become his mother through

105 Bayhaqī reported in *Dalāʾil al-nubuwwa* via Muḥammad b. Abī Suwayd al-Thaqafī, from ʿUthmān b. Abī al-ʿĀṣ who said, 'Fāṭima b. ʿAbd Allāh al-Thaqafīya—one of the female Companions—narrated to me that she was in Āmina's company the night the latter was going through labour. She said, "I looked at the stars coming close and drawing near. Startled, I said, 'They are going to fall upon me!' But when she [Āmina] gave birth, a light came forth from her that lit up the entire house and the surrounding area."'

nursing. Her story, and the well-known miraculous occurrences she saw during the time she nursed the Prophet (Allah bless him and grant him peace), have been recounted in detail in our commentary on the *Hamziyya Ode*.

As for his pure origins and goodly mention that were made clear during his birth, there is no doubt that the Prophet (Allah bless him and give him peace) was the noblest of his people, being born of such a father and mother. Ibn ᶜAbbās (Allah be pleased with him) related that the Prophet (Allah bless him and give him peace) said, 'Truly, Allah divided mankind into two groups'—meaning the Companions of the Right (*Aṣḥāb al-Yamīn*) and the Companions of the Left (*Aṣḥāb al-Shimāl*)—'and He made me the best of them in pedigree; I am therefore the best among the Companions of the Right. Then Allah divided them into three groups and made me the best of the thirds. There are the Companions of the Right, the Companions of the Left, and the Forerunners (*al-Sābiqūn*)—and I am of the Forerunners. Then Allah made each third into tribes and made me the best of them in that respect. Again, Allah has said "*And We have made you into peoples and tribes, that you may get to know one another. The noblest of you in the sight of Allah is the most God-fearing amongst you.*" (Qur'an 49:13) Indeed I am the most God-fearing of the children of Ādam, and the noblest of them in the sight of Allah. Then Allah established households, and He placed me in the best of them. He said "*Allah wants only to remove impurities from you, O members of the Household, and to purify you to the utmost!*"'[106] (Qur'an 33:33)

It is related on the authority of Wāthila b. al-Asqaᶜ that the Prophet (Allah bless him and give him peace) said, 'Allah selected Ismāᶜīl from the children of Ibrāhīm, and selected Banū Kināna from the offspring of Ismāᶜīl, and selected Quraysh from Banū Kināna, and selected Banū Hāshim from Quraysh, and selected me from Banū Hāshim.'[107] (For more details refer to *al-Shifā'* ('The Healing', by al-Qāḍī 'Iyāḍ), for in it lies healing.)

Ibn ᶜAbbās (Allah be pleased with him) related that the Emissary of Allah (Allah bless him and give him peace) said, 'Allah caused me to descend to the earth while in Ādam's loins, and then He placed me in Nūḥ's

106 Bayhaqī, *Dalā'il al-nubuwwa*.
107 Muslim.

loins, and then I was cast into the fire while in Ibrāhīm's loins, and Allah continued to transmit me through noble and pure loins until I was born to parents who had never committed fornication.'[108]

It is also related, on the authority of Ibn ᶜAbbās, that 'Quraysh was a light in the presence of Allah, the Exalted and Sublime, one thousand years before the creation of Ādam. That light glorified Allah, and the angels glorified Allah with its glorification, and when Allah created Ādam He placed that light within Ādam's loins. [The Prophet (Allah bless him and give him peace) said] "So Allah caused me to descend to the earth within Ādam's loins, and then He placed me in Nūḥ's loins, and then in Ibrāhīm's loins, and He continued to transmit me through noble loins and pure wombs."'[109]

Perhaps in saying *the purity of his pedigree,* the author is alluding to this light. Allah Most High knows best.

The Prophet's birth took place on the twenty-seventh or twenty-eighth day of the month of Rabīᶜ al-Awwal. It is also said that he was born on the eighth, or the tenth, or the twelfth. The correct position is that it was the twelfth. Scholars agree that the Prophet (Allah bless him and give him peace) was born on a Monday, and that he was tasked with Prophethood on a Monday, and that he migrated to Medina on a Monday, and that he passed away on a Monday, eleven years after the Migration.

The story of Āmina's marriage to ᶜAbdullāh, and ᶜAbd al-Muṭṭalib's vow to sacrifice one of his sons and his expiation for that vow, are well known, so in the interest of brevity we will not retell them here.

Just as extraordinary events unfolded during the Prophet's birth, other miracles manifested towards the end of his [terrestrial] life and when he passed away. For this reason the author expresses his astonishment by saying, *O how pure were his beginning and his end!* The vocative particle [O] is used to express amazement with the profusion of purity that manifested during his birth and his passing. It is also possible that by saying *end*, the author means the end of the Prophet's [earthly] life, in which case his astonishment applies to all of the miracles of the Prophet (Allah bless him and give him peace), from the time Allah sent him till the time He took his soul. Allah Most High knows best.

108 Abū ᶜUmar al-ᶜAdanī, *Musnad*.

109 Cited by Qāḍī ᶜIyāḍ in *al-Shifāʾ* without a chain of transmission.

يَـوْمٌ تَـفَـرَّسَ فِيـهِ الْـفُـرْسُ أَنَّـهُـمُ ‎ ‎ قَـدْ أُنْـذِرُوا بِـحُـلُـولِ الْـبُـؤْسِ وَالنِّـقَـمِ

On that day the Persians intuited that they
Had been warned of looming misery and retribution.

Intuition (*firāsa*) is a light from Allah and is one of His secrets. With it the believer looks and sees things as if they are present before him. The guidance that a person can acquire from his spiritual intuition is proportionate to the strength of his faith. It is possible that a person of spiritual intuition may predict a future event and it takes shape exactly as he predicted. Spiritual intuition is conveyed through presages and notions (just as a fearful person is given away by certain signs).

A soothsayer (*kāhin*) is one who receives news from jinn that he then informs others. An inspired person (*muḥaddath*) is one who receives news from the angels that he then communicates to others. The difference, therefore, between a soothsayer and an inspired person is that the former receives his information from the jinn while the latter receives his information from an angel. Allah can also create knowledge within the heart of the inspired person—without thought, contemplation or via an intermediary—of what will happen to him in the future. Among such inspired people is ʿUmar (Allah be pleased with him). He appointed Sāriya [b. Zunaym al-Khaljī] as commander over an expeditionary force. Sāriya and his troops made contact with the enemy, but the enemy vastly outnumbered them and nearly wiped them out. Meanwhile in Medina, far away from Sāriya, ʿUmar was addressing the people, when suddenly he began to speak about Sāriya and his troops, and Allah disclosed their plight to ʿUmar's heart and he began to cry out, 'O Sāriya, take to the mountain! O Sāriya, take to the mountain!' Allah conveyed ʿUmar's cry to Sāriya, and Sāriya and the Muslims with him took refuge on the mountain, and that was the cause of their survival. The Emissary of Allah (Allah bless him and give him peace) informed people about ʿUmar's reality when he said, 'Amongst the nations before you there were inspired people [*muḥaddathūn*]; and if there is to be anyone like that in my nation it will be ʿUmar!'[110]

In this couplet the author (Allah have mercy upon him) explains the previous couplet about the signs and extraordinary events that appeared

110 Bukhārī and Muslim

during the Prophet's birth. In other words, it was a tremendous day in which marvels and signs appeared, many of which pertained specifically to the Persians (al-Furs) and their ruler the Khusraw, such as the collapse of the [palace] arch, the extinguishing of their sacred fire and the drying up of the lake—all of which will be recounted in full, Allah willing.

When the Persians witnessed these occurrences (not to mention the prognostications that they had received from the oracles in whom they had absolute confidence and trust) they discerned with their minds that misery was looming upon them, and felt that these were sure signs that their power was to scatter and that their empire was to fall and end in oblivion.

You might object and say 'You stated earlier that *firāsa* is a light from Allah by which a believer sees things, so how can that apply to a disbeliever?' To that I reply: This is not *firāsa*, properly speaking. What the Persians saw were but outward causes and signs from which they inferred—and feared for—the destruction of their empire and their impending doom; as the saying goes, 'The companion of evil suspicion is madly in love.' The reason for the author's use of the word *firāsa* is to introduce wordplay (*jinās*) whereby *firāsa* and *furs* were matched together. The Persians saw only the outward causes that gave rise to their fears; spiritual intuition had nothing to do with it. [True] *firāsa* was beyond their ken, since it is a light from Allah Most High and was far removed from them. *Firāsa* only applies to a perfected believer.

Someone [among the spiritual masters] was asked about *firāsa* and he said, '[*Firāsa* is that which is communicated by] souls that move about in the sovereign realm (*al-malakūt*) and look upon the meanings of unseen realities, whose secrets they then describe in truth with an expression born of direct witnessing and intellective vision, not surmise and deduction.' To quote al-Kattānī, 'Spiritual intuition is an unveiling of the truth and a vision of the Unseen.'

Spiritual intuition is one of the stages of faith (*īmān*). Imam Mālik (Allah have mercy upon him) had extremely powerful intuition. It is narrated that the first time al-Shāfiʿī (Allah have mercy upon him) visited Mālik and set eyes upon him, Mālik looked at him from head to toe and then said to him approvingly, 'Dear son, fear Allah and avoid sin, and something great will come of you for certain!' On another occasion Ibn

Farūkh, Ibn Ghānim and al-Bahlūl b. Rāshid came to see Mālik. He said of the first, 'He is the jurist of his land'; he said of the second, 'He is the judge of his land'; and he said of the third, 'He is the conqueror of his land'—and for all of them [what he said] came true.

It is reported that al-Shāfiʿī and Muḥammad b. al-Ḥasan were in the Sacred Mosque in Mecca when a man entered their presence. Muḥammad b. al-Ḥasan said, 'I intuit that he is a carpenter.' Al-Shāfiʿī said, 'I intuit that he is a blacksmith.' When they asked his profession the man said, 'I used to be a carpenter but these days I am a blacksmith', and so both of them were correct!

Al-Dīnawarī related: 'I was once sitting in the congregational mosque of Baghdad in the company of some poor people. No provision came our way, so I went to see Ibrāhīm al-Khawwāṣ to ask him for something they could eat. When he saw me, and before I had a chance to speak to him, he said, "Let me ask you: the need for which you have come to ask of me—does Allah know of it or not?" I replied, "Of course He knows," whereupon he said, "So be quiet, return from whence you came and do not disclose your need to people!" I made my way back and a short while later Allah granted an opening and provided even more than enough.'

Imam al-Qushayrī (Allah have mercy upon him) related that a young man sought the company of Junayd. Junayd's companions said to him, 'O master, this young man possesses *firāsa* and can read other people's thoughts.' When Junayd learned of this, he asked him, 'What is it that people say about you?' The young man said to Junayd, 'Think of something.' 'I have done so,' said Junayd. The young man told him, 'You thought of such-and-such.' Junayd replied, 'No.' The young man told him, 'Sit down and think of something else.' Junayd said, 'I have done so.' The young man told him, 'You thought of such-and-such.' Junayd replied, 'No.' The young man said, 'Sit down a third time and think of something.' Junayd replied, 'I have done so.' The young man said, 'You thought of such-and-such.' Junayd replied, 'No.' The young man exclaimed, 'Glorified is Allah! You are a truthful man and I do not belie my own heart!' Junayd said to him, 'You were correct all three times, but I wanted to test you in order to see if your heart would change!'

If you ask 'But how could Junayd tell a lie and say "No"?' the answer is that it was not a lie. When he said 'No,' Junayd was in effect saying 'I will not inform you.' He did so in order to examine the young man and ascertain his truthfulness, and to test his character and see if he would change or not.

It is also related that al-Sarrī al-Saqaṭī said to Junayd, 'Go out and preach to people.' At the time, Junayd had a fear of speaking in public because he did not consider himself worthy of the task. Junayd said, 'One night, however, which happened to be a Thursday night, I went to sleep and saw the Prophet (Allah bless him and give him peace) in my dream, and he instructed me, "Go out and preach to people!" When I woke up, I quickly went to al-Sarrī's house and knocked on his door. After he came out and looked at me, he asked me before I had a chance to inform him, "So you did not believe me until you were ordered [by the Prophet]?" "Yes," I replied. The next day I went to the Friday congregational mosque and news had spread that I was going to speak.' And so Junayd began to speak, when a Christian youth in disguise approached him and said, 'Master, what is the meaning of the words of Allah's Emissary (Allah bless him and give him peace), "Beware of the believer's spiritual intuition, for he looks with the light of Allah"?'[III] Junayd lowered his head for a while, then he looked up and said, 'Embrace Islam, for the time for your Islam has arrived.' The young man embraced Islam that very moment. Junayd's spiritual intuition manifested that moment and it became clear that the young man was a Christian who had come in a disguise. Allah Most High knows best.

وَبَاتَ إِيوَانُ كِسْرَىٰ وَهْوَ مُنْصَدِعٌ   كَشَمْلِ أَصْحَابِ كِسْرَىٰ غَيْرَ مُلْتَئِمِ
وَالنَّارُ خَامِدَةُ الْأَنْفَاسِ مِنْ أَسَفٍ   عَلَيْهِ وَالنَّهْرُ سَاهِي الْعَيْنِ مِنْ سَدَمِ

وَسَاءَ سَاوَةَ أَنْ غَاضَتْ بُحَيْرَتُهَا   وَرُدَّ وَارِدُهَا بِالْغَيْظِ حِينَ ظَمِي
كَأَنَّ بِالنَّارِ مَا بِالْمَاءِ مِنْ بَلَلٍ   حُزْنًا وَبِالْمَاءِ مَا بِالنَّارِ مِنْ ضَرَمِ

That night the throne room of Khusraw became cracked,
Khusraw's people, too, crumbled, never to be restored.
The sacred fire, grief-stricken, breathed its last,
And the river [Euphrates] dried up out of worry.
Sāwa was saddened by its lake drying up;

III Tirmidhī, *Sunan*.

the thirsty who went to drink there came back in a rage!
As if the fire, from sorrow, took on the water's wetness
And water assumed the fire's quality of blazing.

In this couplet the author (Allah have mercy upon him) explains the signs and outward causes by which the Persians had sensed the coming loss of their might and the destruction of their empire—signs and causes that warned of looming misery and ruin. What made these signs so astounding was their unprecedented nature. One of these signs is the shaking and splitting of their palace. Their palace shook so violently [on the night of the Prophet's birth] that it cracked and fourteen loges fell from its uppermost part. The palace of the Persians was so well built that they used to say that nothing would topple it except the Trumpet [announcing the Day of Judgment].

Another of these signs is the extinguishment of their sacred fire which they worshipped and venerated. Their sacred fire had been kindled and kept lit for over one thousand years, but it went out at once on the day of the Prophet's birth. One of the governors of Khusraw wrote a letter to him to inform him of what occurred. The date was recorded, and it had taken place on the morning of the Prophet's birth.

The author makes it appear that the fire, when it was extinguished, was in a state of grief and sadness over its worshippers and servants who used to venerate it.

Another of these signs is the drying up and receding of the lake [of Sāwa]. It became so barren and dry that not a single drop of water was left, as if realities had been inexorably altered that day. It was as if the fire took on the quality of the water's wetness, thereby becoming extinguished and doused; and as if the water took on the blazing quality of the fire, thereby catching fire, burning, and drying up.

The ruler of the Yemen at the time received a letter informing him that Lake Sāwa had dried up and receded, and that those who came to drink from it would return distraught as they were unable to fulfil their needs and quench their thirst. In addition, the governor of Syria wrote to the ruler of the Yemen to inform him that the water in the valley of Sāwa had vanished and receded.[112]

112 Imam al-Sakhāwī says, 'Similarly, the lake of the city of Sāwa—a city whose inhabitants were flagrant in their idolatry and oppression—dried up when the Prophet was born. This lake,

Another of these signs was the collapse of all of the idols in the world. In one village an idol had fallen on its face and its inhabitants lifted it back up. As soon as they put it back it fell down once again. They had lifted it back up two or three times when suddenly a voice called out to them, which they could hear but whose source they could not see; and it recited the following lines:

It has fallen thanks to a newborn whose light has shone
On all corners of the earth, east and west.
The idols have toppled because of him;
The hearts of kings east and west have filled with dread.
The fire in the land of the Persians let out its death cry and went dark.
The King of the Persians spent the night suffering the greatest of calamities
The soothsayers, whose jinn would bring news of the unseen,
Now have nothing to report from them, be it truth or lies.
Ah, Quṣayy, abandon your waywardness,
And come to Islam and a welcoming abode!

These, then, are evident signs, clear miracles and extraordinary events that Allah Most High manifested when the Prophet (Allah bless him and give him peace) was born. He manifested these signs out of esteem and divine concern for the Prophet (Allah bless him and give him peace), and they were cause for the felicity of some and the damnation of others; whoever Allah guides will not be led astray, and whoever He leads astray has no guide. O Allah, illuminate our hearts with gnosis of You, and cause us to die with love for this noble Prophet (Allah bless him and give him peace). Amen!

وَالْجِنُّ تَهْتِفُ وَالْأَنْوَارُ سَاطِعَةٌ   وَالْحَقُّ يَظْهَرُ مِنْ مَعْنًى وَمِنْ كَلِمِ

There were jinn calling out, and dazzling lights
As truth was manifested in both word and reality.

wider than a *farsakh* (4.827 km.), was located in the Iraqi kingdom [i.e. western Iran] between Hamdan and Qum, and was a dock for ships and a means to travel to other cities, such as the Fergana Valley [A study of a map will show, this latter notion is not plausible] (p). On the night of the Prophet's birth, this lake dried up and became a barren expanse of earth, as if there had never been any water there before. Their water had dried up and receded to the point that a city was built in the place where it once stood, called Manāra, which remains till this day a well-guarded city…' (See Mullā ʿAlī al-Qārī, *al-Mawrid al-rawī fī mawlid al-Nabī*.)

The word *jinn* is derived from the verb 'concealed'. The calling out of the jinn refers to their screaming and their delivering information to soothsayers. The word 'lights' (*anwār*) is the plural of 'light' (*nūr*), and here denotes proofs and signs, since they exposit the truth and make it clear, and dispel the darkness of ignorance and disbelief, just as physical lights make physical things visible and clear.

The author (Allah have mercy upon him) tells of how the jinn relayed news of the Prophet's imminent appearance in creation, and the arrival of the mission with which Allah Most High had sent him. The author also tells how the lights were radiant. By radiant lights he means the proofs of the Prophet's message and the plethora of evidence showing his veracity, such as the communication of inanimate objects and the information relayed by soothsayers and by the learned among the Jews, Christians and others. So the truth manifested in both word and meaning—both in the mute tongue of expression and the physical tongue of expression. By saying in *reality*, the author alludes to the collapse of the idols, the receding of the waters and the cracking of the [Persian] arches and other signs; and by saying in *word*, he alludes to the reports of the soothsayers, rabbis and priests.

As regards the jinn and their announcement of the Prophet's birth, some authorities have related that when he was born a voice called out to those who were performing rites at the Kaʿba:

I swear that no woman has conceived
And no woman given birth to anyone
Like the esteemed one born of the resplendent woman,
Who honourably eschewed the shame of the clans.

Another jinn, at Mount Abū al-Qays, recited four lines of poetry containing a similar meaning.

There are several recorded incidents of jinn announcing the commencement of the Prophet's mission. One such incident is the story of Sawād b. Qārib, who was a soothsayer in the pre-Islamic period of ignorance [*jāhiliyya*]. He said, 'One night as I was sleeping atop one of the mountains around Sarrāt a jinn came to me and struck my leg and called out, "Get up, Sawād b. Qārib! An Emissary from the progeny of Luʾayy

b. Ghālib has come to you." I raised my head and sat upright, and then it went away while reciting:

I marvelled at the jinn and their demands–
How they saddled their camels
And swept towards Mecca, seeking guidance;
The truthful jinn are not like their liars
Go, then, to the cream of Banū Hāshim;
Their front parts are not like their hind parts!

The same jinn came to me on the second night and struck my leg again, and said, 'Get up, Sawād b. Qārib! An Emissary from the progeny of Luʾayy b. Ghālib has come to you." I raised my head and sat upright, and then it went away while reciting similar lines. The same jinn came to me again on the third night recited similar lines of poetry. When I woke up the next morning I mounted my camel and entered Mecca, and lo and behold the Emissary of Allah (Allah bless him and give him peace) had appeared. I related to him what had happened and pledged my fealty to him.'

In some of the transmission routes of this *ḥadīth* it says that Sawād recited lines of poetry that were similar in meaning to what was recited to him. He said:

After a calm and restful night my medium came to me;
And in my experience he was not one to tell lies.
For three nights in succession he said to me
'A Prophet has come to you from Luʾayy b. Ghālib!'
I raised the corners of my waist wrapper and girded my loins
And hastened to make my way
I testify that there is nothing along with Allah (lā shayʾ ghayruhu)
And that you are the trustworthy bearer of all the unseen
And that you are the closest of the Emissaries in intercession
Unto Allah, O son of the noblest and pure!
Command me with what comes from our Lord's revelation
Even if what you bring causes white hairs,
And be my intercessor on the Day in which there is no intercession
But yours that will benefit Sawād b. Qārib!

A similar incident was mentioned in the story of the Khathᶜams[113]. Abū Hurayra related, 'One day, as the Khathᶜams were standing before one of their idols to which they seek judgements in disputes, they heard a voice call out:

O people, O possessors of bodies,
Who ascribe judgements to the idols!
Are you all suffering from languor?
Do you not see what I see before me?
A resplendent light, piercing through darkness
The scions of the best of humankind!
From Hāshim, at the apex
Disclosing the light in the Sacred Land
Coming to demolish disbelief with Islam
Ennobled by the Merciful. O what a leader!

They remained silent long enough to memorise what was said, then each went their separate ways. Not three days had passed before news came to them of the Emissary of Allah (Allah bless him and give him peace) and the announcement of his message in Mecca.

Our master ᶜUmar b. al-Khaṭṭāb (Allah be pleased with him) recalled a similar incident. He said, 'By Allah, just one month before the advent of Islam, I was close to one of the many idols of the pre-Islamic period of ignorance when a man from the Arabs sacrificed a calf to it. As we were waiting for him to divide up the meat and give us our portion of it, I heard a sound coming from the idol; I never heard anything as clear as it. It said, "I bring you good news of an eloquent man who says there is no god but Allah!"' There are numerous reports of this nature. See [*al-Iktifā bi- sīrat al-Muṣṭafā*] of [Abū al-Rabīᶜ] al-Kalāᶜī.

As for the soothsayers and their prognostications of the Prophet's arrival and mission, their accounts are many and well-known. One of them is the story of Shiqq and Saṭīḥ. The story tells of Rabīᶜa b. Naṣr, King of the Yemen, who saw a troubling dream. He brought together every single soothsayer, astrologer or magician in his kingdom and said, 'I have had a very troubling dream.' 'Relate it to us,' they said, 'so we may tell you its meaning.' He said, 'If I tell you of what I saw in my dream I will

113 An Arab tribe in western Arabia near the border of Yemen.

not be at ease with any interpretation you provide me; no one knows its true meaning but the one who knows what I saw before I relate it.' One of the men in the assembly submitted, 'If this is His Majesty's wish, then let him send for the two oracles, Shiqq and Saṭīḥ, for no one knows of these matters better than them.' The name of Shiqq was Rabīʿ b. Rabīʿa b. Masʿūd, and the name of Saṭīḥ was Muṣʿab b. Yashkur. And so the king bade them to come to his presence. Saṭīḥ arrived before Shiqq, and the King told him, 'I have had a very troubling dream. Tell me what I saw, and if you are correct then you will be able to interpret it correctly.' Saṭīḥ said to the king, 'Very well. You saw blazing coals—which came forth from the darkness—and fell upon the lowlands descending to the sea and devoured there everything with a skull!' The king said, 'You did not miss the mark one bit, Saṭīḥ; what do you think it means?' Saṭīḥ answered, 'I swear by the serpent between the two lava fields that the Abyssinians will swoop down on your land and rule over all of the land from Abyan to Jurash.' The king said to Saṭīḥ, 'By your father, Saṭīḥ, this is indeed distressing and painful for us! When will this take place? In my own time, or in the future?' Saṭīḥ replied, 'Nay, indeed, it will take place some time in the future—after more than sixty or seventy years elapse.' The king asked, 'Will their kingdom endure, or will it be short-lived?' Saṭīḥ answered, 'Nay, it will be cut short after seventy-odd years have passed, and then all of them will be slain or expelled from it as fugitives.' 'Who, then, will assume that task of killing and expelling them?' asked the king. Satīḥ replied, 'Iram of Dhū Yazan, who will march against them from Aden and will not leave a single one of them in the Yemen.' The king enquired, 'Will Iram's dominion there endure, or will it too be short-lived?' Saṭīḥ replied, 'It will indeed be cut short.' The king said, 'And who will cut it short?' He replied, 'A prophet—a pure one to whom divine revelation will come from on high.' The king asked, 'From whom will this prophet hail?' He replied, '[He will hail from] a man from the progeny of Ghālib b. Fihr, son of Mālik b. al-Naḍr. His dominion over his people will last till the end of time.' The king said, 'O Saṭīḥ, will there come an end to time?' He replied, 'Yes, a day on which the first and the last will all be assembled; on that day the righteous will be joyous and the evildoers will be wretched.' The king said, 'Is what you are informing me true, Saṭīḥ?' Saṭīḥ replied, 'Yes, by the redness of the sun at evening, and the onset of the darkness of night and the dawn when it spreads. What I have told you is indisputably true!'

When Saṭīḥ had finished, Shiqq arrived, so the king summoned him and said to him exactly as he said to Saṭīḥ, except that he concealed from him what Saṭīḥ had said in order to see whether the two interpretations agreed or differed. Shiqq said, 'Yes, you saw a skull which came forth from the darkness and fell upon all of the land, meadows and thickets, and devoured everything there that breathes.' The king said to Shiqq, 'Shiqq, you did not miss the mark one bit! So what do you think it means?' Shiqq replied, 'I swear by the men living between the two lava fields that the blacks will certainly descend upon your land and seize every tender one from your hands, and will rule over all of the land, from Abyan to Najran.'

The king exclaimed, 'By your father, Shiqq, this is indeed distressing and painful for us! When will this take place? In my own time, or in the future?' Shiqq answered, 'Nay indeed, a stretch of time after you. Then a mighty one of lofty status, shall rescue you from it and make them taste the deepest abasement.' 'Who is this person of mighty status?' asked the king. Shiqq replied, 'A youth, neither base nor inadequate for what he attempts; he will come forth from the house of Dhū Yazan.' The king said, 'Will his rule endure, or will it be short-lived?' He replied, 'Indeed, it will end when a prophet is sent—who will come with truth and justice—among the people of religion and virtue; and then the rule will remain among his people till the Day of Departure.' 'And what is the Day of Departure?' the king asked. Shiqq said, 'It is the Day on which the rulers will be requited [for what they did in this life]. Calls will be made from the heavens, which both the living and the dead shall hear. It is the Day on which mankind will be gathered together at the appointed place, on which there will be salvation and blessings for those who fear Allah.' The king said, 'Is what you say true, Shiqq?' Shiqq replied, 'Yes, by the Lord of heaven and earth, and the highlands and the lowlands that lie in between. What I have told you is indeed the truth, in which there is no doubt!'

When the king had finished questioning the two men, it occurred to him that what they told him regarding the invasion of the Abyssinians was going to take place so he prepared his two sons and the other members of his family for a journey to Iraq, gathering what they needed, and wrote on their behalf to one of the emperors of Persia called Sāpūr [or Shāpūr], who allowed them to settle at al-Ḥīra. Al-Nuʿmān b. al-Mundhir, the king of al-Ḥīra, was a descendent of Rabīʿa b. Naṣr. Thus ends the citation from [al-Kalāʿī's] *al-Iktifā*.

Another account is that of the dream of Mūbadhān [a Persian judge]. Soon after the arches of Khusraw's palace had collapsed, Mūbadhān had a dream in which scores of powerful camels were leading packs of Arabian horses across the Tigris River and spreading through their lands. Al-Khaṭṭābī said, 'This is taken from the tradition of Hāniʾ b. Hāniʾ al-Makhzūmī, who narrated, "On the night of the Prophet's birth the Arch of Khusraw cracked, causing twelve[114] balconies to collapse; Lake Sāwa had receded; the valley of Samawa (which for years was dried up) was suddenly filled with flowing water; and the fire of the Persians [Zoroastrians], which had been kept lit for over one thousand years, was extinguished. And Mūbadhān had a dream in which scores of powerful horses[115] were leading packs of Arabian horses across the Tigris River and spreading through their lands. When Khusraw [*Anūshīrwān*] awoke [and was informed of the dream] he was deeply troubled, but he remained patient with the foreboding news till his patience wore thin. He finally resolved not to keep the dream to himself, and decided to inform his subjects and advisers. He placed his crown on his head and sat upon his couch and sent for his advisers, and when they assembled and stood before him he asked, "Do you know why I have called you here today?" "No," they replied. "Only if Your Majesty informs us." Just then a letter arrived, informing him that their sacred fire had been extinguished, which added to the king's distress. Khusraw then related to his advisers the dream that had so troubled him. Mūbadhān said, "May God rectify the kingdom! Last night I had a dream in which scores of powerful camels were leading packs of Arabian horses across the Tigris River and spreading through the lands." "What does this mean, Mūbadhān?" asked Khusraw. Mūbadhān, who was the most knowledgeable of them, replied, "It means that an event has taken place among the Arabs. Upon this, Khusraw wrote a letter to Nuʿmān b. al-Mundhir instructing him to

114 Bayhaqī's version mentions fourteen balconies.

115 Bayhaqī's version reads 'roaring camels.'

send a learned man whom he could ask about this matter. Nuʿmān b. al-Mundhir sent ʿAbd al-Masīḥ al-Ghassānī. When ʿAbd al-Masīḥ appeared before Khusraw he was asked, "Do you know what I want to ask you about?" ʿAbd al-Masīḥ replied, "The king may inform me of whatever he likes; if I have knowledge concerning it I will tell him, and if I do not know then I will send for someone who does." Khusraw told him about what had happened, so he said, "The knowledge of this matter is with my maternal uncle who resides in the eastern part of the Levant; he is called Saṭīḥ. [ʿAbd al-Masīḥ went to visit Saṭīḥ and found] that he was near death. ʿAbd al-Masīḥ greeted him but Saṭīḥ did not respond. Then he sung some poetry praising Saṭīḥ, and when Saṭīḥ heard it he raised his head and said, "Has ʿAbd al-Masīḥ come upon a sombre camel to visit Saṭīḥ when he is close to the grave? You were sent by the Sasanid emperor because of the collapse of the arches, the extinguishing of the fire and the dream of Mūbadhān, who saw scores of powerful camels leading herds of Arabian horses across the Tigris River and spreading through their lands. O ʿAbd al-Masīḥ, when divine revelation is recited more, and the Master of the Staff (*Ṣāḥib al-Harāwa*—the Prophet Muḥammad (Allah bless him and give him peace)) appears, and when the valley of Samawa is filled with flowing water, Lake Sāwa recedes, and the Persians' fire is extinguished, then the Levant will not be the same Levant for Saṭīḥ. There will be as many Sasanid kings and queens as loges that collapsed, and then the divine Promise will be realised." Immediately after that Saṭīḥ passed away.

'When ʿAbd al-Masīḥ returned to Khusraw he informed him about what Saṭīḥ had said: "[The dynasty will remain] among you until fourteen rulers among you have assumed power."'

At that time, owing to wars, ten Sassanid rulers had already died, and the four remaining kings and queens ruled [for sixty-seven years], till the Caliphate of ʿUthmān (Allah be pleased with him), after which the Muslims conquered their lands and their kingdom was cut off, and Allah replaced it with Islam. And all praise is for Allah.

Among those who spoke of the Prophet's appearance before he was tasked with the prophetic mission was Sayf b. Dhī Yazan, who was mentioned in the story of Shiqq and Saṭīḥ. When Sayf defeated the Abyssinians and expelled them from the Yemen, the Arabs sent many delegations of their nobles and poets to congratulate him and praise him for his efforts and defence of his people. A delegation of Qurayshī dignitaries came to him, including ʿAbd al-Muṭṭalib, and sought an audience with him in San'aa, which he permitted them. When they entered in to see him, ʿAbd al-Muṭṭalib approached him and sought permission to speak. Sayf b. Abī Yazan said to him, 'If you are among those given leave to speak before kings then speak, for I have granted you permission.' ʿAbd al-Muṭṭalib said, 'O king, Allah has granted you a realm fine, formidable, firm, lofty and fair. He has made you the owner of a garden, the roots of whose trees are pure and whose fruits are sweet and whose base is firm and its branches high. You have been bestowed with a position of greatness and the finest of mines. You, O king, are the head of the Arabs whom they will follow, their firm pillar on whom they will rely, their stronghold in whom [Allah's] servants will find refuge and their spring who makes their land fertile. You have the best ancestors and you are the best to come after them. We, O king, are the people of Allah's Sanctuary and the caretakers of His House. We have come to you because of what has delighted us—the removal of difficulties—and are a delegation sent to congratulate you, not a delegation sent to grumble about our frustrations.'

Sayf said to him, 'Which one of them are you, O spokesman?' He replied, 'I am ʿAbd al-Muṭṭalib son of Hāshim.' Sayf said, 'Are you our cousin from our mother's side?' 'Yes', replied ʿAbd al-Muṭṭalib. Sayf said, 'Come near to me.' ʿAbd al-Muṭṭalib drew near to him and then Sayf turned to him and the people in attendance and said, 'Welcome to all of you! The king has heard your words and recognised your kinship and accepted the one put forward as your intermediary and means of approach [ʿAbd al-Muṭṭalib]. You are welcomed guests day and night and shall be honoured for as long as you stay here, and shall receive plentiful gifts when you prepare your caravans for departure. Go now to the guesthouse reserved for delegations.'

They remained there for one whole month, but during that entire time they were unable to have an audience with the king, nor did he permit them to take leave. Then one day, all of a sudden, the king took notice of the situation and sent for ʿAbd al-Muṭṭalib. Sayf said, 'O ʿAbd al-Muṭṭalib, I am going to disclose to you a secret which I know, a secret that I will not divulge to anyone else besides you. I see that you are a worthy mine for secrets, so I shall relate it to you. Let it remain a secret till Allah permits it to come to pass, for Allah will most certainly cause it to happen. I find within the hidden book and treasured knowledge that we have kept for ourselves a great and momentous piece of news that foretells for all men in general, and for you and your group in particular, a noble life and virtuous death!' ʿAbd al-Muṭṭalib said, 'Only a man of your stature, O king, can impart such a secret and good news. What is it? May the people of the desert be a ransom for you, one after the other!' The king said, 'When a young boy is born in Tihāma [Mecca], between whose shoulders is a mole [the Seal of Prophethood], to him shall belong leadership (*imāma*), and through him you [the clan of Hāshim] shall exercise authority until the Day of Resurrection!' ʿAbd al-Muṭṭalib replied, 'I shall return with news the like of which no delegation has ever received! Were it not for the awe, majesty and honour of the king, I would have requested him to disclose more of his secrets so that my joy might increase!' [Sayf] b. Dhī Yazan then said to ʿAbd al-Muṭṭalib, 'This is the time in which he is to be born, or else he has already been born. His name is Muḥammad. Both his mother and father will die, and his grandfather and uncle will take care of him. His birth will be a secret, but Allah will send him [with the prophetic message] openly, and grant him helpers. Through him, Allah shall honour his allies and abase his enemies. With them, Allah shall smite many a man, and with them He shall take possession of the best territories in the earth. He shall break the idols and extinguish the fires [i.e., the fire of the Persians]; the All-Merciful (*al-Raḥmān*) shall be worshipped [alone] and Satan will be pulverised. His word will be decisive, his rule just. He will enjoin the good and practice it, and forbid the evil and eradicate it.'

ʿAbd al-Muṭṭalib said to him, 'O king, may your status be forever honoured and may your authority prosper, and may your kingdom abide! Has the king any more secrets that he wishes to disclose after this, for he has spoken to me with clarity?' [Sayf] b. Dhī Yazan said, 'By the House with coverings [i.e., the Kaʿba], and the signs and idols of stone, you, ʿAbd al-Muṭṭalib, are his grandfather—and that is no lie!' Hearing this, ʿAbd al-Muṭṭalib fell prostrate. The king then said to him, 'Raise up your head; may your breast be cooled; may your status be exalted. Do you sense anything from what I have disclosed to you?' ʿAbd al-Muṭṭalib replied, 'I had a son who was dear to me, and I married him off to a noble woman from the best of his people. She gave birth to a boy whom I named Muḥammad. His mother and father passed away, and I and his uncle have taken it upon ourselves to care for him.' Ibn Abī Yazan said to him, 'You are saying exactly what I have told you, so see to it that you safeguard him and protect him from the Jews, for they are his enemy. Allah will not give them any way to harm him. Keep all that I have told you confidential and do not disclose it even to this small band that has accompanied you here, for I am afraid that rivalry will spread amongst them and that they will vie for power and cause him great trouble and hatch schemes against him—this they will certainly do, either themselves or their descendants. Alas! Were it not that I know I will die before he is charged with his message, I would have certainly migrated on foot until I arrived at Yathrib, the centre of his kingdom, for I find it written in the Scripture and ancient book that Yathrib shall be where he establishes his mission and finds people of support, and it is where his grave shall be. Were it not for my fear that difficulties and troubles would come his way, I would have announced his arrival despite his young age. But I now bid you farewell without any shortcoming [in rewarding] you and those in your company.'

Then the king ordered that each member of the delegation be given ten male servants and ten female servants, a *ḥalas* (which is a sheer house robe), one hundred camels, five *raṭl*s of gold, ten *raṭl*s of silver, and a container filled with ambergris. The king ordered that ʿAbd al-Muṭṭalib be given ten times the amount given to the others. The king then said to him, 'Come to see me again after a year has passed', but Ibn Dhī Yazan died before a year had elapsed.

ʿAbd al-Muṭṭalib would often say, 'Men of Quraysh, let none of you be jealous of me because of the generous bestowal of the king; for all of that, though plentiful, is set to perish. Instead, be jealous of me because of what shall remain after me and my progeny of goodly mention, pride and honour!' When asked about that he would reply, 'You shall soon come to know!'

Similar to this is the story found in the lengthy *ḥadīth* about Salmān al-Fārisī. At the end of the narration it tells how he was serving a priest at ʿAmūriya [in Byzantium], and when death approached the priest,

Salmān asked him, 'To whom do you advise me to go?' The priest replied, 'By God, I know of no one anywhere who is on the path we are on; however, the time has come for a Prophet who will be sent with the religion of Abraham. He will come from the land of the Arabs. His place of migration lies between two lava tracts between which are date-palm trees. He has clear and unmistakable signs: he eats of gifts and does not eat of charity, and between his shoulders is the seal of prophethood. If you are able to make your way to that land, do so.'[116] Soon after this the priest died. Please refer to the complete *ḥadīth*, which I have cited in full in my commentary on the *Hamziyya*.

Another example of this is the *ḥadīth* of al-Nuʿmān al-Sabānī, who was one of the rabbis of the Jews in the Yemen. When he heard of the arrival of the Prophet (Allah bless him and give him peace) he went to see him and asked him about various matters. Then he said, 'My father took a letter and sealed it [with wax] and said, "Do not read this until you hear of a Prophet coming from Yathrib. When you hear of him, go and open it." I listened to him. So when I heard of you I went and opened the letter, and lo and behold it described your features exactly as I see you this very moment! It mentioned what you permit and what you forbid, and says that you are the best of the Prophets and that your nation is the best of nations. It says that your name is Aḥmad and that your nation is given to frequent praise. [It says] that their sacrifices are their own lives and that their scriptures are in their breasts. [It says] that they do not gather for battle without Gabriel being in their midst. Allah is as tender with them as a bird is with its hatchlings. My father also said to me, "Go to him and proclaim your faith in him!"'

The Prophet (Allah bless him and give him peace) loved having his Companions hear al-Nuʿmān's story from beginning to end. The Prophet (Allah bless him and give him peace) was seen smiling and he said, 'I bear witness that I am the Emissary of Allah.' Al-Nuʿmān was later killed by [the false prophet] al-Aswad al-ʿAnsī. And Allah Most High knows best.

عَمُوا وَصَمُّوا فَإِعْلَانُ الْبَشَائِرِ لَمْ تُسْمَعْ وَبَارِقَةُ الْإِنْذَارِ لَمْ تُشَمِ

They were blind and deaf, so the glad tidings proclaimed
Went unheard, and the warning lightning-flash was not seen

116 Aḥmad.

Because the disbelievers failed to benefit from their faculties of hearing when they heard of the Emissary of Allah (Allah bless him and give him peace) from soothsayers and from Sayf b. Dhī Yazan, and the dream of Mūbidhān and the words of Shiqq and Saṭīḥ—all of which they considered incontrovertible and unequivocally sound—the author (Allah have mercy upon him) describes them as having been blind to the dazzling proofs, the clear signs, the miracles whose fame spread far and wide and the dream visions [heralding his arrival]. They knew all of these and did not entertain any doubts about them, and indeed they witnessed them directly; yet they did not wake from their slumber and did not heed the warnings or benefit from their faculties of hearing and sight. No wonder, then, that the author describes them as blind and deaf, since they share with the blind and the deaf in their inability to see and hear. For this reason Allah has told [us] about them in His Book, saying '*[They are] deaf, dumb and blind...*' (Qur'an 2:18) Here Allah denies their faculties of hearing and sight because they did not benefit from them. As you [now] know, they were aware of what the soothsayers had brought forth, and were aware of the story of Sayf b. Dhī Yazan with ʿAbd al-Muṭṭalib, the dream of Mūbidhān and the marvels that were manifested on the day of the Prophet's birth, and they were eyewitnesses to the Prophet's miracles that appeared after he was tasked with the divine message. Yet none of these were of benefit to them, and they only persisted in their disbelief and misguidance. We seek refuge in Allah from having such an evil state!

All of this is alluded to in the author's couplet. They were blind and unable to see the lightning cloud of warning—in other words, what evoked their fear and warned them with clarity like a flash of lightning—and they were deaf and unable to hear the proclamations of glad tidings heralding the Prophet's arrival, which are too many to enumerate, and some of which have already been mentioned.

مِنْ بَعْدِ مَا أَخْبَرَ الْأَقْوَامَ كَاهِنُهُمْ   بِأَنَّ دِينَهُمُ الْمُعْوَجَّ لَمْ يَقُمِ
وَبَعْدَ مَا عَايَنُوا فِي الْأُفْقِ مِنْ شُهُبٍ   مُنْقَضَّةٍ وَفْقَ مَا فِي الْأَرْضِ مِنْ صَنَمِ

Even after the soothsayers had informed their peoples
That their crooked religion would not endure,
And even after their eyes saw meteors on the horizon
Plunging downwards, as idols were toppled on earth;

The author (Allah have mercy upon him) says that the disbelievers were blind and deaf after the truth was manifest and the matter became clear through the physical and mute tongues of expression. As for the physical tongue of expression, their soothsayers had informed them that their religion was crooked and unable to stand, and that it would soon turn on its heels and be cut off, and that the religion of the Prophet (Allah bless him and give him peace) was upright and firm and unshakable. The author alludes to this in the first couplet [of this section] where he says *His birth made the purity of his pedigree evident.* As for the mute tongue of expression, it is what they had seen directly with their own eyes and had witnessed for themselves, from the shooting stars and their falling from the heavens and their preventing the jinn from eavesdropping, to the toppling and collapse of the idols—all of which had occurred at the time of the Prophet's birth and which we have detailed when discussing the line *His birth made the purity of his pedigree evident.*

As for the reports of the soothsayers and the shooting stars, both took place shortly before the Prophet's arrival. The soothsayers, men and women alike, continued to discover certain details about the Prophet (Allah bless him and give him peace), but the Arabs paid no heed to them until Allah sent the Prophet and the prognostications they had mentioned came true and they recognised them.

Abū Jaʿfar al-ʿUqaylī narrated with his chain of transmission from Lahab b. Mālik who said: 'I was in the presence of the Emissary of Allah and mentioned soothsayers to him. I said, "May my mother and father be sacrificed for you! We were the first to know of the guarding of the heaven, and the prevention of the devils from eavesdropping by the pelting of meteors, and that is because we went to one of our soothsayers named Khaṭar b. Mālik, who was an elderly man some two hundred and eighty years old. He was one of our most knowledgeable soothsayers. We asked him, 'Khaṭar, have you any knowledge regarding these shooting meteors? We are terrified because of them, and fear that some evil will result from them.' He replied, 'Come to me in the late night just before daybreak and I will inform you whether they portend good or harm, safety or danger.' So we left him for the remainder of the day, and later that night, just before daybreak, we went to him and found him standing on his feet and gazing directly towards the heaven. We called out to him,

"Khaṭar, Khaṭar!" whereupon he indicated to us that we should be quiet, so we were. Then a large piece of a meteor from the heaven crashed, whereupon he cried out in a loud voice and said, "He has been struck by misfortune; his chastisement has overcome him; his torment has come swiftly; his blazing meteors have scorched him; his answerer is no more! Alas, woe unto him for his condition! Angst has clutched him confusion has visited him! His force has been severed and his conditions have changed!"

'Then he was quiet for a long time. Then he said, "Men of Banū Qaḥṭān, I inform you with truth and sure proof. I swear by the Kaʿba and the pillars, and by the secure and well-guarded city [Mecca]. The insolent jinn have been thwarted by a flaming meteor in the Hand of Him who possesses authority—this for the sake of one of tremendous status sent with revelation and recitation [Qur'an], and with guidance and a decisive criterion, who will do away with idol worship!"

'I asked him, "Khaṭar, what do you foresee for your people?" He replied, "I foresee for my people what I foresee for myself: that they will follow the best Prophet amongst mankind, whose proof is like the rays of the sun; him who will be sent forth in Mecca, the abode of protection. He will rule by revelation devoid of confusion."

'We said to him, "From whom does he hail, O Khaṭār?" He replied, "By life and living, he is from Quraysh. There is neither inconstancy in his objective nor restlessness in his character. His shall be an army—and what an army!—from the progeny of Qaḥṭān and ʿAysh."

'We said to him, "Tell us, then: from which family of Quraysh will he hail?" He replied, "By the house with its supports, and the cloister and the doves, he is of the scions of Hāshim and from a noble folk. He will be sent with fierce, tumultuous battles and he will slay every oppressor." Then he said, "This is the explanation given to me by the chief of the jinn." Then he said, "Allah is greatest! The truth has come and manifested, and news from the jinn has been cut off!" Then he fell silent and became unconscious, and did not regain consciousness till three days later. Then he said "There is no god but Allah!"

'The Emissary of Allah said, "Glorified is Allah! He has spoken something like prophecy and will be quickened on the Day of Resurrection as a nation unto Himself!"'[117] (What this means is that despite not following a particular religion he was nevertheless a believer, as you can see.)

We have already mentioned the narratives about Shiqq and Saṭīḥ and about other soothsayers who foretold of the Emissary of Allah (Allah bless him and give him peace).

The wisdom behind the pelting of stars was for fear of divine revelation being confused with the news contained within the heavens, and to establish the truth and eliminate specious arguments which might have arisen had the inhabitants of the earth been confused about what had come to them from Allah. Allah informed His Prophet (Allah bless him and give him peace) about the pelting of stars: '*We have adorned the lowest heaven with ornaments, the stars, and as a protection against every insolent devil.*' (Qur'an 37:6–7) And the Most High said, '*Say, "It has been revealed to me that a group of jinn have listened [to this Qur'an] and said 'We have heard an astounding recitation!' ..."*' (Qur'an 72:1) See Sūrat al-Jinn from verse one to verse nine where it says '*And we [the jinn] used to sit in [the heavens] for positions eavesdropping, but he who listens now finds a blazing fire waiting in ambush.*' (Qur'an 72:9)

The Emissary of Allah (Allah bless him and give him peace) once asked a group of the Anṣār, 'What did you use to say regarding the shooting stars?' They replied, 'We used to say, "A king has died, a king has been born, or a child has been born, a child has died."' The Prophet said, 'It is not so; rather, when Allah—Blessed and Exalted is He—decrees something concerning His creation the bearers of the Throne hear it and glorify Him, and those below them glorify Him, and those lower still glorify Him; and this goes on until the glorification descends from heaven to heaven to the lowest heaven where they glorify. Then they ask each other why they are glorifying, and are told "It is because those above us have glorified, so we have too." Then they say to them, "Why do you not ask those above you the reason?" and so it goes in questioning on till they reach the bearers of the Throne, who are asked "What is the reason for your glorification?" and reply, "Allah has decreed such-and-such concerning His creation." The news descends from heaven to heaven till it reaches the lowest heaven where they discuss it, and the devils then eavesdrop and mingle it with conjecture and false information. Then

117 Al-Suhaylī records this in his *al-Rawḍ al-unuf* and comments that its chain contains weakness.

they go and convey it to the soothsayers, and so the soothsayers are sometimes right and sometimes wrong in their information. Then Allah veiled the devils by means of these stars with which they were pelted, so soothsaying has been cut off today.'[118]

If you contend, 'But we still find today soothsayers who inform [people] about unseen matters,' the response is the following: The veiling of the devils was only during the time of the Prophet (Allah bless him and give him peace), and was done in order to prevent people from becoming confused about divine revelation. But once revelation had ceased the devils returned to their eavesdropping, albeit it is now weaker than it was before the Prophet (Allah bless him and give him peace) was sent. The pelting was through flaming pieces separate from the actual stars themselves, and it should not be understood that they were pelted with the stars themselves, because the stars simply pass through their orbit. It may be likened to how a firebrand is taken from a larger fire. Allah Most High knows best.

حَتَّىٰ غَدَا عَنْ طَرِيقِ الْوَحْيِ مُنْهَزِمٌ   مِنَ الشَّيَاطِينِ يَقْفُو إِثْرَ مُنْهَزِمِ

Until devils, routed, from the path of revelation,
Fled in the wake of those who had been overpowered.

Here the author (Allah have mercy upon him) says: Flaming meteors continued to rout the devils and burn them, expelling them from the sitting-places from which they eavesdropped until they were defeated, with some of them fleeing in the wake of those who were defeated before them. In other words, when the jinn sought to eavesdrop they would do so with one positioned over another, stacked up until they reached the heavens, and then, when the one on top was pelted with a flaming star, those beneath him would all flee in defeat. It is said that when the jinn on top was pelted, the one beneath him would rise up and take his place; then he too would be pelted and the one beneath him would rise up, continuing like this all the way to the last jinn.

The scholars disagree about this pelting of the jinn and whether it was limited to ancient times or if it continues. Some say that the pelting still occurs, but others say that it was limited to ancient times and that what occurs today is simply an abundance of shooting stars. Regarding the

118 Aḥmad.

verses '*And we [the jinn] used to sit therein [the heavens] for positions eavesdropping, but he who listens now finds a blazing fire waiting in ambush*' (Qur'an 72:9), Ibn ʿAṭiyya says in his exegesis, 'This necessitates that the pelting occurred in the Age of Ignorance, though it was not for the purpose of completely uprooting them; it was for the sake of guarding [the heavens] and was not severe. But when the revealtion of Islam began the matter intensified to the point that there was only a limited moment…' He said, 'This is proven by the statement of the Prophet (Allah bless him and give him peace), "What did you use to say about shooting stars?" They replied, "We used to say, 'A king has died, a king has been born, or a child has been born, a child has died.'" The Prophet said, "It is not so…"

This is the correct view: what occurs today is simply an abundance of shooting stars. This is proven by the word 'filled' [used in verse eight of Sūra al-Jinn], though the nature of it too is differed over: was it when the Prophet (Allah bless him and give him peace) was sent with his mission, or when he was born? Al-Zamakhsharī cites in his exegesis of Sūrat al-Jinn a narration from Ibn ʿAbbās that 'The devils were not previously veiled from the heavens, but when ʿĪsā (upon whom be peace) was born they were veiled from three heavens, and when Muḥammad (Allah bless him and give him peace) was born they were veiled from all of the heavenly spheres entirely.' This indicates that it occurred when the Prophet (Allah bless him and give him peace) was born, and Allah Most High knows best.

كَأَنَّهُمْ هَرَبًا أَبْطَالُ أَبْرَهَةٍ   أَوْ عَسْكَرٌ بِالْحَصَىٰ مِنْ رَاحَتَيْهِ رُمِي

نَبْذًا بِهِ بَعْدَ تَسْبِيحٍ بِبَطْنِهِمَا   نَبْذَ الْمُسَبِّحِ مِنْ أَحْشَاءِ مُلْتَقِمِ

Fleeing like the brave warriors of Abraha
Or the army pelted by pebbles thrown by his hand,
Cast by him after glorifying Allah in the palm of his hand,
As he who glorified his Lord was cast from the whale.

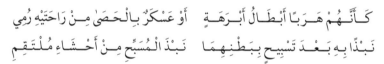

In speaking about the devils and their fleeing and running away from the falling stars cast at them, the author (Allah have mercy upon him) draws a comparison between them and two groups. The first group is the soldiers of Abraha who ran away and fled when torment descended upon them after they had resolved to demolish the Kaʿba. Allah protected His sanctified House and ennobled Kaʿba, and Abraha's forces were defeated and laid to waste on every road. The second group is the army [of the idolaters] during the Battle of Badr who were routed when the Prophet (Allah bless him and give him peace) threw pebbles at them and caused them to reach for their faces and attempt to remove the pebbles from their eyes, which resulted in them being slain and taken prisoner and ultimately defeated. This also occurred during the Battle of Ḥunayn; hence the 'or' in the couplet is for either battle.

It is as if the author were saying: 'If you wish you may compare them to Abraha's soldiers or to the Meccan forces. What unites them all is the fact that the devils were defeated and had fled and were pelted just as Abraha's soldiers had fled and were pelted by stones, and just as the armies were defeated and fled after the Prophet (Allah bless him and give him peace) cast pebbles at them at the battles of Badr and Ḥunayn.'

As for the story of Abraha, it is well-known from works on Prophetic biography. The gist of the story is that he constructed a building in the Yemen to which he wanted to divert the Arabs so they could perform pilgrimage to it [instead of the Kaʿba]. A Bedouin Arab had visited this building constructed by Abraha and defecated inside it. Infuriated, Abraha gathered his forces and mounted an elephant and set out for Mecca, vanquishing every Arabian tribe he encountered along the way. When he finally reached Mecca, the Quraysh fled to the mountains and valley passes and left the city wide open for Abraha's taking, and not a single Arab remained to defend the sacred House and stand guard over it. Then came the decree of the One (*al-Wāḥid*) and the Dominator (*al-Qahhār*), and the seizing of the Almighty and Powerful, for Abraha was now determined to destroy the Sacred House of Allah. But Abraha's elephant knelt down at Dhū al-Ghamīs and refused to go towards Mecca. They [the soldiers] struck it with iron bars but it would still not move against the Kaʿba; yet each time they would pull it in another direction it would run [willingly]. As they were struggling with the elephant, Allah sent against them a large flock of black birds from the sea coast (it is also said that they were inland birds); each bird had with it three stones—one in its beak and one in each claw—and each stone was larger than a lentil seed but smaller than a chickpea. The birds then released these stones against Abraha's forces. When the stones hit they would kill their targets and leave smallpox scars across their bodies. Defeated, Abraha and his surviving troops beat a hasty retreat and made their way back to Yemen, but every last one of them perished along the road, scattered every thirty miles or so, and Abraha's fingernails and limbs continued to rot until eventually he died. Allah protected His Revered House and gave victory to its caretakers.[119]

119 Shaykh Aḥmad Ibn ʿAjība provides more detail in his commentary on al-Buṣīrī's *Hamziyya*, and in his Qur'anic exegesis *al-Baḥr al-madīd*, where he says:

> Abraha b. al-Ṣabbāḥ al-Ashram, viceroy of the Yemen under the command of the Negus [of Abyssinia], had constructed a cathedral in Ṣan'ā, which he named Qulaysh. He wanted it to become the place of pilgrimage [for Arabia]. A man from the tribe of Kināna went to the cathedral one night and defecated inside it. Al-Wāqidī relates that this man, named Nufayl al-Ḥaḍramī, smeared his excrement on the wall of the cathedral and littered it with the carcasses of dead animals. Infuriated, Abraha vowed that he would demolish the Kaʿba in retaliation. Having prepared from Abyssinia, Abraha set off with an extremely large and powerful elephant named Maḥmūd, which, along with twelve other elephants (some say eight), had been given to Abraha by the Negus. When Abraha finally reached Mughammis, ʿAbd al-Muṭṭalib came to him and offered him a third of the wealth of Tihāma on condition that he and his troops leave and go back. Abraha refused. He had drawn up his troops and brought forth the elephant. Nufayl b. Ḥabīb [a guide who had marched in the army caravan and learned some of the command words used for controlling the elephant] took hold of the elephant's ear and bid it to kneel, saying, 'Kneel, Maḥmūd, for you are in Allah's Sacred Precinct. Go back to where you came from.' The elephant kneeled, and each time the troops pointed him in the direction of the Sacred Precinct he would again kneel and remain in his place. When they turned him toward Yemen or any other direction [away from the Kaʿba] he would rise on his feet and move briskly.
>
> Allah sent against them flocks of birds that approached from the sea: each bird had three pebbles (larger than a lentil seed and smaller than a chickpea): one in its beak and one between the claws of each foot. These pebbles would strike a man's head and exit from his anus, and each pebble had written upon it the name of its victim. Defeated, Abraha's troops fled in disarray and perished on the waysides and watering springs. When Abraha was struck, his fingernails and limbs rotted, but he did not die until his chest had split open, revealing his heart. Abraha's minister, Abū Yaskūm, had taken off, but a bird was circling him overhead until he reached the Negus. After he finished relating to the Negus what had taken place, a pebble suddenly struck him and he fell down dead before the Negus.
>
> It is reported that Abraha had seized two hundred camels belonging to ʿAbd al-Muṭṭalib. When ʿAbd al-Muṭṭalib came to him to seek their return, Abraha was impressed by his appearance (for ʿAbd al-Muṭṭalib was handsome and well built). Abraha was informed that ʿAbd al-Muṭṭalib was the chief of Quraysh and the leader of Mecca's caretakers, the one who fed the people of the hollow and the beasts of the mountain tops. So impressed was he by ʿAbd al-Muṭṭalib that Abraha descended from his seat and sat with ʿAbd al-Muṭṭalib on the carpet. Some reports state that Abraha had ʿAbd al-Muṭṭalib sit next to him on the royal seat. Through his interpreter, Abraha asked, 'What is your request?' When ʿAbd al-Muṭṭalib mentioned his request, that he return to him his camels, Abraha responded, 'Your esteem has now fallen in my eyes; I have come to raise the House (the Kaʿba)—the religion of you and your forefathers, and your sanctity and honour from time immemorial—yet you do not speak to me about it and only care that I return what I have taken from you!' ʿAbd al-Muṭṭalib replied, 'I am the lord of the camels, and the House likewise has a Lord who shall defend it.' Abraha

Regarding the second couplet, the author, after mentioning that the Prophet (Allah bless him and give him peace) cast pebbles with his blessed hands, informs us that this casting and throwing came after another sign, and preceded another miracle: namely the glorification of pebbles—meaning pebbles in general, not the specific pebbles that he threw—in his hands. Then the author draws a parallel between the glorifying stones that the Prophet (Allah bless him and give him peace) cast from his hand and the casting of the Prophet Yūnus (upon whom be peace) from the belly of the whale after he glorified Allah. One casting is likened to another; just as the Prophet Yūnus (upon whom be peace) was cast from the belly of the whale after he glorified Allah, likewise the pebbles in the Prophet's hand were cast after they glorified Allah (the Exalted and Sublime). Both the former and the latter were cast out and glorifying Allah.

The glorification of the pebbles in the Prophet's hand is counted amongst his many inimitable miracles (*muʿjizāt*), and the *ḥadīth* report about it is well-known, having been related by Abū Dāwūd, al-Ṭabarānī and others, from Anas (Allah be pleased with him) who said: 'The Prophet (Allah bless him and give him peace) took a handful of pebbles and they began to glorify Allah in his hand to the point that their glorification could be heard by others. Then he put the pebbles in Abū Bakr's hand and they continued to glorify; then he put them in my hand, but they did not glorify.' In another narration it is stated that the pebbles glorified [Allah] while in the hands of ʿUmar, ʿUthmān and ʿAlī—Allah be pleased with them all.

As for the story of the Prophet Yūnus (upon whom be peace), it is Qur'anic, well-known and extraordinary. Yūnus b. Mattā was a Prophet

---

said, 'He shall not defend it against me!' ʿAbd al-Mūṭṭalib said, "We shall see."

Soon after, ʿAbd al-Muṭṭalib returned to the door of the Kaʿba and convened a meeting with a group of Quraysh. They supplicated to Allah, the Exalted and Sublime. Just as they were invoking Allah, suddenly ʿAbd al-Muṭṭalib turned and saw a flock of birds coming from the direction of Yemen. He exclaimed, "By Allah, these are strange birds! They are neither of Najd or of Tihāma. ʿAbd al-Muṭṭalib then dismissed his tribesmen and moved on with his companions to observe what Abraha was going to do. It was at that moment Allah set the birds against the troops and what was narrated took place.

It is said that Abraha was the grandfather of the Negus who lived during the time of the Prophet (Allah bless him and give him peace). ʿĀʾisha (Allah be pleased with her) reported, 'I saw the elephant-rider and the water-carrier: both were blind and crippled and begging for food.' (*al-Baḥr al-madīd*) [t] amongst the Children of Israel. When Yūnus was twenty-eight years old Allah sent him to his people and he invited them to embrace the message he brought, but they did not respond to it. They continued in this fashion for a long time, till Yūnus finally asked Allah to punish them. It was revealed to him that the punishment would descend upon them on such-and-such day, and when Yūnus informed them they said to each other, 'If he leaves us then we will know that the punishment he speaks of will surely afflict us, but if he remains in our midst we will know that he is a liar.' During the evening prior to the promised day of torment, Yūnus made his way out [of the city] and left them behind, and they realised with certainty that punishment was imminent, and knew that Yūnus had been telling the truth all along. All of the inhabitants made their way to the outskirts of the city and took their animals, separating the young from their mothers, and they all repented to Allah and expressed heartfelt submission, so Allah lifted their punishment. By that time Yūnus had already left them and the city behind, and was waiting for Allah to punish them; but when he saw that they were not being afflicted with punishment, and that Allah was not carrying out His divine threat against them, he felt disturbed. At the time he thought that they would interpret the event as proof that he was a liar in everything that he had brought to them, so he swore an oath that he would never return. It is narrated that it was their religious practice to kill people guilty of lying, so Yūnus was afraid of them and fled. Allah reprimanded him for exiling himself, because it was not done with the express permission of his Master (Allah). Now, the Prophets are taken to task for things that others are not, for 'the good deeds of the pious are the sins of those brought nigh', and what is considered a minor fault for others constitutes an enormity for the elect. Having ran away, Yūnus fled to the sea and boarded a ship. It is reported by Ibn Masʿūd that after Yūnus had boarded the ship and sailed some distance, it suddenly became motionless in the sea, even as other ships sailed past it on its left and right. The ship's captain called out, 'There is an escapee on board, someone guilty of an offence! Everyone assemble and let us draw lots.' Each of them took a lot, and they were gathered and cast into the sea. The passengers said, 'O Allah, let the guilty party's lot float and let the other lots sink!' And so it was that Yūnus's lot floated, so they repeated the process three times, but each time it was his lot that floated, so the passengers agreed that they would cast him overboard into the sea.

Yūnus went to the ship's bow to cast himself in the sea, but there he saw a large sea creature lurking in the water and waiting for him. Then he went to the ship's stern to cast himself from there but saw the same creature there, too. Yūnus went around all corners of the ship's deck but no matter where he went the sea creature was following him and lying in wait. He soon realised that it was from Allah, so he threw himself overboard and the creature swallowed him up. It is narrated that the whale swallowed Yūnus up after he entered the water. It is also narrated that Allah (the Exalted and Sublime) revealed to the whale, 'I have not made Yūnus a provision for you; I have made your belly a refuge and prison for him.' Allah's words '*So he was from the losers*' (Qur'an 37:141) means Yūnus was of those who lost when the lots were drawn. The word for loser, *mudḥaḍ*, means a loser in lots or a loser in a race or competition. [Regarding the verse after it '*Then the whale swallowed him, and he was blameworthy*,'] the word for blameworthy (*mulīm*) describes a person who does something that warrants blame.

After some time, Allah Most High saved Yūnus (upon whom be peace) and delivered him from the belly of the whale. There is a difference of opinion as to the length of Yūnus' stay in the belly of the whale. Some say that he remained only for an hour. It is also said that he remained for seven hours, or three days, or seven days, or fourteen days. Al-Suddī said he remained there for forty days.

Allah Most High made glorification (*tasbīḥ*) the means of Yūnus' rescue from the belly of the whale (besides the pre-eternal decree). Scholars differ over what the exact formula of glorification was. Ibn Jubayr said, 'It was his saying "Glorified is Allah (*Subḥān Allāh*)."' Others said that on the contrary, this glorification was Yūnus' supererogatory prayer. Those who hold this latter view differ among themselves further. According to Ibn ʿAbbās and Qatāda, his prayers during times of ease benefited him in his time of difficulty, for the one who invokes Allah in times of ease will attain benefit in times of difficulty. Ḍaḥḥāk b. Qays used to say atop his pulpit, 'Remember Allah in times of ease and He will remember you in times of difficulty. Yūnus was considered a person of remembrance in the sight of Allah, so when difficulty struck him he was profited by his remembrance, as Allah says, "*Were it not that he was of those who glorified [Allah], he would have remained in the belly of the whale until the Day they are resurrected.*" (Qur'an 37:144) Fir'awn, on the other hand, was a transgressor in times of ease, but when he was drowning he said "I believe!" but his faith at that time profited him not. So remember Allah in times of ease and He will remember you in times of difficulty.'

Al-Ḥasan b. Abī al-Ḥasan said, 'Yūnus's glorification was his voluntary prayers inside of the belly of the whale.' It is narrated that the Emissary of Allah (Allah bless him and give him peace) said, 'When Yūnus beseeched [Allah] in the layers of darkness, his call was raised up to the Throne and the angels said, "Our Lord, this is a weakened voice [calling out] from a place of loneliness!" so Allah answered his prayer.'

Ibn Jubayr said, 'The phrase [in the verse] "*were it not that he was of those who glorified*" points to Yūnus's prayer where he said "*There is no god but You; glorified are You, truly I have been one of the wrongdoers!*"' (Qur'an 21:87)

It is narrated that the whale swam through the entire sea until it finally cast Yūnus out near the city of Mosul. Allah tossed him upon an open piece of land. The word used here, *ʿarāʾ*, describes a land without trees. Yūnus was cast out like an infant with tender flesh; it is also said that his skin was extremely tender to the touch, though in a way that did not detract from his [beautiful] physical form. Allah provided him with shelter under the shade of a gourd vine and provided him with a spring of water. It is said that Yūnus would eat from the gourd vine and find in its shade a variety of food. Most people say this was a pumpkin tree (calling it a tree is either figurative or because Allah caused it to develop a trunk as an extraordinary break with natural norms; according to the Arabs, a tree is something that has a trunk, and that which does not have a trunk is called a vine). The pumpkin has many excellent qualities. It provides cool shade, it is soft to the touch, its leaves are large and flies do not come near it; in fact al-Naqqāsh said, 'If its water is sprayed around an area flies will not come near it.'

And so Yūnus (upon whom be peace) recovered and his body healed. It is narrated that one day as he was sleeping there, Allah caused the gourd vine to dry up. Yūnus woke up due to the intense heat of the sun and missed the gourd sorely and felt unease. Thereupon Allah revealed to him, 'Yūnus, do you feel unease due to the drying of the gourd, when you did not feel unease at the destruction of over one hundred thousand people who repented to Me and whom I forgave?' This was a reproach from Allah (the Exalted and Sublime) to His Prophet Yūnus (upon whom be peace) for having asked Allah to punish them, even though they were disbelievers. Yūnus's anger towards them was for the sake of Allah; however, the elect are taken to task for the smallest of things because they are demanded with a level of propriety that is not required of others. Allah Most High says to our Prophet (Allah bless him and give him peace), '*So be patient with the decree of your Lord, and do not be like the Companion of the Whale.*' (Qur'an 68:48)

Then Allah Most High returned Yūnus to his people and sent him to them once again, and they had faith in him and believed him; and he remained amongst them until Allah caused them to pass away. Glorified is He whose dominion never fades and whose Life never ends!

CHAPTER 5

The Prophet's Miracles ﷺ

جَاءَتْ لِدَعْوَتِهِ الْأَشْجَارُ سَاجِدَةً   تَمْشِي إِلَيْهِ عَلَىٰ سَاقٍ بِلَا قَدَمِ

كَأَنَّمَا سَطَّرَتْ سَطْرًا لِمَا كَتَبَتْ   فُرُوعُهَا مِنْ بَدِيعِ الْخَطِّ بِاللَّقَمِ

Trees came prostrating to him when he called,
Walking towards him on trunks without feet
As though they had inscribed lines of splendid calligraphy
With their branches along the path.

THE AUTHOR (Allah have mercy upon him), after mentioning the miracle of the throwing of the pebbles and how they defeated the [enemy] army, as well as the pebbles that glorified [Allah] while in the Prophet's hands, goes on to mention the miracle of the tree's prostration to the Prophet (Allah bless him and give him peace) and its response to his call and submission to his command. He uses the word 'prostrate' to describe the tree's submission and pliancy, since it is not established that it literally prostrated; what is certain is that it was a camel and a sheep that literally prostrated themselves before the Prophet (Allah bless him and give him peace). Abū Hurayra (Allah be pleased with him) reported, 'The Emissary of Allah once entered a walled compound and a camel approached and prostrated before him…'[120] Similar reports have been transmitted on the authority of Jābir [b. ʿAbd Allāh], Yaʿlā b. Murra and ʿAbd Allāh b. Jaʿfar, the last of whom reported, 'No one would enter the compound without the camel putting up resistance, but when the Prophet entered and called it, it placed its trunk on the ground and kneeled before him and addressed him. The Prophet then said, "There is nothing within the

120 Aḥmad.

heavens or the earth but testifies that I am the Emissary of Allah, except for the rebellious amongst jinn and mankind."'[121]

Another narration tells how the Prophet (Allah bless him and give him peace) had asked the owners about it, and they informed him that they wanted to slaughter it.[122] Anas (Allah be pleased with him) related, 'The Emissary of Allah along with Abū Bakr and ᶜUmar, entered a walled compound belonging to one of the Helpers (*Anṣār*). Once they were inside, a sheep prostrated itself before him, whereupon Abū Bakr said, "O Emissary of Allah, we have more right to prostrate to you than this sheep!" ...'

With regard to the tree, what is transmitted is that it spoke to [the Prophet (Allah bless him and give him peace)] and that he called it and it responded. It is recorded in a rigorously authentic *ḥadīth* that the Emissary of Allah (Allah bless him and give him peace) would call out to trees and they would obediently and submissively respond to him, going so far as to move to stand before his presence. They would testify to the veracity of his message and then he would order them to go back to where they had come from.[123] ᶜĀʾisha (Allah be pleased with her) related that the Emissary of Allah said, 'After Jibrīl came to me with the divine message I would not pass by a tree or a stone without it saying "Peace be upon you, O Emissary of Allah!"'[124]

The point that the Shaykh [al-Būṣīrī] is alluding to is what [Qāḍī] ᶜIyāḍ mentioned in *al-Shifā*, with his chain of transmission going back to Ibn ᶜUmar (Allah be pleased with him), who narrated: 'We were with the Emissary of Allah on a journey and a Bedouin came up to him and he asked, "O Bedouin, where are you going?" The Bedouin replied, "To my family." He said, "Do you want something good?" The Bedouin inquired, "And what might that be?" He said, "That you bear witness that there is no god but Allah, who is alone and without partner, and that Muḥammad is His servant and Emissary." The Bedouin asked, "Who will bear witness to the truthfulness of what you say?" He replied, "This

121 Ṭabarānī, *al-Muᶜjam al-awsaṭ*.

122 Qāḍī ᶜIyāḍ, *al-Shifāʾ*.

123 Ibn Ḥibbān

124 This *ḥadīth* could not be traced but Muslim reports a *ḥadīth* with a similar meaning from Jābir b. Samura in which the Prophet said 'Indeed, I know of a stone in Makka that would greet me before *biᶜtha* (prophethood) [and] I still recognise it now'.

mimosa tree; call it and it will come to you." The Bedouin called out to the tree, and suddenly it advanced from the edge of the valley, cleaving the earth until it stood before him and he asked it thrice to bear witness, which it did and then returned from whence it had come.'

Burayda (Allah be pleased with him) related, 'A Bedouin asked the Prophet for a sign and he said to him, "Tell that tree that the Emissary of Allah calls it." The tree then leaned to the right and left, in front and behind, pulled up its roots and came cleaving the earth and dragging its dust-covered roots until it stood before the Emissary of Allah. It said, "Peace be upon you, O Emissary of Allah!" The Bedouin said, "Command it to return to its place." It then returned, sank its roots back [into the ground] and became still. The Bedouin said, "Give me permission to prostrate to you!" The Prophet replied, "Were I to command anyone to prostrate to another, I would have commanded a woman to prostrate to her husband."[125] The Bedouin said, "Then give me permission to kiss your hands and feet!" and the Prophet granted him permission.'

There are several narrations that convey this meaning. Now the author's statement *Walking towards him on trunks without feet* is a hyperbolic way of conveying the inimitability [of this miracle], since feet help one to walk, though these trees came walking towards him without any feet at all. The author expresses this point with amazement and astonishment after having affirmed [the Prophet's] inimitable miracles. Allah Most High knows best.

Then in the second couplet the author draws a comparison between calligraphy and the lines that the trees etched in the earth with their trunks along the path. What lends force to this simile is the fact that it describes the surface of the earth as if it were a tablet or a sheet of paper for those lines, describes the branches of the trees as being a scribe, and describes the roots that cleave the earth with the act of writing that calligraphy. So the roots of the trees etched the lines and the branches masterfully wrote upon them with splendid calligraphy. Allah Most High knows best.

مِثْلَ الْغَمَامَةِ أَنَّىٰ سَارَ سَائِرَةً   تَقِيهِ حَرَّ وَطِيسٍ لِلْهَجِيرِ حَمِي

Like the cloud that hovered over him wherever he went,
Shielding him from the intense oven of the midday heat.

125 Tirmidhī, *Sunan*.

Here the author (Allah be pleased with him) is alluding to another miracle, the shade that the clouds provided [to the Prophet (Allah bless him and give him peace)]. This miracle, however, came before the prophetic mission [*biʿtha*], so it is called a harbinger [*irhāṣa*]; it did not occur after the Prophet (Allah bless him and give him peace) was tasked with the prophetic mission. Reports suggest that clouds shaded the Prophet (Allah bless him and give him peace) from the sun on several occasions, and that as they accompanied him as he travelled, if they [the caravan] stopped by a shady tree, they would leave the tree to provide him with shade. The reports that speak of this before the prophetic mission are numerous and well-known. They were witnessed by the Prophet's servant Maysara as they were on the way to the Levant (Shām); they were also seen by Buḥāyra the monk when they [Abū Ṭālib's caravan] disembarked under a tree near his home, after which the tree casted its shade upon the Prophet (Allah bless him and give him peace); and Khadīja witnessed the clouds providing the Prophet (Allah bless him and give him peace) with shade as he returned from his journey—and that, as is stated in the science of the Prophetic Biography, was what moved her to marry him. The author said in his *Hamziyya*:

As if the clouds had escorted him,
Which had taken shade from him from the heat!

There are two reasons why the clouds shaded the Prophet (Allah bless him and give him peace). The first is physical and the second is spiritual. The first reason is that the shading served as a precursor and herald of his prophethood, and a proclamation of the divine care and honour he was to receive. The second reason is that the shading signalled that whoever of his nation follows him and seeks his shade will attain complete security and everlasting honour. In spite of this, the Prophet (Allah bless him and give him peace) is free of need for the shade of clouds—rather he is a shade and source of security for all mankind!

Taking the outward reality into consideration, the shading of the Prophet (Allah bless him and give him peace) served as an additional protection and safeguard, and a reflection of the providential care for his status, and an admonition [to others] that his sanctity must be upheld and that he must be revered. For if the clouds were subjected to him even though they are inanimate, and yet they escorted him and shielded him, what do you think should be done by those endowed with intelligence? Allah selects for His mercy whom He wills, and Allah is the possessor of immense bounty!

أَقْسَمْتُ بِالْقَمَرِ الْمُنْشَقِّ إِنَّ لَهُ مِنْ قَلْبِهِ نِسْبَةً مَبْرُورَةَ الْقَسَمِ

I swear by the [Lord of the] moon that was split in two a true oath: it has truly a connection with his heart.

Here the author (Allah have mercy upon him) is alluding to the miracle of the splitting of the moon, as well as the splitting of the Prophet's breast, and brings the two together in a beautiful manner, phrasing it as an oath. He tells us that he swears by the splitting of the moon and what followed from it that whenever he suffers from the dark vicissitudes of time and seeks the Prophet's aid he receives his succour and rescuing help at once and without delay. Then the author mentions the subject of his oath and says that there is a link between the Prophet's heart and the moon. It is this connection that led the author to hold the moon in so much esteem that he swore an oath by it. That is because the Arabs only swear by things that are revered, and since the author (Allah have mercy upon him) reveres the moon on account of its connection to the heart of the Emissary of Allah (Allah bless him and give him peace), he swears by it here.

Now, the connection between the moon and the Prophet's heart is that both were split; just as the splitting of the moon was a miracle in support of the Prophet (Allah bless him and give him peace), so too was the splitting of his breast, when the two angels came to him and washed his heart with Zamzam water, and came to him another time with a bowl carrying ice and snow. So the author observes that the moon attained honour and esteem and therefore split just as the breast of Allah's Emissary (Allah bless him and give him peace) was split. If a person makes an oath it is obligatory upon him to fulfill it, and that is why the author says a true oath: it has truly a connection with his heart. This means the oath must be fulfilled, or the oath is true.

As for the splitting of the moon, the reports concerning it are both mass-transmitted [*mutawātira*] and Qur'anic, and have been narrated by the majority of the Companions. Allah Most High said, '*The Hour has drawn near and the moon has split. And when they see a sign they say, "It is continuous magic!"'* [Qur'an 54:1–2] Allah (Glorified and Exalted is He!) speaks about the splitting of the moon using the past tense. And in the rigorously authentic collection [of al-Bukhārī] it is reported that Ibn Masᶜūd (Allah be pleased with him) said, 'The moon split in two during the time of Allah's Emissary: one part was behind the mountain and the other part was on this side of the mountain. The Emissary of Allah said, "Bear witness." ...'

Another narration states, 'And then I saw the mountain above the two pieces of the moon. The disbelievers of the Quraysh scoffed, "Ibn Abī Kabsha (i.e., the Prophet) has bewitched you!" One of them said, "Though Muḥammad may have bewitched us, his sorcery cannot encompass the entire world; ask those who come to you from other lands whether they saw this." Later, when some travellers arrived and were asked about it, they said that they too had witnessed it.'[126]

Anas related, 'The Meccans had asked the Emissary of Allah to show them a sign, and so he showed them the moon splitting into two pieces so far apart that they could see Ḥirāʾ between the two pieces.'

As for the splitting of the Prophet's breast, it is recorded in the rigorously authenticated ḥadīth that the Companions of the Emissary of Allah (Allah bless him and give him peace) said, 'O Emissary of Allah, tell us about yourself.' He replied, 'Yes. I am the answer to Ibrāhīm's supplication; I am the glad tidings of my brother ᶜĪsā that he delivered to his people; and I am the embodiment of my mother's dream in which she saw herself giving birth, with a light emitting from her that shone upon the palaces of the Levant. I was suckled among Banū Saᶜd b. Abī Bakr. One day [there], while I was with a foster-brother of mine shepherding some of the animals that belonged to us, there came to me two men wearing white garments and carrying a golden bowl filled with snow. Then they took me and opened up my belly, then extracted my heart and split it; then they removed from it a black morsel and threw it away; then they washed my heart and my belly with that snow until they had thoroughly cleaned them. One of the men said to the other, "Weigh him against ten people of his nation," and when he weighed me I outweighed them all; then he said, "Weigh him against one hundred people from his

126 Bukhārī.

nation" and when he weighed me I outweighed them all; and he then said, "Leave him be, for if you weighed him against his entire nation he would outweigh them all!"'[127]

According to Ibn Ḥajar al-Haytamī, the Prophet's chest was split open on four separate occasions. The first time was in [the incident] narrated above, when he was a young boy. The wisdom behind it was to purify him of the deficiencies of youth so he could take on the most perfected qualities of manhood, and this is why he lived in the best of all possible states.

The second time his chest was split was when he was ten years of age, according to the narrative about him and [his paternal uncle] Abū Ṭālib, narrated by Abū Nuʿaym in *Dalāʾil* [*al-Nubuwwa*] and by ʿAbdullāh son of Imam Aḥmad in the reports [*zawāʾid*] he transmitted from his father.

The third time his chest was split was in the cave of Ḥirāʾ when the revelation began. This was narrated by al-Ṭayālisī, al-Ḥārith [b. Abī Usāma], and Abū Nuʿaym—although it is weak.

The fourth time his chest was split was during the miraculous Night Journey [*al-Isrāʾ*]. The narration concerning this is rigorously authenticated and agreed upon; it was narrated by al-Bukhārī and others.

The splitting that took place in this extraordinary and awe-inspiring fashion was given exclusively to the Prophet (Allah bless him and give him peace), and while it is unquestionably true that the hearts of all the previous Prophets were purified, none of them underwent this. And with Allah is all success.

وَمَا حَوَى الْغَارُ مِنْ خَيْرٍ وَ مِنْ كَرَمٍ   وَكُلُّ طَرْفٍ مِنَ الْكُفَّارِ عَنْهُ عَمِي

And by the goodness and nobility contained in the cave
While the disbelievers' every glance was blind to him.

After swearing an oath by the splitting of the moon, the author (Allah have mercy upon him) adds to it another oath, this time swearing by what was contained in the cave. It is as if he were saying: 'I swear by the moon and by the nobility and excellence contained in the cave,' since it contained the Emissary of Allah (Allah bless him and give him peace) and his close companion Abū Bakr. Allah protected them inside the cave and

127 Bukhārī and Muslim.

blinded the eyes of the disbelievers from seeing them, despite the disbelievers' best efforts and keenness to apprehend them. The disbelievers had even promised a large bounty to whoever could bring them back [to Mecca], but Allah veiled them [both], concealing them from the disbelievers despite their extreme closeness to the cave. How excellent are the words of al-Būṣīrī who said in his *Hamziyya*:

> He was hidden from their view despite his nearness;
> The most apparent things are often hidden!

And so Allah protected His Prophet (Allah bless him and give him peace), enabled him to complete his migration (*hijra*), and gave victory to his religion. The story of the cave is both mass-transmitted and Qur'anic. The gist of the story is that the Emissary of Allah (Allah bless him and give him peace) was awaiting Allah's permission to migrate from Mecca. Abū Bakr had left the protection provided by Ibn al- Dughunna [who escorted him back to Mecca under his guarantee of protection after his attempted migration to Abyssinia] and soon resolved to leave Mecca. Then the Emissary of Allah (Allah bless him and give him peace) told him, 'Perhaps Allah will appoint for you a travel companion.' When Allah granted His Emissary (Allah bless him and give him peace) permission to leave, he readied himself for the journey while in Abū Bakr's house, and both of them later set out and spent three nights in the cave on Mount Thawr. Abū Bakr said to the Prophet (Allah bless him and give him peace), 'If any of them should even look at his feet he will see us!' The Prophet (Allah bless him and give him peace) replied, 'What do you think of two for whom Allah is the third?'

The reason why the Prophet (Allah bless him and give him peace) left Mecca as an immigrant to Medina, besides the fact that it was pre-eternally decreed, was that Quraysh conspired to harm him and were in a position to do so after the death of the Prophet's uncle Abū Ṭālib. They had convened an assembly in the Dār al-Nadwa to plan what they were going to do against the Prophet (Allah bless him and give him peace), when Satan appeared before them in the form of a respectable old man and stood by the door of the Dār. When they saw him they asked, 'Who is the elder?' and he replied, 'I am one of the people of the highlands of Najd who has heard of your plan against him [the Prophet] and has come to hear what you have to say. Perhaps you will hear me out and let me offer my opinion.' 'But of course' they replied. So Satan, in the guise of an old man, entered their company and found the chieftains of Quraysh gathered. One of the men said, 'You are well aware of what has come of this man. By Allah, we are not safe against him launching a sudden attack against us with those who have joined him, so determine the best course of action to be taken against him.' They consulted one another and one of those present advised, 'Put him behind bars and lock the door behind him, and wait until the same fate befalls him as befell his like among the poets before him, Zuhayr and Nābigha, and he dies just as they died.' The old man of the Najd objected, 'By Allah, this should not be your course of action! By Allah, if you imprison him the news of it will spread behind his prison door and it will not be long before they launch a sudden attack against you and free him from your control and overcome you. So consider another course of action!'

Another man among them said, 'Let us expel him from our midst and exile him from our lands, so when he leaves us we will not care where he goes.' The old man of the Najd objected once more, 'By Allah, this should not be your course of action! Have you not observed his fine speech and beautiful diction and his compelling nature that affects the hearts of men? By Allah, if you do that you will not be safe from him settling among some tribe of the Arabs and winning them over with his statements and speech, until they pledge fealty to him and he leads them to you and they seize power from your hands and do with you as they wish! Consider another course of action.'

Abū Jahl then said, 'By Allah, I have a suggestion that none of you have yet proposed.' Those in attendance asked, 'What is it, Abū al-Ḥakam?' He said, 'We should take from every clan a young and powerful youth from a prominent family and give him a sharp sword, then have them all go forth and strike him with the sword-blow of a single man, killing him. After that has been done his blood will be evenly divided between all of the clans and Banū ʿAbd Manāf will be unable to wage war against all of them and will settle with accepting blood-money, to which we will all contribute.' The old man of the Najd proclaimed, 'In my opinion this is the only acceptable course of action!' The assembly then dispersed, having come to this decision.

Soon thereafter Jibrīl (upon whom be peace) descended to the Emissary of Allah (Allah bless him and give him peace) and said, 'Do not sleep in your bed tonight.' Later that night they assembled at his door and waited for him to go to sleep so they could fall upon him. When the Prophet (Allah bless him and give him peace) saw them lying in wait he said to ᶜAlī, 'Sleep on my bed and wrap yourself up in this mantle of mine, for nothing will befall you.' The Prophet (Allah bless him and give him peace) then took a handful of dust into his hand, sprinkled it over the heads of the young men lying in wait, and recited Sūra Yāsīn from the beginning till he reached the verse '*And We have placed before them a barrier and behind them a barrier, and We have covered them so they do not see.*' (Qur'an 30:9) Allah averted their eyes from seeing the Prophet (Allah bless him and give him peace), and there was not a single one among them but had dust on his head. Then the Prophet (Allah bless him and give him peace) went as he pleased and a man came to them and said, 'What are you waiting for?' They replied, 'We are waiting for Muḥammad.' The man said, 'Allah has frustrated your plans! By Allah, he came out to you and put dust on the head of every single man among you!' The men put their hands on their heads and felt the dust upon them.

Allah revealed about this incident, '*And when those who disbelieve hatch a plot against you to silence you or kill you or expel you, they plot and Allah plots; and Allah is the best of plotters.*' (Qur'an 8:30) It was at this time that Allah commanded His Prophet (Allah bless him and give him peace) to migrate and the Prophet permitted Abū Bakr to be his travel companion. Abū Bakr said, 'O Emissary of Allah (Allah bless him and give him peace), here are two camels that I have readied for this!' No one knew when the Emissary of Allah (Allah bless him and give him peace) was migrating except for ᶜAlī and Abū Bakr. The Prophet (Allah bless him and give him peace) instructed ᶜAlī to stay behind to return on his behalf the goods that others had deposited with him for safekeeping (anyone who had property whose care was cause for worry would deposit it in the Prophet's care, for he was known for his truthfulness and trustworthiness).

Then the Emissary of Allah (Allah bless him and give him peace) began his migration. He and Abū Bakr headed for a cave in a mountain below Mecca and entered it. Abū Bakr entered it before the Emissary of Allah

(Allah bless him and give him peace) and felt around inside, looking for snakes or poisonous insects, wanting to protect the Emissary of Allah (Allah bless him and give him peace) from them with his own person. ᶜAbdullāh the son of Abū Bakr stayed back and was to listen to what Quraysh were saying and then make his way by night to the Prophet (Allah bless him and give him peace) and Abū Bakr and inform them of what he had heard. ᶜĀmir b. Fuhayra would also make his way out to them at night and bring some of Abū Bakr's sheep which they would then milk and slaughter for food.

Asmāʾ the daughter of Abū Bakr said, 'When Abū Bakr and the Emissary of Allah (Allah bless him and give him peace) left, a group of Quraysh, including Abū Jahl, came [to our home] and stood at the door. I came out to them and they asked, "Where is your father, O daughter of Abū Bakr?" I replied, "I do not know," whereupon Abū Jahl, who was a vile and dissolute man, raised his hand and struck me upon my face so violently that my earrings flew off.'

Once Quraysh realised that the Prophet (Allah bless him and give him peace) and Abū Bakr had left they offered a reward of a hundred she-camels for whoever would return them [to Mecca]. Surāqa b. Juᶜshum was eager to receive such a reward. He said, 'I hoped to be the one to bring them back and receive the hundred she-camels, so I rode out in their pursuit and when just my horse was going at a swift pace it stumbled and threw me off and I fell down. I then took out my divining arrows—these being three arrows that were used as a type of omen, the first of which it is written "Do not do it", the second of which it is written "Yes" and the third of which is written "Void". I pulled out the divining arrows and got the result I did not want, "Do not do it"; but I refused the decision and pulled them out again, only to get the same result a second and third time. I continued in pursuit until my horse's forelegs became stuck in the ground and threw me off again. As my horse pulled its legs out of the ground, smoke arose from the holes. When I saw that I knew that he [the Prophet] was protected against me, so I called out to him, "I am Surāqa son of Mālik. Grant me respite and allow me to speak with you, for by Allah I will not bring you any harm!" I asked him to give me something that would be a sign between him and me, so he instructed Abū Bakr to write something. I took the writing and put it in my quiver and returned to

Quraysh. Upon my return I mentioned nothing of the matter. I said, "I saw no one."

Quraysh continued their pursuit of the Prophet (Allah bless him and give him peace) until they reached the cave, whereupon Allah shielded the Prophet (Allah bless him and give him peace) by causing a bush to grow in front of the cave, placing two doves at the mouth of the cave, and causing a spider to weave a web over it. When Quraysh reached the cave and saw the doves and the spider's web, some of them thought to go inside, but Umayya b. Khalaf said, 'Why bother when it is covered with a spider's web older than Muḥammad himself?' (They [scholars] say that the Prophet (Allah bless him and give him peace) forbade killing spiders since they are among Allah's soldiers.) And so those in pursuit turned away. Allah blinded their vision, diverted their hearts and protected His Prophet (Allah bless him and give him peace) from them, desiring to honour him and exalt his religion.

Abū Bakr and the Prophet (Allah bless him and give him peace) remained inside the cave for three days. Surāqa kept the Prophet's letter in his possession. [Surāqa said] 'Then when the Prophet conquered Mecca and went on to Ḥunayn and Ṭāʾif, I went out to meet him with the letter. I met up with him in Jiʿrāna and got among a platoon of the Anṣār, who began to hit me with their spears and say "What do you want?" I then got near to the Emissary of Allah (Allah bless him and give him peace) as he was sitting atop his she-camel, and by Allah his shank in his stirrup looked like the trunk of a palm tree. I lifted my hand with the letter and said, "O Emissary of Allah (Allah bless him and give him peace), this is your letter and I am Surāqa b. Juʿtham." The Emissary of Allah (Allah bless him and give him peace) said, "This is the day of repayment." I stood before him [and embraced Islam], after which I returned to my people and delivered charity to the Emissary of Allah (Allah bless him and give him peace).'

When the Emissary of Allah (Allah bless him and give him peace) reached Medina, the Immigrants [al-Muhājirūn] soon joined him, and none remained in Mecca except those who were detained or those who were beguiled. Many miracles and signs were manifested for the Prophet (Allah bless him and give him peace) on his migratory journey, and they have been cited by the biographers. And with Allah is enabling grace.

فَالصِّدْقُ فِي الْغَارِ وَالصِّدِّيقُ لَمْ يَرِمَا   وَهُمْ يَقُولُونَ مَا بِالْغَارِ مِنْ أَرِمِ

Truthfulness and the True One in the cave wavered not
While they said 'No one who breathes is in the cave!'

In this couplet the author informs us that *Truthfulness*—meaning the Prophet himself—remained in the cave along with *the True One* [Abū Bakr], and that when the disbelievers reached the cave in their pursuit of him they said, '*No one who breathes is in the cave*' Allah protected His Prophet (Allah bless him and give him peace) by means of what the disbelievers saw (i.e. a spider's web and doves), but had He so willed He could have blinded their eyesight without there being any spider or doves. Nevertheless, Allah Most High willed to create a material diversion that would prevent them from discovering the Prophet, so they would feel certain that no one could be near such a freshly built nest and web. Allah made these two things means by which their hopes were dashed. He diverted them by His wisdom; and Allah is All-Wise, All-Knowing.

ظَنُّوا الْحَمَامَ وَظَنُّوا الْعَنْكَبُوتَ عَلَىٰ   خَيْرِ الْبَرِيَّةِ لَمْ تَنْسُجْ وَلَمْ تَحُمِ

They supposed that a dove would never perch,
Or a spider would spin its web, for the Best of Creation.

Having stated in the previous line that those outside said to one another '*No one who breathes is in the cave*', the author produces an imaginery person who asks him 'Why did they say that?' He replies, 'When they saw a dove hovering over the mouth of the cave, and when they saw that a spider had cast its web over the entrance, they thought it was empty and that no one was inside,' for normally doves will not settle around a cave occupied by people. When one of the men approached and saw two doves at the entrance, he returned to his companions and said, 'There is no one in the cave! I saw two doves at the entrance.' Likewise, spiders normally spin their webs in areas where few things pass, and it takes some time before they appear. So the men [pursuing the Prophet (Allah bless him and give him peace)] did not attempt to enter the cave; when one of them said 'Go inside,' Umayya b. Khalaf said, 'Why bother when it is covered with a spider's web older than

Muḥammad himself?' And so they returned from whence they came, as we detailed earlier.

In saying that the spider spun its web to help the Best of Creation (Allah bless him and give him peace), the author also intends the Prophet's companion Abū Bakr. His name was omitted since it was already known, and this is similar to the [elliptical] statement of the Most High '*And* [He has] *made for you garments that protect you from the heat*' (Qur'an 16:81)—in other words, garments that protect you from heat *and* from cold. Alternatively, the author might be alluding only to the Prophet (Allah bless him and give him peace), because he is the centre [of the story] and Abū Bakr was merely following. The author mentions the verb 'think' twice for the sake of emphasis. Allah Most High knows best.

وِقَايَةُ اللَّهِ أَغْنَتْ عَنْ مُضَاعَفَةٍ   مِنَ الدُّرُوعِ وَعَنْ عَالٍ مِنَ الْأُطُمِ

Their protection by Allah absolved them of need for additional armour or for lofty fortresses.

Here the author (Allah have mercy upon him) says that Allah's protection of the Prophet (Allah bless him and give him peace) and Abū Bakr (Allah be pleased with him) in the cave saved them from needing coats of armour or lofty fortresses. Allah Most Glorified protected them without armour and without well-built citadels, even though normally they are the only two means for guaranteeing survival. Consider how protection was secured using the weakest of things, a spider's web, about which Allah Most High says, '*And verily the flimsiest of dwellings is the dwelling of the spider.*' (Qur'an 21:80) When a servant is under the watchful care of Allah and receives His concern and protection, he will not be harmed by those who take him as an enemy, and he will not need a coat of chainmail or an impenetrable fortress, and Allah will save him from need for tribes and kinsfolk. But if a servant is not under the protective care of Allah, he will not profit from either coats of chainmail or impenetrable fortresses. According to a *ḥadīth* related from the Prophet (Allah bless him and give him peace): 'Know that if creation were to gather together with the intention of benefiting you, they would not be able to benefit you except with what Allah has decreed for you; and if creation were to gather together with the intention of harming you, they would not be able to harm you except with what Allah has decreed for you. So when you ask, ask Allah; and when you seek help, seek help from Allah. And know that with patience comes victory and that with hardship comes relief and with difficulty comes ease'[128] [He also said] 'One difficulty will never overcome two eases.'[129] So depend upon Allah in all of your affairs and be of strong certitude in your reliance upon Him in your movements and stillness, and you will behold such astounding displays of Allah's power as the mind cannot fathom.

It is related that Abū Ḥamza al-Khurasānī took a covenant with Allah that he would not entrust his destiny to any of creation or ask a human being for any of his needs, and that he would sever all intermediaries between him and his Lord. One day as he was walking, his foot slipped and he fell into a well. It occurred to him at that moment that he should call out to a passer-by and ask for help and rescue from certain death, but he remembered the covenant he had taken with his Lord, so he refrained. He then said, 'I will not violate the covenant I have taken with my Lord; I am surely under His care and He sees me and knows my condition.' His certitude was remarkable, and he remained inside the well waiting for relief when a group of people passed by and one of them said to his companions, 'Come over here and let us cover the opening to this well so no one falls in.' They came together to move [a stone or wooden plank] to cover the well, and Abū Ḥamza said to himself, 'It looks as though this will be the end of me!' and it occurred to him that he should break the oath he had taken with Allah; and yet Allah had strengthened his certitude and faith and he kept silent as he saw them covering the opening of the well. After they covered it they went away, meanwhile Abū Ḥamza had resigned his fate to Allah's divine pre-ordainment and knowledge. But then suddenly he heard growling outside of the well, and the cover over the well was moved. When he looked up, Abū Ḥamza saw that it was a lion. The lion then lowered its tail inside of the well and Abū Ḥamza grabbed hold of it and pulled himself out, after which the lion growled and went away. After this, a voice called out to Abū Ḥamza saying, 'O Abū Ḥamza, the real wonder is that We have rescued you from one mortal danger by another mortal danger!'

128 Tirmidhī, *Sunan*.

129 ʿAbd al-Razzāq, *al-Muṣannaf*.

Look at the certitude of this master! He exposed himself to imminent death, yet he refused to violate the oath that was between him and his Lord. May Allah allow us to benefit from his blessings, and may He bestow upon us what He bestowed upon him! If you ask 'Is it permissible for someone to do as he did?' the answer is 'No. It is not allowed unless someone has certitude like that of Abū Ḥamza; in any other situation this would be considered suicide'. So, if you have a level of certitude like Abū Ḥamza then do so without a care, for Allah will deliver you and provide a way out for you!

It is related that one of the Sufis said, 'My companions and I once held a retreat (*iʿtikāf*) inside a mosque for the sake of dedicating ourselves to devotions and seeking divine openings. We remained therein for some days but no divine opening came. Eventually hunger took its toll upon us and we were too weak to continue our devotions, and we were afraid we would perish. Because of our dire need we agreed that one of us should go out and seek provision and beg. It was I who went out for that purpose. [As I was begging] one of the elect [saints] encountered me and I greeted him. Immediately he said, "Let me ask you: the need for which you have come to ask of me—does Allah know of it or not?" I replied, "Of course He knows", whereupon he said, "Then take your need to Him and show proper etiquette [with Him], and do not take your need to created beings!" I returned [to the mosque] and not an hour had passed before Allah blessed me with a divine opening!'

The foundation of this is having strong certitude and reliance upon Allah Most High. If you are like these folk then do as they did; but if not, beware of such perilous acts. There are many stories of this nature mentioned in the relevant sources, and from Allah comes all enabling grace.

مَا سَامَنِي الدَّهْرُ ضَيْمًا وَاسْتَجَرْتُ بِهِ   إِلَّا وَنِلْتُ جِوَارًا مِنْهُ لَمْ يُضَمِ

Never, when fate oppressed me, have I sought refuge in him
but that I found sanctuary with him and was oppressed no more.

Here the author (Allah have mercy upon him) says that fate has never visited him with misfortune, and no affliction has ever descended upon him, nor has he experienced fear, after which he sought sanctuary with the Emissary of Allah (Allah bless him and give him peace) and sought refuge in his exalted person and unassailable honour, and took his magnificent status and noble rank as means of approach, but that he [then] enjoyed safety and protection from all that he feared, was delivered from all that troubled him, and entered, as a result, an impenetrable and well-fortified fortress. How could this not be, when he has sought refuge in the Master of all created beings and the well-spring of nobility and generosity? There is no doubt that whoever gains sanctuary with the Emissary of Allah (Allah bless him and give him peace) will attain salvation and honour, and will be surrounded by divine protection and safeguard in this world and the Next.

It was a common practice of the Arabs of old to offer sanctuary (*jiwār*). Once they had granted a person sanctuary, as Abū Bakr al-Ṣiddīq and others did, no one would be able to harm them.

We mentioned in the introduction to this commentary that the author suffered a heart attack that left him bedridden and with one side of his body paralysed, and that he composed this ode and Allah healed him through the blessings of the Prophet (Allah bless him and give him peace). Likewise, all who seek refuge with the Prophet (Allah bless him and give him peace) in times of difficulty and hardship will find assistance nearer to them than their own selves—especially for those who frequently invoke blessings upon him.

The righteous Shaykh Mūsā al-Ḍarīr (Allah have mercy upon him) relates the following incident: 'We boarded a ship in the ocean and were soon assailed by a powerful wind they called *al-Iqlābiyya*, and which seldom left behind survivors who did not drown. People began to shout out of fear of drowning. Just then I was overcome by sleep and in my dream I saw the Prophet (Allah bless him and give him peace), and he said to me, "Tell the passengers in the ship to say the following one thousand time: 'O Allah, bless Muḥammad with a blessing that will deliver us from every terror and tribulation, fulfil for us every need, purify us from every sin, raise us to the loftiest spiritual degrees, and cause us to attain the most laudable aims in all matters of goodness in this life and after death.'" When I had awoken I told the other passengers what I had seen, and by the time we had recited the supplication three hundred times, the tempest, by the blessings of invoking prayers upon the Prophet (Allah bless him and give him peace), had subsided.' (This is taken from the commentary upon *Dalāʾil al-khayrāt*.)

Abū ʿAbdullāh b. Abī al-Khiṣāl related that when he became infirm he took a piece of paper and wrote down a plea seeking the Prophet's intercession, and sent it with someone to take to the Prophet's grave. When the paper was placed before the noble grave he was instantly healed. The plea reads as follows:

> This is a writing from one ailing, infirm
> Seeking healing by the grave of Allah's Emissary,
> Sought by one long infirm and encumbered
> Unable to do anything but point with his head
> And when he sees visitors set out to draw near
> While he is kept away from you by his ailment and weakness
> In sadness he bids the caravan farewell as they set out at daybreak—
> A sincere greeting, leaving a waft of fragrance in their midst
> O Seal of the Emissaries, Intercessor before your Lord,
> This is a prayer of one rising, of one submissive in heart and sight.

And at the end of his poem he said:

> It is in you that we hope, in life and in death,
> To avert calamities which, if removed, will keep terror at bay.

Ibn al-Jalāʾ (Allah be pleased with him) said, 'I entered the City of the Emissary of Allah (Allah bless him and give him peace) and was suffering from want, so I presented myself before the Prophet's grave and invoked salutations upon him and his Companions, Abū Bakr and ʿUmar next to him. Then I said, "O Emissary of Allah, I am in need, and I am your guest tonight." I then turned and went to sleep between the grave and the pulpit (*minbar*). As I was sleeping, the Prophet (Allah bless him and give him peace) came to me and handed me a loaf of bread, of which I ate half. When I awoke, I found the second half with me!' It is said that Ibn al-Jalāʾ lived for forty years after this incident, and, thanks to the blessings of what he had eaten [from the Prophet], he never once felt the need for food or drink.

وَلَا الْتَمَسْتُ غِنَى الدَّارَيْنِ مِنْ يَدِهِ إِلَّا اسْتَلَمْتُ النَّدَى مِنْ خَيْرِ مُسْتَلَمِ

And never have I sought wealth in both worlds from his hand
Without receiving largesse from the best of givers.

The author (Allah have mercy upon him) essentially says: Never does one aspire to something in this world and the Next and entertain hope that Allah will combine both for him, taking the Prophet (Allah bless him and give him peace) as an intermediary, or seeking intercession through his rank, but that he will, generally speaking, attain his desire. This couplet is akin to saying, 'No one seeks wealth in both Abodes from the hand of Allah's Emissary (Allah bless him and give him peace) except that he attains his hope and desire.'

The reason why the author links the verb to himself is that he realised it through direct experience and thus speaks about it with certainty and as tried and true. Because the Prophet (Allah bless him and give him peace) is the Supreme Means *(al-Wasīlat al-ʿUẓmā)* in these areas of pursuit, and it is through him that they are obtained and by his exalted rank that they are acquired, the author describes them as coming directly from the Prophet's hand and falling under his dominion. It is narrated, 'Seek a means of approach [to Allah] by my rank, for in His sight my rank is immense.'[130] It is also narrated, 'If anyone desires to ask Allah for a need, let him begin and conclude his request with prayers upon me, for Allah accepts the request that falls between the two prayers and He is too generous to ignore what falls between them.'[131] Ibn Masʿūd (Allah be pleased with him) said, 'When one of you wishes to ask for the fulfilment of a need, let him begin by praising Him [Allah] and lauding Him as He merits, then invoke blessings upon our Patron Muḥammad, and then present his need.'

These narrations apply to worldly needs, and we have already mentioned the story of Ibn al-Jalāʾ who, thanks to the blessings of the food he received from the Prophet's hands, was absolved of need for food and drink.

As for needs pertaining to the Hereafter, if one had gained only worldly and Next-Worldly honour reserved for those who praise and invoke

130 Shaykh ʿAbdullāh al-Talīdī states that this *ḥadīth* is without basis.
131 This is not a *ḥadīth*, but a saying of Abū Sulaymān al-Dārānī.

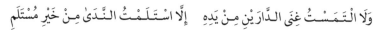

blessings upon the Prophet (Allah bless him and give him peace), that would suffice him. The Prophet (Allah bless him and give him peace) said, 'Jibrīl came to me and said, "Are you not pleased that your Lord, the Exalted and Sublime, says, 'Truly no one of your nation invokes blessings upon you without my invoking ten blessings upon him; and no one of your nation invokes salutations upon you without my invoking ten salutations upon him'?"'[132] And in another narration, 'Whoever invokes one blessing upon you, Allah will invoke upon him ten blessings the like thereof; and whosoever invokes a single blessing upon you, Allah will record for him ten good deeds, efface ten bad deeds, and raise him by ten spiritual degrees.'[133]

There are numerous *ḥadīth* reports that speak of Allah invoking ten blessings upon anyone who invokes a single blessing upon the Emissary of Allah (Allah bless him and give him peace), narrated by Muslim and others. Qāḍī Abū ʿAbdullāh al-Bilālī said, 'Know that a blessing from Allah is a mercy, and for whoever Allah gives a single portion of mercy, it will be better for him than the world and all it contains. What, then, is one to say about a person who receives ten mercies? How many afflictions and tribulations are averted because of them, and how many subtle graces and blessings are obtained by virtue of their blessings!'

Shaykh Ibn ʿAṭāʾ Allāh (Allah be pleased with him) said, 'Whover invokes a single blessing upon the Prophet, Allah will suffice him for his worldly and Afterworldly concerns; so how much more for the one who invokes ten blessings upon him!'

Ibn Shāfiʿ said:

> The Prophet's eminence is so vast that the one who invokes blessings upon him receives this immense portion; for when would you receive blessings from Allah upon you otherwise? Had you spent your entire life performing every act of obedience, and had Allah then sent upon you a single blessing, that single blessing would outweigh all of the [acts of] obedience you performed throughout your entire life! That is because you invoke blessings [upon the Prophet (Allah bless him and give him peace)] according to your capacity, but Allah sends blessings upon him according to His Lordship—and this is speaking of a single

132 Aḥmad.
133 Ibid.

blessing, so what can one say if Allah sends ten blessings upon you for every blessing that you invoke?

Regarding the meaning of the couplet, the author is saying that he never sought wealth in this world or the Hereafter from the Prophet's hands—in other words, he never sought through the Prophet (Allah bless him and give him peace) to be granted well-being through having sufficient wealth in this world and safety from illnesses and afflictions, and never sought through him wealth in the Hereafter by having immense reward and the pleasure of the Majestic King—save that he received it and procured it, and it reached him from the best hand that gives: the hand of the Prophet (Allah bless him and give him peace). Because he received those things by virtue of the Prophet (Allah bless him and give him peace) and by seeking a means of approach through him, the author describes them as if they were from the Prophet; and since blessings are usually received in the hand, the author says *from his hand* figuratively and means that he received them from the Prophet. In speaking about what he obtained the author uses the word *istilām*, which is used figuratively to describe receiving, and he states that the blessing and generosity he received as largesse was taken from the *best of givers*, meaning from the Prophet's noble hand.

لَا تُنْكِرِ الْوَحْيَ مِنْ رُؤْيَاهُ إِنَّ لَهُ   قَلْبًا إِذَا نَامَتِ الْعَيْنَانِ لَمْ يَنَمِ

Do not deny the revelations he received in his dreams;
For though his eyes slept, he had a heart that slept not.

After speaking about the miracle of the splitting of the Prophet's chest the author mentions what came about as a result of it, namely the Prophet's purification and his being readied for the descent of divine lights and revelation. Consequently, it was not possible for him to be overcome with sleep. So the author (Allah have mercy upon him) addresses those who can understand, and essentially says: Do not deny the revelations the Prophet (Allah bless him and give him peace) received from his dreams, for his heart is awake even when his eyes are sleeping.

It is related in the *Ṣaḥīḥ* [of al-Bukhārī] that ʿĀʾisha (Allah be pleased with her) asked, 'O Emissary of Allah, do you go to sleep before performing the *witr* prayer?' He replied, "ʿĀʾisha, my eyes sleep but my heart does not sleep.' When the Prophet (Allah bless him and give him peace) was asleep, no one would wake him up before he woke on his own, because they did not know the state he would be in at that time. It is stated in a *ḥadīth* report that 'The dreams of the Prophets are revelation.'[134]

Know that dreams are the comprehension of a reality and they constitute a true form of knowledge. The state that a person is in remains with him in wakefulness or in sleep, so if his state is one of confusion and idle play with others it will be reflected in his dreams; and if his wakeful state is one of knowledge and actualisation (*taḥqīq*), that will be reflected in his dreams, and the angel in charge over dreams will instruct him with things that reflect his actualisation. Dreams, therefore, are closer to the truth because they are received through the medium of an angel, and the angel possesses naught but the truth; hence true dreams are a portion of prophethood because it is the angel who instructs one through them. For this reason, dreams are considered glad tidings, as they are news that the angel brings from Allah Most High. The reason why the dreams of some people are untrue is that heedlessness overwhelms them and they are engrossed in the appetites of their stomachs and private parts, so when they sleep they are inundated by their passions and see nothing, much like someone who is confused or in a drunken stupor.

As for the state of the Prophet (Allah bless him and give him peace), outwardly he is human and inwardly he is angelic, so in all of his states he is upon truth and realisation, and with the Angel [Jibrīl] on every path. Regarding the incident in the valley pass when the Prophet (Allah bless him and give him peace) slept past the Morning Prayer—which according to Ibn al-ʿArabī [al-Mālikī] happened several times—the answer to it is from many angles. Firstly, the Prophet's statement 'My eyes sleep, but my heart does not sleep' means that it was his predominant state, and this incident was a rare occurrence in which Allah (the Glorified) caused him to remain asleep past the prayer, willing that the Prophet (Allah bless him and give him peace) explain the *sunna* in that situation. This is proven by the *ḥadīth* of al-ʿAlāʾ, who reported that the Prophet (Allah bless him and give him peace) said, 'Had Allah willed He would have woken us, but He willed that this be a practice (*sunna*) for those who come after you.' And

134 Hakim, *al-Mustadrak*.

this is why Ibn ᶜAbbās has said, 'I would not be happy to possess the world and all that it contains in exchange for praying the Morning Prayer *(Fajr)* with the Emissary of Allah (Allah bless him and give him peace) after the sunrise!' This is a great dispensation that Allah has taught us, for someone who sleeps past the time of prayer is not guilty of sin.

Secondly, the rising of the sun can only be perceived by eyesight, which is taken during sleep, while the heart does not perceive the rising of the sun even when it is awake. The heart only perceives the spiritual realm (*ᶜĀlam al-Malakūt*).

Thirdly, the meaning of the Prophet's statement 'but my heart does not sleep' is that it does not sleep because it is receiving revelation at that time. So his heart could be busy hearing the revelation and understanding it from Allah Most High and thus unable to look elsewhere and engage [with the outside world] at the same time. Allah Most High knows best.

It is recorded in a rigorously authenticated *ḥadīth* that 'a righteous person's dream is one of forty-six parts of prophethood.'[135] This means that the Prophet (Allah bless him and give him peace) received revelation for twenty-three years, and for six months of that period, before the Angel [Jibrīl] descended, he would see dreams that would appear as the breaking of dawn—as stated in a *ḥadīth*.[136] Six months in relation to twenty-three years is one forty-sixth part, and hence, righteous dreams formed one of forty-six parts of prophethood in their soundness and truthfulness. All the same, a revealed text [a verse of Qur'an or a *ḥadīth*] is required in order to ascertain if the Prophet (Allah bless him and give him peace) had in fact received true dreams for a six-month period prior to the appearance of the Angel.

Furthermore, another narration states that 'a righteous person's dream is one of seventy parts of prophethood'; another narration says 'one of forty parts of prophethood'; and yet another says 'one in forty-five parts of prophethood.' The correct response to reconcile these narrations was indicated by al-Ṭabarī, who remarked that these discrepancies are with respect to the various states of the dreamers concerned. The righteous believer's dream is one of forty-six parts (and sometimes one of forty

135 Bukhārī.
136 Ibid.

parts) and the corrupt sinner's dream is one of seventy parts, others being situated between these two according to their respective states. Al-Ṭabarī said, 'And for this reason the Prophet (Allah bless him and give him peace) said in the narration about seventy parts "the righteous dream (*al-ruʾya al-ṣāliḥa*)" and did not say "from a righteous person." It is not a condition that the one seeing the dream be righteous.' [Qāḍī] ʿIyāḍ (Allah have mercy upon him) said in response to this:

> It is said that dreams are guides and that the forms of guidance contained in dreams are sometimes subtle and sometimes clear. So when [the Prophet (Allah bless him and give him peace)] mentioned the seventy parts he meant subtle [guidance]; and when he mentioned the forty or forty-six parts he meant clear [guidance]. It is also said that a dream is one of forty-six parts [of prophethood] for him who is of those who perform complete ablutions when ablutions are difficult [i.e., during extreme cold] and who are patient during difficulties, and who wait after one prayer for the next. Accordingly, a person's dream will be between seventy and forty parts of prophethood, and not less than forty.

The upshot of this, on the basis of the various narrations, is that the relation of a dream to revelation is with respect to its truthfulness and soundness, which in turn depend on the condition of the dreamer. Allah Most High knows best.

وَذَاكَ حِينَ بُلُوغٍ مِنْ نُبُوَّتِهِ فَلَيْسَ يُنْكَرُ فِيهِ حَالُ مُحْتَلِمِ

That was when he attained his Prophetic status;
the night dreams of mature men cannot be denied!

The author (Allah have mercy upon him) says that the veracity of the above-mentioned Revelation, which the Prophet (Allah bless him and give him peace) received in the form of dreams, was undeniable since they appeared [as clear] as day. He would see these dreams at the beginning of the process of Revelation as well as when he reached the pinnacle of his prophecy; all of which were the precursors of Revelation and glad tidings. In this couplet the author (Allah have mercy upon him) employs a double entendre, and says that the Prophet's dreams took place when he attained prophethood, and that they were a sign of his prophethood just as *iḥtilām* (nocturnal emission) happens when one has attained manhood and is a sign of his maturity. So owing to the soundness of the sign of his prophethood he should not be denied.

Ibn Isḥāq said:

> When Allah willed to honour him with prophethood, the Emissary of Allah (Allah bless him and give him peace), when going out for a need, would head out to where he could no longer see the outlines of houses, and would go towards the mountain passes and valleys of Mecca. The Emissary of Allah (Allah bless him and give him peace) passed by no stone or tree without it calling out to him, 'Peace be upon you, O Emissary of Allah!' On hearing this, the Emissary of Allah (Allah bless him and give him peace) would look around him, to his right and to his left, behind him and in front of him, but see nothing there but trees. The Emissary of Allah (Allah bless him and give him peace) remained in this state, seeing and hearing, for as long as Allah willed. Then, one Ramaḍān as he was inside the cave of Ḥirā', the Angel Jibrīl (upon whom be peace) came to him with revelation by Allah's generosity.

تَبَارَكَ اللّٰهُ مَا وَحْيٌ بِمُكْتَسَبٍ   وَلَا نَبِيٌّ عَلَىٰ غَيْبٍ بِمُتَّهَمِ

Blessed is Allah! Revelation is not something acquired!
Nor can a Prophet's knowledge of the Unseen be deemed suspect.

The author (Allah have mercy upon him) prefaced his statement by saying *Blessed is Allah*. This is similar to the words of the Prophet (Allah bless him and give him peace), 'Glorified is Allah—the believer is never impure!'[137] It also expresses astonishment (*taʿajjub*) at the statement of one who claims that this noble station can be acquired and gained through personal effort. Then the author opens with the statement *Revelation is not something acquired,* that is, it is not obtained through acquisition or stratagems; it comes only through the unique bestowal of the Great and Exalted One. 'He selects for His mercy whom He wills' and does in His kingdom as He wishes.

The position of the people of Islam [Muslims] is that prophethood is not acquired. This [couplet] is a refutation of the philosophers who maintained that divine revelation could be had through personal effort.

137 Ibid.

This is utterly false, because Allah (Glorified is He) is free from needing His creation. He is neither benefited by obedience nor harmed by disobedience, yet He bestows His favours upon whomever He wills of His servants. Allah Most High said about the Emissaries, '*We are but men like you, but Allah bestows His favour on whomever He wills of His servants.*' (Qur'an 14:11) Allah Most High has also said, '*Say, "I am but a man like yourselves, to whom it is revealed that your God is but one God…"*' (Qur'an 18:110) There are many other verses to that effect.

As for sainthood [*wilāya*], some scholars maintain that it is obtained through works and spiritual struggle—meaning that Allah creates those things within a person and strengthens him with them till he attains what Allah apportioned for him in pre-eternity. This is the station of spiritual wayfaring (*sulūk*) and the rank of spiritual wayfarers. As for those who are enraptured (*al-majdhūbūn*), the path of wayfaring is folded up for them, and they attain [unto the divine] purely through Lordly concern.

Then the author says, *Nor can a Prophet's knowledge of the Unseen be deemed suspect*. By *the Unseen* he means revelation and news from the heavens that is hidden from the inhabitants of the earth. In other words, it is not possible to hold a Prophet suspect regarding the revelation and unseen news that he brings—by accusing him of subtracting or adding to it, or saying something from his own opinion—because it is necessary that a Prophet have complete trustworthiness and be divinely protected from error. Allah Most High says about our Prophet (Allah bless him and give him peace), '*And he is not a withholder of [knowledge of] the Unseen.*' (Qur'an 81:24) This means he is not held suspect. Allah Most High also says, '*And he does not speak from selfish desire; it is but a revelation revealed.*' (Qur'an 53:3–4) The link between this couplet and the previous couplet is obvious; and Allah Most High knows best.

كَمْ أَبْـرَأَتْ وَصِبـًا بِاللَّمْسِ رَاحَـتُـهُ   وَأَطْـلَـقَـتْ أَرِبـًا مِـنْ رِبْـقَـةِ اللَّـمَـمِ

How many sick people were healed by the touch of his hand;
how many released from the tight knots of madness!

The author (Allah have mercy upon him) is essentially saying: 'On numerous occasions the Prophet (Allah bless him and give him peace) placed his blessed hand on those suffering from sicknesses and debilitating illnesses, and they would experience instant healing by his blessings (Allah bless him and give him peace); and on numerous occasions the Prophet (Allah bless him and give him peace) set free and unfettered those suffering from madness, removing what had afflicted them.'

The author ascribes this to [the Prophet's] hand figuratively; what he intends is that Allah willed to heal them through the means of the Prophet's hand, and restore sanity by means of the Prophet's touch. This may be likened to Allah's words, '*Until they made you forget Our remembrance.*' (Qur'an 23:110) This means 'until you forgot—because of them—My remembrance.'

The word *knot* is a metaphor for madness because when a person is afflicted by jinn possession, it is as if he were fettered and bound by the jinn, and thus akin to someone tied up. So when that person is released from the grip of madness it is as if he were unfettered and released from bondage.

In the first line of this couplet the author alludes to the narrations that tell how, when the Prophet (Allah bless him and give him peace) passed his noble and blessed hand over a sick person, Allah would heal that person and restore his health. That was one of the inimitable miracles of the Prophet (Allah bless him and give him peace). An example of this is mentioned by [Qāḍī] ʿIyāḍ (Allah be pleased with him), who cited [a report] that the Prophet (Allah bless him and give him peace) placed his hand upon the head of Ḥanẓala b. Ḥazīm and blessed him. A man was brought to Ḥanẓala whose face had swollen, and a sheep whose udders had swollen. They were placed on the spot where the Prophet's hand had touched, and the swelling went down.

The Prophet (Allah bless him and give him peace) touched the head of a young boy who was suffering a [scalp] ailment, and the boy's hair grew out evenly.

Shurayḥīl al-Jaʿfī had a large cyst on his hand that prevented him from gripping his sword and the reins of his horse. He complained about this to the Prophet (Allah bless him and give him peace), and the Prophet continued pressing and rubbing the cyst with his hand until he had removed it, leaving behind no trace of it at all.[138]

138 Bayhaqī, *Dalāʾil al-nubuwwa*.

It is related that during the Battle of Uḥud, Qatāda b. al-Nuʿmān sustained an injury to one of his eyes, causing it to come out of its socket and dangle upon his cheek. The Prophet (Allah bless him and give him peace) pushed it back [into the socket] and it became Qatāda's stronger eye.[139]

Al-Nasāʾī narrated from ʿUthmān b. Ḥunayf that a blind man said to the Emissary of Allah, 'Pray to Allah that he restore my sight!' The Prophet said, 'Go and perform ablutions, [then come to the Mosque, perform two units of prayer] and say "O Allah, I ask You, and turn to You through our Prophet Muḥammad, the Prophet of Mercy. O Muḥammad, I turn through you to my Lord that He restore my sight. O Allah, grant him intercession for me."' He [ʿUthmān b. Ḥunayf] said, 'And soon thereafter Allah restored his sight.'

In the second line of this couplet the author alludes to the narration of the Prophet (Allah bless him and give him peace), reported by Ibn ʿAbbās (Allah be pleased with him and his father) who said, 'A woman came to the Emissary of Allah with a son of hers who had been possessed by a jinn. The Emissary of Allah rubbed the boy's chest, and the boy let out a sound like a bleating sheep; and a small black figure like a dog came out of him and scurried away.'[140]

It is related on the authority of Ṭāwūs that whenever the Prophet (Allah bless him and give him peace) was brought someone touched by madness and jinn possession, he would touch their chests and the madness and possession would leave them. It is related in the *Ṣaḥīḥ* [of al-Bukhārī] that a woman suffering from epilepsy came to the Prophet (Allah bless him and give him peace) and pleaded, 'O Emissary of Allah, invoke Allah for me!' He said to her, 'If you wish you can be patient and the Garden of Paradise is yours; and if you wish I can invoke Allah [to cure you].' She chose to be patient and enter Paradise, and then said, 'O Emissary of Allah, [when I experience seizures] my nakedness is exposed;' so he prayed to Allah, asking Him that she not be uncovered, and his prayer was answered. Incidents of this nature are many and well-known. Whoever would like healing in this regard should refer to the *Shifāʾ*.

139 Abū Nuʿaym, *Dalāʾil al-nubuwwa*.

140 Aḥmad.

وَأَحْيَتِ السَّنَةَ الشَّهْبَاءَ دَعْوَتُهُ حَتَّىٰ حَكَتْ غُرَّةً فِي الْأَعْصُرِ الدُّهُمِ

His supplication brought life to a grey year [of drought] –
Marked it out from dark years like [a horse's] white blaze.

In this couplet the author (Allah have mercy upon him) alludes to the miracle of the Prophet's supplications being answered when he prayed for rain. There is no doubt that the Prophet's supplications were answered when he prayed for rain and other things. Accounts of his praying for rain are numerous and repeated throughout the authentic *ḥadīth* collections. In [the *Ṣaḥīḥ* of] al-Bukhārī, Masrūq related, 'We were with ʿAbdullāh b. Masʿūd and he said, "When the Prophet saw that the people [Quraysh] were turning away he supplicated, 'O Allah [give them] seven years like the years of Yūsuf,' and soon thereafter they were struck with a famine in which everything became barren, so much that they ate animals hides, carrion and other decaying animals. So famished they were that when one of them would look upwards to the sky he would see what appeared to be smoke. During this famine, Abū Sufyān went to the Prophet (Allah bless him and give him peace) and pleaded, 'Muḥammad, you command [people] to obey Allah and show filial piety, and your people are dying. Pray to Allah for them!' Then Allah revealed, '*So watch for the Day when the sky brings forth a visible smoke that covers the people; this is a painful torment. [They shall say,] "Our Lord, remove the torment from us; verily we are believers!" How shall there be a reminder for them when there has already come to them a clear Emissary? Then they turned away and said, "He is taught [by another] and is a madman!" [Then] We will remove the punishment a little, [and] you [rejecters] are returning [to your old ways]. On the Day We strike with the great assault; indeed We are vengeful!*' (Qur'an 44:10–16) The great assault was the battle of Badr. All of these—the smoke, the assault and the sign of the Byzantine victory [*Rūm*]—came to pass."'

Al-Bukhārī and Muslim both recorded in their rigorously authenticated collections on the authority of Anas (Allah be pleased with him) that: 'One Friday, as the Emissary of Allah was delivering a sermon, a man entered the mosque and faced him directly and said, "O Emissary of Allah, our wealth has suffered ruin and our families are starving and the paths have been severed. Supplicate to Allah that He send us rain!" So the Emissary of Allah raised his hands up in prayer and said thrice, "O Allah give us succour." By Allah, at that time we could not see a single still or wind-driven cloud, or anything in fact, and neither home nor hearth stood between us and the sky, when suddenly a large cloud shaped like a shield rose behind the Prophet. It continued to move upwards and spread larger until it began to rain. By Allah, we did not see the sun for an entire week. The next Friday, as the Emissary of Allah was delivering a sermon, another man entered the mosque from the same door as the man from the week before, and he stood before the Emissary of Allah and said, "O Emissary of Allah, our wealth has suffered ruin, our homes have been destroyed, and the paths have been cut off [by the immense rainfall]; supplicate to Allah to withhold the rain!" So the Emissary of Allah raised his hands up in prayer and said, "O Allah, on our outskirts and not upon us; on our hillocks and our low and high valleys, and on the roots of the trees!" After that supplication the rainclouds dispersed, and we went out and walked around in the sunlight.'[141]

The author alludes to this narration and its likes by saying, *His supplication brought life to a grey year*. The *grey year* is a reference to drought. A drought is described as grey because there is no rain and it results in crop failure. A dry and rainless year of drought when nothing grows is called a 'grey year' or a 'white year'.

The author's line *Marked it out from dark years like [a horse's] white blaze* means that people had sought refuge in the Emissary of Allah (Allah bless him and give him peace) when rains were withheld from them in that grey year, and so he supplicated for them. Allah, through the blessings of the Prophet's supplication, removed the affliction that had struck them. As a result of the Prophet's supplication, that grey year of drought was filled with beauty, fertility, resplendence and blessings, and when compared to the previous years of drought it stood out like the white blaze on a horse's brow.

The years of drought are described as dark because the Arabs are averse to blackness and dislike it. When they speak of difficult years they say 'It was a black year,' or 'They were black years.' They also say about a fertile year coming after years of drought, 'This year compared to the dark years is like a white blaze on a horse's brow.' And because blackness is

141 Bukhārī and Muslim.

disliked by Arabs, you will find that they seek a good omen by using the word white metonymously in its place. A poet said:

> Like charcoal, called white for a good omen;
> But the self knows what it really is.

The Arabs also dislike and are averse to dry spells because with them come straitened means and neediness. May Allah, out of His grace, grant us refuge from them!

بِعَارِضٍ جَادَ أَوْخِلْتَ الْبِطَاحَ بِهَا   سَيْبٌ مِنَ الْيَمِّ أَوْ سَيْلٌ مِنَ الْعَرِمِ

With generous rainclouds, so much that you would have thought
That the valleys flowed with sea water or the flood of ʿArim.

This couplet is a completion of the one before it. Here it is said that the life mentioned above—the greenery of the flora—was caused by the generous clouds that brought plentiful rains, and was so much, O listener, that you would have thought that the valleys were flowing with water from the sea or from the torrential rain that was sent against the people of Sabaʾ which caused their dam to burst. You might ask: 'But the flood of ʿArim was destructive, so how can it be used as a comparison here?' To this I reply: The simile applies only in respect of abundance, not destructiveness, since the intent here is hyperbole. And Allah Most High knows best.

لَمَّا شَكَتْ وَقْعَهُ الْبَطْحَاءُ قَالَ لَهُ   عَلَى الرُّبَا وَالْهِضَابِ انْهَلَّ وَانْسَجِمِ

فَأَدَّتِ الْأَرْضُ مِنْ رِزْقٍ أَمَانَتَهَا   بِإِذْنِ خَالِقِهَا لِلنَّاسِ وَالنَّعَمِ

وَأُلْبِسَتْ حُلَلًا مِنْ سُنْدُسٍ وَلَوَتْ   عَمَائِمًا بِرُؤُوسِ الْهَضْبِ وَالْأَكَمِ

فَالنَّخْلُ بَاسِقَةٌ تَجْلُو قَلَائِدَهَا   مِثْلَ الْبَهَارِ عَلَى الْأَبْصَارِ وَالْعَنَمِ

§ وَفَارَقَ النَّاسَ دَاءُ الْقَحْطِ وَانْبَعَثَتْ   إِلَى الْمَكَارِمِ نَفْسُ النِّكْسِ وَالْبَرِمِ

When the valley [Medina] complained of [its lack of rain]
He said, 'Pour down and flow over hillocks and mountains!'
The earth fulfilled its trust, bringing forth provision
For men and livestock by the permission of her Creator
She was adorned with a fine dress, and had wound

Turbans around her mountains and hills.
Lofty date-palms displayed themselves with necklaces,
Which dazzled the eye like yellow spice on the mountain.
When the drought's malady departed, the people,
Formerly weighed down and stingy, were freed up for virtues!

These five couplets (and the four couplets after them) are not found in many copies of the *Burda*, and have not been explained by many of the commentators. The Shaykh and polymath jurist Abū ᶜAbd Allāh b. Marzūq, said, 'The author of these lines was the Shaykh, jurist and man of letters, Abū al-Ḥasan ᶜAlī b. al-Jiyāb, who was the chief of the literati (*udabāʾ*) in Andalusia.'

He [Shaykh Abū al-Ḥasan ᶜAlī b. al-Jiyāb] alludes here to the complete story of the miracle of seeking rain, which is recorded in the rigorously authenticated *ḥadīth* collections. The wording used by al-Bukhārī, on the authority of Anas (Allah be pleased with him), reads: 'One Friday, as the Emissary of Allah was delivering a sermon, a man entered the mosque and faced him directly and said, "O Emissary of Allah, our wealth has suffered ruin and our families are starving; supplicate to Allah that He send us rain!" So the Emissary of Allah raised his hands up [in prayer]. At that time we did not see a single wind-driven cloud, but by Allah, no sooner had he lowered his hands than large mountainous clouds began to appear, and he remained upon his pulpit till I saw rain dripping down from his beard. We received rain that entire day, and the day after, and the day after—until the next Friday. One week later, that Bedouin (or another person) stood up and said, "O Emissary of Allah! Our homes have been destroyed by water, and our wealth has been ruined. Supplicate to Allah for us!" The Prophet raised his hands and supplicated, "O Allah, [let it rain] around us on our outskirts." No sooner had he pointed towards an area of dense cloud coverage, it split apart and dispersed, becoming like scattered seeds; and the valley floor, and the valley of Qanāt, flowed with water for one month, and no one came from any outlying area but spoke of plenty [thanks to the abundant rains].'

Another narration adds, 'He said, "On our hillocks and our low and high valleys, and on the roots of the trees!"'

In the first couplet the author (Allah have mercy upon him) alludes to the statement of the Bedouin who asked the Emissary of Allah (Allah bless him and give him peace) for the rain to stop when it became too much: 'O Emissary of Allah, our homes have been destroyed by water, and our wealth has been ruined...' He ascribes the complaint to the valley metaphorically, as if to say 'When the people of the valley complained of the withholding of rain.' It is also possible that it is used as the 'mute tongue of expression' (*lisān al-ḥāl*)—in other words, when the rainwater became so plentiful that the valley was nearly engulfed, the Emissary of Allah (Allah bless him and give him peace) said to the rain, 'Pour down atop hillocks and mountains.' The reason why these particular places were mentioned in the request is that heavy rainfall benefits them since they retain water and greenery grows upon them, and when mountains receive heavy rains their springs provide abundant water. Likewise, when hillocks receive heavy rains they produce abundant greenery. The above narration mentions the low valleys too, since abundant rainfall therein causes water to remain, and provides nourishment to the roots of trees.

The gnostic Ibn Abī Jamra (Allah be pleased with him) said about this *ḥadīth*:

> This *ḥadīth* contains the following lessons in jurisprudence. [Firstly] alleviation should not be sought from something injurious except in the amount that is ascertained to be harmful. In this context, that was the amount [of rain] that destroyed homes and drowned wealth (camels), since it causes them to become stuck in mud, and does not benefit them in the least. [On the other hand,] when desert areas receive rain they benefit greatly in their future and there is an increase in pastureland, water and other benefits.
>
> [Secondly,] in this *ḥadīth* there is proof that Allah (Glorified is He!) gave His Prophet (Allah bless him and give him peace) great perceptiveness and intuition regarding what is good.
>
> [Thirdly,] in [Anas'] statement 'No sooner had he pointed towards an area of dense cloud coverage, it split apart and dispersed' there is proof of the Prophet's tremendous miracles in that regard, as the clouds were subjected to him each time he pointed at them, and they submitted to his instruction without him needing to resort to speech. That is because the Prophet's speech is intimate discourse with the Real

[Allah], while his communication with the clouds was [merely] by pointing. Were it not that the clouds were ordered to obey him they would not have obeyed, because they move and float wherever and for however long they are commanded.

[Fourthly,] in [Anas'] saying 'large mountainous clouds appeared' there is proof of the immense power of the Majestic and Sovereign King. This is understood from the speed with which He created the giant clouds in such a short span of time, Exalted and Sublime is He!

[Fifthly,] this also proves the tremendous sanctity of the Prophet (Allah bless him and give him peace), as seen from the swiftness with which his request was granted.

[Sixthly,] this also proves that supplication (*duʿāʾ*) is one of the greatest means of goodness. This is taken from the speed at which the Prophet's supplication provided benefit. The Prophet (Allah bless him and give him peace) has said, 'He who is inspired to make supplication has the doors of providence opened for him.' This is why the Sufis say that supplication is goodness in and of itself, and that the fulfilment of need is but a side effect of it.

[Seventhly,] in [Anas] saying that they received rain from one Friday to the next there is proof that bestowal is proportionate to the sanctity of the intercessor. Since the intercessor here was the possessor of immense sanctity, the rains came down in succession until the people received the benefits they had sought after. This is why the Prophet (Allah bless him and give him peace) said, 'Your leaders are your intercessors, so consider well who will intercede on your behalf.' The Sufis say, 'Put your beloved before you in your request, and you will find what you seek.'

In the second couplet and the couplets after it, the author (Allah have mercy upon him) alludes to the benefits of those rains, and the usefulness of the torrents. He says that the rains, because they brought forth from the earth the provision that it retained as a trust—meaning the provision that it held—and because the earth safeguarded the provision by the permission of its Lord, it was like a faithful keeper of a trust. Allah Most High said, '*And We have sent down blessed rain from the heavens and made to grow thereby gardens and grains for harvest.*' (Qur'an 50:9) And Allah said to humans and livestock, '*Have they not seen that We drive water [in clouds] to barren land, and bring forth crops from which their livestock and they eat? So do they not see?'* (Qur'an 32:27)

The author's statement *She was adorned with a fine dress...* means the earth clothed itself in a variety of growth and appeared like finery, winding—that is, wrapping a turban or crown from the light of trees and various flowers—around the tops of mountains and hillocks. The growth that Allah causes to come forth out of the earth by means of rain is likened to green raiment that clothes the earth, and the light and radiance on the mountains and hillocks are likened to white turbans surrounding them.

Among the things that grow are date-palms, which is why [the author] then said *Lofty date-palms*—that is, tall date-palm trees which are spread out—*displayed themselves with necklaces* as a bride wears fine jewelled necklaces around her neck. Here the stalks that are attached to the date-palm are likened to jewelled necklaces around the neck of a bride that is adorned on her wedding, and these necklaces are like *bihār*, which is a plant that produces a sweet scent, and ᶜ*anam*, which is a tree that produces a red fruit. That is to say, these necklaces bring forth a fine scent and turn red that are like *bihār* and ᶜ*anam* in smell and in colour. This is the apparent meaning of the author's couplet; but to describe a date-palm tree as scented is questionable (though his description of dates as red is acknowledged).

So when the rains fell, abundant blessings were brought forth, and people were relieved of the drought's malady—meaning famine and hardship—by obtaining ease and plenty, they were free to acquire virtues, meaning the virtues of generosity and largesse, particularly those who were avaricious and weak and suffering despair (as the word *burum* here means one who is so weighed down by despair and sorrow that he is unable to keep company with others). Alternatively, this could refer to one who was afraid lest others ask him for something, as the Prophet (Allah bless him and give him peace) said, 'The stingy person is distant from Allah and distant from people, while the generous person is close to Allah and close to people, and distant from Hellfire.'[142]

142 Tirmidhī, *Sunan*.

§ إِذَا تَتَبَّعْتَ آيَاتِ النَّبِيِّ فَقَدْ   أَلْحَقْتَ مُنْفَخِمًا مِنْهَا بِمُنْفَخِمِ

If you follow the miracles of the Prophet
You will but add one splendour to another.

Here the author (Allah have mercy upon him) says: If you followed all of the Prophet's inimitable miracles (*muᶜjizāt*) and the breaks with normality (*khawāriq al-ᶜādāt*) that were manifested at his hands, you would find that all of them are magnificent and splendid. Some of his miracles pertained to the celestial realm, such as the splitting of the moon, the heavenly ascension, and the sending of rain; other miracles of his pertained to the terrestrial realm, such as his speaking to a lizard, gazelle and camel and other animals, as well his receiving greetings from stones and trees, and the flowing of water [from his blessed fingers], and the weeping of the date-palm trunk, and other miracles that occurred with inanimate objects; and accounts of them are many. Speaking on this, the author said in his *Hamziyya*:

> One of your miracles is the sheer inability
> To describe you, as your description defies enumeration.
> How can your nature be expressed in speech?
> Can a ladle ever scoop out the oceans' water?
> There is no limit to your description that I may seek,
> Though words have limits and ends.
> Truly your virtues are ever renewing like time itself,
> And your signs that we enumerate are but a single moment there-from.

Thus, if you carefully follow the signs of the Prophet (Allah bless him and give him peace) and add them all together, you will but add one splendour to another, as Allah Most High said about the miracles of our master Mūsā (upon whom be peace), '*And We showed them no sign but that it was greater than its like.*' (Qur'an 43:48) Allah Most High knows best.

قُلْ لِلْمُحَاوِلِ شَأْوًا فِي مَدَائِحِهِ   هِيَ الْمَوَاهِبُ لَمْ أَشْدُدْ لَهَا زِيَمِي

وَلَا تَقُلْ لِي بِمَاذَا نِلْتَ جَيِّدَهَا   فَمَا يُقَالُ لِفَضْلِ اللَّهِ ذَا بِكَمِ

§ لَوْلَا الْعِنَايَةُ كَانَ الْأَمْرُ فِيهِ عَلَى   حَدِّ السَّوَاءِ فَذُو نُطْقٍ كَذِي بِكَمِ

Tell the one who tries to outstrip my praises of him,
'They are gifts—I did not exert myself in their composition.'
Don't ask me, 'How have you obtained such excellent verse?'
No one says of Allah's grace, 'How much exactly?'
But for Allah's divine concern they would be the same,
and one with a voice would be like one who is mute.

Here the author (Allah have mercy upon him) says: Say, O listener, to anyone who tries to surpass and outdo my praises of the Prophet (Allah bless him and give him peace) that he has no hope of succeeding, because my panegyric verse is not within my power of acquisition and effort; it is simply a gift. I do not force it or exert myself in its composition. If it could be acquired with effort alone, one could simulate it and produce the like of it. Do not ask me, 'How have you gained such proficiency and skill and shown such rhetorical prowess in your praise of the Prophet (Allah bless him and give him peace)?' for Allah's grace is not dependent on any external causes that it might be enquired as to what they were—far exalted is the pre-eternal ruling above being linked to external causes and means! Were it not for Lordly care and the pre-eternal divine will, the vocal and the mute would be equal in [ability to] praise the Prophet (Allah bless him and give him peace).

What this means is that rationally, the act of praising the Prophet (Allah bless him and give him peace) can either exist or not exist, since it is a 'possibility' like every other act of obedience; therefore, one who has received pre-eternal divine concern is no different from a mute person in this regard. Allah Most High knows best.

CHAPTER SIX

The Nobility of the Qur'an and its Merit

دَعْنِي وَوَصْفِي آيَاتٍ لَهُ ظَهَرَتْ ظُهُورَ نَارِ الْقِرَىٰ لَيْلًا عَلَىٰ عَلَمِ

Let me describe to you the signs that were manifested for him,
Visible like the village beacons lit atop hills at night.

THE AUTHOR (Allah have mercy upon him) says: Let me describe these manifest signs and radiant proofs that demonstrate the Prophet's truthfulness. Here I give free rein to my expressiveness and loosen my tongue, and I delight in recounting the Prophet's clear and inimitable miracles and the brilliant proofs of his prophethood—proofs that have filled every horizon and gained renown, becoming as clear and as visible as village beacons lit atop mountains, establishing the truth and proving his veracity. Those who were decreed felicity in pre-eternity were guided aright through these miracles, while those who were destined for ruin were led away from them. We ask Allah, Glorified is He, to cause us to die loving this noble Prophet (Allah bless him and give him peace), and to unite us with him in the Abode of Blessing. Amen!

فَالدُّرُّ يَزْدَادُ حُسْنًا وَهْوَ مُنْتَظِمٌ وَلَيْسَ يَنْقُصُ قَدْرًا غَيْرَ مُنْتَظِمِ

Though a pearl is more lovely when strung [with others],
Its value is not diminished when alone and unstrung.

The author (Allah have mercy upon him) says: All the miracles of the Prophet (Allah bless him and give him peace) represent the epitome of glory and exquisiteness, and can be likened to pearls and rubies. There is no doubt that after a precious jewel has reached the peak of beauty and is strung together with other jewels it becomes even more beautiful and exquisite than it was when it was alone before being strung with others. The same may be said of the miracles of our Master (Allah bless him and give him peace): when arranged and strung together they are increased in beauty and exquisiteness, and they leave an indelible impression within the heart, and occupy a firm place within the soul.

Even if the miracles are mentioned in a disjoined and unarranged manner that does not decrease their value or diminish their rank or greatness, in the same way that a pearl or ruby is not diminished in value [when alone]; the same cannot be said for other commodities, for when they are gathered together and adorned they increase in value, and if they stand alone and disjoined their value diminishes. Allah Most High knows best.

فَمَا تَطَاوُلُ آمَالِ الْمَدِيحِ إِلَى مَا فِيهِ مِنْ كَرَمِ الْأَخْلَاقِ وَالشِّيَمِ

To what hope can the giver of praise aspire
Of doing justice to his noble qualities and traits?

The author (Allah have mercy upon him) says: Since it is impossible for anyone to describe the full extent of the Prophet's qualities or reach their limit, what hope does one have in actually attaining his qualities of character and adorning himself with his beautiful traits, given that he cannot reach them or even fully praise them despite his best efforts? How can one grasp the quality of the one about whom Allah Most High said, ascribing to him two of His own attributes: '*Full of Pity, Merciful*' (Qur'an 42:10)? Indeed, it is impossible, as the poet said:

If Allah—Majestic is His Might—has said about him
'Full of Pity' and 'Merciful' in His divine Speech.
Who, then, shall compete with revelation inimitable
Employing [mere] skill in poetry or prose?

Since it is the wont of every person who aspires to something to raise his head and outstretch his neck in pursuit of it, the author expresses that hope and ambition to praise, and uses the word *aspire*. He speaks of the giver of praise and the hope to which he aspires, as well as the longing he has to laud and extol this noble Prophet (Allah bless him and give him peace) and to gather his qualities together [in verse]. But then the author disapproves of him, casts the veil over him and shuts the door in his face; it is as if the author were saying to the giver of praise, 'How can you aspire to [do justice to] something that you are unable to enumerate and whose qualities you cannot encompass?' We quoted the couplets of Shaykh Ibn Juzayy [al-Kalbī] earlier, in commenting on the line *For the worth of Allah's Emissary has no limit, That could be expressed by a human mouth.*

آيَاتُ حَقٍّ مِنَ الرَّحْمَانِ مُحْدَثَةٌ   قَدِيمَةٌ صِفَةُ الْمَوْصُوفِ بِالْقِدَمِ

Signs of truth from the All-Merciful—revealed within time
Yet pre-eternal; the attribute of Him who is pre-eternal.

Because the author (Allah have mercy upon him) has said earlier *Let me describe to you the signs that were manifested for him*, and since he means by *signs* the miracles and signs of the Prophet (Allah bless him and give him peace) mentioned before, he informs us here that the greatest of those signs is the Magnificent Qur'an, for it is the Speech of Allah Most High and is one of His divine attributes that He revealed to the Prophet (Allah bless him and give him peace), and with which He sent him to mankind.

The miracles of the Qur'an cannot be limited to one thousand, or thousands, in number, because the Prophet (Allah bless him and give him peace) challenged others with [the inimitability of] its verses. The shortest chapter in the Qur'an is Sūrat al-Kawthar, and every verse in the Qur'an is considered an inimitable miracle in and of itself. Furthermore, as scholars have explained, each miraculous verse contains other miracles; so the author mentions this tremendous miracle—the Qur'an—in isolation and separately from the other signs. Some commentators opine that the word *signs* is an explanation of the earlier line *his noble qualities and traits*, and an allusion to the statement of ʿĀʾisha (Allah be pleased with her), 'His character was the Qur'an; he was pleased when Allah was pleased, and he was angered when Allah was angered.'[143] But this explanation is questionable, since the Magnificent Qur'an is not limited to character and proprieties: it also comprises knowledge of the ways of those in the past,

143 Bukhārī.

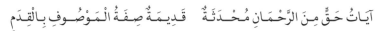

the stories of bygone nations, exhortations, pieces of wisdom, information about the realm of the Hereafter, and many other things—including this [the Prophet's character]. It seems as if the author [in composing this line] was motivated by the fact that the Qur'an was not mentioned amongst the Prophet's signs in the earlier couplet where he said *Let me describe to you the signs that manifested for him*, and seeing that the two were not connected, he needed to go out of his way and mention it here.

It is likely that the connection [between this couplet and the earlier couplet *Let me describe to you the signs that were manifested for him*] lies in the fact that when he said *Let me describe to you the signs*... he anticipated that a questioner would ask 'When describing these signs, do you include amongst them the Prophet's noble qualities of character?' So he responded by saying *To what hope can the giver of praise aspire*...? Then, after observing that no one can praise the Prophet (Allah bless him and give him peace) fully by mentioning all of his qualities, he mentions a proof in support of his contention and says that the Prophet was given the Magnificent Qur'an whose miracles are endless, and that it was one of many miracles vouchsafed to him.

The author says *Signs of truth*. This means that to him are vouchsafed true signs; his ascription of truth to the signs is a form of hyperbole, just as one can say 'a man of truth' and 'a man of justice' for someone who is known for his abundant truthfulness and justice.

From the All-Merciful means the verses were revealed from the All-Merciful (*al-Raḥmān*) because they are from His divine speech. When he says *revealed within time* (*muḥdatha*) he is referring to the verses' descent, as Allah Most High said, '*No fresh reminder comes to them from their Lord but they listen to it while they are at play*.' (Qur'an 21:2) And when he says *Yet pre-eternal* he is speaking in reference to the verses in and of themselves, since they are an attribute of Allah (Glorified and Exalted is He!), to Whom [alone] pre-eternality (*qidam*) is ascribed. The attribute of the Pre-Eternal is also pre-eternal.

Some have objected to the author's use of the expression *revealed within time* to describe the Qur'an, and have said that it gives a misleading impression. But it has been argued that the author removed any obscurity from the issue when he said *Yet pre-eternal; the attribute of Him who is pre-eternal*. The reason why the author composed this couplet in such a manner was to preserve the eloquence and expressiveness of the poem, as it is impossible for something to be both contingent and pre-eternal. By linking the verses to the All-Merciful, the author conveys the idea that they were revealed as a mercy to [His] servants. In addition, there is congruity and agreement with [this couplet] and the Qur'an in the verse '*No fresh reminder comes to them from their Lord but they listen to it while they are at play*.' Allah Most High knows best.

لَمْ تَقْتَرِنْ بِزَمَانٍ وَهْيَ تُخْبِرُنَا   عَنِ الْمَعَادِ وَعَنْ عَادٍ وَعَنْ إِرَمِ

They are not connected with time, yet they inform us
About the Resurrection, and about ʿĀd and Iram.

The author (Allah have mercy upon him) says that these verses—the verses of the Qur'an—are neither connected nor joined to time, because time is contingent (*ḥādith*) and the Qur'an is Allah's speech. Allah's speech is one of His attributes, and is pre-eternal because all of His attributes are pre-eternal, and therefore not connected to time or place. Nevertheless, the divine verses relate details of past and future events because those events are in Allah's knowledge, as is stated in the authentic *ḥadīth* according to which the Prophet (Allah bless him and give him peace) said, 'Verily Allah has revealed this Qur'an to command and forbid. In it He has revealed the ways of those in the past and similitudes that are struck. It contains news concerning you and news concerning those that will come after you. It contains decisions on matters that arise amongst you. It is not worn down by repetition, nor do its counsels ever expire, nor do its wonders ever cease. It is decisive and not a jest. Whoever quotes from it speaks the truth; whoever rules according to it acts justly; whoever acts upon it is rewarded; whoever holds firmly to it will be guided to a straight path; whoever seeks guidance from other than it will be led astray by Allah; and whoever judges by other than it will be broken by Allah. It is the wise reminder, the clear light, the straight path and Allah's powerful rope. It is a protection for those who hold fast to it, and a salvation for those who follow it. It contains no crookedness needing to be set aright, and no deviation that requires correction. The learned are never sated by it. Hearts are never misled by it. Tongues cannot confound it. When they heard it, the jinn said, "*Verily we have heard a marvellous recitation that guides to the right way, and so we have believed in it. And we shall associate naught with our Lord."* (Qur'an 72:1–2)'[144]

This *ḥadīth* encapsulates several of the benefits found in the Immense Qur'an. One of them, mentioned by the author, is that it contains news of the past and future—the Resurrection here referring to the future and Iram and ᶜĀd referring to the past. There is no doubt that the revealed verses have informed about the events that shall unfold on the Day of Resurrection, and have detailed the terrors and severities that it contains, as well as its delights and pleasures, all of which are inevitable. This is one of the examples of the Qur'an's inimitability (*iᶜjāz*), wherein it speaks of unseen realities and events that have yet to occur. There are several places where the Qur'an speaks about unseen realities that came to pass exactly as they had been described, such as the statements of the Most High '*You shall indeed enter the Inviolable Mosque, Allah willing, safely.*' (Qur'an 48:27), '*And they, after their defeat, will be victorious in a few years.*' (Qur'an 30:3–4) and His statement '*That He make it manifest over all other religions...*' (Qur'an 40:28). There are several examples like these.

Another example of the Qur'an's inimitability is that it tells of past events and bygone nations and mentions defunct earlier laws which only isolated scholars among the Christians and Jews had known about (and that in only single narratives). Yet the Prophet (Allah bless him and give him peace) related these matters accurately and in their exact wording, causing scholars to acknowledge the soundness and fidelity of what the Prophet related and to admit that such things were not acquired by learning.

The People of the Scripture knew that the Prophet (Allah bless him and give him peace) was unlettered and neither read nor wrote nor engaged in formal study and instruction. None of the People of the Scripture were unaware of the Prophet's state. In fact, many of them would ask him about these matters and soon thereafter revelation from the Qur'an would be sent down to him and he would recite it to them. Examples of this include the narratives of the past Prophets and their folk, and similar matters. For more on this, refer to *al-Shifā*. Allah Most High knows best.

144 Ahmad and Tirmidhī, *Sunan*.

The story of ʿĀd is mentioned repeatedly in the Immense Qur'an. It is reported that Allah (Glorified is He!) gave them bodily strength, authority in the lands and abundant wealth such as He had not given to any previous nation. But when they transgressed throughout the lands and sowed therein much corruption, Allah sent Prophet Hūd (upon whom be peace) to them. But they belied him and persisted stubbornly with their ways, so Allah withheld rains from them for three years. They were an agricultural and farming community in Northern Arabia, so when rains were withheld, resulting in severe shortages, Prophet Hūd instructed them to seek forgiveness and repent, and promised them that rains would come if they obeyed, as Allah informed in His statement '*O my people, seek your Lord's forgiveness and repent unto Him; then He will send down upon you rain in torrents and add strength to your strength.*' (Qur'an 11:52) The Prophet Nūḥ (upon whom be peace) did the same with his people before him, and they too refused. The people of Hūd (upon whom be peace) sent a group to Mecca to pray for rain, but once there they began to occupy themselves with idle play and wine-drinking, until one of their compatriots woke up and reminded them [of the purpose of their journey], whereupon they prayed for rain. There and then, Allah Most High sent a powerful wind to their land. When the people saw the dense cloud passing over their valleys they were overjoyed and said, 'This cloud has come to bring us rain!' The rain clouds were hovering over the area where they normally received rains, whence their delight upon seeing them in the area. Allah Most High said (it is also opined that it is a quotation from the Prophet Hūd) '*Nay, rather it is what you sought to hasten*' (Qur'an 46:24) in response to their challenge '*Then bring us what you promise, if what you say is true.*' (Qur'an 46:22). Allah [then said] '*A tempest in which there was a painful torment, destroying everything by the leave of its Lord. And naught was seen at morning save their dwellings.*' (Qur'an 46:24–25).

The tempest carried them and shattered their skulls and demolished their dwellings, leaving them a pile of rubble. It is reported that the gusts of wind entered through their mouths and exited through their anuses, and would sever their limbs one by one and lift them up into the sky despite the strength they had possessed. Ibn ʿAṭīyya related that the tempest struck all of the people there, both transgressors [and innocent], but that it would [only] carry away the transgressors. We seek refuge with

Allah from His displeasure and wrath! When a gust of wind blew, the Prophet (Allah bless him and give him peace) would say 'O Allah, make it winds, and not wind.'[145] That is because the word wind, when singular, refers to a punishment, but when used in the plural form it refers to mercy. Allah Most High knows best.

دَامَتْ لَدَيْنَا فَفَاقَتْ كُلَّ مُعْجِزَةٍ   مِنَ النَّبِيِّينَ إِذْ جَاءَتْ وَلَمْ تَدُمِ

They remained with us, thus surpassing every miracle
Of the other Prophets, which came but did not last.

Here the author (Allah have mercy upon him) says: The miracles of the previous Prophets and Emissaries, despite their abundant numbers, faded when those Prophets went away. Not so the inimitable miracles of the Qur'an and its dazzling signs and resplendent lights; they shall remain forever, preserved by Allah Most High. The Most Exalted and Sublime says, '*Verily We have revealed the Reminder, and verily We shall safeguard it.*' (Qur'an 15:9) The Prophet (Allah bless him and give him peace) said, 'There is no Prophet but he was given something by which people believed in him, and that which I have been given is revelation revealed to me by Allah; so among them I hope to have the most followers on the Day of Resurrection.'[146]

Indeed, the Qur'an is preserved until the Day of Resurrection. It is a penetrating proof. Its signs are dazzling. It is impossible to put forward objections to it. Throughout the ages there have been a multitude of rhetoricians and masters of eloquence and scholars well-versed in the Arabic language and fluent and articulate, many of them disbelievers eager to voice their opposition to the Qur'an. And yet not one of them was able to muster an effective refutation. Nay, by merely hearing it they were captivated by its splendour. Anyone who attempts to compete with it will come up with nothing but drivel that makes him a laughing-stock until the Day of Judgement.

If you retort 'But the Torah and the Gospel also remain still today', the answer is that Allah Most High did not reveal the Torah or the Gospel as inimitable miracles. He revealed them so that laws and rulings could be

145 Tabarani in *al-Muʿjam al-kabīr.*

146 Bukhārī and Muslim.

made clear—unlike the Qur'an, which Allah Most High revealed as an inimitable miracle in the arrangement of its expressions, and for clarifying legal rulings with its meanings. Within a single verse can be found inimitability as well as legal rulings, sciences and mystical secrets. May Allah give us a taste of the sweetness of its meanings and secrets. Amen.

Because Allah has taken it upon Himself to safeguard the Qur'an, it will remain preserved and protected till the Day of Resurrection – unlike the Torah, which Allah entrusted to the rabbis amongst the Jews, tasking them with its preservation. Allah Most High says, '*By it, the Prophets who had submitted had judged the Jews, as did the rabbis and scholars by that with which they were entrusted of the Book of Allah…*' (Qur'an 4:44) But they replaced and changed the scripture, and moved words from their proper places. This is why the author says *They remained with us*—meaning, they will not disppear so long as this world remains—*thus surpassing every miracle, Of the other Prophets*, which ended with the passing of those Prophets, and of which nothing remains but their narratives, and *which came but did not last*. The Mighty Qur'an, on the other hand, remains now as it was when first revealed, and likewise its legal rulings shall remain till the Day of Resurrection. And with Allah is enabling grace.

مُحَكَّمَاتٌ فَمَا تُبْقِينَ مِنْ شُبَهٍ   لِذِي شِقَاقٍ وَمَا تَبْغِينَ مِنْ حَكَمِ

Unequivocal verses leaving no doubt to remain in dissenters, and requiring no arbiter.

Here the author (Allah have mercy upon him) says: These verses of the Immense Qur'an are unequivocal (*muḥkamāt*)—that is, they are clear-cut and explicit, and no specious doubt, confusion or misgiving can remain for the opponent and obstinate dissenter, for their proofs and evidence are as Allah says, '*without doubt*.' (Qur'an 2:2)

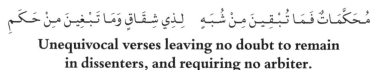

Alternatively, you can say that the expressions and meanings of the verses are masterful and wondrous (this is the interpretation given to the words of the Most High '*A Book whose verses have been perfected…*' (Qur'an 11:1)). The first meaning, however, is considered the stronger: that its verses leave no specious doubt to remain for a dissenter or opponent. That is because of the Qur'an's pristine clarity and the lucidity of its meanings and expressions, which have rendered eloquent speakers powerless and left those skilled in rhetoric utterly dumbfounded. Hence no specious argument remained for the opponent, and no misgiving remained for the doubtful; rather, they yielded and acknowledged this reality despite the intensity of their hatred and their keenness to belie it. Mankind is completely incapable of opposing it or producing the like of it. So he who is granted enabling grace is he for whom felicity has been decreed, and he who is wretched and envious is he for whom damnation has been decreed: '*Is, then, he against whom the decree of torment justly due [equal to him for whom felicity has been decreed?]. Would you, then, rescue one who is in Hellfire?*' (Qur'an 39:19)

The disbelievers who had reached the pinnacle of eloquence and rhetorical skill acknowledged that the Immense Qur'an cannot be the work of men or within creation's ability to produce. Its verses therefore left no specious doubt or misgiving to remain for the opponent. When [Walīd b.] Mughīra heard the Prophet (Allah bless him and give him peace) recite the verse '*Verily Allah enjoins justice and excellent conduct…*' (Qur'an 16:90), he said, 'By Allah, it contains a sweetness and elegance; its roots are deep and its branches are fruit-bearing. It is surely not the word of man.'[147]

One of the disbelievers said, after hearing someone recite the verse '*Then, when they despaired of him, they retired, conferring privately together*' (Qur'an 12:80): 'I testify that no created being is capable of producing the like of that!'

It is also related that ʿUmar b. al-Khaṭṭāb (Allah be pleased with him) was once at the mosque when he saw a man standing up and proclaiming the testimony [of faith]. When ʿUmar asked him who he was, the man informed him that he was one of the patriarchs of Byzantium and fluent in Arabic and other languages. The man told ʿUmar that he heard a man reciting a verse from the Qur'an. He said, 'I contemplated its meaning and realised that it mentions exactly what Allah revealed to ʿIsā son of Maryam concerning the conditions of this life and the Hereafter. The verse was Allah's statement "*And whoever obeys Allah and His Emissary and has reverential fear and mindfulness of Him, it is they who are the triumphant!*"' (Qur'an 24:52)

147 Ḥākim, *al-Mustadrak*.

Al-Aṣmaʿī once heard a slave-girl speak and, amazed at her, said, 'How eloquent you are!' She replied, 'Does any eloquence remain after the eloquence of Allah's words "*Suckle him; but when you fear for him, cast him in the river and fear and grieve not. We shall return him to you and make him one of the Emissaries*"?' (Qur'an 28:7) Indeed, in this verse Allah brings together two commands, two prohibitions, two predicates, and two glad tidings. There are many examples of this nature that are too lengthy to cite here; anyone who would like healing in this regard should refer to *al-Shifā'*. (I have quoted from it in full in my commentary on the *Hamziyya*.)

If you contend 'But how can [the author] assert that its verses leave no specious doubt for the wretched when it is found that many people of misguidance and error are characterised by such doubts, as well as arrogance?' the response is: In terms of what they deserve and merit, the verses leave no specious doubt. It is as if the author were saying: If the verses are considered on their own merit, there should be no doubt about them, so if anyone expresses doubts about them then it is only due to his own misguidance and lack of divine success (*tawfīq*]). As for the verses in and of themselves, there are no doubts about them, because their proofs are so lucid and clear, and their inimitability is so perfect and complete. That, then, is the meaning of Allah's words '*That is the Book in which there is no doubt*.' (Qur'an 2:2)

The author's statement *and requiring no arbiter* means these verses do not seek out a judge to decide between them and those who oppose and go against them. Rather, it is the verses that judge others. The Most High says, '*Shall I seek a judge besides Allah, when it is He who has sent down to you the Book, explained in detail?*' (Qur'an 6:114) This means: whose rulings have been explicated and detailed. The Most High also says, '*Verily it is a decisive statement, and it is not a trifling amusement*.' (Qur'an 86:14) And with Allah is [all] enabling grace.

مَا حُورِبَتْ قَطُّ إِلَّا عَادَ مِنْ حَرَبٍ أَعْدَى الْأَعَادِي إِلَيْهَا مُلْقِيَ السَّلَمِ

No implacable foe has attacked them
But that he retreated from battle and sued for peace.

Here the author (Allah have mercy upon him) says: No one has tried to oppose these noble verses and contend with them and claim the ability to produce the like thereof without then being forced to acknowledge his incapacity and turn on his heels; and anyone who was their implacable foe and unwavering in his opposition to them was forced to yield to them and admit his inability to go against them and to acknowledge the inimitability of their sheer eloquence. This admission, as a result, removed his obstinacy; and because of the clarity provided by the verses, his stubbornness was eliminated—except for the envier, for his envy and obstinacy endure even if he knows the truth, as it has been said:

> You may have hopes of any enmity being removed
> Save the enmity of him who hates you out of envy!

The fact that they are unable to resist the verses is unequivocal proof of the veracity of the Emissary of Allah (Allah bless him and give him peace), and a proof that they are indeed from Allah. That is because the opponents [of the verses] were adept at and proficient in the Arabic language, and were masters of eloquence; they were given what no other nation had been given, as Allah made linguistic skill a part of their natural disposition and aptitude, and a talent that made them the most eloquent of all nations. In their speech they would present the most astounding [expressions] and lawful magic. Eloquence was their forte and rhetorical force their unbridled skill.

While that was their condition, with eloquence as their ken, a noble Emissary (Allah bless him and give him peace) came to them with a mighty book: '*No falsehood can approach it from before or behind it; it is sent down by One All-Wise, All-Praiseworthy*.' (Qur'an 41:42). Its verses were perfected, its words detailed. It came to them in their own language, in which they would converse with one another, and came with eloquence, which was their own craft. Time and again it would call out to them loudly and challenge them publicly: '*Say, "Then bring ten chapters like it that are invented..."*' (Qur'an 11:13) Then it lowered the standard and challenged them to produce [only] one chapter, thus making it easier for the fabricator and inventor. It continued to thrash them with this challenge and condemn their false deities, while they were utterly incapable of mustering opposition to it, and were flummoxed and unable to produce anything like it. They were beguiling themselves when they said '*This is but magic from days of old. This is but the statement of a mere man*' (Qur'an

74:24–25); when they said '*This is but tales of the ancients!*' (Qur'an 6:25); and when they said '*Had we willed we could have said the like of this.*' (Qur'an 8:31). That was a mere claim on their part, so Allah told them that they will be unable [to produce anything like it]: '*Say: "Were the whole of mankind and the jinn to gather together to produce the like of this* Qur'an, *they would not be able to produce the like of it, even if they lent help and support to each other.*"' (Qur'an 17:88)

Those amongst their foolish ones who did attempt to produce something like it (such as the false prophet Musaylama al-Kadhdhāb) were exposed for all to see and brought nothing but folly that made them a laughing-stock till the Day of Resurrection. The majority [of the Arabs] yielded and acknowledged their inability [to produce anything like it].

It was not hidden from the masters of rhetoric and eloquence amongst them that the Qur'an was not in the same mode as their eloquence, and not from the same rhetorical mould as their speech. That is what was said when [Quraysh] assembled for the purpose of fomenting opposition [to the Prophet (Allah bless him and give him peace)]. It is related that when al-Walīd b. al-Mughīra heard the Prophet's words and his recitation of the Qur'an to him, he was affected by it. When Abū Jahl criticised him, al-Walīd said, 'By Allah, there is no one amongst you more knowledgeable about poetry than me. By Allah, what he recites does not resemble poetry in the least!'

In another report it is related that when Quraysh came together during the *Mawsim* festival, al-Walīd b. al-Mughīra said, 'Delegations of Arabs will come, so come to a common agreement about this man [Muḥammad (Allah bless him and give him peace)] so that none of you belie the other.' They replied, 'Let us say that he is a soothsayer.' Al-Walīd said, 'By Allah, he is no soothsayer, for he does not have the unintelligent murmuring and rhymed speech of a soothsayer.' They said, 'Then let us say that he is possessed.' Al-Walīd replied, 'No, he is not possessed, for he does not suffer the spasmodic movements and whispering of one possessed.' They said, 'Then let us say that he is a poet.' Al-Walīd replied, 'He is not a poet; we know poetry in all its forms and metres.' They said, 'Then let us say he is a sorcerer.' Al-Walīd replied, 'He is not a sorcerer, for he does not blow incantations or tie knots.' They said, 'So what shall we say about him?' Al-Walīd replied, 'You can say nothing of the suggestions mentioned except that I know they are untrue.' The nearest thing to the truth is for you to say that he is a sorcerer who [with his message] separates a man from his son and his brother and wife and kin.' After this meeting they parted ways and began to sit along the roadsides, warning people [against the Prophet (Allah bless him and give him peace)] Thereafter, Allah revealed about al-Walīd, '*Leave Me [to deal] with him whom I created alone*...' (Qur'an 74:11–26)

When he heard the Qur'an being recited, ʿUtba b. Rabīʿa said, 'O people, you all know very well that I have not left a single thing without studying it and knowing it. By Allah, I have heard a statement; by Allah, I have heard nothing like it before. It is neither poetry nor sorcery, nor is it the divination of a soothsayer!' Al-Naḍr b. al-Ḥārith expressed similar sentiments.

In the *ḥadīth* about Abū Dharr's embracing of Islam and his description of his brother Unays, Abū Dharr said, 'By Allah, I did not hear poetry from my brother Unays; indeed, he had defeated twelve of the poets of the Age of Ignorance.' Abū Dharr's brother went to Mecca and brought Abū Dharr information about the Prophet (Allah bless him and give him peace). Abū Dharr asked him, 'What are people saying?' Unays replied, 'They are saying that he is a poet and a soothsayer and sorcerer, but I have heard the words of soothsayers and it is not their words. I have compared it to the poetic metres, and no one has come, or ever will come, with the like thereof. Verily, he is truthful and they are liars!'[148]

Reports of this nature are many, so we will suffice with these. The author's statement *No implacable foe has attacked them* is a metaphor, in which war stands for opposition, and suing for peace stands for submission and retreat.

رَدَّتْ بَلَاغَتُهَا دَعْوَىٰ مُعَارِضِهَا رَدَّ الْغَيُورِ يَدَ الْجَانِي عَنِ الْحُرَمِ

Their sheer eloquence refutes the claim of their opponent,
As a jealous man wards off an assailant's hand from his wife.

Here the author (Allah have mercy upon him) says: Anyone who claims to refute the verses, or who attempts to refute them, will find that their sheer eloquence and rhetorical strength repudiates his claim and frustrates his effort, for the verses of the Qur'an represent the pinnacle of

148 Muslim.

eloquence and reached the degree of inimitability. Therefore, no one can muster strength to oppose these verses or produce anything like them. Those among the foolish ones of the Arabs who attempted such a futile endeavour were exposed and disgraced before all of creation. Allah stripped the eloquent Arabs and skilled rhetoricians of articulateness when standing before it. It was not hidden from the discerning amongst them that the eloquence of the Qur'an was not in the same mode as theirs and did not resemble the rhetorical mould of their speech. They [either] turned on their heels and fled from it or came to it submissively, and were [either] guided or astray.

Because of this, when [al-Walīd] b. al-Mughīra heard the Prophet (Allah bless him and give him peace) recite the verse '*Verily Allah enjoins justice and excellent conduct...*' (Qur'an 16:90), he said, 'By Allah, it contains a sweetness and elegance; its roots are deep and its branches are fruit-bearing. It is surely not the words of man.'

Abū ʿUbayd stated that a Bedouin Arab once heard a man recite the verse '*Proclaim openly that which you are commanded...*' (Qur'an 15:94), whereupon he prostrated. He said, 'I prostrated because of its sheer eloquence!'

Another man [amongst the disbelievers] heard someone recite the verse, '*Then, when they despaired of him, they retired, conferring privately together*' (Qur'an 12:80), whereupon he said, 'I testify that no created being is capable of producing the likes thereof!' (We mentioned this earlier.)

Scholars differ over how exactly the Qur'an is inimitable. Most maintain that the Qur'an's rhetorical force, eloquence of expressions, beautiful arrangement, succinctness and marvellous composition and style are such that it is not within the realm of human power, and that it is miraculous and beyond the ability of creation to replicate—like other miraculous breaks with normal phenomena, such as quickening the dead, transforming a staff into a serpent, pebbles glorifying, and so on. Shaykh Abū al-Ḥasan [al-Ashʿarī] held that producing the like of it does fall within the scope of human power and that Allah is capable of granting humans the ability to do so, but that He did not and it will not occur, and so Allah has prevented them and made them utterly incapable of doing it. (For example, a person may have the ability to speak, or the ability to stand,

and the Prophet (Allah bless him and give him peace) could say to him, 'My miracle is that you will be unable to speak', and thereupon he is unable to speak; or he could say, 'My miracle is that you will be unable to stand', and thereupon he is unable to stand although previously he was able to.)

That was the opinion of a number of his [Shaykh Abū al-Ḥasan al-Ashʿarī] companions. Others amongst them believed that it *was* within human capacity [to produce something like the Qur'an], but that the exigencies of the time diverted them from it. But this opinion is [to be] rejected, since it is proven that there were some who claimed to have produced, or attempted to produce, something similar to the Qur'an, such as Musaylama and his ilk. Thus there remain but the two aforementioned opinions, according to both of which the Arabs were incapable of [producing anything like the Qur'an]. To establish the proof against them by confronting them with something that is ostensibly in the realm of human power, and challenging them to replicate it, is a most decisive evidence and a far more intense way of making it inimitable and leaving an impression. Establishing the proof against them by challenging them to produce something [seemingly] within the power of humans is the most dazzling sign and most convincing of proofs.

In any case, they were unable to muster a response, and instead they were forced to endure hardship and killing, and swallowed the bitter drink of ignominy and humiliation. For more on this subject, refer to *al-Shifā'*.

The author then compares the refutation to the response of a protectively jealous man who violently wards off the hand of someone who wishes to trespass against his folk and violate them. He compares it to warding off by hand because crimes are usually committed by the hands. As for what has been recorded about those who countered, or attempted to counter, these verses, we have Ibn al-Muqaffaʿ, the most eloquent man of his time, who endeavoured to produce something similar to the Qur'an, but soon afterwards, as he was walking, he passed by a young boy who was reciting the verse '*And it was said, "O earth, swallow up thy water, and O sky, withhold [thy rain]!"*' (Qur'an 11:44). Thereupon he returned home and erased what he had written, saying 'I bear witness that this [Qur'an] cannot be opposed, and that it is not from the words of man!'

It is also related that Yaḥyā b. Ḥakam al-Ghazāl, the eloquent speaker of Andalusia in his time, tried something similar and looked at Sūra al-Ikhlāṣ and replicated it—or so he claimed, for how can a human being possibly [express] the majesty and perfection of divinity? It is said that soon afterwards he was overwhelmed by fear and dread that drove him to repent and mend his ways.

There are several stories of this nature. May Allah safeguard us from partaking in frivolity!

If you contemplate the words of the Most High '*And if you could but see when they are terrified but there is no escape...*' (Qur'an 34:51); and '*Repel [evil] by that which is better; thereupon the one whom between you and him is enmity will become as though he were a close friend.*' (Qur'an 41:34); and '*And it was said, "O earth, swallow up thy water..."*' (Qur'an 11:44); and '*So we seized each for his sin...*' (Qur'an 29:40)—if you contemplate these verses, it will become clear to you that each expression contains several threads and a multitude of points. This is the essence of [the Qur'an's] eloquence that dazzled the Arabs and rendered them unable to muster any opposition, and left hopelessly unable to bring forth the likes thereof. Thus opponents are left without hope or ability, and all praise belongs to Allah, the Lord of the Worlds!

لَهَا مَعَانٍ كَمَوْجِ الْبَحْرِ فِي مَدَدٍ وَفَوقَ جَوْهَرِهِ فِي الْحُسْنِ وَالْقِيَمِ

They contain meanings like the sea's bountiful waves,
And surpass the sea's jewels in beauty and value.

Here the author (Allah have mercy upon him) says: The meanings contained in the verses of the Qur'an are limitless and cannot be encompassed, and each of its expressions contains a multitude of sublime meanings, sciences and warnings, only some of which have filled volumes upon volumes—so much so that our master ʿAlī (Allah be pleased with him) has said, 'If I wished to fill one hundred camel-loads with exposition on the meanings of the Opening of the Book [Sūra al-Fātiḥa], I could do so.' The possessors of spiritual insight and hearts whom Allah has blessed with knowledge and understanding of His Book are bestowed with a deep grasp of it that cannot be delimited or enumerated; nevertheless, those of its meanings that escape them, and which only Allah and

His Emissary (Allah bless him and give him peace) know, are far greater and more numerous.

Al-Ḥasan has said, 'Allah has revealed one hundred and four scriptures. He deposited their sciences in four of them [that remained]: the Torah, the Gospel, the Psalms and the Criterion [the Qur'an]. Then he deposited the sciences of the first three in the Criterion.' Al-Shāfiʿī (Allah be pleased with him) said, 'Everything that the *Umma* says is a commentary upon the Sunna, and everything said in the Sunna is a commentary upon the Qur'an.' Someone else said, 'There is nothing near or far and no judgement that the Prophet (Allah bless him and give him peace) declared but its origin is found in the Qur'an.' Someone else said, 'There is nothing in the world except but is mentioned in the Qur'an.' He was asked, 'Where, then, is there mention of inns?' He replied, 'In the words of the Most High, "*And there is no sin upon you if you enter uninhabited houses.*"' (Qur'an 24:29) (The 'uninhabited house' can refer to an inn.) Someone else said, 'For one whom Allah Most High grants enabling grace, there is nothing but can be extrapolated from the Qur'an—even the age of Allah's Emissary (Allah bless him and give him peace), which was sixty-three. This is extrapolated from the end of Sūrat al-Munāfiqūn, since it is the sixty-third chapter, and is followed by Sūrat al-Taghābun (Mutual Loss and Gain), inasmuch as mutual loss became apparent on the day of the Prophet's passing.'

Someone else said, 'No one has encompassing knowledge of the Qur'an save its Speaker [Allah]. Apart from that which He preserved [exclusively] in His own divine knowledge, Allah has detailed its meanings to His Prophet (Allah bless him and give him peace), and that knowledge was later inherited by the bulk of the Prophet's Companions (Allah be pleased with all of them), even though there were disparities amongst them in its understanding (according to their degrees of knowledge). They include Abū Bakr, who was the most knowledgeable amongst them, and ʿAlī (may Allah ennoble his countenance), about whom the Prophet (Allah bless him and give him peace) said, 'I am the city of knowledge and ʿAlī is its gate.'[149] Ibn ʿAbbās (Allah be pleased with him) said, 'All of the exegesis that I have disclosed to you has come from none but ʿAlī (Allah be pleased with him).'

149 Ḥākim, *al-Mustadrak*.

They also include Ibn ᶜAbbās himself, about whom the Prophet (Allah bless him and give him peace) said, 'O Allah, grant him deep understanding of the religion and teach him the interpretation [of the Qur'an].'[150] And in another narration: 'and teach him wisdom.'[151] Ibn ᶜAbbās said, 'Had my hobbling cord [*ᶜiqāl*] been lost I would have found it in the Book of Allah.'

Most of this knowledge was later inherited by the Followers [*Tābiᶜūn*], after which aspirations began to weaken and were incapable of carrying all of the sciences and disciplines mastered by the *Salaf*, and so they arranged the Qur'an's sciences into distinct areas of study so that each group could systematise them. For the most part, each of these sciences was later set out in detail in distinct works, too numerous to count.

Some have said that the sciences of the Qur'an are 77,450 in number, which can then be multiplied by four, since each word in the Qur'an contains an outward *(ẓāhir)* meaning, an inward (*bāṭin*) meaning, a norm (*ḥadd*) and an anagoge (*maṭlaᶜ*).[152] Word pairs could also be added to this, but none of this can be encompassed by any save the Speaker [Allah]. Others have said, 'The Qur'an embraces knowledge of all things, since Allah Most High says "*We have neglected nothing in the Book.*"' (Qur'an 6:38)

As for sciences, you will not find any matter that it is not alluded to in the Qur'an. The Qur'an mentions the marvels of creation, the dominions of the heavens and the earth, what is contained in the higher celestial realms, and what is buried in the depths of the earth. It details the genesis of creation and the names of famous Prophets and well-known angels, and provides accounts of the bygone nations. It mentions the Prophet (Allah bless him and give him peace) and his expeditions and the events of his life up to the time of his passing, and also mentions his nation and what shall happen to them after him. It describes the beginning of man's creation and his death. It speaks of the portents of the Final Hour and the states that will be experienced in the intermediary realm (*barzakh*) and at the Resurrection, as well as Paradise and Hell. It demonstrates how one should present rational arguments according to the way of the debaters amongst the theologians. Indeed, it is full of syllogisms and rational conclusions, and even geometry and other disciplines too numerous to

150 Aḥmad.

151 Tirmidhī, *Sunan*.

152 Making the total number of sciences 309,800. [t]

mention here. Whoever empties his heart for the purpose of pondering deeply on the Qur'an will find this true—and with Allah is [all] enabling grace!

The author's comparison of [the Qur'an's] sublime meanings to the waves of the sea is beautiful; when a wave comes from the sea and is seen by an onlooker, he stares attentively at it, and no sooner does it come than another, even greater and more massive, follows in its wake, and so the onlooker looks on even more. The same may be said with regard to a single verse of the Qur'an: no sooner does a knowledgeable contemplative discover a meaning within it than another meaning comes to him that is greater than the one preceding it. That, of course, is in proportion to the degree of one's knowledge. These meanings that are disclosed, compared to those that are not disclosed, are but like a drop in the ocean. This is with respect to the erudite scholars who possess penetrating insight and expertise in the sciences and who have plunged into the depths of complex meanings and abstruse concepts; although it is quite possible that there may come someone who is more knowledgeable than them, who is granted more than them, and who discovers precious meanings and marvels that they were unaware of, for '*above every person of knowledge is one more knowledgable still*' (Qur'an 12:76).

The author compares the meanings derived from the verses of the Qur'an to the waves of the sea, in that they are bountiful and unending. So just as the waves of the sea roll in, one after the other, in succession without end, it is likewise with the sublime meanings contained in the verses of the Qur'an. They too are without limit or end, and no matter how far someone engrossed in knowledge may reach, he has no hope of ever encompassing the meanings contained therein, for there is no degree of understanding, no level of extrapolation, except that beyond it lies what is far greater (and what is hidden from the eminent scholars at the forefront in every discipline is even greater and more abundant). Allah confers His bounty upon whomever He wills.

If you ask: 'How can he compare the meanings of verses, which are not ephemeral, to waves of the sea which are?' I respond from two angles. The first angle is to say that the resemblance (*tashbīh*) is in abundance as such, even if it is true that 'the thing compared therewith' [the waves] is ephemeral. This is just like the words of the Most High '*They shall abide therein eternally, as long as the heavens and earth remain…'* (Qur'an 11:107) The dwelling [in Paradise] shall be eternal, while the heavens and the earth shall fade, so it is said that the point here is the import of the statement, not the actual duration [of the heavens and the earth]. The greatest 'abiding' in this world is reserved for the heavens and the earth, because we see that many bygone nations have passed and many generations have perished, one after the other, yet the heavens and the earth remain as they were when first created. So because of their lengthy existence, 'eternal abiding' is given as their length of duration.

The second angle is to say that what are intended by 'meanings' here are the meanings known to mankind—meanings known by the scholars of repute and the experts amongst the *Umma*—which have reached them and which they have understood. These, it is said, resemble the waves of the sea in abundance.

In saying that they surpass precious jewels in their beauty and value, the author means that the meanings that are extracted from the Qur'an surpass, in their beauty and value, the precious jewels that are extracted from the sea. The beauty of jewels is perceived through the physical senses, while the beauty of the Qur'an's meanings bring great delight to the one who listens to it and extracts benefits from it, and he finds great joy and delight when understanding the verses. Such a person attaches no value to jewels in comparison to this delight; indeed, some scholars would jump up and utter ecstatic words out of extreme joy at understanding an abstruse or recondite question in the Mighty Qur'an. Al-Zamakhsharī spoke along these lines when he said:

> My swaying to and fro in delight at solving a complexity
> Is more pleasurable to me than wine-bibbing!

If a seeker had acquired a piece of knowledge that he understood well and which expanded his breast, and was offered vast sums of money in return for him taking it out of himself and giving it to another (assuming that was within his power), he would not allow himself to hand it over, and would not offer it for sale even if the price were the entire world and all that it contains; for in his eyes the value of that piece of knowledge is far more to be treasured and its worth far nobler. May Allah, out of His bounty and largesse, allow us to taste the goodliest portion thereof!

فَمَا تُعَدُّ وَلَا تُحْصَىٰ عَجَائِبُهَا   وَلَا تُسَامُ عَلَى الإِكْثَارِ بِالسَّأَمِ

Their marvels can neither be counted nor numbered,
And frequent repetition never gives rise to tedium.

This couplet is a completion of what was expressed in the preceding couplet. Since the meanings of the Qur'anic verses and all the marvels and precious jewels they contain are limitless and akin, in their bountifulness, to the waves of the sea, how can their marvels possibly be counted or enumerated? As the *ḥadīth* mentioned earlier states, 'nor do its counsels ever expire, nor do its wonders ever cease…' The first line of this couplet, then, is a continuation of what was said in the couplet before it.

As for the second line in this couplet, it carries an added meaning since it informs us that the frequent recital of these verses does not cause weariness or tedium; rather, their frequent recitation engenders an increase in love and yearning for them. Other forms of lofty and metrical speech, though they might reach the apex of fluency and rhetorical beauty and be delivered with a wondrous melody and lovely tune that captures the hearts of the listeners, and though their sound might affect the soul and bring it to rapt attention, would still give rise to boredom and weariness if repeated again and again. Such speech can scarcely be repeated two or three times before people's inner constitutions discard it and grow weary of it and disdainful of hearing it, and its repetition becomes burdensome. The verses of the Mighty Book, on the other hand, are not worn out through frequent repetition, and their reiteration is not wearisome; the repetition of the verses only increases them in beauty and splendour, as stated [by Imam al-Qāsim b. Fīrruh al-Shāṭibī] in *Ḥirz al-amānī*[153]

[It is] the best companion: one never tires of its speech,
And its repletion only increases its beauty!

This, in fact, is one of the aspects of the Qur'an's inimitability, by which I mean that one who recites it never grows bored with it, and the listener never grows weary with it; rather, its frequent recitation increases one in sweetness, and its repetition engenders love for it, and it remains succulent and fresh.

153 *Ḥirz al-amānī wa Bulūgh al-tahānī*, also known as al-*Shāṭibīyya*, is a didactic poem on the canonical modes of Qur'anic recitation. [t]

قَرَّتْ بِهَا عَيْنُ قَارِيهَا فَقُلْتُ لَهُ لَقَدْ ظَفِرْتَ بِحَبْلِ اللهِ فَاعْتَصِمِ

They delighted the one who recited them, so I told him, 'You have the Rope of Allah, so hold fast to it!'

Here the author (Allah have mercy upon him) says: He who recited them was filled with delight—that is, he was filled with joy and happiness when reciting the verses—because of what he had gained, such as having his breast expanded and his heart illumined with their cautions and commands, and their prohibitions and exhortations and narratives, all of which led to an increase in faith and strengthening of certitude, in addition to the divine rewards that are given for each letter recited of the Qur'an: ten for each letter. The Prophet (Allah bless him and give him peace) said, 'I do not say that *Alif Lām Mīm* is one letter; rather, *Alif* is a letter, *Lām* is a letter and *Mīm* is a letter.'[154]

Furthermore, tranquillity descends when one recites the verses of the Qur'an, and one's home is illumined and the angels rejoice, as do the believers amongst the jinn and those who live in his home. Al-Bukhārī and Muslim both recorded in their rigorously authenticated collections, on the authority of Usayd b. Ḥuḍayr, who said that one night as he was reciting the Qur'an, 'I saw what appeared like a cloud containing lamps. It ascended in the sky until I could no longer see it, whereupon I went to the Emissary of Allah [and informed him]. He said, "Those were the angels listening to your recitation; had you continued reciting, people would have seen it and it would not have been concealed from them."'[155]

154 Tirmidhī, *Sunan*.

155 Shaykh Aḥmad Ibn ʿAjība relates this *ḥadīth* in its meaning and not its exact or full wording. The complete *ḥadīth* in *Ṣaḥīḥ al-Bukhārī* reads: 'It is reported that Usayd Ḥuḍayr said that while he was reciting Sūrat al-Baqara one night with his horse tethered beside him, the horse became agitated. As soon as he was silent, the horse became quiet, but when he recited again the horse became agitated once more. He fell silent and the horse became quiet. Then he recited again and the horse became agitated, so he stopped. His son Yaḥyā was near the horse and was afraid that it might step on him. When he moved him and looked towards the sky, he could not see it. In the morning, he told the Prophet (Allah bless him and give him peace), who said, "Recite, Ibn Ḥuḍayr! Recite, Ibn Ḥuḍayr!" He said, "O Emissary of Allah, I was afraid that it would trample on Yaḥyā since he was close to it. I lifted my head and went over to him, then I looked up to the sky and I saw what appeared like a cloud containing lamps. It ascended in the sky until I could no longer see it." He asked, "Do you know what it was?" "No", replied Usayd. "Those were the angels listening to your recitation; had you continued reciting, people would have seen it and it would not have been concealed from them."'

There is no doubt that a person who recites the Qur'an will have his heart filled with joy and his breast expanded by the rewards and recompense he receives for its recitation. His home will be illumined, and the angels and those residing in the home will experience delight and will supplicate for him. This is especially true if the reciter is granted understanding [of the verses], and is given the ability to act [on them], for then he will be told 'Indeed you have the Rope of Allah!' That is to say, 'Yours is the rope that allows one to reach the Sacred Way, and you have obtained the supreme means and guarantor of felicity and triumph with eternal bliss in the Hereafter; so hold fast to it and keep it firmly in your grip. Safeguard it and strive against your lower self by reciting the Qur'an and listening attentively to it and practicing the commands contained therein; for the Book of Allah Almighty is the clear light, the firm cord, the straight path, the light of hearts and the repose of souls. It is the expander of breasts and the key to felicity for those who hold fast to it. O Allah, expand our breasts with the Qur'an, and make it the verdant spring of our hearts, the light of our vision, and the remover of all our stresses and anxieties. This we ask You of Your largesse, O Most Merciful of the Merciful!

إِنْ تَتْلُهَا خِيفَةً مِنْ حَرِّ نَارِ لَظَىٰ   أَطْفَأْتَ نَارَ لَظَىٰ مِنْ وِرْدِهَا الشَّبِمِ

If you recite them out of fear of a blazing fire's heat
from their cool wells they will quench the blazing heat

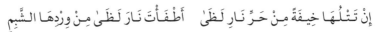

Here the author (Allah have mercy upon him) addresses all who can be addressed, and says: Reciter, if you recite these verses with a true intention and sound aim and then seek a means of approach [to Allah] by reciting them and turn to them out of fear of the blazing fire, you will have extinguished the fire's heat by the verses' cool water. This is a metaphor: as reciting the verses saves one from the heat of the blazing fire and protects one from its torment, it is as if they were cool water; and since they are a means of deliverance from the blazing fire, they assume the same position as one who extinguishes it. In any case, the fire of Hell is not actually put out, so what is meant here is that the reciter of the verses is saved from it and is not punished by it, so the verses, as far as he is concerned, are like swift mounts since he was not harmed by the fires of Hell.

It behoves the reciter to read the Qur'an in a measured pace whereby he is able to understand the verses and contemplate their meanings, for the outpouring of its meanings is proportionate to the degree of one's deliberation, tranquillity and contemplation. That is why Allah Most Exalted commanded His Prophet (Allah bless him and give him peace) to recite in a measured pace: '*And recite the* Qur'an *in a measured pace.*' (Qur'an 73:4) This verse means: Recite the Qur'an with a measured pace and with propriety and contemplation, for that is more conducive to presence, so the mind finds ample space to examine and understands its meanings. As for those who recite the Qur'an in a hurried and disorderly manner and fail to give each letter its correct pronunciation, they will never be able to contemplate and ponder its meanings. Our master ʿAlī (Allah be pleased with him) said, 'There is no good in a recitation devoid of contemplation, and there is no good in worship devoid of understanding the law therein.' Because of this, many of the *Salaf*, when they passed by a verse mentioning mercy or punishment, would repeat it again and again. It is related that al-Ḥasan al-Baṣrī spent an entire night standing in prayer and reciting Sūrat al-Nabaʾ, repeating it over and over while weeping.

Al-Alyūrī said:

> Our Shaykh, al-Ustādh Abū Sahl (Allah be pleased with him), said, 'In public teaching sessions there was a discussion in which invocation and recitation were compared and the question was asked which of the two is more beneficial and which leaves a deeper impact upon the heart. The Shaykhs amongst the Sufis enjoin invocation and prefer it to recitation because remembrances are oft-repeated, which they maintain leaves a deeper impact upon the heart. I spent a good portion of the night thinking about this and considering which of the two is more beneficial. I retired to my bed without coming to a reliable conclusion on the matter, and after I fell asleep I had a dream in which someone said, "Arise and sing!" "What shall I sing?" I replied. The person told me to sing:
>
> "When lovers are unable to meet
> There is no communication better than a book!"

'When I had awoken I said to myself, "That was a message from Allah to teach me that reciting His Book is the most meritorious act by which one can draw near to Him, and more beneficial than invocation." When morning came he recounted this in his public gathering.

كَأَنَّهَا الْحَوْضُ تَبْيَضُّ الْوُجُوهُ بِهِ   مِنَ الْعُصَاةِ وَقَدْ جَاءُوهُ كَالْحُمَمِ

Like the Pool, they brighten the faces of the sinful,
Though they had come to it as black as charcoal.

The author (Allah have mercy upon him) compares the verses of the Qur'an that are recited by the reader—verses which expand breasts and illuminate and brighten hearts after they were blackened—to the Pool (*Ḥawḍ*) which will brighten the faces of the disobedient folk against whom the divine Threat will be carried out, and who will come out from Hell by the intercession of Allah's Emissary (Allah bless him and give him peace). That intercession will be for the disobedient folk against whom the divine Threat was carried out, and who will come out [of Hell] blackened like charcoal.

The author is alluding to the *ḥadīth* recorded by al-Bukhārī and others, on the authority of Abū Saʿīd al-Khudrī (Allah be pleased with him), who related that the Prophet (Allah bless him and give him peace) said: 'When the inhabitants of Paradise enter Paradise, and the denizens of Hell enter Hell, Allah—Blessed and Exalted is He—will proclaim, "Bring out [of Hell] all who have faith in their hearts equal to the weight of a mustard seed." They will be brought out and will appear like scorched skeletons and turn into charcoal. Then they will be tossed into the River of Life and will grow like seeds in a silt left by a flood. Do you not see how they emerge, yellow and curved?'

However, as you can see, this *ḥadīth* only speaks about those who will be tossed into the River of Life. If by 'Pool' the author intends a limitless body of water which would include the River of Life, his statement here is uncontested; but if he means the Pool of Allah's Emissary (Allah bless him and give him peace) then he stands in need of a revealed text to support it. Allah Most High knows best.

The blackening of the hearts due to disobedience and the brightening of hearts due to recitation and obedience are both mentioned in the *ḥadīth* recorded by al-Tirmidhī and others, in which the Prophet (Allah bless him and give him peace) said, 'When a servant commits a sin a black spot is inscribed in his heart. If he expresses remorse and seeks forgiveness, his heart is polished, thereby removing the spot. But if the black spot continues to grow larger it will spread till it covers the entire heart. This is the 'stain' mentioned by Allah when He says "*Nay, that which they earned has brought a stain to their hearts.*"' (Qur'an 83:14)

It is obligatory to believe in the Pool. The Prophet (Allah bless him and give him peace) mentioned it by saying, 'My Pool is [as great as the distance] from Aden to Amman. It is cooler than ice and sweeter than honey. Whoever denies it today (in this life) will not take drink from it on that Day.'[156]

[Abū al-Walīd] al-Bājī was asked, 'Is it [the Pool] before or after the Traverse?' He replied, 'I do not know.' Abū Ḥāmid [al-Ghazālī] said, 'The Pool will be after the Traverse. Its quality is that it is cooler than ice and sweeter than honey. It is said that its extent is a month's journey and that its cups are as numerous as the stars. Whoever drinks from it shall never feel thirst again.' Abū Ḥāmid's opinion that the Pool comes after the Traverse runs counter to the position of the majority of scholars, and Allah Most High knows best.

وَكَالصِّرَاطِ وَكَالْمِيزَانِ مَعْدِلَةً فَالْقِسْطُ مِنْ غَيْرِهَا فِي النَّاسِ لَمْ يَقُمِ

Like the Traverse and like Scales in justice;
True justice amongst men cannot be upheld from any other source.

Here the author (Allah have mercy upon him) says that just as the verses of the Qur'an resemble the Pool in that they brighten and illumine faces, they also resemble the Traverse (*Ṣirāṭ*) and the Scales (*Mīzān*) in that they establish justice. Indeed, no justice has been established save through these verses, and the divine injunctions and prohibitions and duties imposed upon the servants [of Allah] are only known through them. From the verses of the Qur'an it is known what is lawful and prohibited. From them there is knowledge of the first and the last [nations], the first Scripture, and the ancient Revealed Books. Allah Most High says, '*We have neglected nothing in the Book.*' (Qur'an 6:38)

156 Aḥmad.

According to the Ahl al-Sunna (People of the Sunna), the Traverse and the Scale are both physical entities and belief in them is obligatory. As for the Traverse, mankind will be tested by crossing it, with some securing passage across it safe and sound, and others plunging to their destruction. Saʿīd b. Abī Hilāl said, 'It has reached us that the Traverse on the Day of Resurrection will be finer than a strand of hair for some people, while for others it will be wider than an expansive valley.' It is stated in a number of *ḥadīth* reports that the distance [across it] is three thousand years: one thousand years climbing it, one thousand years descending it and one thousand years traversing its flat portion. (Another version gives five hundred years for ascending, five hundred for descending and five hundred for traversing its flat portion).

People vary as to how rapidly they will be saved. The first group will cross it as fast as lightning; those who come after them will cross it as fast as the wind, followed by those who cross as fast as a bird, then others as fast as a swift steed, and others as fast as a man with a quick pace. All of these levels and degrees are according to [the measure of] their good deeds.

The Prophet (Allah bless him and give him peace) said, 'O Allah, grant safety, grant safety!' ʿĀʾisha (Allah be pleased with her) said, 'O Emissary of Allah, will a person remember his loved one on the Day of Resurrection?' He said to her, 'At three stages he will not: at the Traverse, at the Scales, and when the scrolls are folded up and placed in either left or right hands.'[157] This means that at those three stations one will be completely preoccupied. It is reported that Allah will order the Angel Jibrīl to stand upon the Traverse and not give anyone permission to cross it till he has asked them three questions: about his life and how he spent it; his youth and how he put it to use; and his wealth and from where he earned it and on what he spent it.

The author also compares the verses, in their justice and lack of injustice, to the Scales that will weigh actions on the Day of Resurrection. Indeed, anyone who confines himself to the verses of the Qur'an treads the Straight Path, and anyone who judges according to them is a just, fair and equitable ruler. According to the Ahl al-Sunna, the Scales are also a physical entity. According to the *ḥadīth* accounts, the Scales possess two scale-pans and a tongue, and will place the scrolls of good deeds in one

157 Aḥmad.

scale-pan and the scrolls of sinful deeds in the other, and then Allah will cause whichever side He wills to be heavy or light.

If you contend: 'But how can it be conceived that deeds are weighed when they are abstract entities (*maᶜānī*)?' the answer is from two angles: The first angle is to say that what is weighed are the scrolls and pages on which actions are recorded, as mentioned earlier. The second angle is to say that the conditions of the Hereafter represent a complete break from the normal patterns [of this world] and it is not inconceivable, therefore, that Allah should create light in the scale-pan of good deeds and create darkness in the scale-pan of sinful deeds —and that He knows [beforehand] which of the two will outweigh the other.

There is a third angle as well, and it is to say that the actions themselves will take on physical forms in the Hereafter. For it is reported that a man's actions will enter his grave with him, he will ask them 'Who are you?' and they will reply, 'We are your good deeds', or 'We are your evil deeds.'[158] Regarding the verse '*And his striving shall certainly be seen*' (Qur'an 53:40), some say it means that the person will see his striving in a physical form, perhaps whilst in his grave. It is related that the Prophet Dāwūd (upon whom be peace) once asked Allah Most High to show him the Scales. When Allah showed them to him, Dāwūd saw that they filled the entire expanse between the heavens and the earth, whereupon he fainted. When he woke up he said, 'My Lord, who can possibly fill such a thing?' Allah Most High replied, 'When I am pleased with My servant I will fill it even with [merely] an atom's weight [of goodness].' The *ḥadīth* [of the parchment [*biṭāqa*][159] corroborates this report.

By saying that true justice amongst men cannot be established from any other source, the author means that whoever seeks justice from anything other than the Qur'an will never be able to establish justice, and his judgements will never be upright. We have already cited the *ḥadīth* which says 'It is decisive and not a jest. Whoever quotes from it speaks the truth; whoever rules according to it acts justly; whoever acts upon it will be rewarded; whoever holds firmly to it will be guided to a straight path; whoever seeks guidance from other than it will be led astray by Allah...' Allah Most High knows best.

158 Aḥmad.
159 Ibid.

لَا تَعْجَبَنْ لِحَسُودٍ رَاحَ يُنْكِرُهَا تَجَاهُلًا وَهْوَ عَيْنُ الْحَاذِقِ الْفَهِمِ

Do not be amazed at an envious person who denies them
Feigning ignorance, though he has perception and understanding.

Here the author (Allah have mercy upon him) says: Do not be amazed, O addressee, at the obstinate envier who denies these verses after their inimitability has been made clear, and who is blinded to their beauties after their lights have dawned, and who—affecting ignorance and displaying jealousy even though he is perfectly intelligent and able to understand—accuses them of being the product of sorcery and divination, for envy prevents one from being fair. As Allah Most High says, '*We certainly know that you are grieved by what they say. Verily they do not belie you; rather, the wrongdoers deny the verses of Allah.*' (Qur'an 6:33) And Allah Most High says about the Jews, '*[Many of the People of the Scripture wish that they could turn you back into disbelievers after your faith], out of envy from themselves, even after the truth has become clear to them…*' (Qur'an 2:109)

The disbelievers knew unequivocally that the verses of the Qur'an were not in the same mode as their speech and that no one in creation was able to produce anything like them. This was acknowledged by most of their prominent speakers who were known for their eloquence and articulateness and giftedness in speech. Any of them who did not acknowledge this fact and instead concealed it did so by affecting ignorance, desiring to extinguish the light of Allah with his mouth; but Allah refuses except to complete His light and exalt the word of His Prophet, even though the idolaters hate it. They strove to deny [the Qur'an] and feign ignorance, and they said, '*If we wished, we could utter words the like thereof.*' (Qur'an 7:31) They also said, '*Do not listen to this Recitation!*' (Qur'an 41:26) as well as '*And in our ears there is a covering.*' (Qur'an 41:5)

They affected ignorance even though each of them was perfectly intelligent and capable of understanding, and each of them was fully cognisant of the Qur'an's meaning and aware that it was not from the mode of human speech. Their only motive for affecting ignorance was envy. Abū Jahl admitted as much when he said, 'We and Banū ʿAbd Manāf were both given nobility; they sacrificed [animals for the pilgrims] and we sacrificed as well; they provided food [for the pilgrims] and we provided food as well; they freed [slaves] and we freed some as well. But then, just as we were about to outstrip them, they proclaimed "There is a Prophet amongst us who receives revelation from the heavens." How can that be outdone? By Allah, we will never believe in him!'

قَدْ تُنْكِرُ الْعَيْنُ ضَوْءَ الشَّمْسِ مِنْ رَمَدٍ   وَيُنْكِرُ الْفَمُ طَعْمَ الْمَاءِ مِنْ سَقَمِ

For the eye, when inflamed, may be averse to the sun's light;
And the mouth, when ailing, may loathe water's taste.

The author brings this couplet as a validation of the previous couplet where he says one should not be amazed at the envious person who, feigning ignorance, denies the verses even though he is intelligent and possesses understanding. Essentially, he is saying that the absence of certain realities for a person suffering an ailment is not proof of their actual absence. Though a sick person cannot perceive what a healthy person can, it does not follow that the thing he is unable to perceive must not exist in actuality. Do you not see how the sun is utterly visible and how it provides many benefits for creation; yet an inflamed eye, because of its ailment and inability to benefit from it, may reject its light? The fault, therefore, is with the eye, not with the sun, and the eye's ailment can in no way detract from the reality of the sun's light. The same may be said with regard to sweet water: the mouth of a sick person might loathe its taste and find it bitter, but that is because of his sickness and not the sweet water. An example of this is found in the statement of the poet:

> He whose mouth is suffering owing to illness
> Will find fresh, sweet water bitter to taste.

And another poet said:

> How many detractors has Laylā, though they've not seen her face!
> [Their] denial says, 'What has already passed is enough for you.'

So just as an eye suffering from inflammation is averse to the light of the sun and experiences pain because of it, despite its visibility and utility to man, likewise an envious and obstinate person will deny these noble verses and their sublime meanings, transcendent eloquence and inimitable style, even though their beauty is plain to see and their miraculous style is evident. The one who feigns ignorance of these wonders does so only because of the sickness within his heart and his envy which is plain to see. So do not be astounded or amazed at such a person, for he is akin to an eye suffering inflammation, which is the closest comparison that can be made. Do you not see how an inflamed eye is averse to the light of the sun and abhors looking at it? That is because of the weakness of his eyesight and his dislike of looking at the light. His aversion to the sunlight in no way detracts from it, and in no way does it diminish or undermine the value of the sun.

A person who suffers from an ailment in his eyes may be likened to an envious and obstinate person who suffers from an ailment in his heart. Like the light of the sun for a person suffering an ailment of the eye, the beauty and light of the Qur'an's verses and the expansion they bring to the heart are in no way undermined by the sickness of the envier and his denial of them, and are not diminished or lessened in rank.

The author did not limit himself to a single simile; he followed this up with another, chiding the denier further and adding more clarity. He says: *And the mouth, when ailing, may loathe water's taste*; in this line, the author mentions the sickness that causes one to loathe the taste of water and deem it bitter (even though it is sweet) and compares it to the heart of a disbeliever that is sick with the disease of hypocrisy and disbelief, which lead it to detract and find fault with the noble verses—despite their beauty and the sublimity of their expressions and the expansiveness they bring to the heart. So just as none are prevented from tasting the sweetness of fresh water but those who are sick in body and taste, likewise none deny the beauty of the Qur'an's verses but those whose hearts are sick from the diseases of disbelief and hypocrisy. We ask Allah for safety, outwardly and inwardly. Amen!

CHAPTER 7

The Prophet's Miraculous Night Journey and Celestial Ascension ﷺ

يَا خَيْرَ مَنْ يَمَّمَ الْعَافُونَ سَاحَتَهُ   سَعْيًا وَفَوْقَ مُتُونِ الأَيْنُقِ الرُّسُمِ

O best of those to whose courtyard seekers turn to
Hastening on foot or the backs of strong camels!

AFTER DESCRIBING THE Prophet (Allah bless him and give him peace) and mentioning some of his miracles, the author (Allah have mercy upon him) employs a rhetorical shift and seeks a means of approach by calling upon him. He concludes his call by mentioning traits that will stir a noble person to respond. He says: *O best of those to whose courtyard seekers turn to, Hastening on foot or the backs of strong camels*. In this couplet, the author mentions those on foot before those who ride, in conformity with the order mentioned in the noble verse '*[And proclaim to mankind the pilgrimage.] They will come unto you on foot and on every lean camel; they will come from every deep ravine.*' (Qur'an 22:27) [He also mentions those on foot before those who ride] because the former receive greater rewards than the latter.

When the pilgrims come within sight of the Sacred House [the Prophet's Mosque of Medina] or the noble *Rawḍa*[160], they dismount from their animals and walk on foot, out of reverence for that exalted station and lofty place. When Abū al-Faḍl al-Jawharī journeyed to Medina and neared its houses, he climbed down off his mount and began to weep while singing the following lines:

160 Literally, 'the verdant garden of Paradise', which lies between the Prophet's home and his pulpit. [t]

When we saw the traces of the one who left our hearts
So enamoured that we couldn't recognise the traces or the bricks,
We dismounted and walked out of honour
For the one for whom we mounted beasts for travel.

And the author excelled in conveying this sense when he said in his *Hamziyya*:

You see caravans flying, out of extreme yearning,
In journey to Ṭayba [Medina], with loud voices
So it is as though the visitors were neither touched by harm
Nor made to undergo difficulties.
Every soul with its broken pleading and begging
And its supplication and longing and seeking.
And sighing so loud that you think
It is the regular tweeting of birds,
With perspiring bodies so filled with awe
It was as if they had bathed in sweat;
With faces so bashful that it was as though
Their complexions changed like chameleons;
With tears so profuse it was as though
They came from eyes of high and low hanging clouds

In the author's words, there is an allusion to visiting the Prophet's grave. Visiting the Prophet's grave is one of the most important of good deeds that draw one near [to Allah], and one of the most profitable of callings and most virtuous of pursuits. When one undertakes a journey to visit the Prophet (Allah bless him and give him peace), he should invoke copious blessings and salutations upon him. He should also intend to pray inside of the Prophet's Mosque and seek blessings from his *Rawḍa*, his pulpit, his grave, his place of sitting, and the places he touched and walked upon with his blessed feet, as well as the pillar that he used to lean on and where Jibrīl would come down to bring him divine revelation. One should also seek blessings from those who filled the mosque, amongst the Companions and the Followers (*Tābiʿūn*), and the Imams of the Muslims, and should take lessons from all of these things.

[The commendation] of visiting the Prophet's grave is a matter of scholarly consensus, and it is highly encouraged. Anas (Allah be pleased with him) stated in one *ḥadīth*, 'The Emissary of Allah said, "Whoever visits me in Medina in anticipation of reward shall be in my close company, and I will be an intercessor for him on the Day of Resurrection."'[161] Indeed, there are a multitude of *ḥadīth* reports that show the merit of visiting the Prophet (Allah bless him and give him peace).

وَمَـنْ هُـوَ الْآيَةُ الْكُبْرَىٰ لِـمُـعْـتَـبِـرٍ   وَمَنْ هُوَ النِّـعْـمَـةُ الْـعُـظْـمَىٰ لِـمُـغْـتَـنِـمِ

O Greatest Sign for those who contemplate!
O Supreme Grace for those who seek to gain!

Here the author (Allah have mercy upon him) completes the petition to him [the Prophet (Allah bless him and give him peace)] by ascribing to him two tremendous qualities appended to the previous couplet. In other words: 'O you who are sought by the seekers who received the good fortune of finding what they were looking for; O you who are the Greatest Sign for the one who contemplates what Allah has uniquely given you by way of praiseworthy actions, noble features, consummate form, beautiful countenance and handsomely proportioned limbs!' As someone has said:

> Were there not a single sign within him,
> His countenance alone would bring you the news!

Allah made the Prophet (Allah bless him and give him peace) the Greatest Sign for those who contemplate and ponder deeply. That is because the Prophet (Allah bless him and give him peace) came with dazzling miracles and evident proofs and weighty matters; it is therefore fitting that he be called the Greatest Sign. His miracles include the splitting of the moon, bringing the sun to a standstill, giving life to the dead, healing the sick and infirm, relating the details of past generations and bygone nations, having knowledge of the sacred Scriptures of earlier and later nations and the narratives of the past Prophets. Water flowed from his fingers and food was multiplied thanks to his blessings. A tree spoke to him, bore witness to his prophethood, and answered his call. A date-palm trunk moaned [for him]. Pebbles glorified [Allah] while in the palm of his hand. A wolf spoke with him, as did the ewe who asked for him to

161 A variant of this *ḥadīth* is narrated by Ibn Khuzayma and Bazzār.

intercede for it with the Bedouin [who had captured its young]. A lizard spoke with him and proclaimed its faith in him. A camel prostrated itself to him. A sheep informed him that it was poisoned. His hands conferred blessings on all that they touched or that came into contact with them. Material objects would transmute themselves for him, such as the stripped palm branch that he handed to ʿAbdullāh b. Jaḥsh during the battle of Badr. Once it was in his hand, the branch changed into a sword. The same thing happened with ʿUkkāsha [b. Miḥṣan] when a wooden club that was in his hand turned into a long sword. That sword remained in his possession until he was killed during the Apostasy Wars.

Other miracles of the Prophet (Allah bless him and give him peace) include his relaying information from the angels and jinn, his enjoyment of Allah's support in the form of angels, and being protected from his enemies who wished him harm.

[Other miracles include] the multiple congruous statements of soothsayers and the rabbis and priests from the scholars of the People of the Scripture regarding the Prophet's description, the description of his mother, his name and his sign, and his Seal that was between his shoulders, as well as the signs that were to appear at the time of his birth. [Other miracles include] the amazing incidents reported by his mother and others who were present at his birth.

All of these miracles have been mentioned earlier, and were it not for fear of being longwinded I would have mentioned even more and explored the details of each of these signs as they have been discussed in their relevant places. Al-Qāḍī [ʿIyāḍ] has certainly provided healing (*shifā'*) in this regard [in his book *al-Shifā'*]. Thus, for him who contemplates and ponders deeply, there should be no doubt whatever that the Prophet (Allah bless him and give him peace) is the Greatest Sign.

As for him being the Supreme Grace for those who seek gain, there is nothing hidden about that reality for those who possess spiritual insight and intellect, for Allah Most Exalted has graced creation with him, and sent him as a mercy to all of the worlds. Allah Most High says, '*Allah has indeed bestowed favour upon the believers in sending amongst them an Emissary who recites to them His verses...*' (Qur'an 3:164) The Prophet (Allah bless him and give him peace), then, is a bestowal and a gift of mercy. Shaykh Abū al-ʿAbbās al-Mursī (Allah be pleased with him) said:

> The Prophets were created from mercy, while our Prophet (Allah bless him and give him peace, and exalt him and glorify and ennoble him) is the essence of mercy [*ʿayn al-raḥma*]; as the Most High says, "*And We have not sent you but as a mercy unto the worlds.*"' (Qur'an 21:107) The Prophet (Allah bless him and give him peace) called people to Allah with clear insight, firm proofs and with the nearest of reaches and ways. He urged others to travel the path of right guidance and to shun lowly paths. He did not leave anything that draws one near to Allah without calling [people] to it, and he did not leave a single point of etiquette that a servant should adopt with Allah without encouraging [people to do] it. He did not leave anything that takes one away from Allah without warning against it, and he did not leave a single deed that alienates one from Allah without removing people from it. He was unceasing and indefatigable in his sincere counsel to deliver [Allah's] servants from the mires of alienation and loci of destruction, until the dark night of polytheism faded and its alterities were cut off, and the daylight of faith shone and its lights dawned. The Prophet (Allah bless him and give him peace) raised the banner of the religion, completed its order, established its obligations and rulings, and explained what is lawful and unlawful in it. Just as he explained legal rulings to [Allah's] servants, he also expanded their horizons of understanding. One narrator even said, "We do not see a bird flying in the sky after the Emissary of Allah has left us but that we have some knowledge of it that we gained from him through the sayings of Allah Most High, '*There is no compulsion in religion; right guidance has been made clear from error*' (Qur'an 2:256) and '*Today I have completed for you your religion.*'"' (Qur'an 5:3)

The words of the Shaykh [author] above, *those who seek to gain*, refers to the believers, since it is they who seek gain through the Sacred Law of the Chosen One (Allah bless him and give him peace), and seek gain through emulation of him and through sending copious prayers and salutations upon him during the remainder of their lives, thereby achieving success with perpetual triumph and eternal bliss in the close company of the one through whose law and emulation they sought gain (Allah bless him and give him peace). Since the Prophet (Allah bless him and give him peace) is the Supreme Grace, seekers repair to his courtyard and location, and thus the author connects this couplet with the previous one. Allah Most High knows best.

سَرَيْتَ مِنْ حَرَمٍ لَيْلًا إِلَىٰ حَرَمٍ كَمَا سَرَى الْبَدْرُ فِي دَاجٍ مِنَ الظُّلَمِ

You journeyed by night, from Sanctuary to Sanctuary
as the full moon travels through the pitch black sky.

Here the author (Allah have mercy upon him) addresses the Emissary of Allah (Allah bless him and give him peace), saying: You journeyed by night from the Sanctuary of Mecca (may Allah ennoble it) to the Sanctuary of Bayt al-Maqdis, which is the Furthest Mosque (*al-Masjid al-Aqṣā*). It was called the Furthest Mosque in that time because it was the furthest of Allah's select houses [of worship]. The author describes Bayt al-Maqdis as a 'sanctuary' (*ḥaram*), which means it is hallowed and revered because it enjoys a level of inviolability and veneration that other mosques do not have, it being one of the three most sanctified mosques. The Emissary of Allah (Allah bless him and give him peace) said, 'No journey is worth undertaking [exclusively for worship] except to three mosques: this Mosque of mine, the Inviolable Mosque [of Mecca] and the Furthest Mosque (al-Masjid al-Aqṣā).'[162]

The author compares the Prophet's Night Journey (*isrāʾ*) to the moon travelling through the pitch-black sky. The sphere of comparison here is guidance, because both the Prophet (Allah bless him and give him peace) and the moon provide guidance. Consider the story of the Bedouin who had lost his she-camel and became fatigued from searching for it and lost hope of ever finding it, until the full moon rose, by which he was able to find it. When he finally found his she-camel he looked up at the full moon and sung these lines:

What shall I say when my words are in your presence,
And you save me from needing to provide details and sentences?
Should I say 'You are forever raised' it would apply to you;
Should I say 'My Lord has adorned you', it is He who did so!

If you ask, 'Guidance through the Prophet (Allah bless him and give him peace) is far greater than guidance through the full moon, so how can he

162 Bukhārī.

possibly be likened to it?' the response is: The reason why he is likened to the full moon is that the full moon is perceptible (*maḥsūs*) and visible to all, whereas guidance through the Prophet (Allah bless him and give him peace) is abstract (*maʿnawī*) and known [only] to the elect of mankind. Hence, the abstract has been likened to the perceptible, and that which is subtler has been likened to something more readily apparent.

The phrase *by night* is superfluous since the word *isrāʾ* applies solely to journeys taken by night. Nevertheless, he mentions it here to emphasise that he has derived the meaning of this couplet from the Qur'anic verse [about the Night Journey], and since the verse mentions both words he has chosen to do so as well.[163] The answers provided by the exegetes regarding this verse can also be applied to the statement of the author here. One of the answers to this is to say that [Allah] mentioned the word 'night' in an indefinite form to indicate the short duration of the Night Journey; as if to say that He took the Prophet (Allah bless him and give him peace) for only a small portion of the night from Mecca to the Levant, which [ordinarily] is a forty-day journey. On the other hand, an indefinite noun, as al-Zamakhsharī said (Allah have mercy upon him), could indicate abundance, and that is indicated in the [non-canonical] recitation of Ibn Masʿūd who recited the verse in question as '*on a Night Journey by the night*'—in other words, by some of the night, as Allah said [in another verse] '*and in the night offer prayer with some of it* [recitation of the Qur'an]...' (Qur'an 17:79)

The incident of the Night Journey is well-known in the religion and there is no difference of opinion amongst the *Umma* about it; it is explicitly mentioned in the Tremendous Qur'an, and is described in detail in rigorously authenticated *ḥadīth* reports. Within the Night Journey we find many marvellous occurrences and numerous breaks with worldly norms (*khawāriq*). There are a multitude of narrations concerning the Night Journey, all of them widely known. I shall mention only a sample of them for the sake of brevity, and also because the author refers to some of the details in subsequent lines. One of these narrations about the Night Journey is that of Muslim, on the authority of Thābit al-Bunānī, who reported on the authority of Anas b. Mālik (Allah be pleased with

163 The Qur'anic verse referred to is the first verse of Sūrat al-Isrāʾ: '*Transcendently Glorious is He who took His servant on a journey by night from the Inviolable Mosque to the Furthest Mosque whose surroundings We have blessed...*' (Qur'ān 17:1) [t]

him), who related that the Emissary of Allah said, 'I was brought the Burāq, which is a tall white beast larger than a donkey but smaller than a mule. It would place its hoof at a distance equal to the furthest range of its sight. I mounted it and rode till I arrived at Bayt al-Maqdis, whereupon I tethered it to the tethering-ring used by the Prophets. I then entered the Mosque and prayed two cycles of prayer; then I came out, and Jibrīl brought me one vessel containing wine and another vessel containing milk. I chose the vessel containing milk, and Jibrīl said, "You have chosen the primordial way (*al-fiṭra*)."

'Then Jibrīl ascended with me up into the lower heaven and sought permission to enter. It was asked, "Who are you?" and he responded, "It is Jibrīl." Then it was asked, "Who is with you?" and he said, "Muḥammad." It was asked, "Has revelation been sent to him?" Jibrīl replied, "Indeed revelation has been sent to him." Then the door was opened for us and suddenly I found myself with Ādam. He welcomed me and prayed for my well-being.

'Then Jibrīl ascended with me up into the second heaven and sought permission to enter. It was asked, "Who are you?" and he responded, "It is Jibrīl." Then it was asked, "Who is with you?" and he said, "Muḥammad." It was asked, "Has revelation been sent to him?" Jibrīl replied, "Indeed revelation has been sent to him." Then the door was opened for us and suddenly I found myself with my two cousins from the maternal line, ʿĪsā son of Maryam and Yaḥyā son of Zakariyyā. They both welcomed me and prayed for my well-being.

'Then Jibrīl ascended with me up into the third heaven and sought permission to enter. It was asked, "Who are you?" and he responded, "It is Jibrīl." Then it was asked, "Who is with you?" and he said, "Muḥammad." It was asked, "Has revelation been sent to him?" Jibrīl replied, "Indeed revelation has been sent to him." Then the door was opened for us and suddenly I found myself with Yūsuf, and he was given half of all beauty. He welcomed me and prayed for my well-being.

'Then Jibrīl ascended with me up into the fourth heaven [and the same discussion transpired as above] ... and suddenly I found myself with Idrīs (upon whom be peace). He welcomed me and prayed for my well-being. Allah Most High says, "*And We have raised him to a high place!*" (Qur'an 19:57)

'Then Jibrīl ascended with me up into the fifth heaven [and the same discussion transpired as above] ... and suddenly I found myself with Hārūn. He welcomed me and prayed for my well-being.

'Then Jibrīl ascended with me up into the sixth heaven [and the same discussion transpired as above] ... and suddenly I found myself with Mūsā (upon whom be peace). He welcomed me and prayed for my well-being.

'Then Jibrīl ascended with me up into the seventh heaven [and the same discussion transpired as above] ... and suddenly I found myself with Ibrāhīm (upon whom be peace), who was leaning his back on the Bayt al-Maʿmūr (The Celestial House), in which seventy thousand angels enter daily [to pray], never to return [once they leave it].

'Then I was taken to the Lote Tree of the Utmost Boundary (Sidrat al-Muntahā), whose leaves are like the ears of elephants and whose fruits are like large clay jars. When it was covered by tremendous, indescribable colours [created] by Allah it was transformed in such a manner that none of Allah's creation could describe its beauty.

'Then Allah revealed to me what He revealed, and imposed upon me fifty prayers each day and night. Then I descended to Mūsā and he asked, "What did Allah impose upon your nation?" I replied, "He imposed fifty prayers." Mūsā said, "Go back to your Lord and ask Him to reduce them, for your nation is unable to bear that; I have lengthy experience with the Children of Israel and have tested them!" So I went back to my Lord and said, "O Lord, please reduce [the number of prayers] for my nation!" He then reduced their number by five. I went back to Mūsā and informed him that Allah had reduced their number by five for me. He said, "Your nation is unable to bear that. Go back to your Lord and ask Him to reduce them. I kept going back between my Lord Most High and Mūsā until Allah said, "O Muḥammad, they are five prayers each day and night; each prayer is equal to ten prayers, making them equivalent to fifty prayers. Whoever thinks to do a good deed but does not do it shall have written for him a single good deed, and if he does it he shall have written for him ten good deeds. And whoever thinks to do a bad deed but does not do it shall have nothing written against him, and if he does it then he shall have written against him a single bad deed." I descended back down to Mūsā, and when I informed him of this he said, "Go back to your Lord and ask Him for a reduction!" I have returned to my Lord until I felt ashamed before Him.'[164]

Qāḍī ʿIyāḍ (Allah have mercy upon him) said: 'Thābit considered this *ḥadīth* [on the Night Journey] to be the best, and no one has transmitted a more correct form than what is found here. Others have blended different narrations and combined them with this *ḥadīth*...' Then he went on to mention various points, some of which will be discussed where the author alludes to them.

There is no disagreement that the Night Journey took place after [the Prophet (Allah bless him and give him peace) received] revelation. Several authorities have said that it took place one year before the Migration (*hijra*), while others have said that it was earlier than that. The *Salaf* and the learned differ over whether the Prophet (Allah bless him and give him peace) was taken on the Night Journey in his physical body or [just] his soul. They hold three different opinions. The first opinion is that he was taken on the Night Journey in his physical body in a waking state. This is the view of the majority of the *Salaf* and the Muslims in general. Qāḍī ʿIyāḍ said, 'This is the truth and has been stated by Ibn ʿAbbās, Jābir, Anas, Ḥudhayfa, ʿUmar, Abū Hurayra, Mālik b. Ṣaʿṣaʿa, Abū Ḥābba al-Badrī, al-Ḍaḥḥāk, Ibn Masʿūd, Saʿīd b. Jubayr, Qatāda and Ibn al-Musayyab...' Qāḍī ʿIyāḍ went on to name a large group of authorities, too many to cite here.

The second opinion is that the Prophet (Allah bless him and give him peace) was taken on the Night Journey with his soul, and that it was a dream vision (while it is acknowledged that the dreams of the Prophets are true and are considered a form of revelation). This was the opinion of Muʿāwiya and some others.

The third opinion is that the Night Journey to al-Bayt al-Maqdis was made in the Prophet's physical body, and that the ascension to the heavens was with his soul.

Qāḍī ʿIyāḍ said:

> The true and sound position, Allah willing, is that the Night Journey was in both body and spirit for the entire event. This is what is substantiated by the Qur'anic verses and rigorously authenticated *ḥadīth* traditions and well-considered opinions. One should not part from the lit-

164 Muslim.

eral and apparent [meaning of a revealed text] and resort to figurative interpretation (*taʿwīl*) unless the former is [rationally] impossible; but there is nothing [rationally] impossible in the Prophet (Allah bless him and give him peace) being taken on the Night Journey in his body in a wakeful state. Nay, had it been a dream [only], Allah would have said '*who took* the soul *of His servant*', and not '*who took His servant*...' Allah also says, '*The sight did not swerve, nor did it transgress*' (Qur'an 53:17), so had it only been a dream, it would not be considered a sign or an inimitable miracle, and the disbelievers would not have thought it far-fetched and rejected it; nor would some feeble Muslims have apostasised and been led to doubt because of it. Dreams of this nature are not subject to such denial. Furthermore, had they not known he was relating to them what occurred with his body in a waking state, they would not have denied it to be so.

And Allah Most High knows best.

وَبِتَّ تَرْقَىٰ إِلَىٰ أَنْ نِلْتَ مَنْزِلَةً   مِنْ قَابِ قَوْسَيْنِ لَمْ تُدْرَكْ وَلَمْ تُرَمِ

That night you ascended till you reached a station
Of Two Bows' Length—one never attained or hoped for!

Here the author (Allah have mercy upon him) addresses the Emissary of Allah (Allah bless him and give him peace), saying: On the Night Journey you ascended, rising higher and higher until you reached a station never attained by either an angel brought nigh or a Prophet sent forth, nor was it sought after or attempted or coveted by any other.' His reason for saying *or hoped for* is because a person might not reach something yet still covet it and try to reach it; so in this line the author negates that and says *a station*...*one never attained or hoped for*, emphasising the exaltedness and loftiness of that station.

By saying *Of Two Bows' Length*, the author means that the Prophet (Allah bless him and give him peace) rose and drew near till he was at the distance of two Arabian bows' length or nearer, as Allah Most High said, '*And then he approached and descended, and was at the distance of Two Bows' lengths or closer.*' (Qur'an 53:8–9) The exegetes disagree over the outward meaning of this verse and what it says regarding 'approach' and 'descent'.

Most of them say that the approach and descent refer either to our Prophet (Allah bless him and give him peace) or to Jibrīl (upon whom be peace); or that one is particular to the Prophet and the other is particular to Jibrīl; or that both terms are describing the Lote Tree of the Utmost Boundary. Ibn ʿAbbās said, 'It was Muḥammad (Allah bless him and give him peace) who approached and descended near to his Lord.' It is said that the word 'approach' here means 'draw near' and that 'descend' means 'increase in proximity'. It is also said that the words are synonymous and mean 'drew near'.

Al-Makkī and al-Māwardī both report that Ibn ʿAbbās (Allah be pleased with him) said that it refers to the Lord, Exalted is He. Thus it means: 'He descended to Muḥammad': that is to say, 'His divine exaltation and command descended to him.' Al-Naqqāsh related that al-Ḥasan [al-Baṣrī] said, 'He drew near to His servant Muḥammad and descended, coming close to him and showing him what He willed to show him of His omnipotence and immensity.' Ibn ʿAbbās said, 'He was put forwards and back: the Carpet-spread drew near to Muḥammad on the night of the Ascension and he sat upon it, then it was taken up and he drew near to his Lord. He said, "Jibrīl parted ways with me and all sounds were cut off from me, and then I heard the speech of my Lord..."'

It is recorded in the *Ṣaḥīḥ* [of al-Bukhārī] from Anas that 'Jibrīl ascended with him to the Lote Tree of the Utmost Boundary, and the All-Dominating (al-Jabbār), the Lord of Honour, drew near till He was at the distance of Two Bows' Length from him or nearer, then He revealed to Him what He willed, and then He revealed to him the fifty prayers.'

Jaʿfar b. Muḥammad [al-Ṣādiq] said, 'Allah's "drawing near" is without limit, while [His] servants' "drawing near" is limited.' He also said, 'When it comes to the "drawing near" modality (*kayfiyya*)[165] is inapplicable; do you not see that Jibrīl was veiled from his "drawing near"? Muḥammad drew near to the gnosis and faith deposited in his own heart, thereby descending with tranquil heart with what he knew to be near, with doubt and misgivings being removed from it.'

After citing these reports, Qāḍī Abū al-Faḍl ʿIyāḍ (Allah have mercy upon him) says:

165 The 'howness' of the drawing near. [t]

> Know that what is said here about 'drawing near' and proximity to or from Allah Most High has nothing to do with nearness of place or proximity of space. As we mentioned from Jaᶜfar al-Ṣādiq, this is not a 'drawing near' that entails a [physical] limit; rather it is the Prophet's drawing near to his Lord. His nearness to his Lord is made clear by his position, the honour of his rank, the splendour of the lights of his gnosis, and his witnessing of the secrets of Allah's unseen Realm of Omnipotence. From Allah to him came benevolence, intimacy, expansion and generosity. Figurative interpretation (*taᶜwīl*) must be resorted to here just as it is when explaining the statement of the Prophet (Allah bless him and give him peace), 'Our Lord descends from the nearest heaven…'[166], which is a descent of generous bestowal, beauty, acceptance and favour.

The *Salaf* differ over whether the Prophet (Allah bless him and give him peace) saw his Lord. ᶜĀʾisha (Allah be pleased with her) denied it, while the position of Ibn ᶜAbbās was that the Prophet (Allah bless him and give him peace) saw Allah with his eyes. Al-Māwardī said, 'It is said that Allah apportioned [His] vision and speech between Muḥammad (Allah bless him and give him peace) and Mūsā (upon whom be peace). Muḥammad (Allah bless him and give him peace) saw Him twice and Mūsā spoke with Him twice.' Qāḍī [ᶜIyāḍ] says:

> The truth of the matter, in which there is no doubt, is that it is rationally possible to see [Allah] in this world. The proof that it is permitted in this world lies in the fact that Mūsā asked for it. It is impossible for a Prophet to be ignorant of what is [rationally] permitted for Allah and what is not; Mūsā only asked for what is permitted. Nonetheless, the occurrence of such a vision is [a matter] of the Unseen that is known only to Allah or to one taught by Allah. [Those who say it is forbidden] do not have a proof in the statement of the Most High '*Eyesight does not apprehend Him*' (Qur'an 6:103), because its meaning is that eyesights do not encompass Him, or that the eyesights of the disbelievers [will not see Him]. Mālik (Allah be pleased with him) said, 'He cannot be seen in this world because He is Enduring (Bāqī), while the eyesights of worldly beings are ephemeral. When the Day of Resur-

166 Muslim.

rection arrives they will be provided with enduring sight, so the Enduring will be seen by the enduring.' These are excellent words and there is nothing in them to indicate that the beatific vision is [rationally] impossible; rather [they affirm] that the vision has not occurred [in this world] because of the weakness of faculties. If Allah strengthens whomever He wills of His servants and gives him the power to bear the rigours of the vision, it will not be impossible for him; and Allah Most High knows best.

وَقَدَّمَتْكَ جَمِيعُ الْأَنْبِيَاءِ بِهَا   وَالرُّسْلِ تَقْدِيمَ مَخْدُومٍ عَلَىٰ خَدَمِ

There all the Prophets and Emissaries gave you precedence,
As a master is given precedence by those who serve him.

Here the author (Allah have mercy upon him) addresses Allah's Emissary (Allah bless him and give him peace), saying: So exalted is your station, so tremendous your rank and so sublime your proximity to your Lord that no other Prophet besides you—despite their honour and lofty level—has attained your degree, and so they put you forward and gave you precedence over themselves. Because of your distinguished rank over them, and because of their knowledge of the favoured position and honour that Allah has conferred upon you, they deemed it fitting that you should be at the head. The best of a people is their leader, so the Prophets and Emissaries put the Prophet Muḥammad (Allah bless him and give him peace) forward as intercessor for them. Abū Hurayra (Allah be pleased with him) reported that the Emissary of Allah said, 'I saw myself in a gathering of Prophets and then I led them in prayer.'[167] This is the strongest proof of the tremendous esteem the Prophet (Allah bless him and give him peace) had in their eyes, for they had chosen him for the imamate, and that was because they knew him as the Best of Creation in the sight of Allah.

In the author's line where he says *There all the Prophets and Emissaries gave you precedence*, a general term is used where a specific one is actually intended. That is because the Prophet (Allah bless him and give him peace) was not given precedence by *all* of the Prophets, nor were all of them present at Bayt al-Maqdis. Narrations state that Jibrīl took the

167 Muslim.

Prophet (Allah bless him and give him peace) to see various signs as he descended from the heavens to the earth, until finally he reached Bayt al-Maqdis wherein he found Ibrāhīm, Mūsā, ʿĪsā and a number of other Prophets who had gathered for him and whom he led in prayer. What seems apparent [from the narrations] is that the Prophet (Allah bless him and give him peace) led them in prayer at Bayt al-Maqdis as well as in the heavens. One tradition states that an angel took the Prophet (Allah bless him and give him peace) by his hand and put him forward, whereupon he led the inhabitants of the heaven in prayer, among whom were Ādam and Nūḥ. It appears, therefore, that this [line] is a general statement subject to qualification (*ʿāmm makhṣūṣ*), as where the Most High says '*Demolishing everything by the command of its Lord*' (Qur'an 46:25), even though the destruction was limited to the people against whom it was sent.

The positioning of Emissaries after Prophets in this couplet is a positioning of the specific after the general. To mention something in specific terms after mentioning it in general terms indicates that thing's nobility, so that it is mentioned twice. In the line where he says *As a master is given precedence by those who serve him*, the author is saying that in giving him precedence, the action of the Emissaries and Prophets resembles the action of servants who give precedence to their master by putting him forward and revering him. Some have commented that this line is distasteful and unbecoming, but it can be argued in the author's favour that the simile drawn here is with respect to precedence alone. Therefore, just as one who is served is given precedence by those who serve him, likewise our Prophet (Allah bless him and give him peace) is given precedence over all of the other Prophets and Emissaries, since Allah has made him the noblest and most honoured among them. And Allah Most High knows best.

وَأَنْتَ تَخْتَرِقُ السَّبْعَ الطِّبَاقَ بِهِمْ   فِي مَوْكِبٍ كُنْتَ فِيهِ صَاحِبَ الْعَلَمِ

You traversed the seven heavens with them [behind you]
In a procession wherein you were the standard-bearer.

Here the author (Allah have mercy upon him) addresses the Emissary of Allah (Allah bless him and give him peace), saying: O Emissary of Allah (Allah bless him and give him peace), during the Night Journey you traversed the seven heavens and crossed through one heaven after another with the Prophets in a group wherein you were the most prominent and notable, in the position of the standard-bearer who is followed.

That is the gist of what the author is saying. This couplet, however, presents a problem since it implies that the Prophets and Emissaries who were in the heavens had traversed the seven heavens with the Prophet (Allah bless him and give him peace), while the *ḥadīth* only establishes that Jibrīl and the Emissary of Allah traversed the heavens. The response to this is to say that the author's phrase *with them* is the 'state' (*ḥāl*) of the subject (*fāʿil*) of the verb 'traverse': in other words, he traversed while keeping company with and passing by each Prophet in his respective heaven. This is because there is no heaven that does not have a Prophet in it. This line is only problematic if the phrase *with them* is linked with the verb *traversed*.

The procession in which the Prophet (Allah bless him and give him peace) was the standard-bearer was a procession of angels. The Prophets were not with him. It is also said that the author is referring both to Jibrīl and to the Prophet (Allah bless him and give him peace) with him.

حَتَّىٰ إِذَا لَمْ تَدَعْ شَأْوًا لِمُسْتَبِقٍ   مِنَ الدُّنُوِّ وَلَا مَرْقًى لِمُسْتَنِمِ

Until your proximity left no space for the avid seeker,
Nor any higher summit for one seeking elevation.

Here the author (Allah have mercy upon him) also addresses the Emissary of Allah (Allah bless him and give him peace), saying: You have attained such degrees and stations as have been attained by no other, and reached a pinnacle that is unreachable by any other man, so that your proximity left no space for the avid seeker. You have surpassed everyone, leaving not a single lofty summit or peak for one seeking elevation. Indeed, you have risen and ascended all of them.

In this couplet, the author is alluding to the Prophet's elevation during the Night Journey and his reaching a place that was never reached by any other, where he heard the scratching of the Pens [of destiny]. Glorified is the One who bestows on whomever He wills whatever unique favours He wills, and has '*elevated some of them in degrees over others in ranks of honour*.' (Qur'an 2:253)

خَفَضْتَ كُلَّ مَقَامٍ بِالْإِضَافَةِ إِذْ   نُودِيتَ بِالرَّفْعِ مِثْلَ الْمُفْرَدِ الْعَلَمِ

You surpassed all other stations in comparison
When acclaimed on high as 'The Matchless and Eminent'–

Here the author (Allah have mercy upon him) says: You surpassed all other stations and all other positions held by the other Prophets in comparison to yours. This surpassing is in relation to the stations of the other Prophets, not to speak of the stations of the saints! Indeed you, O Prophet (Allah bless him and give him peace), have surpassed all stations entirely because Allah has elevated you to the loftiest of degrees and raised you to the noblest of positions, you are named with titles of sublimity and exaltation, and you have attained what no other has; so it is as if you are *The Matchless and Eminent* One. This is an excellent play on words: the author gives the impression that he is speaking about the 'lowering' of a word in a genitive construction (*iḍāfa*), while what he really means is the lowering of stations [in comparison to the Prophet's]. He also gives the impression that he is speaking about the 'raising' [*rafʿ*] of a proper noun [in the nominative case], while what he really means is the raising of the object named and his lofty rank in the sight of his Lord.

The play on words occur twice here. The first is when he says *You surpassed*, intending a metaphorical 'lowering' and employing the grammatical term *khafḍ*; he adds to that the term *comparison* (*iḍāfa*), since the grammatical *khafḍ* only occurs through *iḍāfa*, and the genitive construction is either one noun joined with another or a verb joined with a noun (the latter having with a preposition in between).

The second play on words is when he says *on high* (*rafʿ*), intending metaphorical loftiness, meaning honour and nobility, and employing the grammatical term *rafʿ*, which is one of the terms used in the science of inflection (*iʿrāb*). Poets and men of letters often play on words using grammatical terms, an example being this statement by a poet:

And, believing that leadership is shown by pride,
He became despised, unknowingly
He drags the tails of vanity, seeking exaltation;
How strange is he who seeks to rise *(rafʿ)* by dragging *(jarr)*!

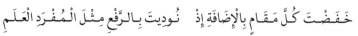

كَيْمَا تَفُوزَ بِوَصْلٍ أَيِّ مُسْتَتِرٍ عَنِ الْعُيُونِ وَسِرٍّ أَيِّ مُكْتَتَمِ

So that you might triumph through a tryst hidden
From sight. How hidden a secret that was!

This explains the reason behind the earlier couplets where the author described how the Prophet (Allah bless him and give him peace) journeyed by night from one Sanctuary to another and ascended and traversed the seven heavens, and how he surpassed all other stations till he was addressed in terms of loftiness and exaltation. All of this, he says, is so that you, Emissary of Allah (Allah bless him and give him peace), should triumph with union and proximity to your Lord who has conferred such gracious favours upon you and blessed you with such pre-eminence and status, through which He has manifested your supreme rank and distinction over all of the other Prophets and selected you for the hidden secret that He has disclosed to no other Emissary or Prophet.

Perhaps this hidden secret is what is referred to in Allah's statement '*Then He revealed to His servant what He revealed.*' (Qur'an 53:10) Allah disclosed to the Prophet (Allah bless him and give him peace) secrets and unseen realities, he beheld what he beheld of the celestial and terrestrial kingdoms and the Highest Assembly (*al-Malāʾ al-Aʿlā*), and saw the greatest Signs of his Lord. In one report it is related that the Prophet (Allah bless him and give him peace) said, 'During the Night Journey my Lord taught me a multitude of knowledges. One portion of that knowledge I was obliged to conceal; another portion I was given the choice of whether to conceal it or divulge; and another portion I was commanded to convey.'[168] ʿAlī (may Allah ennoble his countenance) said, 'The Prophet confided in Abū Bakr, ʿUmar, ʿUthmān and me secrets which he was given the option to conceal or divulge.' Now, this narration has been quoted by a number of commentators, but al-Maḥallī stated, 'I have not discovered any basis for it in the books of *ḥadīth*.'

It is also possible that this couplet is an explanation of the reason behind the author's statement *You surpassed all other stations in comparison*—in other words, you surpassed all other stations so that you alone might triumph with the exalted rank and position that was not reached by any of the Prophets before you.

168 Shaykh ʿAbd Allāh al-Talīdī notes that this narration is without basis.

The hidden union refers to when the Prophet (Allah bless him and give him peace) reached a point where he heard the scratching of the Pens and when he was told 'Calm your terror, Muḥammad, and draw near!' This is a noble station of union and proximity that was not reached or attained by any Prophet before him; and Allah is the Possessor of great bounty![169]

فَحُزْتَ كُلَّ فَخَارٍ غَيْرَ مُشْتَرَكٍ وَجُزْتَ كُلَّ مَقَامٍ غَيْرَ مُزْدَحَمِ

So you received every glory without rival
And gained every station alone, unbeset.

Here the author (Allah have mercy upon him) addresses the Emissary of Allah (Allah bless him and give him peace), saying: When you surpassed all other stations you received every praiseworthy quality and attained every splendid action, and no Prophet or Emissary or angel shared with you in any of them. You received every lofty rank and were alone and unbeset during every noble station that you crossed through in the heavens on the Night Journey. That is because you are alone and without partner in them, since crowding only occurs when there is co-sharing, not when someone is alone.

وَجَلَّ مِقْدَارُ مَا وُلِّيتَ مِنْ رُتَبٍ وَعَزَّ إِدْرَاكُ مَا أُولِيتَ مِنْ نِعَمِ

How glorious is the worth of the ranks you were given
How difficult it is to grasp the graces conferred!

Here the author (Allah have mercy upon him) addresses the Emissary of Allah (Allah bless him and give him peace), saying: Sublime is the measure of what Allah has given you by way of tremendous ranks, noble stations and exalted miracles. It is exceedingly rare, or impossible, for anyone other than you to comprehend the numerous graces and exquisite bounties that Allah Most High has granted you and bestowed upon you! Allah Most High says, '*And He taught you what you did not know, and the bounty of Allah towards you is tremendous!*' (Qur'an 4:113)

169 Qāḍī ʿIyāḍ, *al-Shifā'*.

بُشْرَىٰ لَنَا مَعْشَرَ الإِسْلَامِ إِنَّ لَنَا مِنَ الْعِنَايَةِ رُكْنًا غَيْرَ مُنْهَدِمِ

Glad tidings for us, O people of Islam,
For we have an indestructible pillar of divine care.

The author, after addressing the Prophet (Allah bless him and give him peace) by saying *O best of those to whose courtyard seekers turn to* and mentioning his Night Journey and and its events: miracles, intimate discourses, meetings with the Prophets and leading them in prayer, ascending to the Lote Tree of the Uppermost Boundary, and what he saw of his Lord's greatest signs—after mentioning all that, he says here: People of Islam, complete joy and everlasting happiness are ours, because we have a sturdy, indestructible pillar of divine care and good fortune from Allah Most High, that being the nobility and solicitude and honour He has granted us through the Prophet (Allah bless him and give him peace) and for the Prophet's sake. Just as our Prophet (Allah bless him and give him peace) is the best of the Prophets, likewise his nation is the best of nations. Allah Most High says, '*You are the best nation raised for mankind.*' (Qur'an 3:110). Allah Most High also says, '*And so We have made you a middle nation.*' (Qur'an 2:143)[170] This means: He has made you a most balanced and preferred nation, that you may be witnesses against mankind. Had this nation's nobility and superiority been only because its witnessing against the previous nations is accepted, that would have been a most decisive proof of its pre-eminence and superiority over the other nations. If you argue 'But how can it bear witness over those they have not seen, as the other nations preceded them?' the reply is as follows: They came to know, and gained incontrovertible knowledge of what they testified to, from the Book of Allah Most High, which informed them of the conditions experienced by the previous Emissaries with their respective nations and how their nations responded to their calls. So they bore witness to what was told to them by the Veracious and Trustworthy One, who relayed from Allah Most High.

Other examples of this nation's superiority include the unique favours bestowed on it by Allah, such as the lightening of the burdens that had been imposed upon earlier nations. Allah will accept our repentance as

170 It is noteworthy that Sūrat al-Baqara has 286 verses, making this the middle verse in the chapter. [t]

long as we feel remorse and resolve never to return to the sin, whereas the repentance of the earlier nations required death. Likewise, the preceding nations were taken to task for mistakes and forgetfulness, but both of these have been lifted from us. Allah has covered [the faults] of this nation and has not exposed it, and has ordered it to cover its faults and the faults of others. Perhaps that is the intended meaning of the *ḥadīth* 'I covered it for you in this world and I shall forgive it for you Today.'[171] Allah Most High knows best.

لَمَّا دَعَا اللَّهُ دَاعِينَا لِطَاعَتِهِ   بِأَكْرَمِ الرُّسْلِ كُنَّا أَكْرَمَ الْأُمَمِ

When Allah named the one who called us to obey Him
The Noblest of Emissaries, we became the noblest of nations!

After stating in the previous couplet that we, the people of Islam, possess an indestructible pillar of divine care and a lofty station, the author (Allah have mercy upon him) posits an abstract individual who asks him 'Why do you all possess this divine care and rank?' He answers: We became the noblest of nations when Allah Most High gave His Prophet the name Muḥammad (Allah bless him and all the Prophets and give them peace) and enjoined us to obey Him by means of that most noble of Emissaries. In other words, because the Prophet (Allah bless him and give him peace) is the noblest of Emissaries, it follows that his nation is the noblest of nations. The fruits and effects of this divine care have been manifested for us to see. When previous nations performed a good deed, one good deed—or less—would be written on their accounts, but for this nation good deeds are multiplied from tenfold up to seven hundredfold, though a single sin remains one. The good deeds of this nation are incalculable and immeasurable, like the good deeds earned through fasting and patience. The Most High says, '*Only the patient shall receive their reward in full without measure.*' (Qur'an 39:10) And He says about fasting, 'Fasting is Mine, and it is I who give its reward.'[172] There are many other unique qualities [of this nation] that have been mentioned earlier. Another unique favour bestowed on this nation by divine care is the Night of Power (*Laylat al-Qadr*), for good deeds performed during that

171 Aḥmad.
172 Ibid.

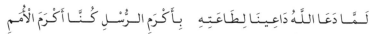

night equal good deeds performed over a span of a thousand months, and standing in prayer in that night is better than standing in prayer for a thousand months in which there is no Night of Power. Allah Most High knows best and is the Noblest.

CHAPTER 8

The Prophet's Jihad[173] ﷺ

رَاعَتْ قُلُوبَ الْعِدَا أَنْبَاءُ بِعْثَتِهِ   كَنَبْأَةٍ أَجْفَلَتْ غُفْلًا مِنَ الْغَنَمِ

The news of his being sent had cast fear into the hearts of foes as heedless sheep are startled by sudden noise.

HERE THE AUTHOR (Allah have mercy upon him) says that the disbelievers were unaware of the news about the Emissary (Allah bless him and give him peace) and heedless of it, but once they heard from rabbis, soothsayers and speakers amongst the jinn of his impending arrival (before he became known) their hearts were soon filled with fear and dread. Likewise those who heard news of the Prophet (Allah bless him and give him peace) after he became known were filled with terror and fear. When the disbelievers heard the news of the Prophet (Allah bless him and give him peace) they were like heedless, oblivious sheep who, upon hearing a loud noise, became startled; their unity was dispersed, their group was dispersed, and their hearts were filled with fear. Had the disbelievers not been unaware of the imminent prophetic mission it would not have startled them so, and had they taken notice of the arrival of the Prophet (Allah bless him and give him peace) they would have enjoyed security and not have been so terrified by it.

173 Jihad in this context refers to the Prophet's martial struggles against people who had opposed and oppressed him and his small community of followers for over a decade. As Shaykh Hamza Yusuf notes: 'The true object of war fought for God is peace. We can only truly establish justice with force because injustice is only perpetuated with force. The world has always been that way, and there is no reason to think it will change any time soon. What Islam demands is that Muslims fight for a just cause only.' (*The Burda of al-Busiri: The Poem of the Cloak,* London: Sandala Ltd., 2002). Hence, Islam allows the use of force but the rules of engagement are extremely stringent which includes the prohibition of targeting civilians, non-combatants, women and children as well as religious institutions and cultivation. [p]

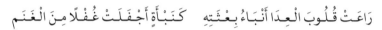

It is recorded in a *ḥadīth* in the two rigorously authenticated collections [of al-Bukhārī and Muslim] that the Prophet (Allah bless him and give him peace) said, 'I have been granted victory through dread at a month's distance.' And al-Ṭabarānī records, 'Verily I have been granted victory through dread at two month's distance.' The intended meaning of this was stated by al-Maḥallī in *Sharḥ al-ʿUmda*:

> We have reported [the wording] 'I was granted victory through dread at one month's distance in front of me and at one month's distance behind me.' This is comparable to the left and the right [sides], so the meaning of the first narration [a month's distance] is a month in any of the cardinal directions [north, south, east or west].

It bears mentioning that the purpose of the Prophet's mission was to unite a scattered and divided people, provide safety from fear, and announce felicity. Nevertheless, Allah willed in His pre-eternal knowledge that [the disbelievers] not attain success. Hence they were invited but refused to answer the invitation; they were given sincere advice but refused to accept it; they were urged to come together in unity but they scattered and became deaf to the truth and blind to the signs and clearest of miracles. This was despite their intelligence and wit. Indeed, 'when Allah wills to carry out His decree and preordainment, He strips the intelligent of their intellects and executes His will'[174]—'*Had We willed We could have given every soul its guidance.*' (Qur'an 32:13)

مَـا زَالَ يَـلْـقَـاهُــمُ فِي كُـلِّ مُـعْـتَـرَكٍ حَـتَّـىٰ حَكَوْا بِالْقَـنَـا لَـحْـمًا عَلَىٰ وَضَمِ

He continued to meet them on every battleground
Until spears cut them, like meat on a butcher's block.

Here the author (Allah have mercy upon him) says that the news of the Prophet's arrival had cast fear into hearts of his adversaries. He had come to them with plain evidence and clear miracles that proved his veracity; and he spared no effort to advise them and deliver them from Hellfire; yet they expressed aversion and denial, so Allah kept their hearts from accepting the truth. Because of their damnation, which was known [to Him] pre-eternally, Allah set the Prophet (Allah bless him and give him

174 A *ḥadīth* recorded by Abū Nuʿaym, Bayhaqī and Daylamī.

peace) against them and he decimated and vanquished them till his way of life was ascendant, Allah honoured Islam and its people by His Emissary, and disbelief and its hosts were humiliated.

The Prophet (Allah bless him and give him peace) continued to meet them for combat on every battleground, so much that the sword-wounds inflicted upon them by the Muslims made their flesh resemble raw meat cast on a butcher's block. The swords did to them what a butcher's blade does to meat on a chopping-block, so their flesh was cut piece by piece as a butcher slices meat.

The Prophet (Allah bless him and give him peace) participated directly in fighting the idol-worshippers and waged war and took part in personal combat. He was renowned for his bravery and valour; he was present during extremely difficult battles from which even valiant and armour-clad warriors fled; and he remained therein, unflinching and leading from the front without turning away.

Our master ʿAlī (may Allah ennoble his countenance) said, 'In the heat of battle, when both armies clashed head on, we sought shelter behind the Emissary of Allah, and so none was closer to the enemy than he was; the most courageous of us in battle was the one who was close to the Emissary of Allah when the enemy drew near.'[175]

Anas (Allah be pleased with him) related, 'The Emissary of Allah was the best of people, and the most generous and courageous of them. One night the people of Medina were terrified by a loud sound, and when they set out in the direction of the sound [to investigate] the Emissary of Allah saved them the trouble and met them on his way back, having gone towards the sound ahead of them. He went to investigate [the sound] while riding the horse of Abū Ṭalḥa without a saddle and with a sword slung around his neck. He said, "Fear not."'[176]

ʿImrān b. Ḥuṣayn (Allah be pleased with him) said, 'Never did the Emissary of Allah meet a regiment in battle but that he was the first to strike.'[177]

When Ubayy b. Khalaf saw the Prophet (Allah bless him and give him peace) during the battle of Uḥud he shouted, 'Where is Muḥammad? May I not survive if he survives!' When Ubayy had been ransomed on

175 Nasāʾī

176 Bukhārī.

177 Recorded by Abū al-Shaykh in *Akhlāq al-Nubuwwa*.

the Day of Badr, he said, 'I have a horse that I feed several measures of corn daily and I shall kill you while riding on it! The Prophet (Allah bless him and give him peace) said to him, 'I shall kill you, if Allah wills.' When Ubayy saw the Prophet (Allah bless him and give him peace) on the Day of Uḥud, he urged the horse on after the Emissary of Allah. Some of the men among the Muslims tried to block his way but the Prophet (Allah bless him and give him peace) said 'Make way for him' and took hold of a spear belonging to al-Ḥarth b. al-Ṣimma, and he shook it in such a way that those around him took flight as flies fly off the back of a camel when it shakes itself. Then the Prophet (Allah bless him and give him peace) turned to face Ubayy and pierced him in the neck, causing him to fall from his horse. It was said that he had broken one of his ribs. When he returned to Quraysh he said, 'Muḥammad has killed me!' They said, 'There is nothing wrong with you at all!' He replied, 'Had everyone here received the injury that I have they would all be killed! Did he not say "I shall kill you"? By Allah, had he spat upon me it would have killed me!' Ubayy died in Sarif as the caravan was making its way back to Mecca.[178] (This is recorded in *al-Shifā'*.)

If you ask 'Why did the caliphs, in their reigns, not follow the Prophet's Sunna in this regard and participate directly in fighting as the Prophet (Allah bless him and give him peace) did?' the answer is: The customary practice of rulers of avoiding direct participation in battles is correct and part of wise governance, for were a king to engage in battle directly he might be struck by a stray arrow, which would then be a cause for the Muslims to suffer defeat and would blunt their military might. At the beginning of his mission the Prophet (Allah bless him and give him peace) was guarded and people feared for his safety, but when Allah Most High revealed '*And Allah shall protect you from people*' (Qur'an 5:67) and he was promised victory and conquest of the lands, he began to participate directly in fighting without concern [for his well-being], because he had complete confidence in the promise of his Lord and knew that he would not suffer harm or grievous injury—none of which can be said for other rulers. Allah Most High knows best.

178 Cited by ʿUqba b. Mūsā in his *Maghāzī* collection, Ibn Isḥāq in his *Sīra* and Ibn Kathīr in *al-Bidāya wa al-nihāya*.

وَدُّوا الْفِرَارَ فَكَادُوا يَغْبِطُونَ بِهِ   أَشْلَاءَ شَالَتْ مَعَ الْعِقْبَانِ وَالرَّخَمِ

They longed to flee, almost jealous of
The dead flesh carried off by hawks and vultures.

Here the author (Allah have mercy upon him) says that when Allah gave victory to His Emissary (Allah bless him and give him peace) over the disbelievers and he [and his followers] put their swords to their necks and decimated them in battle, the disbelievers wished to run away and longed to be saved by any means at their disposal. So severe was their condition and so painful were the beating and onslaught they received that they saw pieces of flesh from their fallen comrades in arms being carried off by hawks and vultures and were almost jealous of them, and began to wish that they too were carried off like the dead flesh borne away by the hawks.

Something similar to this description took place during the battle of Badr (as well as the other campaigns of the Prophet (Allah bless him and give him peace)). Many of Quraysh and others thought to go back [to Mecca]; one of them even said 'I see only that this confrontation will usher in certain death!' Dread would enter the hearts of the Prophet's enemies before they met him in battle, and the same dread would be felt when others met his Companions in battle after him, such as during the battle of Yarmouk and the Battle of Qādisiyya. Allah Most High knows best.

تَمْضِي اللَّيَالِي وَلَا يَدْرُونَ عِدَّتَهَا   مَا لَمْ تَكُنْ مِنْ لَيَالِي الْأَشْهُرِ الْحُرُمِ

The nights passed with them unaware of their number,
Apart from the nights of the Sacred Months.

Here the author (Allah have mercy upon him) says that the disbelievers, because of the severe grip of war waged against them by Allah's Emissary (Allah bless him and give him peace) and his Companions and because of the distress and anxiety that afflicted them, would experience several nights pass by whilst they were unable to keep count of them, so forgetful were they because of the shock, terror and intensity they were forced to endure. The only exception was the period of the Sacred Months, whose nights they were able to count because they then enjoyed safety from war and fighting. During the Sacred Months their hearts would return to them and their terror would abate. They would repose during that time and wait till they were over before the return of toil and hardship and the tribulations and vicissitudes to which they had grown accustomed. Their souls would take rest in the days of the Sacred Months, and their hearts and minds, earlier overcome and driven mad with fear, would return to them. During that period they were able to take count of the days. They counted the days of relaxation because they, and the rest they brought, were short-lived. They did not count the days of hardship and fighting because they were beside themselves with worry.

Nights are mentioned here in particular, either because mentioning them alone is sufficient (since night is a concomitant of day) and the new months begin at night, or because forgetfulness at night is more common than forgetfulness in daytime, night being a time of repose and rest. So if they forgot the passing days, that shows how intense and frequent their forgetfulness was.

When it comes to counting days, people aspire to a variety of ends. Some count the days out of anxiety over their passing... Abū Bakr [al-Shiblī] related, "ᶜĀṭāʾ al-Maqdisī said, "I had a Sufi Shaykh who would take a single almond and place it in a nosebag [used to feed an animal] if his entire day had been spent in righteousness. When asked his age, the Shaykh would take out the nosebag, count the number of almonds in it, and say "This is how old I am."" This Shaykh considered his true age to consist of the days he filled with righteous works. Those are the days that will be in his favour and which merit counting, not the days that go by bereft of benefit, which should be discounted.

Concerning the words of the Most High '*And remind them of the Days of Allah*' (Qur'an 14:5), [al-Qāḍī Abū Bakr] Ibn al-ᶜArabī said:

> These are the days of well-being and blessings. That is the intended meaning [of the verse]. Unfortunately, however, what is found most commonly today is that people count the days of toil and difficulty. You will see a sick man count the days of his sickness, and a debtor count down how many days have passed and how many remain before he must pay off his debt, while he may neglect to count the days of well-being [that he enjoyed], or else the days of sorrow. In the former case, it is because of luxury and ease: his heart is preoccupied with

> experiencing pleasure, so he does not recount them. In the latter case, it is because of his toil and the successive concerns that distract him from attending to his most important and pressing concerns, let alone counting [the days of sorrow]. Hence he forgets to count, because his heart is preoccupied.

The Prophet (Allah bless him and give him peace) would seek to avoid fighting against the disbelievers during the Sacred Months, until Allah revealed '*And fight against the idolaters entirely, as they fight against you entirely*.' (Qur'an 9:36) From that point on, the Prophet (Allah bless him and give him peace) would fight against them in any month [including the Sacred Months]. Saʿīd b. al-Musayyab reported: 'Before Sūrat al-Tawba was revealed, the Emissary of Allah used to forbid fighting during the Sacred Months since Allah had revealed verses proscribing it.' This narration is cited by al-Ṭabarī. The words of Allah Most High '*So do not wrong yourselves therein*' (Qur'an 9:36) refer to acts of disobedience. This is an ennoblement of time in particular, for otherwise wrongdoing is unlawful in any period of time. Allah Most High knows best.

كَأَنَّمَا الدِّينُ ضَيْفٌ حَلَّ سَاحَتَهُمْ   بِكُلِّ قَرْمٍ إِلَىٰ لَحْمِ الْعِدَا قَرِمِ

As if the religion were a guest that had arrived at their courtyard,
With every honoured chieftain eager for the flesh of their foes.

Here the author (Allah have mercy upon him) compares the religion to a guest that has arrived at the courtyard of the disbelievers with every honoured chieftain desirous and eager for their flesh. The chieftains are keen and fervently want to look for them, and their foes treat them to their selves and their flesh. The word *chieftain* here refers to the Prophet (Allah bless him and give him peace) and his noble Companions. This is an excellent couplet and is close in meaning to the statement of the poet:

> She said, 'What is this emaciation, what is this gauntness?'
> I answered her with words of the enraptured and lovelorn:
> 'Love for you has come to me as a guest,
> So I gave it my flesh as food and blood as drink!'

And the opposite meaning to this is found in the couplet:

She said, 'Why is your body so supple and soft?
My experience of lovers' bodies is that they are sick.'
I answered her, 'My heart has not divulged its love for you
To my body, so my body knows not what love is.'

يَجُرُّ بَحْرَ خَمِيسٍ فَوْقَ سَابِحَةٍ   يَرْمِي بِمَوْجٍ مِنَ الْأَبْطَالِ مُلْتَطِمِ

Bringing forth a sea of soldiers on swift steeds,
Tossing wave upon wave of onrushing heroes.

The author (Allah have mercy upon him) says that this religion, which has arrived at the courtyard of the disbelievers seeking to have its noble guests (the chieftains) given what they desire of the flesh of the disbelievers, has brought forth an immense sea, this sea being brave soldiers who surge as waves upon waves atop swift battle-steeds. In this couplet the author uses the sea as a metaphor for soldiers because they resemble the sea with their lustrous armour and shining swords. Then the author ascribes the sea to the word soldiers alone, in a way similar to how you might say 'I saw the moon of your face.' Then, to take the metaphor further, he describes the sea by saying that it is riding atop horses. And since he describes the soldiers as being like a sea—and one of the qualities of the sea is that it tosses waves—he goes on to say that the soldiers themselves are tossing wave upon wave; those waves, however, are waves of brave warriors, because brave warriors resemble waves insomuch as they come in successive waves and bring disarray and cut down the ranks of their foes one by one like the successive waves of the sea. The author uses the word *swift* in allusion to the steeds that come one after the other as the waves of the sea come crashing one after the other (it is clearer to designate *swift* as 'the thing compared to' (*al-mushabbah bihi*)).

In this couplet the author is speaking about the victory granted to the Emissary of Allah (Allah bless him and give him peace) and how his religion was made uppermost, and how his sword and the swords of his Companions gained the upper hand against the enemies of the religion and the deniers of the Prophets and Emissaries, until Islam had overwhelmed its foes and gained ascendency over all other religions.

The description of the Prophet (Allah bless him and give him peace) and his Companions as *onrushing heroes* is well known and does not stand in need of any inference, since Allah Most High has described them as being severe towards the disbelievers, saying: '*Severe towards the disbelievers, merciful between themselves*' (Qur'an 48:29), and '*Soft with the believers and stern towards the disbelievers.*' (Qur'an 5:54) When you hear of their battles and contemplate the wars they fought and their efforts and striving with their wealth and lives to give victory to Allah's religion, it will be clear to you that they fully merit being described as valiant and that [this attribute] is theirs specifically to the exclusion of all others.

They are the true men, so let it not be said
That those devoid of their qualities are men!

Were I to mention their qualities and descriptions I would need to devote several volumes [to the subject]. May Allah benefit us by them and allow us to dwell amongst them [in Paradise]!

مِـنْ كُلِّ مُنْتَدِبٍ لِلَّهِ مُحْتَسِبٍ   يَسْطُو بِمُسْتَأْصِلٍ لِلْكُفْرِ مُصْطَلِمِ

All responding to Allah's call and anticipating reward,
Boldly charging on, and uprooting disbelief.

Here the author (Allah have mercy upon him) says that this army which tosses wave upon wave of brave warriors is responding to the call of Allah Most High and answering His invitation to fight when He says '*O you who believe, fight the disbelievers who are near you...*' (Qur'an 9:123)[179] —in addition to other verses to that effect—doing so for the sake of Allah Most High, and seeking His reward and to give victory to His religion; not for the sake of show, fame, tribalism (*ḥamiyya*) or desire for wealth and prestige. They vanquished the disbelievers with their swords and eradicated disbelief with their lances, till disbelief turned its back and fled and the banners of Islam were ascendant. May Allah reward them with goodness on behalf of the people of Islam!

179 This verse was a command to the Prophet (Allah bless and give him peace) to fight those disbelievers who posed an immediate threat to the political stability of the Arabian Peninsula.[p]

حَتَّىٰ غَدَتْ مِلَّةُ الإِسْلَامِ وَهْيَ بِهِمْ مِنْ بَعْدِ غُرْبَتِهَا مَوْصُولَةَ الرَّحِمِ

Until the religion of Islam was, through them,
Reunited in kinship after being in exile.

Here the author (Allah have mercy upon him) says: The Emissary of Allah (Allah bless him and give him peace) and his Companions continued fighting against the disbelievers and vanquishing them with their swords, and persisted in their Jihad for the sake of Allah—striving for His sake truthfully to give victory to His religion and hoping in His reward and anticipating His divine recompense—until His religion was made manifest, His Sharīʿa was made dominant, His word was made uppermost and its followers became numerous, so that the religion of Islam and the law of faith were united in kin after a period of exile and separation. It appears as if the author is alluding to the statement of the Prophet (Allah bless him and give him peace), 'Islam began as something strange, and shall return to being something strange as it began; so glad tidings to the strangers!'[180]

This couplet compares Islam to an exiled woman who was without family or kin with whom she could be reunited. When Islam became widespread, the religion—praise be to Allah—became like a woman reunited with her kin. Before Islam gained ascendency the Muslims were fearful of open displays of their faith; they would worship Allah in secrecy for fear of harm coming to them. The disbelievers would torture anyone who embraced Islam, such as ʿAmmār, Ṣuhayb, Bilāl and Khabāb. During that period the Prophet (Allah bless him and give him peace) would supplicate 'O Allah, grant honour to Islam through either ʿUmar b. al-Khaṭṭāb or Abū al-Ḥakam b. Hishām.'[181] The Prophet's supplication was answered through ʿUmar (Allah be pleased with him), and from the day ʿUmar embraced Islam, the religion became an open affair and the Muslims were able to worship Allah in public. In the early days of Islam disbelief was intense and its adherents had strength and dominance; they attempted to extinguish the light of Allah with their mouths, but Allah refuses but to complete His light, even if the idolaters be averse to it. How eager and keen they were to kill the Prophet (Allah bless him and

180 Muslim.
181 Tirmidhī, *Sunan*.

give him peace)! They placed rewards on his head, enlisted the help of armies, and laid trap upon trap for him, but none of their plots availed them against the will of Allah. Allah is dominant over what He destines!

This couplet alludes to maintaining ties of kinship (*ṣilat al-raḥm*), which is enjoined in the Sharīʿa. The Prophet (Allah bless him and give him peace) said [in a Ḥadīth Qudsī]: 'I am Allah, and I am al-Raḥmān (the All-Merciful). I created the womb (*al-raḥm*) and gave to it from My Name; whoever keeps its ties, I will keep ties with him; and whosoever breaks its ties I will break ties with him.'"[182] And in another *ḥadīth*, the Emissary of Allah (Allah bless him and give him peace) said, 'The womb is attached to the Throne and says, "O Allah, keep ties with whoever keeps ties with me, and cut ties with whoever cuts ties with me!"'[183] There are several other *ḥadīths* along the same lines.

مَكْفُولَةً أَبَدًا مِنْهُمْ بِخَيْرِ أَبٍ ‌ ‌ وَخَيْرِ بَعْلٍ فَلَمْ تَيْتَمْ وَلَمْ تَئِمِ

Forever protected from [foes] by the best of fathers and husbands,
So that she was no longer an orphan or a widow.

Here the author (Allah have mercy upon him) says: The Emissary of Allah (Allah bless him and give him peace) and his Companions after him continued to defeat the disbelievers through battle, capture and eviction until the religion of Islam was reunited with its kin after being exiled (as mentioned earlier). She is forever protected from her foes and cared for by the best of fathers and husbands, who attend to her needs, as a woman with a father and a husband is cared for, with the father securing her provision and needs and the husband fulfilling her rights.

The author compares the religion of Islam—when the Muslims established it dutifully, acted upon its precepts, carefully followed its laws and kept to its obligations—to a woman who enjoyed the guardianship of the best of fathers and husbands. He places the Muslims who establish the religion in the position of her father and husband, they being the best of fathers and the best of husbands. The reason why he compares the religion to a woman under the guardianship of both father and husband, rather than just one, is that when she is cared for by both she will lack

182 Bayhaqī, *al-Sunan al-Kubrā*.

183 Bukhārī and Muslim.

nothing and will be in the best of conditions. On the other hand, if she is cared for by only of them she may be somewhat lacking in her needs.

The author mentions the father and the husband as guardians specifically because guardianship is best when undertaken by them. He calls them the best of fathers and husbands because guardianship may take different forms depending on how they are; if they are as described here, the guardianship will be as it should and will be upheld in the best of manners.

Then the author says: *So that she was no longer an orphan or a widow*. Undoubtedly, if she has a father and a husband then she is neither an orphan nor a widow. Here the word *orphan* is linked with the father and the word *widow* is linked with the husband. This is an outstanding couplet that uses an analogy called 'compound metaphor' (*majāz murakkab*).

هُمُ الْجِبَالُ فَسَلْ عَنْهُمْ مُصَادِمَهُمْ   مَاذَا رَأَىٰ مِنْهُمُ فِي كُلِّ مُصْطَدَمِ

They were mountains! Ask those who came to blows with them
What they saw from them on every field of battle.

Here the author (Allah have mercy upon him) says: These folk, who responded to the call and anticipated reward and recompense from Allah and rose up to give victory to Him and elevate His religion, were like firm and unshakable mountains when in battle with their foes. On the battlefield they neither fled nor budged, and when standing in the frontlines of tumultuous fights they were as firm and unflinching as mountains; that is why the author compares them to mountains. Then he provides proof for the validity of his claim by citing the agreement of the enemy whose wont is to reject and deny the positive qualities, praiseworthy traits and noble merits of his opponents, yet is unable to; their virtues are so famous and have filled the horizons and become as evident as the sun, so there is no way for him to deny them, because sense faculties would prove him a liar. So ask [those enemies or theirs] about these virtues, and they will inform you. Excellent indeed is the statement of the one who said:

Merits attested to by the enemy are preferred,
Since the truth is what enemies [must] acknowledge.

It is natural for an enemy to deny his opponent's virtues, as recognising them will cause him to raise the opponent's status. An enemy focuses on taking things to their extreme limit and belittling his opponent, so he only bears witness to a virtue of his opponent when there is no scope for him to deny it and when he feels that anyone who denies it will be proven a liar by sense faculties.

The author amplifies his praise for the Companions and their good qualities and goes beyond the norm in citing the testimony of their enemies whose wont is to deny and reject. He says: If you ask those who came to blows with them they will tell you of their intrepidness and bravery on the battlefields and in places of combat. They cannot deny this because it is so well-known.

The author compares the Companions to mountains in accordance with the custom of the Arabs, who often compare something that is firm and steady and immovable to a mountain whose nature is firmness and stability. Allah Most High says, '*And they hatched their plot, and their plot was with [in the knowledge of] Allah, and their plotting was such as almost to move mountains!*' (Qur'an 14:46). Since it is not possible to remove mountains or move them from their places, Allah Most High stresses the nature of the plotting of the disbelievers and says that it is such as to nearly move the mountains (this is based upon the Qur'anic reading *(qirāʾa)* whereby the *fatḥa* vowel is recited with the *lām* in the present tense verb).

In saying *Ask those who came to blows with them*, the author means those who came to blows with them on the battlefield and were tested by fighting them: Ask them and they will tell you what they encountered from them by way of things they could neither endure patiently nor bear. If you ask 'Their enemies and opponents are dead, so how can he ask them?' the answer is: Their stories and narratives are well-known and have been transmitted and passed down from the early generations on, so the events described in their stories are like your means of hearing them from the enemy at first hand. The author avoids instructing us to read their narratives directly from the books and instead bids us ask them and hear their testimony to the truth of his words, since that emphasises their acknowledgement and shows that they are in no position to reject or deny. Alternatively, this couplet could mean that if they were alive and present they would have no alternative but to acknowledge what has been said. Allah Most High knows best.

وَسَلْ حُنَيْنًا وَسَلْ بَدْرًا وَسَلْ أُحُدًا   فُصُولَ حَتْفٍ لَهُمْ أَدْهَىٰ مِنَ الْوَخَمِ

Ask Ḥunayn, ask Badr, ask Uḥud—
Seasons of death, more disastrous for them than the plague!

Here the author (Allah have mercy upon him) says, intending hyperbolic effect to show the truthfulness of his claim: *Ask Ḥunayn, ask Badr, ask Uḥud*, all of which were seasons of death and demise for them. They will inform you of what severe frights and immense calamities the disbelievers met with at the hands of the Emissary of Allah (Allah bless him and give him peace) and his Companions. Supposing these seasons could speak, they would answer in this way and their mute tongue of expression (*lisān al-ḥāl*), more eloquent than the tongue of speech (*lisān al-maqāl*), would tell us so.

Because these battles took place in different months, some of which were in the spring, some in the autumn and some in the summer, the author describes them as seasons of death. Since [the unbelievers'] death and destruction came about by means of the sword in these seasons, they are described as seasons of death more calamitous for them than the plague. The questions are referred to these places [rhetorically] for the purpose of hyperbole; the Arabs only ask questions of inanimate objects that cannot reply when it is done for the purposes of emphasising the truth of what is said and showing that the matter is truth and without doubt.

As for the battle of Ḥunayn, it took place after the conquest of Mecca, in the last ten days of Ramaḍān in the eighth year after the Migration. The story in short is as follows. There were ten thousand Companions with the Emissary of Allah (Allah bless him and give him peace) during the conquest of Mecca, and after its conquest two thousand more—from among those who were set free—joined them, making their total number twelve thousand. When the disbelievers among the Arab [clans] heard this they were perturbed, so Hawāzin consolidated their forces with Mālik b. ʿAwf al-Muḍarī as their leader, and [the clan of] Thaqīf gathered with ʿAbd Yālīl b. ʿAmr as their commander; and when the different groupings of people came together they numbered thirty thousand in total. The Emissary of Allah (Allah bless him and give him peace) marched out against them until they all gathered at Ḥunayn. After the idolaters advanced from the opposite side of the ravine from where the Muslim forces were, they were defeated. Qatāda said, 'It was rumoured that those who had been set free [in Mecca] had fled [the battle] with the intention of bringing defeat to the Muslims.'

The Prophet (Allah bless him and give him peace) was riding upon a white mule that day. Abū ʿAbd al-Raḥmān al-Fihrī reported: 'I was with the Emissary of Allah as he was riding upon a horse that had been owned by his paternal uncle al-ʿAbbās and his cousin Abū Sufyān b. al-Ḥārith b. ʿAbd al-Muṭṭalib. Along with him was Ayman, the son of Umm Ayman, who was killed during the course of battle—Allah have mercy upon him. When the fighting grew intense, the Prophet took a handful of soil and cast it towards the faces of the disbelievers, saying "May faces be disfigured!"' Abū ʿAbd al-Raḥmān al-Fihrī continued, 'The Prophet descended from his steed and took a handful of the earth, whereupon the *Sakīna* (Tranquillity) descended to give him victory and he called out to the Anṣār and ordered al-ʿAbbās to call out "Where are those who pledged fealty under the tree [during *Bayʿat al-Riḍwān*]? Where are the people of Sūrat al-Baqara?' whereupon they all redoubled their efforts as a unified whole, and the idolaters were routed.'[184]

Yaʿlā b. ʿAṭāʾ said, 'The sons [of the idolaters who fought at Ḥunayn] related to me that their fathers had said "There were none of us left without some of that soil entering their eyes."'

That is the story of Ḥunayn in brief. Anyone who would like all of the details should consult the biographical works.

As for the battle of Badr, the victory of the Muslims there is famous. It took place on Friday, the seventeenth of Ramaḍān, just twelve months after the Migration, and resulted in the killing of several of the chieftains of Quraysh. As for its cause, the Emissary of Allah (Allah bless him and give him peace) heard that Abū Sufyān was making his way back [to Mecca] from the Levant carrying goods and wares acquired for Quraysh, so he urged the Muslims to set out against him. The Emissary of Allah (Allah bless him and give him peace) went with three hundred or so men

184 Aḥmad.

from amongst the Migrants (Muhājirūn) and the Helpers (Anṣār) to confront Abū Sufyān. Their initial intention was not to engage in fighting—they only had with them a steed belonging to Zubayr (Allah be pleased with him)—but when Abū Sufyān got wind that the Emissary of Allah (Allah bless him and give him peace) had set out to meet him, he hired a man to go to Quraysh and call out for help. The man rushed back to Mecca and pleaded for Quraysh's help, whereupon they set out. When they had descended to the farthest side of the valley, Abū Sufyān then redirected his caravan and took another path. When the Emissary of Allah (Allah bless him and give him peace) was informed of Abū Sufyān's move and Quraysh's approach, he consulted with his Companions. Some of them said, 'O Emissary of Allah (Allah bless him and give him peace), we did not come out to fight anyone; lead us back [to Medina] and let us wait till they come to us.' Others said, 'No, let us meet our enemies head on!' Miqdād b. al-Aswad al-Kindī said, 'O Emissary of Allah (Allah bless him and give him peace), we shall not say to you, as the Children of Israel said [to Mūsā], "*Go, you and your Lord, and let the two of you fight; we shall sit right here.*" (Qur'an 5:26) Rather, we say, "Go, and we shall go with you and fight on your right and on your left side! If you led us to the ocean and bade us enter it, we would enter it with you!' Miqdād's words delighted the Emissary of Allah (Allah bless him and give him peace) and he said, 'Proceed with Allah's blessings.'

The Emissary of Allah (Allah bless him and give him peace) marched on until he reached the wells of Badr, [the army of] Quraysh being at the furthest slope beyond ʿAqanqal. When the Emissary of Allah (Allah bless him and give him peace) finally saw them he supplicated, 'O Allah, here are Quraysh. They have come in their pride and vanity, opposing and belying Your Emissary. O Allah, grant me the victory You have promised me. O Allah, destroy them at daybreak!'

When the Prophet (Allah bless him and give him peace) saw ʿUtba b. Rabīʿa among the fighters and riding atop a red camel he said, 'If there be any man of good and virtue among them they will listen to the man atop the red camel and be guided.'

A group of Quraysh made their way to the cistern that the Emissary of Allah (Allah bless him and give him peace) had built, among whom was Ḥakīm b. Ḥizām. The Prophet (Allah bless him and give him peace) said, 'None shall drink from it but will be slain—except Ḥakīm, for he shall be safe.' (Ḥakim later embraced Islam and was a good Muslim, and he would later swear, 'By Him who saved me on the Day of Badr!') Ḥakīm said to Abū al-Walīd [ᶜUtba], 'Abū al-Walīd, you are senior chieftain of Quraysh and one who is obeyed. Would you like to be remembered with praise amongst them till the end of time?' ᶜUtba said, 'How shall that be?' Ḥakīm replied, 'Lead the people back and take upon yourself the matter of your slain ally ᶜAmr b. al-Ḥaḍramī.' He said to him, 'Your ally here wants to lead the people back, and you have seen your force with your own two eyes.' ᶜĀmir b. al-Ḥaḍramī, whose brother ᶜAmr had been killed [at Nakhla], stood up and shouted at the top of his lungs, 'Alas for ᶜAmr!' and the fever of war began to rise and the situation of the people became confused. When Abū Jahl's words reached ᶜUtbā, ᶜUtba said, 'That coward will soon find out whose lungs are swollen, his or mine!' Then ᶜUtba looked for a helmet to put on his head, but his head was so large that he could not find among the army any helmet that would fit it, so he took a piece of cloth that was with him and wound it around his head.

Al-Aswad b. ᶜAbd al-Aswad al-Makhzūmī came out to the battle, and he was an ill-tempered and vicious man. He swore a solemn oath by Allah that he would drink from the cistern or else he would destroy it or die in the process. When he drew near to the cistern Ḥāmza b. ᶜAbd al-Muṭṭālib went out to confront him and the two met in combat. Near the cistern, Ḥamza struck him with such force that his foot was sliced off from the mid-shin mark, whereupon he stumbled over to the cistern and fell in, as if still trying to fulfil his oath. Ḥamza followed closely behind him and dealt the death blow, killing him as he lay inside the cistern.

Next came ᶜUtba b. Rabᶜīa, followed by al-Walīd and his brother Shayba, who issued the challenge to individual combat (*al-barāz*). An equal number of men from the Anṣār came out to respond to their challenge, to which the men of Quraysh said, 'We have no need of you!' Then they called out, 'O Muḥammad, send forth against us peers from our own tribe!' The Prophet (Allah bless him and give him peace) said, 'Arise, ᶜUbayda b. al-Ḥārith; arise, Ḥamza; arise, ᶜAlī.' When the three drew near, the enemy asked 'Who are you?' They replied, 'We are so-

and-so, sons of so-and-so', to which the three men of Quraysh said, 'Ah, now we have peers and nobles!'

ʿUbayda b. al-Ḥārith, who was the oldest of the three, duelled with ʿUtba b. Rabīʿā; Ḥamza duelled with Shayba; and ʿAlī duelled with al-Walīd b. ʿUtba. Ḥamza, sparing not a moment, immediately slew Shayba, as did ʿAlī with al-Walīd; but al-Ḥārith traded blows with ʿUtba, and each struck the other twice. Ḥamza and ʿAlī then turned their swords against ʿUtba and finished him off. They then carried their wounded companion back to his camp; but he died, Allah have mercy upon him.

Soon after that, the people [i.e. the armies] began to advance and draw near to one other. The Prophet (Allah bless him and give him peace) ordered his Companions to hold their fire and not attack until he gave the order. The Emissary of Allah (Allah bless him and give him peace) was with Abū Bakr in the hut [that had been constructed for him]; he went out to organise the battle ranks of his Companions, and when he passed by Sawād b. Ghaziyya, who was standing out of line, he poked him [in the belly] with an arrow in his hand and said, 'Line up straight, Sawād!' Sawād said, 'You hurt me, Emissary of Allah, and Allah has sent you with the truth, so let me retaliate!' The Emissary of Allah (Allah bless him and give him peace) exposed his stomach and said, 'Retaliate, Sawād', whereupon Sawād embraced him and kissed his stomach. The Prophet (Allah bless him and give him peace) asked him, 'What motivated you to do that, Sawād?' Sawād replied, 'O Emissary of Allah, the battle, as you see, is near approaching [and I may not survive], so it was my wish that my last encounter with you be with my skin touching yours!' The Prophet (Allah bless him and give him peace) prayed for him to obtain goodness.

The Prophet (Allah bless him and give him peace) then returned to his hut and began beseeching his Lord for the victory He had promised. He prayed, 'O Allah, if this band should perish today You will be worshipped no more!' Abū Bakr said to him, 'Surely your Lord will answer your prayer, for Allah will fulfil His promise to you!' Then the Prophet (Allah bless him and give him peace) took a light sleep, and when he had awoken he said, 'Be of good cheer, O Abū Bakr, for Allah's help has come to you. Here is Jibrīl holding the rein of his horse and leading it.'

Then the Prophet (Allah bless him and give him peace) went out to encourage the Muslim forces and rouse them for battle. He said, 'By the

One in whose Hand is my soul, no man will be slain this day fighting against them with steadfast courage, advancing and not retreating, but that Allah will enter him into Paradise!' A man from Banū Salima was eating some dates [and when he heard the Prophet's words] he said, 'Hurrah! There is nothing between me and my entering Paradise save to be killed by these men!' He flung the dates from his hand, took hold of his sword, and fought against the enemy till he was slain.

The Emissary of Allah (Allah bless him and give him peace) took a handful of small pebbles and turned towards Quraysh and said, 'May faces be disfigured, may faces be disfigured!' Then he threw the pebbles and ordered his Companions, 'Charge!' The enemy was defeated. Allah slew many of Quraysh's chieftains and took captive many of their nobles. The Prophet (Allah bless him and give him peace) ordered that ᶜUtba b. Rabīᶜa, Shayba b. Rabīᶜa, Umayya b. Khalaf, ᶜUqba b. Abī Muᶜīṭ and Abū Jahl b. Hishām be flung into a pit. Then he stood over their corpses and called each of them by name, saying 'O so-and-so son of so-and-so, have you found what your Lord promised you to be true? For truly I have found what my Lord promised me to be true!' ᶜUmar asked the Prophet (Allah bless him and give him peace), 'O Emissary of Allah, how can you speak to lifeless bodies?' The Prophet (Allah bless him and give him peace) replied, 'By Allah, you do not hear what I am saying better than they do, but they cannot reply.'

[After giving the order for their bodies to be thrown into the pit] the Prophet (Allah bless him and give him peace) looked at the face of Abū Ḥudhayfa, the son of ᶜUtba b. Rabīᶜa, and saw that his complexion had changed. He said, 'Abū Ḥudhayfa, perhaps you are feeling grieved over your father.' Abū Ḥudhayfa replied, 'No, O Emissary of Allah (Allah bless him and give him peace), I swear by Allah that I entertain no doubts or misgivings about his demise. Yet I knew him as a wise, virtuous and forbearing man, and had hoped that Allah might guide him to Islam because of those qualities; but once I saw what had befallen him and that he had died as a disbeliever I was taken by grief.' The Prophet (Allah bless him and give him peace) was quiet for a while, then he supplicated for Abū Ḥudhayfa and prayed for his good.

[We now turn to the background of the battle of Uḥud.] After the aforementioned men had been thrown into a pit and the idol-worshippers had suffered defeat at Badr, ʿAbdullāh b. Rabīʿa, ʿIkrima b. Abī Jahl and Ṣafwān b. Umayya walked with the men whose fathers and sons had been killed at Badr, and they spoke to Abū Sufyān and those who had had merchandise in that caravan and sought their sympathy, describing what had taken place: 'Men of Quraysh, Muḥammad wronged you and killed the best of your men, so help us with this money to fight him so that we may hope to get our revenge for those we have lost.' So Quraysh gathered the other tribes that would obey them and resolved to wage war against the Emissary of Allah (Allah bless him and give him peace).

Soon after that, the Emissary of Allah (Allah bless him and give him peace) had a dream. He said, 'I have had a dream in which a cow was slaughtered; I saw a dent in the blade of my sword; and I saw that I had thrust my hand into a strong coat of mail. As for the cow, I interpreted it to mean men from my Companions who shall be slain; as for the dented blade, I interpreted it to mean a man from my family who shall be killed; and as for my hand thrusting into a strong coat of mail, I interpreted it as meaning Medina. If you think it well to stop in Medina and leave [the enemy] where they have encamped [we may do so], for if they halt they will have halted in a bad position and if they try to enter the city, we can fight them there.' One of the Muslim men who was to be honoured with martyrdom [at Uḥud] said, 'Emissary of Allah (Allah bless him and give him peace), lead us to fight against our idol-worshipping enemies, lest they think that we are too cowardly and weak to fight them!'

Those who wanted to fight kept urging the Prophet on until he went in his house and put on his armour. This was on a Friday after he had finished the prayer. Meanwhile, the people were remorseful, thinking that they had persuaded the Prophet (Allah bless him and give him peace) against his will and objected to the plan that he considered appropriate. When he came back out they said, 'We pressured you against your will, O Emissary of Allah (Allah bless him and give him peace), when we should not have! If you wish, remain [in Medina] and do as you see fit.' The Prophet (Allah bless him and give him peace) replied, 'It is not fitting that a Prophet who has put on armour for his nation should lay it aside until he has fought.' So the Prophet (Allah bless him and give him peace) marched out with a thousand of his Companions and appointed ʿAbdullāh b. Umm Maktūm to lead the people [of Medina] in prayer.[185]

Quraysh had readied themselves [for battle]; they were three thousand men and had with them two hundred cavalry. At the right of the cavalry was Khālid b. al-Walīd, and at their left was ʿIkrima b. Abī Jahl.

The Prophet (Allah bless him and give him peace) had said, 'Who will take this sword with its right?' The Companions asked, 'What is its right, O Emissary of Allah (Allah bless him and give him peace)?' He said, 'That you smite the enemy with it until it bends!' Abū Dujāna called out, 'I shall take it with its right!' [One of the Companions said] 'Abū Dujāna was a brave man who would act conceitedly and proudly during battle, and whenever he wrapped his red band of cloth around his head we knew he was ready to fight.' They said, 'Abū Dujāna took out his red band of death, and after wrapping it around his head he came out between the two battle ranks and began to strut conceitedly. The Prophet (Allah bless him and give him peace) said, "That is a gait which Allah detests except in a situation like this."'

When the two sides drew near to each other, Hind b. ʿUtba stood up with the women who were with her and they began to beat tambourines while urging the men to fight. Hind's brother and father had both been slain during the battle of Badr, so her hatred and thirst for revenge were strong.

Ḥamza fought gallantly on that day and attained the great richness [i.e., martyrdom], as did Abū Dujāna. When the battle intensified the Prophet (Allah bless him and give him peace) sat down under the standard of the Anṣār and sent for ʿAlī to come forward with his standard. ʿAlī came forth with the standard and said, 'I am Abū al-Qaṣm', whereupon a man [from the enemy] called out to him, 'Dare you accept my challenge to individual combat?' ʿAlī replied, 'Yes!' The two of them then duelled between the ranks and traded blows until ʿAlī dealt a final blow and knocked him to the ground. ʿAlī then left without finishing him off. When he was later asked about that, he said, 'When he fell down his nakedness was exposed and my compassion for him held me back.'

Soon thereafter, Allah sent down His help upon the Muslims and fulfilled His promise to them, and they slew the enemy with their swords

185 A variant is narrated by Bayhaqī in *Sunan al-kubra*.

and cut them off from their camp until they were routed. The Prophet (Allah bless him and give him peace) then put ʿAbdullāh b. Jubayr, brother of Banū ʿAmr b. ʿAwf, in charge over the archers, who numbered fifty men, and had them sit behind the army. He said, 'Remain behind us and do not leave your position!' But when the disbelievers had suffered defeat, those [of the archers] with ʿAbdullāh said, 'The spoils, the spoils!' ʿAbdullāh reminded them of the order given to them by the Emissary of Allah (Allah bless him and give him peace), but they refused to listen to him and got up and left their positions, and only ʿAbdullāh and around ten other men remained. Shortly after that, Khālid b. al-Walīd made his approach [on horse] and killed ʿAbdullāh b. Jubayr and his men and then came up behind the people [the Muslim troops]. A caller cried, 'O servants of Allah, behind you!' The people turned around and began fighting. ʿUtba b. Abī Waqqāṣ struck the Emissary of Allah (Allah bless him and give him peace) and knocked out his molar tooth and wounded his bottom lip, and ʿAbdullāh b. Shihāb struck his face.

The battle of Uḥud was a tribulation and trial by which Allah tested the believers and exposed the hypocrites who had proclaimed Islam verbally. Through this battle, Allah honoured certain people with martyrdom. Allah Most High revealed sixty verses in the Qur'an—in Sūrat Āl ʿImrān—about the battle of Uḥud. In those verses Allah detailed the experiences of that day of theirs [the Muslims] and reproached a number of them. Allah, the Blessed and Most Exalted, said to His Prophet (Allah bless him and give him peace), '*And [remember] when you left your family in the morning to post the believers at their stations for the battle, and Allah is All-Hearing and All-Knowing*' (Qur'an 3:121)—till the end of the series of verses that come after this.

This is but a brief account of the battles mentioned by the author. He mentioned these in particular because of their prominence, and because the confrontations with the enemy in these battles were more intense than others.

اَلْمُصْدِرِي الْبِيضِ حُمْرًا بَعْدَ مَا وَرَدَتْ   مِنَ الْعِدَا كُلَّ مُسْوَدٍّ مِنَ اللِّمَمِ

White swords returned, dripping red after taking drink
From beneath the black heads of all their enemies.

Here the author (Allah have mercy upon him) says that the Companions returned from battle with their swords red with blood from all the disbelievers they had slain and injured with them, though before the swords were unsheathed and wielded they had been white from their polish and shine. After the battles their swords returned dripping red from taking drink from the heads of their foes. This was the result of all that had led up to the Muslims meeting the disbelievers in battle, and shows their bravery since it means they had charged against them with their swords. The idea conveyed by the author in this couplet was expressed before him by ʿAmr b. Kulthūm, who said:

O Abū Hind, do not be hasty with us!
Wait and watch for us to inform you with certainty
That we shall enter the fray with white standards
And return with them dripping red having quenched their thirst!

The author mentions heads in particular, and that is what he means when he says *From beneath the black heads of all their enemies*. He says *black heads* to convey the sense that the disbelievers who were fighting were young men skilled in combat and practiced in the ways of war. Nevertheless, despite the strength and numbers of the disbelievers, Allah gave the Companions victory over them.

وَالْكَاتِبِينَ بِسُمْرِ الْخَطِّ مَا تَرَكَتْ أَقْلَامُهُمْ حَرْفَ جِسْمٍ غَيْرَ مُنْعَجِمِ

Like scribes with wielded spears for pens,
Leaving no letter of a body unmarked with dots.

The author (Allah have mercy upon him), having described the Companions of the Emissary of Allah (Allah bless him and give him peace) and [their] enemies and saying that the Companions' swords would return red with the blood from the heads of the disbelievers, says that their spears too were pens with which they wrote dotted letters on the bodies of the disbelievers. The 'writing' refers to the effect of the blows and the 'dots' refer to the spattered blood that came from the wounds. The pens – meaning the spears – left no part of their bodies unmarked with dots. This simile of the author's had been used before among the Arabs. One poet said:

Brother in arms, had you witnessed my bearings
As the horses stood beneath the spears, heads lowered,
You would have read what was marked by the hand of tumult;
What the white sword wrote of letters, and what the spear marked of dots!

This poet describes the white sword as making inscriptions because of its striking power and reach (for it leaves wounds like inscriptions), and describes the spear as marking with dots because it leave puncture wounds in the body (which bear the most resemblance to dots). This couplet conveys this meaning more effectively.

The meaning of the author's couplet is that the swords (mentioned in this line and the one before it) did what was most fitting for them, just as the spears did what was most fitting for them. He says that writing pens have left the marks and dots, and this is one of the best and sweetest couplets in this poem.

§ إِنْ قَامَ فِي جَامِعِ الْهَيْجَا خَطِيبُهُمُ   تَصَامَمَتْ عَنْهُ أُذْنَا صِمَّةِ الصِّمَمِ

When their orator stood amidst the noise of battle,
Their ears would feign deafness to his cry.

After describing the Companions as having used their spears to write on the disbelievers—with their large stab wounds appearing like writing and their small stab wounds appearing like dots—the author then mentions what results from writing: that is, reading. He says: If their orator stands in their midst reading aloud to them what he has inscribed on their bodies, he will find that they are dead, or he will find that they are completely oblivious [to him] because of the horror they are experiencing, and so cannot hear anyone's words. So if the ears of brave warriors feign deafness, what about the ears of the cowardly!

What is meant here by *orator* is a Companion who stands over the disbelievers after their defeat, though it may also refer to an orator of their own. [Following the latter interpretation] the couplet means: If any orator among them stands and encourages them to fight on, the brave ones in their ranks will feign deafness and, owing to the horror that has descended upon them, he will find no one listening to him. The former interpretation, however, is more fitting.

This couplet is missing from many copies [of the *Burda*], and none of the commentators whose works I have come across made mention of it. Allah Most High knows best.

شَاكِي السِّلَاحِ لَهُمْ سِيمَا تُمَيِّزُهُمْ   وَالْوَرْدُ يَمْتَازُ بِالسِّيمَا مِنَ السَّلَمِ

Well-armed, they were distinguished by a clear sign,
as a rose differs from an acacia tree in its features.

Here the author (Allah have mercy upon him) says: Because of their intense focus on Jihad, eagerness for battle and bravery, the Companions had great concern for weaponry that would assist them in Jihad. They would sharpen their blades and remove rust from them. They had a sign that set them apart from others. As Allah Most High said in His description of them: '*Muḥammad is the Emissary of Allah, and those with him are stern against the disbelievers, merciful among themselves. You see them bowing and prostrating, seeking bounty from Allah and [His] good pleasure. Their distinguishing mark is on their faces from the trace of prostration.*' (Qur'an 48:29) The scholars disagree about the meaning of this 'distinguishing mark' that Allah mentions in this verse. Mālik said, 'Their foreheads were covered in dust from frequent prostration on the ground.' Others have suggested that it is a divine promise about their condition on the Day of Resurrection, and that Allah Most High will grant them light on that Day from the traces of prostration just as He will cause the parts of their bodies washed in ablution to shine. Others have said that this 'distinguishing mark' is their pleasant demeanour—meaning their humility that shows upon their faces—which is the condition of those who offer many prayers. Others have said that this 'distinguishing mark' is the paleness and sallow complexion that marks sleepless faces.

After this, the author appends another likeness by which the Companions are distinguished from others. He says that just as a rose is distinguishable from a tree, likewise the Companions are set apart by salient features that distinguish them from other fighters. Those features are their humility, self-effacement and pleasant demeanour. May Allah bring us benefit through their blessings!

تُهْدِي إِلَيْكَ رِيَاحُ النَّصْرِ نَشْرَهُمُ   فَتَحْسِبُ الزَّهْرَ فِي الأَكْمَامِ كُلَّ كَمِي

The winds of victory bring you their scent as a gift;
You would think each armed hero a flower in bud!

Here the author (Allah have mercy upon him) addresses all who can be addressed, saying: The winds of victory and support give you the fragrance and fine scent of the Companions, so that you reckon each brave warrior among them to be, because of their virtues and merits, a flower in bud. The author uses fine scent as a metaphor for the widely diffused virtues and honours of the Companions. And because it is in the nature of scent that it is wafted and carried by the winds, the author informs us that this scent was wafted by winds of victory. He uses wind as a metaphor for victory. And because it is in the nature of a scent to be contained in a flower, the author describes the Companions as flowers in bud. The reason he compares them to flowers in bud is that they were concealed beneath their armour, so he put them in the same position as a flower concealed within its bud. The souls are like buds and the Companions are like flowers, and that is why the author says: *You would think each armed hero a flower in bud*! And Allah Most High knows best.

كَأَنَّهُمْ فِي ظُهُورِ الْخَيْلِ نَبْتُ رُبًا   مِنْ شِدَّةِ الْحَزْمِ لَا مِنْ شَدَّةِ الْحُزُمِ

As if, riding their steeds, they were flowers on a hill-top
Held firm not by strong stirrups, but by strength of resolve.

After describing the Companions in the preceding couplets, the author compares their strength, relentlessness and firmness when riding their steeds to flowers upon hillocks. This proves their chivalry and courage. Their firmness on steeds, he says, was not because they secured themselves with straps, stirrups or any other novel strategy, for such techniques are only used when there is fear and weakness and ignorance of the ways of chivalry. They did nothing of the sort; rather, their firmness on their steeds was a result of their bravery and knowledge of martial skills, as well as their eagerness for combat, firm resolve and discipline. They suffered neither dread nor terror, and neither fled from the battlefields nor budged. How could one not have energy and remain steadfast when he has certain knowledge that he will attain one of two goods, either victory over his enemy or martyrdom, both of which are excellent merits? Such a person will have either a blessing in this life, namely victory and spoils of war, or an eternal blessing in the Hereafter, namely triumph through martyrdom and multiplied rewards. The Most High says, '*Say, "Do you anticipate anything for us but one of two goods…?"*' (Qur'an 9:52)

The author compares the Companions' firmness and relentlessness to flowers upon hillocks and not to flowers that grow in the lowlands because the former are strong and firm, unlike the latter which are not firm and which can easily and quickly be uprooted. Allah Most High knows best.

طَارَتْ قُلُوبُ الْعِدَا مِنْ بَأْسِهِمْ فَرَقًا   فَمَا تُفَرِّقُ بَيْنَ الْبَهْمِ وَالْبُهَمِ

Their forceful onslaught so put their foes' hearts to flight
that you could not have told a herd from a warrior.

Here the author (Allah have mercy upon him) says: The [disbelievers'] hearts took flight and their minds were scattered out of the fear and panic brought on by the intrepidness and bravery of the Muḥammadan troops. So intense was the shock visited upon the disbelievers that they were completely beside themselves with fear, and so severe was their mental stupor that they were unable to distinguish between realities, and could not tell the difference between a herd of sheep and cattle and the brave warriors among the Companions. As a result of this terror and stupor they would flee when seeing a herd of sheep, thinking them to be the [Muslim] horsemen.

وَمَنْ تَكُنْ بِرَسُولِ اللَّهِ نُصْرَتُهُ   إِنْ تَلْقَهُ الْأُسْدُ فِي آجَامِهَا تَجِمِ

For the one whose help comes from the Emissary of Allah
Even lions finding him in their dens will be loth to face him.

Here the author (Allah have mercy upon him) says: Do not deny that the hearts of the enemy took flight out of fear when meeting the Companions of Allah's Emissary (Allah bless him and give him peace) in battle; and do not deny the Companions' courage, bravery, prowess in combat and skill on the battlefield. For he who is given victory through the Emissary of Allah (Allah bless him and give him peace) and who gives aid to his religion and turns to him in his affairs and concerns, it is only fitting that everything should fear him and that all of creation be afraid of his force. If one of them were to attack ferocious lions in their dens, the lions, despite their aggressiveness and rapacity (especially in their dens), would be loth to fight with him.

In this line the author is referring to the bravery of the Companions and the strength of their force and onslaught against their foes. If one who is given aid through the Emissary of Allah (Allah bless him and give him peace) is feared by lions in their dens and lions are loth to fight with him, how can they not cause fear to fighters whose hearts had taken flight out of dread and who were in such a stupor that they could not distinguish between a herd and a brave warrior?

He who is given victory through the Emissary of Allah (Allah bless him and give him peace) is given victory through Allah, because obedience to the Emissary of Allah is obedience to Allah. The Most High says, '*Whoever obeys the Emissary has obeyed Allah*.' (Qur'an 4:80) He who is given victory by Allah will never be vanquished by any foe.

It is related that a group of Companions, among whom was ʿAbdullāh b. ʿUmar, were walking when a lion appeared before them. ʿAbdullāh b. ʿUmar walked up and took the lion by its ear and moved it off of the path. [When asked about what he had done] he said, 'If you fear Allah [truly] everything will fear you.'

It is also narrated that when Safīna, the freed bondsman of the Emissary of Allah (Allah bless him and give him peace), encountered a lion on his path and said to it, 'I am the freed bondsman of the Emissary of Allah!' the lion purred and showed him the way.

Some have reported that [once] a man had set out to visit a saint when he was confronted by a lion on the road. When he complained of this to the saint, the saint went out to the lion and pinched its ear and said to it, 'Did I not tell you to stop bothering my guests?

A story is also told of a saint who would summon a lion and ride on its back as crowds looked on. Indeed, whoever obeys Allah will be obeyed by everything. You shall be with the cosmos for as long as you do not witness the Creator, but when you witness the Creator, all of the cosmos will be with you. With Allah is enabling grace, and there is no might or power except with Allah, the Exalted and Magnificent!

وَلَنْ تَرَىٰ مِنْ وَلِيٍّ غَيْرَ مُنْتَصِرٍ   بِهِ وَلَا مِنْ عَدُوٍّ غَيْرَ مُنْقَصِمِ

You will not see one saint who is not victorious through him;
Or a single foe of his who is not dealt mortal blows.

Here the author (Allah have mercy upon him) says: You will never see a believer who is not given victory over his physical and spiritual foes through the Emissary of Allah (Allah bless him and give him peace); and you will never see an enemy who is not made to suffer mortal blows at the hands of him whose victory is through the Emissary of Allah (Allah bless him and give him peace). Because the Companions attained victory through the Emissary of Allah (Allah bless him and give him peace) more than others, they were feared by lions in their dens and by kings in their seats of power.

It is said that the meaning of this couplet is as follows: You will not see a believer who does not gain victory through the Emissary of Allah (Allah bless him and give him peace) and rely upon him in all of his affairs; and you will not see a disbeliever—an enemy to the Emissary of Allah—who is not cut off from the Emissary of Allah and who gains victory through him or relies upon him. The former meaning is more fitting in view of the preceding couplet; but Allah Most High knows best.

أَحَلَّ أُمَّتَهُ فِي حِرْزِ مِلَّتِهِ   كَاللَّيْثِ حَلَّ مَعَ الْأَشْبَالِ فِي أَجَمِ

He gave his nation sanctuary in the stronghold of his faith,
As a lion settles in with its cubs in a thicket.

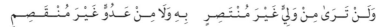

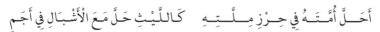

Here the author (Allah have mercy upon him) says that because of his intense compassion and care for his nation, the Prophet (Allah bless him and give him peace) asked Allah to grant them victory and power over the lands so that He might confer upon them honour, authority and safety, remove their fear, and enter them into the impenetrable fortress and sanctuary of his religion—all by them defeating their foes and gaining power in their lands. Through the blessings and care of the Prophet (Allah bless him and give him peace) they enjoyed much safety and security after fear, and became many after being few, thus being like a lion cub in the care of its father. When a lion is with its cubs no one will dare trespass against it or try to do anything harmful to it or its cubs, as its cubs enjoy protection and safekeeping. Similarly, anyone who believes in the Emissary of Allah (Allah bless him and give him peace), and who embraces his religion and enters his sanctuary, will not suffer harm or abasement, and will not be touched with fear, and no one will dare subject him to harm. May Allah make us of those who seek the sanctuary of the Prophet's law and hold fast to him. Amen!

كَمْ جَدَّلَتْ كَلِمَاتُ اللّٰهِ مِنْ جَدِلٍ فِيهِ وَكَمْ خَصَمَ الْقُرْءَانُ مِنْ خَصِمِ

How often have Allah's words felled his opponents,
And how often the Qur'an has defeated its enemies!

Here the author (Allah have mercy upon him) says: How often has an obstinate, quarrelsome person argued over the state of the Prophet (Allah bless him and give him peace) and his status and what he brought, only to be defeated and felled by the words of Allah and to have his ostensible proofs invalidated by the Mighty Qur'an, leaving him without any proofs or specious doubts. And how many a quarrelsome opponent has been defeated by signs that prove the Prophet's truthfulness, such as the water that poured from his fingers, the splitting of the moon, the glorification of the pebbles [in his blessed hand] and other resplendent signs and unequivocal proofs that appeared by his hands, leaving no denier or argumentative foe—except those for whom damnation was predestined—any choice but to acknowledge his prophethood and veracity!

The Jews would often ask the Prophet (Allah bless him and give him peace) about what was contained in their scriptures; the intent behind their questions was simply stubbornness, but the Qur'an would reveal the answers to their questions and rebuke them. An example of this is when they asked about the soul (*rūḥ*) and about Dhū al-Qarnayn, and about the People of the Cave (*Ahl al-Kahf*) and what Isrāʾīl (the Prophet Yaʿqūb) made forbidden for himself. The Qur'an revealed the answers to all of their questions and refuted their provocations.

كَفَاكَ بِالْعِلْمِ فِي الْأُمِّيِّ مُعْجِزَةً فِي الْجَاهِلِيَّةِ وَالتَّأْدِيبِ فِي الْيُتُمِ

The erudition of an unlettered one is miracle enough
in an Age of Ignorance, as is an orphan's education.

In the previous couplet the author (Allah have mercy upon him) stated that the Mighty Qur'an has felled those who argued against it and revealed answers that refuted the provocations and stubbornness of its opponents, and that the clear miracles and breaks with natural phenomena that manifested at the Prophet's hands defeated and silenced opponents. Because those proofs are innumerable, the author says here: When you furnish proof, it is enough for you to mention two magnificent and inimitable miracles that took place in the Age of Ignorance. The first of these miracles is the fact that the Prophet (Allah bless him and give him peace) was the most knowledgeable of all when it came to this life and the Next, the past nations and bygone generations, and the first and the last—although he was unlettered and could neither read nor write, and was never afforded the chance to study or peruse books. He did not look into the books of the early nations, and did not read their exploits or study their narratives and accounts; nevertheless, he relayed information concerning the past and spoke of what is to come in the future up to the establishment of the Final Hour, and related the knowledge of the first and the last which was only known to individual learned scholars among their rabbis and priests—of which they only knew in a piecemeal fashion and acquired only after spending their entire lives in study and learning it. This was during the Age of Ignorance in which all such details were completely unknown. It had been a long while since people were familiar with Prophets, and they had altered and changed the content of Allah's sacred Scriptures by either adding to them or subtracting from them or concealing them; but then came the Prophet (Allah bless him and give him peace), who exposed them, confirmed the past sacred laws and belied those who had denied any part of them. This alone is enough to prove the soundness of his claim and the truth of his prophethood, for although the Prophet (Allah bless him and give him peace) did not read (or even try to read or study) or receive from someone who could read, there manifested from him such divinely vouchsafed sciences and branches of knowledge, such masterful governance of creation in all their diversity, such all-embracing knowledge of all worldly and religious benefits, such absolute embodiment of every excellent quality of character and every perfection possible for mankind, and such pre-eminence in every kind of knowledge, judgement and wisdom, that they render all of creation utterly incapacitated and his unique position is made manifest to all.

The Prophet (Allah bless him and give him peace) was a clear sign and dazzling proof. His unletteredness was a manifest perfection in his case, for reading and writing are ancillary means whose end purpose is to attain knowledge, so if the fruit is already obtained there is no need for them. Moreover, had the Prophet (Allah bless him and give him peace) been able to write, that would have been cause for doubt since it might be thought that his writing would obviate the need to meet him face to face. As the Most High says, '*And you did not recite a Scripture before it, and you did not write it with your right hand, for then the falsifiers would have had [reason] to doubt.*' (Qur'an 29:48). Since complete unletteredness is inextricably connected with prophethood (*nubuwwa*), the term 'Unlettered' has not been mentioned except in conjunction with the term 'Prophet', so the former should not be mentioned in isolation from the latter. (As for the author, he mentions it here in isolation because he is speaking of it as an inimitable miracle, so there is no objection to be made against him.)

The second of these miracles is what the Prophet (Allah bless him and give him peace) had by way of the highest levels of manners (*ādāb*) and loftiest degrees of good character, as described here and there throughout the rigorously authenticated reports and well-known *ḥadīth* traditions. ᶜAlī (Allah be pleased with him) described the Prophet (Allah bless him and give him peace) [thus]: 'His heart was the soundest of hearts, his speech was the most truthful of speech, and he was the gentlest of all people in nature and the noblest of them in relations...'[186] There are many other *ḥadīth* of this nature. Nevertheless, the Prophet (Allah bless him and give him peace) had no one to teach him or instill in him good character. His father had died while his mother was pregnant with him, and after he was born he remained with his mother and grandfather under Allah's care and protection; Allah, wanting to honour him, caused him to grow up beautifully.

When the Prophet (Allah bless him and give him peace) was six years of age his mother passed away and he was left in the care of his grandfather ᶜAbd al-Muṭṭalib. ᶜAbd al-Muṭṭalib would have a cushion placed for him in the shade of the Kaᶜba. Out of respect for him, none of his sons would sit upon it. The Emissary of Allah (Allah bless him and give him peace) would come and sit upon it and his uncles would remove him

186 Tirmidhī, *Shamāʾil*.

from it, but his grandfather told them, 'Leave him be, dear sons, for by Allah, something tremendous indeed shall come of this son of mine!' Then he would sit the Prophet (Allah bless him and give him peace) next to him and rub his back and show his happiness with what the Prophet was doing.[187]

When the Prophet (Allah bless him and give him peace) was eight years of age ʿAbd al-Muṭṭalib died. The Emissary of Allah (Allah bless him and give him peace) was then under the care of his uncle, Abū Ṭālib. Allah, wanting to honour the Prophet and give him His divine message, protected him and safeguarded him from the filth of the Age of Ignorance as he grew into maturity, till he entered adulthood as the most virtuous man of his people, the best of them in character, the noblest of them in pedigree, the finest of them in company, the greatest of them in clemency, the most truthful of them in speech, the most trustworthy of them in rendering trusts and the furthest of them from immorality—till Allah ultimately chose him to be the recipient of His divine message and selected him for His tremendous favour, Allah bless him, honour him, ennoble him and give him peace!

The Prophet (Allah bless him and give him peace) despite being raised an orphan, attained an undeniable level of propriety, moral virtues and well-pleasing qualities of character, all of which have been presented in *al-Shifā'* and other works. Anas said, 'I served the Prophet for ten years and never once did he say "Fie!" to me; nor did he ever ask me, if I did something, "Why did you do that?" or if I failed to do something, "Why did you not do that?"'[188] The Prophet (Allah bless him and give him peace) would respond to those who called him, and no one would call out to him but he would say 'At your service!' He used to joke with his Companions and mingle with them, and would converse with them and play with their children. He would respond to the call of a servant or poor person. He would visit the sick. He would accept the excuse of one seeking pardon. Whenever anyone shook his hand he would never be the first to release it; he would release it only after the other person released his. He would initiate greetings of peace to those who he met and would be the first to shake hands. He never interrupted people when they were

187 This is taken from a *ḥadīth* recorded by al-Bayhaqī in *Dalāʾil al-Nubuwwa*.
188 Bukhārī.

speaking. Whenever anyone sat near him while he was at prayer, he would lighten his prayer. Then [after finishing his prayer], he would inquire about the person's need and then return to his prayer. May Allah bless him and give him peace!

CHAPTER 9

Seeking Intercession through the Prophet ﷺ

خَـدَمْـتُـهُ بِـمَـدِيحٍ أَسْـتَـقِيـلُ بِـهِ   ذُنُـوبَ عُـمْـرٍ مَـضَىٰ فِي الشِّعْرِ وَالْـخِدَمِ

By this euology I have served him, seeking absolution
For the sins of a life spent in poetry and patronage.

HERE THE AUTHOR (Allah have mercy upon him) says that he has served the Emissary of Allah (Allah bless him and give him peace) and has sought a means of approach through praising him, lauding him, and mentioning his beautiful life story, praiseworthy attributes, virtuous morals, sanctified merits and dazzling miracles—seeking absolution for past sins and forgiveness for the misdeeds of days gone by. He seeks absolution for the sin of going to excess and overpraising others in his poetic tributes, which he did for the sake of gaining their favour, and out of desire for their ephemeral worldly possessions. He replaced all that with a eulogy dedicated to the Master of the two abodes (this life and the Next) and the noblest of the two rational species [of men and jinn]. There is no doubt that a person who seeks a means of approach to Allah through praise of His beloved will attain what he seeks and obtain what he desires. The Most High says, '*O you who believe, have consciousness of Allah and seek the means of approach to Him.*' (Qur'an 5:35) Indeed, there is no means greater than the Emissary of Allah (Allah bless him and give him peace), for he is Allah's greatest door. [Ibn al-Wafā says:]

You are the door to Allah; whoever attempts to enter [the Divine Presence]
From any door other than yours shall not enter It.

The Prophet (Allah bless him and give him peace) would bestow generous rewards on those who praised him. He would say to Ḥassān [b. Thābit], 'O Allah, aid him with the Holy Spirit!'[189] The Prophet (Allah bless him and give him peace) also said that to Ḥassān after he recited the line in his ode in which he told some of the disbelievers among Quraysh:

You lampooned Muḥammad and I responded;
And with Allah shall be the reward.

إِذْ قَلَّدَانِيَ مَا تُخْشَى عَوَاقِبُهُ   كَأَنَّنِي بِهِمَا هَدْيٌ مِنَ النَّعَمِ

For these two have yoked me, with consequences I fear;
as if I were, on their account, a ritual lamb for slaughter.

Here the author (Allah have mercy upon him) says that he did not have a pious objective behind the poetry he had [previously] composed, as it was not in praise of the Prophet (Allah bless him and give him peace) or dedicated to one of the sacred sciences or other forms of wisdom, [the exposition of] which is a good deed. Instead, he says, his poetry was about vain worldly matters such as flattery of kings and so on, all of which entails hyperbole and exaggeration, and which cause one to tell lies and say things that are impermissible, this being the prohibited form of poetry and the type described in the words of the Most High '*And the poets—followed by the erring...*' (Qur'an 26:224). As for poetry that contains wisdom or exhortation, or praise for one by praising whom good deeds are earned, all of that is good, and that is what the Prophet (Allah bless him and give him peace) meant when he said 'Verily in some poetry there is wisdom.'[190] Al-Shāfiʿī said, 'Poetry is [a form] of speech: [what is] good in it is good and [what is] bad in it is bad.'

Likewise, his cultivation of rulers was not for a praiseworthy end; rather, it was for the sake of finding favour and benefaction, and seldom is one free from those intentions. He feels, therefore, that he has been yoked with poetry and patronage and led by them to a final consequence that is to be feared; though his poetry and patronage have adorned him in this life, their end result is doom and abject loss. That is why he says

189 Bukhārī.
190 Bukhārī and Muslim.

that *For these two have yoked me*—that is, the sins of poetry and seeking the patronage of kings, the end results of which are to be feared. Then he compares himself in that regard to a ritual lamb that is garlanded. So just as a ritual lamb is garlanded and festooned right before its death and slaughter or sacrifice, likewise the author says that his poetry and patronage have raised him up high in the world and led him to enjoy outward distinction among his peers, even though inwardly these have led him to destruction and ruin—unless, of course, he obtains pardon from the Generous Sovereign [Allah]. This is one of the most excellent couplets in this ode, and none have preceded him in it. Allah Most High knows best.

أَطَعْتُ غَيَّ الصِّبَا فِي الْحَالَتَيْنِ وَمَا   حَصَّلْتُ إِلَّا عَلَى الْآثَامِ وَالنَّدَمِ

In both I obeyed the reckless folly of youth,
And gained nothing except sins and regrets.

Here the author (Allah have mercy upon him) says: In my poetry and praise of people I have obeyed the drive and reckless folly of youth. I have spent my life seeking the patronage of others and composing poetry to praise them, but by going to excess in such a way that it is not without lies. From all of that I have gained nothing but perdition and sin, and have sacrificed my honour and taken advantage of creation for a few fleeting days whose ignominy and ill-consequence will linger on after the respect and prestige I earned from panegyric poetry is long gone and vanished. [From this couplet] it appears as though the author encountered an apparition bringing a secret.

All of this happened during the time of his youth; as he aged, his reason returned to him and he awakened from his heedlessness and expressed remorse at what had passed, and he realised that what was coming had already arrived. In this [couplet] the author acknowledges his past sins and expresses scorn towards his ego in the presence of the one he is asking, so that it might be a cause for pardon, forgiveness and mercy.

A servant [of Allah], during the period of youth, is not impervious to folly, since [as the saying goes] 'Youth is a branch of madness', unlike the period of maturity, which is usually characterised by a weakened urge towards carnal desires along with a strengthened intellect. For this reason one *ḥadīth* includes the statements, 'Your Lord is amazed at a young man who is without folly.'[191] It is also narrated that 'When the servant [of Allah] reaches forty years of age but has yet to repent and abandon [sin], Satan drags his hand along his forelock and says to him, "Ah, welcome to a face that will not succeed!"'[192] It is also reported that the Prophet (Allah bless him and give him peace) said, 'There are four [types of people] despised by Allah, Exalted and Sublime is He: a seller of merchandise who swears oaths to sell his wares, a conceited poor person, an elderly fornicator, and a tyrannical leader.'[193] May Allah protect us from the destinations of the damned. Amen!

فَيَا خَسَارَةَ نَفْسٍ فِي تِجَارَتِهَا   لَمْ تَشْتَرِ الدِّينَ بِالدُّنْيَا وَلَمْ تَسُمِ

Alas, what abject loss for a soul in its transaction!
It did not buy the Next World at the price of this – or even try to!

Here the author (Allah have mercy upon him) openly expresses the regret and remorse contained in his heart, pitying his own condition and acknowledging his remissness and neglect. He mourns because of the abject loss for his soul, and grieves over it because of a lifetime spent in superficialities wherein it sold what is precious and valuable—that being religion, by means of which a person secures ease in this world and bliss in the Next, and which is the foundation of all profit and the epitome of happiness—in exchange for a paltry and short-lived piece of the lower world. It has preferred what is valueless over what is valuable, and what is insignificant over what is of the utmost significance, purchasing the world at the price of the religion instead of purchasing this world to secure the Next. Averse to the religion and desirous of the world and its ephemeral vanities and fleeting adornments, it did not occur to [his soul] that it should seek to acquire religion, much less purchase it.

One of the wise has said, 'Had this world been of gold but set to vanish, and had the Hereafter been of mud but set to remain, the intelligent person would choose what shall remain over what shall vanish, especially

191 Aḥmad.
192 Al-Ḥāfiẓ al-ʿIrāqī says in *al-Mughnī ʿan ḥaml al-asfār fī al-asfār* that this *ḥadīth* has no basis.
193 Ibid., this *ḥadīth* has no basis.

considering that the opposite is true.' May Allah grant us enabling grace to do what He loves and is pleased with.

If you ask 'How can he say that he did not buy, or even attempt to buy, this world for the Next when that is the state of someone who has not obtained anything of faith?' the reply is as follows: The author did not say that he failed to buy the religion or that he failed to attempt it. Rather he says that he did not buy, or seek to buy, the religion at the price of this world. His failure to buy the religion at the price of this world does not necessarily mean he did not attain it in other ways. His objective here is only to describe his lack of non-attachment to the world, and in doing so he produces this couplet for hyperbolic effect. He did attain faith through his conviction and good deeds and his pronouncement [of the testimony of faith]. But he is expressing his outrage over his soul, describing himself as one clinging tenaciously to the world and jealously vying with others over it, and says that he has not reached the level of the ascetics. And Allah Most High knows best.

وَمَنْ يَبِعْ آجِلًا مِنْهُ بِعَاجِلِهِ   يَبِنْ لَهُ الْغَبْنُ فِي بَيْعٍ وَفِي سَلَمِ

Anyone who sells the Hereafter for the ephemeral
Will be cheated in their present and future transactions.

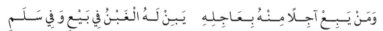

This couplet completes the meaning expressed in the previous couplet. It is as if he were saying: 'How can one not suffer abject loss in his purchase and be cheated in his transaction if he sells an immortal kingdom and inexhaustible bliss in exchange for insipid and short-lived goods that are made loathsome with faults and illness, and that dwindle, wane and suffer change, as is the wont of the lower world and its people?' For death lies in wait at every moment and heralds the loss of everything familiar, of wealth and kin, children and homeland, where everything that is to come is near at hand, and anyone who lived for a thousand years would be like someone who lived for a single year. How deserving is this soul of abject loss, and how deserving is this seller of being cheated! We are all that man. May Allah (Glorified is He!) deal with us with His grace and benevolence, and give us the ability in these short moments that remain to make amends for what has passed us by! He who denies that he has been cheated and suffered loss in his transaction is ruined, while he who confirms and knows that he has suffered loss in his transaction is a fool whose actions are those of one without intellect. For indeed anyone who sells perfect delight, perpetual happiness and inexhaustible bliss in return for a short-lived and ephemeral pleasure should be considered a fool.

In the light of such realities, it behoves an intelligent person to weep. The defrauded person will only uncover the fraud when the covering is lifted and the good-doer is rewarded for his good and the evil-doer is requited for his evil. On that Day, pain shall be grievous and the bereft person will experience regret though it will avail him naught, and he will wish to make up for what he missed but will find no way to do so. On that Day, tears will be shed in torrents, hearts will quiver, and people will long for return [to the world]—but that is absolutely out of the question! O Generous in Pardoning, O Immensely Kind One, deal with us with Your generosity and kindness, O Most Merciful of the Merciful!

إِنْ آتِ ذَنْبًا فَمَا عَهْدِي بِمُنْتَقِضٍ مِنَ النَّبِيِّ وَلَا حَبْلِي بِمُنْصَرِمِ

I have sinned, yet my pledge to the Prophet is unbroken;
Nor has the rope binding me to him been severed.

Here the author (Allah have mercy upon him) consoles himself and says: Were I to commit sins and engage in acts of disobedience and commit enormities, none of that would break the pledge to which I am bound or the covenant I have taken with my Lord: to have faith in Allah and belief in His Emissary (Allah bless him and give him peace) and all that he has brought, and to be committed and maintain my belief in this life and after death. My hope in my Lord is strong, and my opinion of Him is good. I seek a means of approach [to Him] through His most eminent beloved and supreme Emissary (Allah bless him and give him peace); I hope, by His immense divine concern, that I shall not be disappointed and that He will accept my means of approach to Him. For I continuously seek his [the Prophet's] intercession and hope in it, and hope to be delivered from entanglement in sin. For even though I have committed enormities, I still have the basis of faith and the belief of a monotheist.

The Prophet (Allah bless him and give him peace) said, 'Whosoever says as his last words "There is no god but Allah" will enter Paradise.'[194]

The author uses the word *rope* as a metaphor for 'pledge' since a pledge, like a rope, is a means of reaching something. By pledge he means the pledge of faith; it is also possible that the pledge refers to the covenant taken on the Day [when Allah said to humanity] '*Am I not your Lord?*' (Qur'an 7:172)

You may object: 'Using the word "if" implies that he is not certain, but in the previous lines he complained of his sins, so the context dictates that he use the word "when".' The response is as follows: There is an ellipsis in the author's statement, and the full meaning is: Even if I were to become known as an open and flagrant sinner, I would still have a pledge that would not break and a rope that could not be severed. (And indeed, the author was not known to be a flagrant sinner.) Allah Most High knows best.

فَإِنَّ لِي ذِمَّةً مِنْهُ بِتَسْمِيَتِي مُحَمَّدًا وَهُوَ أَوْفَى الخَلْقِ بِالذِّمَمِ

For I have a protective covenant with him owing to my name—Muḥammad—and he is the most loyal of mankind to covenants.

Here the author (Allah have mercy upon him) amends his earlier claim when he spoke of *the rope binding me to him* and explained why it could not be severed. He says: How could my rope of connection to the Prophet (Allah bless him and give him peace) be severed? I have security and protection afforded by him, which have come as a result of receiving the same name as the Prophet (Allah bless him and give him peace)—Muḥammad—and he is the most loyal of mankind in keeping trusts and fulfilling pledges.

It is narrated in *ḥadīth* reports that the Prophet (Allah bless him and give him peace) will intercede for everyone whose name is Muḥammad. It is reported that Surayj b. Yūnus said, 'Allah Most High has angels whose [form of] worship is to roam and visit every house containing a person named Aḥmad or Muḥammad.' Another report asks, 'What harm is there for you in having in your homes one, two or three people named Muḥammad?' It is reported on the authority of Jaʿfar al-Ṣādiq that his

194 Muslim.

father said: 'On the Day of Resurrection a caller will cry out, "Hearken! Let him stand whose name is Muḥammad and enter Paradise on account of the nobility of the Prophet's name in the sight of Allah!"'[195]

People are wont to use lineages or regional proximity or mutual acquaintances or commonality of age as means of seeking favour. It is related that al-Faḍl b. Yaḥyā was visited by a man who said to him, 'I have come to you with means of approach.' Al-Faḍl asked, 'And what might these means be?' The man replied, 'We share the same name, the same region and the same age.' Al-Faḍl said to him, 'As for region, all people share in it; as for name, many have the same name; and as for age, how do you know my age? How old are you?' The man replied, 'Thirty-five'—which was the same age as al-Faḍl. 'Who told you that we are the same age?' al-Faḍl asked him. The man replied, 'My mother.' Al-Faḍl said, 'Then what prevented you from drawing near to me with these means before today?' The man replied, 'I am now in dire need of you giving me one hundred dinars.' Al-Faḍl then gave the man thirty-five hundred dinars.

Ibn Bashkuwāl quoted a *ḥadīth* that says 'Whoever makes an intention that if he has a child he will name it Muḥammad, he will have naught but a male child.' *Ḥadīth* reports of this kind, though they may be weak, should not be neglected. Consider the *ḥadīth* of the man suffering from leprosy, who complained to the Prophet (Allah bless him and give him peace) and to whom the Prophet said, 'Does not the statement "The Emissary of Allah said" suffice you?'—and others like it, especially in matters that pertain to virtuous actions. Allah Most High knows best.

إِنْ لَمْ يَكُنْ فِي مَعَادِي آخِذًا بِيَدِي فَضْلًا وَإِلَّا فَقُلْ يَا زَلَّةَ الْقَدَمِ

If, in the Hereafter, he does not take me by the hand
From pure grace, what a terrible slip of the foot!'

Here the author (Allah have mercy upon him) addresses the Prophet (Allah bless him and give him peace) and seeks his affection, saying: If you do not take me by the hand at that stage, and if you do not intercede

195 There are many *ḥadīths* narrated about the Prophet's intercession for anybody named Muḥammad; Shaykh ʿAbd Allāh al-Talīdī notes that the majority of these are fabricated and some are weak.

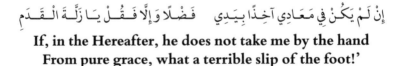

for me in that place of standing with your eminent rank—out of pure largesse and in upholding the protective covenant mentioned earlier, not because I merit or deserve it—then alas, what an evil condition I shall be in, and what abject loss my soul shall suffer!

This 'taking by the hand' is a metaphor for deliverance from intensities and receiving help and assistance; likewise, 'a horrible slip' is a metaphor for destruction, ruin, and suffering intensities and difficulties. For someone who suffers an intensity or difficulty is like a person who slips from a high place or fall into an abyss. The author ascribes the slip to the foot because it is by means of the feet that a person can stand firm; so if person's feet are secure he will be safe, and if he slips he will fall. We ask Allah for protection from slips in statements and actions. Amen!

حَاشَاهُ أَنْ يَحْرِمَ الرَّاجِي مَكَارِمَهُ أَوْ يَرْجِعَ الْجَارُ مِنْهُ غَيْرَ مُحْتَرَمِ

Far be it for him to deprive one hopeful of his generous gifts,
Or for a neighbour to turn back without being honoured by him!

Here the author (Allah have mercy upon him) says: The Prophet, I declare, in whom all the virtues are combined, is completely exalted, and his ennobled rank is far too great for him to deprive one who hopes in him or to refuse and leave empty-handed one who eagerly seeks his noble gifts. How deserving is the one who seeks a means of approach through him, and who holds fast to him, keeps him close company and relies upon his rank and providential care to have his pact honoured, his prayers answered, his means of approach accepted and his desires fulfilled; and to gain his Prophet's intercession, immense concern, and noble company!

By *one hopeful* the author means all who are hopeful, or himself. In other words [it is as if he were saying]: I declare the Prophet (Allah bless him and give him peace) far too exalted to forsake me and not intercede for me after I have praised him, sought refuge with him and depended upon him for deliverance, besides which I have the same name as his; and I declare him far too exalted to turn away anyone from his nation who clings to his presence and enters his protection, and to not show immense concern and care for him and intercede for him! That could not be, and would not befit with the exalted station of Prophethood.

In some copies of the *Burda* the word *intercession* occurs in place of *honoured*. The Prophet's general and specific intercessions have already been discussed. May Allah bless us to enter the Prophet's protective sanctuary and intimate company, as his greatness and rank merit. Amen!

وَمُنْذُ أَلْزَمْتُ أَفْكَارِي مَدَائِحَهُ   وَجَدْتُهُ لِخَلَاصِي خَيْرَ مُلْتَزِمِ

Ever since I have focused my thoughts on his praises,
I have found him the one most committed to my salvation.

Here the author (Allah have mercy upon him) says: Ever since I have focused my thoughts upon, and devoted myself to praising the Emissary of Allah (Allah bless him and give him peace), there is nothing of the affairs of this world or the Hereafter that I ask for, taking him as my means of approach, without it being fulfilled. Never have I sought intercession through him during times of difficulty and tribulation—whether in relation to this world or the Hereafter—without finding him the best assurance of my deliverance therefrom, the best one to seek and the best whose succour is sought for.

This is not exclusive to the author. Anyone afflicted with a concern who seeks the Prophet's protective care will find him the best whose succour is sought, and will find that relief comes to them swiftly.

If you ask 'It is clear that he could be delivered from tribulations and the like in this life as a result of him seeking a means of approach through the Prophet (Allah bless him and give him peace). The Hereafter, however, is unseen; so how can he say this with certainty?' the response is that it is according to his good opinion and hope in the Prophet (Allah bless him and give him peace). Just as the Prophet (Allah bless him and give him peace) rescued him in this life, he hopes that he will also rescue him in the Hereafter, especially since the author was one of those who have served the Prophet (Allah bless him and give him peace) and is linked to him because of his praise of him and preoccupation with his right. There is no doubt that anyone who is among the servants of the Prophet (Allah bless him and give him peace) and counted among his slaves must be revered and honoured for his sake, and that causing them harm or wronging them must be avoided. To make this clear to you, consider a servant who is known to be close to a sultan and enjoy his high esteem;

the intimate care he receives is not hidden, so he should not be opposed or treated with anything but the highest regard. ʿAlī b. al-Muwaffaq performed several pilgrimages [to Mecca] for the Prophet (Allah bless him and give him peace) [i.e. donating their reward to him], and saw him in a dream. The Prophet (Allah bless him and give him peace) said to him, 'Here is my hand of support for you, and I shall suffice you with it on the Day of Resurrection. I shall take you by the hand on the concourse of judgement and enter you into Paradise while the rest of humanity are undergoing the rigours of divine reckoning!'

Someone who occupies himself with praising the Prophet (Allah bless him and give him peace) has taken a hand of support from the Prophet by which he shall be sufficed, because the Prophet is the noblest of people in this world and in the Hereafter, as the author said in the second line. Indeed, this is what motivated us to pen this commentary despite the paucity of our knowledge and our dearth of learning. Perhaps we may be joined among the ranks of the Prophet's servants, for honourable people might allow in one who intrudes upon them; and whoever loves a group of people will be resurrected with them. And Allah is Possessor of Great Bounty!

وَلَنْ يَفُوتَ الْغِنَىٰ مِنْهُ يَدًا تَرِبَتْ   إِنَّ الْحَيَا يُنْبِتُ الْأَزْهَارَ فِي الْأَكَمِ

His wealth will not overlook a dusty, needy hand;
For showers cause flowers to bloom on hill-tops.

Here the author (Allah have mercy upon him) says that thanks to the Prophet's natural generosity and virtuous character towards the one who turns to him and seeks refuge with his largesse, wealth will not pass him up nor will he suffer want or poverty in this world or the Next. As for his wealth in this world, it is wealth of the heart, even though he might be lacking materially. True wealth does not consist of abundance of material objects: true wealth is inner wealth, which is the 'goodly life'. As for his wealth in the Next Life, it consists in his enjoying the protective sanctuary of the one to whom all of creation shall turn to seek refuge, in whose hand is the Standard of Praise (*Liwāʾ al-Ḥamd*), and whose nobility and pre-eminence shall manifest.

After expressing these sentiments the author coins a simile for the Prophet's generosity and says that showers bring flowers upon hillocks.

In other words, one should not deny this or deem it farfetched, for it is possible for rains to bring flowers to heights that do not typically have flowers even if those heights do not soak up water and even if [flowers] grow mainly on lowlands. The Prophet's generosity may be likened to a vast and far-reaching rain shower that brings growth to areas that do not typically produce greenery, and bring goodness everywhere. Likewise with the Prophet (Allah bless him and give him peace), his blessings and goodness extend to all, making the materially poor rich of heart and content, and enriching those who are dead and poor as regards good deeds through his intercession and blessings. This is because of the Prophet's kindness and mercy for his entire nation, especially those who put themselves at his service and those who love him. May Allah, out of His largesse and generosity, grant us a goodly portion of that by the Prophet's rank and lofty measure. Amen!

وَلَمْ أُرِدْ زَهْرَةَ الدُّنْيَا الَّتِي اقْتَطَفَتْ   يَدَا زُهَيْرٍ بِمَا أَثْنَىٰ عَلَىٰ هَرِمِ

I sought not the flowers of this world
Which Zuhayr picked for his praise of Harim.

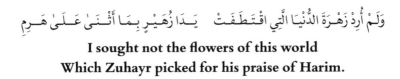

The word 'wealth' (ghina) [in the previous couplet], when used without qualification, refers to the trappings of this world and an abundance of money; likewise, the word 'poverty' refers to scarcity and want. The author (Allah have mercy upon him) was afraid that his interlocutor might misunderstand his intent and think that he wishes to praise the Prophet (Allah bless him and give him peace) in order to acquire worldly wealth, so he disabuses him of this notion by saying: 'I have not sought in my praise for the Emissary of Allah (Allah bless him and give him peace) the acquisition of the adornments of this world or its ephemeral trappings, in which case I would have been like Zuhayr the panegyrist of Harim b. Sinān.' Zuhayr's praise was for the sake of worldly adornments and gifts, of which he received from the object of his praise, Harim, far beyond his expectations; yet all of it faded away and disappeared, as is the nature of worldly trappings, which are quick to wilt and waste away. It is narrated that the daughter of Zuhayr went to see ʿUmar b. al-Khaṭṭāb, who asked her, 'What did Harim b. Sinān give to your father when he praised him in extreme terms?' She replied, 'He gave him goods and wares that wilted away under the vicissitudes of time.' ʿUmar said, 'But, that which your father gave will not be wilted by the vicissitudes of time!' So the author does not intend by his praise what Zuhayr intended by his. Instead, he desires to gain nobility and intercession in the Hereafter so he may become wealthy after being poor in good deeds.

CHAPTER 10

Intimate Discourse and the Petition of Needs

يَا أَكْرَمَ الْخَلْقِ مَالِي مَنْ أَلُوذُ بِهِ   سِوَاكَ عِنْدَ حُلُولِ الْحَادِثِ الْعَمِمِ

O Noblest of Creation, whose protection can I seek
But yours, when the Universal Event comes to pass?

HERE THE AUTHOR (Allah have mercy upon him) is addressing the Emissary of Allah (Allah bless him and give him peace), seeking his affection and bringing to mind his presence while calling out using his title of nobility. The relationship and connection between this couplet and the one before it is clear since, as was explained, the author did not seek worldly gain from his panegyric; what he sought was reward in the Hereafter. He mentions Zuhayr and Harim to convey that every panegyric poet will obtain a reward, but the reward of the one who praises people of the material world will only be ephemeral and passing—as the daughter of Zuhayr said to ʿUmar—whereas the panegyrist who has received divine providence in this world and the Next will obtain a reward that will never vanish or pass; its blessings will permeate this life and the Next.

Then, after explicitly mentioning the Prophet's nobility as his means of approach, the author demonstrates the proficiency of his opening and calls out to the Prophet (Allah bless him and give him peace), presenting his need. The import of this couplet is that the author will most certainly obtain a reward, since earlier he spoke of how he attained rewards for praising those of lesser status. How, then, could he not be rewarded for praising the one of superior status, who is truly characterised by generosity and nobility, especially after expressing his utter devotion to him and looking to naught besides him?

The apparent meaning of generosity here is the Prophet's rank and station in the sight of Allah, for the Prophet (Allah bless him and give him peace) is the noblest of creation in the sight of Allah, and the most beloved of them to Allah. It is also plausible that generosity here is referring to the Prophet's largesse and munificence, because, as we have shown in detail elsewhere, the Prophet (Allah bless him and give him peace) was the most generous and benevolent of people. The proof that the Prophet (Allah bless him and give him peace) is the noblest of creation is the *ḥadīth* of Anas (Allah be pleased with him) who reported, 'The Emissary of Allah said: "I am the first person to come out [of the grave] when mankind is quickened; I am their speaker (*Khaṭīb*) when they all fall silent; I am their leader when they assemble in delegations; I am the one to bring them glad tidings when they despair; and I shall be their Intercessor when they are taken to reckoning. On that day, the Standard of Generosity will be in my hand, [and on that day, the keys to Paradise will be in my hand.] I am the noblest of the children of Ādam in the sight of his Lord Most Exalted, and that is no boast. [I move among one thousand servants that appear as if they are hidden pearls.]"'[196] And the Prophet (Allah bless him and give him peace) also said, 'I am the Master of the children of Ādam on the Day of Resurrection, the first person whose grave will be split open, the first intercessor and the first whose intercession shall be accepted; and that is no boast.'[197] There are several *ḥadīth* reports of this nature which prove the Prophet's supremacy in this life and the Hereafter. The mention of the Hereafter in particular within these *ḥadīth* reports is an indication that the Prophet (Allah bless him and give him peace) alone will have leadership on that Day, and that even the great Prophets and Emissaries will find none but him to intercede. On that Day, the Prophet's sovereign rank over all of humanity will be manifest.

وَلَنْ يَضِيقَ رَسُولَ اللَّهِ جَاهُكَ بِي إِذَا الْكَرِيمُ تَجَلَّىٰ بِاسْمِ مُنْتَقِمِ

O Emissary of Allah, your rank will not be diminished
By me when the Generous One appears, named as the Avenger.

196 Tirmidhī, *Sunan*.
197 Bukhārī.

Here the author (Allah have mercy upon him) says: The rank of the Emissary (Allah bless him and give him peace) is immense, his station is exalted, his intercession is accepted, and his honour in Allah's sight is well-known. So the greatness of your rank will not be diminished by the likes of me, for your intercession encompasses the throngs of humanity, and your rank is not lessened by the vast number of petitioners. When the All-Compelling (al-Jabbār) becomes wrathful and takes on the qualities of rigour and majesty and vengeance against those who had disobeyed Him and contravened His commands, it is then that your rank will manifest, and it is then that your solicitude will be clear for all of creation to see. Silenced are those who had made [false] claims, and manifest are the unique positions of the sincere ones!

The author has penned this couplet to show the perfection he is seeking. He is not seeking [the Prophet's] rank when mercy in particular is made manifest (since that encompasses all of creation), rather he is seeking his solicitude when that of all other claimants is cut off, when the Creator, Exalted is He, takes on the divine name 'the Avenger' (al-Muntaqim). Indeed, Allah is Almighty and the 'Possessor of Vengeance' (Dhū al-Intiqām); and the time He shall manifest with this name will be the most tremendous time of the Day of Judgment, in which He will be angry as never before. 'The Avenger' is one of Allah's names and means Him who punishes whomever He wills. 'The Generous' is also one of Allah's names and means 'the Magnanimous', in which case it is one of the attributes of divine action. It is also said that 'the Generous' means He who is manifest in His Essence and Lofty in His attributes. It is also said that:

> Al-Karīm is the One who pardons when He decrees and protects when He binds. When He gives to someone, He increases him beyond hopes and does not care how much He gives and to whom He gives. If anyone besides Him is petitioned for a need He will not be pleased, and if someone offends Him He will lightly rebuke him and not take it to the utmost limit. He does not fail the one who seeks refuge and protection in Him, and He suffices [one] from all intermediaries and intercessors. He who combines all these [qualities] in himself, without affectation, is considered generous in the absolute sense.[198]

198 Abū Ḥāmid al-Ghazālī, *al-Maqṣad al-asnā*.

Now, these qualities will not find their complete expression except in a perfected soul with lofty qualities. The Shaykh [al-Būṣīrī] mentions this name in order to strengthen hope; no one will despair of the Generous One's pardon when He exacts vengeance. Allah Most High knows best.

فَإِنَّ مِنْ جُودِكَ الدُّنْيَا وَضَرَّتَهَا وَمِنْ عُلُومِكَ عِلْمَ اللَّوْحِ وَالْقَلَمِ

For this world and its companion, the Next, come from your bounty,
And part of what you know is knowledge of the Tablet and Pen.

Here the author (Allah have mercy upon him) explains his reasoning for having mentioned the Prophet's expansive and undiminishing rank in the previous couplets. In essence he says: 'How can I not be included in your rank when the cosmos is but from your bounty, since both this world and the Hereafter were only created for your sake?' The author included this world and the Next as being from the Prophet's bounty because they were both created because of him and for his sake, and therefore it is as if he had bestowed them out of his munificence.

It is also possible that the verbal noun [bounty] is linked to an object-noun, in which case it means: 'For among the things bestowed upon you are this world and the Hereafter.' There is no doubt that Allah bestowed upon the Prophet (Allah bless him and give him peace) this life and the Hereafter. As for this life, Allah permitted for him the spoils of war (which He had not permitted anyone else before him); He granted him victory through dread at a month's distance; He made the earth a place of prostration [prayer] and purification for him; the mountains of Tihāma also offered to turn themselves into gold and silver for him; and more. As for the Hereafter, the Prophet (Allah bless him and give him peace) shall receive the Praiseworthy Station, and shall have the unfurled Banner, the quenching Pool, Exalted Rank, and words that are listened to.

The author's statement, *And part of what you know is knowledge of the Tablet and Pen* is a form of hyperbole [*mubālagha*]. There is no doubt that Allah taught the Prophet (Allah bless him and give him peace) knowledge of the past and future peoples and past and future events, and disclosed to him the conditions of the Intermediate Realm (*al-Barzakh*) and the Day of Resurrection. So because the Prophet (Allah bless him and give him peace) had all-embracing knowledge of the past and the future, the author says that it is as if the Tablet and the Pen derive their knowledge from him. Allah Most High knows best. (The Tablet and Pen are real and not figurative, but their modality is not known to any but Allah Most High.)

يَا نَفْسِ لَا تَقْنَطِي مِنْ زَلَّةٍ عَظُمَتْ　　إِنَّ الْكَبَائِرَ فِي الْغُفْرَانِ كَاللَّمَمِ

O soul, despair not over a fault that is immense;
Enormities, with divine forgiveness, are like minor errors.

Here the author (Allah have mercy upon him) addresses his own soul, seeking to solace it and make things easy for it: O soul, do not despair over major sins and slips, for enormities, with divine forgiveness, are like minor sins, as mercy encompasses them and envelopes them. Allah Most High says, 'Say, "O My servants who have transgressed against yourselves, despair not of Allah's mercy. Verily Allah forgives all sins entirely."' (Qur'an 39:53)

One of the poets has said:

Though my sins, Lord, be enormous and immense
I know for certain that Your pardon is greater!

And another poet said:

When my heart grew hard and my ways became narrow
I made my hope in Your pardon a ladder.
My sin appeared immense, but when I compared it
To Your pardon, O Lord, Your pardon was more so!

We read in the *Ḥikam*, 'There is no minor sin when His divine justice confronts you, and there is no enormity when His grace meets you.' And Yaḥyā b. Muʿādh (Allah be pleased with him) said, 'When He confers His grace upon them no sin of theirs remains; and when He executes His justice no good deed of theirs remains.' O Allah, make our sins the sins of those whom You love, and do not make our good deeds the good deeds of those with whom You are angered!

لَعَلَّ رَحْمَةَ رَبِّي حِينَ يَقْسِمُهَا　　تَأْتِي عَلَىٰ حَسَبِ الْعِصْيَانِ فِي الْقِسَمِ

Perchance my Lord's mercy, when He apportions it,
Will be distributed in accordance with the measure of sins.

After consoling himself in the previous couplet by stating that enormities are like minor sins when it comes to divine forgiveness, the author (Allah have mercy upon him) then expresses his hope in attaining it and says, in essence: 'Perhaps the mercy of my Lord, being the hundred forms of mercy that He shall send to His servants on the Day of Resurrection—will be distributed in accordance to the measure of disobedience and sins, and sinners will obtain it in equal measure to their misdeeds so that those with the most sins will receive the most mercy.'

According to a rigorously authenticated *ḥadīth*, 'Verily Allah (Exalted and Sublime is He!) possesses a hundred mercies. He has kept ninety-nine portions of mercy with Himself and released one portion in this world. Because of this one portion of mercy, creation shows mercy to one another, to the extent that a horse will lift up its hoof from its foal for fear of harming it. On the Day of Resurrection, Allah will combine the single portion of mercy [in the world] with the remaining ninety-nine and distribute them amongst creation. Had the disbeliever known the mercy that is with Allah he would never have despaired of entering Paradise, and had the believer knows the punishment that is with Allah, he would never have felt secure from Hellfire.'[199]

The author alludes to this mercy when he says *Perchance my Lord's mercy...* The intended meaning of *mercy* here is its genus (*jins*), so it applies to the one hundred portions of mercy that Allah will distribute to His creation. The author believes that he has many sins, but perchance he may obtain divine mercies in multitude. This is humility on the author's part, for 'the good deeds of the pious are the sins of those brought near.' No attention should be given to anyone who argues that mercy, if distributed in accordance with the measure of sins, will result in loss for the Godfearing. The Godfearing will attain levels and degrees in Paradise that the disobedient will never reach, because the disobedient will be in need of two forms of mercy, the mercy of deliverance and the mercy of divine bounty, whereas the Godfearing will need only the mercy of divine bounty. Allah Most High knows best.

199 Bukhārī.

يَا رَبِّ وَاجْعَلْ رَجَائِي غَيْرَ مُنْعَكِسٍ   لَدَيْكَ وَاجْعَلْ حِسَابِي غَيْرَ مُنْخَرِمِ

O my Lord, let not my hope in You be overturned
And do not make my account devoid of value.

Here the author (Allah have mercy upon him) says: *O my Lord, let not my hope in You be overturned* so that You grant me whatever I crave [in this life] and cause me to despair of attaining my hopes [in the Hereafter]. How could that ever be when You have said, 'I am as My servant thinks of Me'?[200] Far be it, then, from Your Generosity and largesse to dash the hopes of those who hope [in You], or to drive away petitioners.

The author also says: O Lord, *And do not make my account devoid of value* by severing my proof, exposing my feebleness, and laying bare my iniquities. Though the rights of my opponents weigh heavily upon me, You are able to make them pleased with me by giving them from Your divine graces. In the *Ṣaḥīḥ* [of al-Bukhārī] it is recorded that the Emissary of Allah (Allah bless him and give him peace) said: 'Whoever has wronged his brother, let him make amends now, for in the Hereafter there shall be neither dirhams nor dinars. [Let him seek his forgiveness] before some of his good deeds are taken away and given to his brother, and if he has no good deeds the sins of his brother are taken and cast upon him, and thus he is cast into the Hellfire.' Also according to the *Ṣaḥīḥ* [of al-Bukhārī], the Emissary of Allah (Allah bless him and give him peace) said in the presence of his Companions, 'Do you know who is the bankrupt person (*muflis*)?' They replied, 'The bankrupt person is one who has neither dirham (money) nor wares.' The Prophet said, 'The bankrupt person is the one who will arrive on the Day of Resurrection with copious good deeds, but who arrives on that Day having struck this person, shed the blood of that person and pilfered the wealth of this person—and so this one and that one [of his victims] will take from his good deeds until, when his good deeds are used up, he is made to take from their sins and as a result is cast into the Hellfire.'[201]

It is on the basis of this meaning found here that the author pleads compassionately for his own self and essentially says: 'O My Lord, let

200 Bukhārī.
201 Muslim.

not my hope in You be overturned, and let not my heart by filled with sins and misdeeds that invalidate my proof at the Reckoning!'

A NOTE OF BENEFIT

If someone is burdened with owing many rights to others, he should say the following supplication frequently (it is said that this supplication came down from the heavens to a man): 'O Allah, I seek Your forgiveness and repent unto You of the many wrongs I have committed against Your servants. For any of Your servants whom I have wronged, whether in his body or his wealth or his honour, which I am unable to redress, make him pleased with me by any means You will, however You will and whenever You will, and grant it to me, O Lord. What have You to do with punishing me when Your mercy has encompassed everything? Nothing remains but for You to honour me with Your mercy. Do not abase me with Your punishment. Lord, it does not diminish You in the least if You treat me as I have asked; and You are the Creator of all things!'

وَالْطُفْ بِعَبْدِكَ فِي الدَّارَيْنِ إِنَّ لَهُ   صَبْرًا مَتَى تَدْعُهُ الأَهْوَالُ يَنْهَزِمِ

Be gentle with Your servant in this life and the Next;
For his patience flees when he is visited by terrors.

Here the author (Allah have mercy upon him) asks Allah to be gentle with him in the worldly abode, beseeching Him to act benevolently and protect him from its pitfalls, tribulations and trials. And he asks Allah to be gentle with him in the Next World and grant him safety in its inescapable terrors that descend upon [His] servants, such as the interrogation by the two angels [Munkar and Nakīr], the reckoning, the Scales, the crossing of the Traverse (Ṣirāṭ), standing in wait for the presentation [of one's deeds], and so on. In order to face these terrors, the servant needs an increase in divine benevolence and kindness. The apparent meaning [of these lines] would seemingly require the author to say 'Be gentle with me', but here he has imbedded the apparent meaning within a pronoun ['Your servant'] for the sake of humbling and lowering himself so that it may serve as a means of having his prayer answered.

Then he goes on to explain his condition and says that he has no patience, and that if a calamity or difficulty were to befall him he would be terrified, and that if worldly terror or harm were to strike him he would be unable to stand firm; and likewise if he sees the dreadful terrors of the Day of Resurrection he will be unable to face them, since he is lacking in patience. He is comparable to a coward who, on seeing warriors engaged in combat, turns on his heels and runs away, and when called upon to engage in individual combat, turns around and reverses course. Patience is extremely difficult for man, and that is why it is a branch of faith. It is narrated that one half of faith is patience and the other half is gratitude. Because of its extreme difficulty for man, patience brings abundant and limitless reward. The Most High says, '*Certainly the patient shall be given their reward without measure!*' (Qur'an 39:10) May Allah, out of His generosity and largesse, grant us a goodly portion of it. Amen!

وَأْذَنْ لِسُحْبِ صَلَاةٍ مِنْكَ دَائِمَةٍ   عَلَى النَّبِيِّ بِمُنْهَلٍّ وَمُنْسَجِمِ

And may clouds of Your blessings rain down constantly
Upon the Prophet, pouring down in abundance.

Here the Shaykh (Allah be pleased with him) asks Allah Most High to bestow constant blessings upon the Prophet (Allah bless him and give him peace) just as heavy rainclouds hover and pour forth rain. The intent behind seeking Allah's leave is to ask for increase in [His] mercy upon His Prophet (Allah bless him and give him peace) and incessant and unique blessings upon him. It is also possible that the author is seeking leave for himself, as if saying: 'O Allah, grant me leave to invoke continual blessings upon the Prophet (Allah bless him and give him peace), and enable me to invoke blessings at all times, so that I fill all of my moments, as much as possible, with blessings upon him!' The first meaning is better: in other words, he asks Allah to send perpetual blessings upon the Prophet (Allah bless him and give him peace) that pour down upon him as clouds pour down rain. In this couplet the author uses the word *clouds* as a metaphor for prayers and then he links the word *clouds* to *blessings*, as you would say 'I saw the moon of your face.' Then, after using the word *clouds* for *blessings*, he adds to it *pouring down in abundance*.

مَا رَنَّحَتْ عَذَبَاتِ الْبَانِ رِيحُ صَبَا   وَأَطْرَبَ الْعِيسَ حَادِي الْعِيسِ بِالنَّغَمِ

For as long as the east wind stirs the branches of willows,
And camel-drivers bring joy to their camels with melody.

This couplet is a completion of the one before it. After asking his Lord to send abundant blessings upon the Prophet (Allah bless him and give him peace), the author (Allah have mercy upon him) then asks Him to make them abiding for as long as the east wind stirs willow branches, and as long as a camel-driver brings joy to camels with melodies. His intention here is that those blessings upon the Prophet (Allah bless him and give him peace) be continual and never-ending, everlasting and abundant. For the blowing winds will not cease until the world ends, and likewise the singing of the camel-driver. So it is as if the author were asking for blessings to be conveyed to the Prophet (Allah bless him and give him peace) for as long as the world abides. As for the Hereafter, it is a realm not of deeds, but of recompense. The reason why the author chose these two things [breezes and the singing of cameleteers] is that they are subtle and gentle. It is also an indication that praising the Prophet (Allah bless him and give him peace) with beautiful melodies increases the listener in yearning and energy, and evokes love and joy.

What the author says about the singing of camel-drivers and the camels' response to melodies is well-known among the Arabs. A reliable person once narrated that he saw tears of blood flowing from the eyes of some camels as they listened to the songs of a camel-driver urging them on. Singing to camels energises them, makes them light-footed, and allows them to travel great distances at a quickened pace. When sung to, camels can cross vast swathes of territory in a short amount of time. This is well-known and knowledge of it is widespread. If a camel-driver has a beautiful voice it is possible that the camels he spurs on will push themselves beyond their physical capacities and perish, or nearly perish, on the way before arriving at their destination. Someone once told a story of how he was a guest with a Bedouin Arab with whom he was acquainted. He said that when he entered the Bedouin's home he called for some food and the two of them ate and talked together. Shortly afterwards, the host had to leave the house to attend to a sudden need. He sought his guest's pardon and asked him to stay until he returned. The Bedouin then went to attend to his need, leaving his guest alone in the house. A voice in the interior of the house called out to the guest, and he could hear it but not see who it was. It said, 'O servant of Allah, intercede for me with my master and you shall be rewarded!' The guest replied, 'Who are you and what have you done wrong?' The voice replied, 'I am my master's servant; he became angry with me and has locked me up inside this house!' When the servant's master finally returned, the guest said to him, 'I adjure you by Allah that you fulfil my need and accept my intercession for this servant and object of anger, and release him from bondage!' The host said, 'Sir, his crime is severe and your intercession will not suffice.' The guest asked, 'What is his crime?' The host replied, 'He killed over twenty of my camels, even after being warned and forbidden to time and time again.' The guest felt that such crimes were indeed severe. He asked, 'How did he kill them?' The host replied, 'He has a beautiful voice and a sweet and pleasant melody; he used to urge the camels on with song. The camels were fastened with heavy chains, and no sooner had they covered a day's journey than they would die. Some of them even perished before covering a day's journey!' The guest said, 'I was astonished to hear this and did not consider it possible, so I asked the servant to let me hear his voice. The master loosened his chains and, accepting my intercession for him, he released him from bondage. He then instructed him to let me hear his voice. He began to sing:

When I set out to visit Saᶜdā in her homeland
I saw the ground fold up and its distant parts come near.
She who sat upon it longed for goodness
When our conversation was to be repeated.

'My ears never heard a voice more beautiful or a melody sweeter than his, and I never heard anything that so affected the soul!'

The author concludes his ode with a prayer invoking blessings upon the Emissary of Allah (Allah bless him and give him peace), in hope of it and the supplications it contains being accepted. It is reported that supplications are veiled, and that Allah does not answer them until one invokes blessings upon the Prophet (Allah bless him and give him peace). It is related that Ibn Masᶜūd (Allah be pleased with him) said, 'When any one of you wishes to ask Allah Most High, let him start by praising and lauding Him as He deserves, then let him pray for blessings upon the Prophet (Allah bless him and give him peace); and then ask, for it is more likely to succeed."[202]

202 Daylamī, *Musnad al-Firdaws*.

Ibn ᶜAṭāʾ said, 'Supplication has pillars, means, wings and times. With the pillars it is strengthened; with the wings it takes flight; and by the means it succeeds. Its pillars are presence of heart, mildness and tranquillity, the heart's connection to Allah and the heart's non-attachment to material causes. Its wings are sincerity, its times are late at night before dawn, and its means are blessings invoked upon the Prophet (Allah bless him and give him peace).'

It is stated in a *ḥadīth* (cited by al-Alyūrī) that 'A supplication said between two prayers upon the Prophet is never rejected.' Jābir reported that the Prophet (Allah bless him and give him peace) said, 'Do not make me like the water-skin of a rider. The rider fills his water-skin and seals it when done. If it contains water he will drink as much as he needs or perform ablution with it and then pour out the rest. Instead, put me [i.e. prayer for blessings upon me] at the beginning, middle and end of [your] supplication.'[203]

[ᶜAbdullāh] b. ᶜAmr narrated, 'I heard the Emissary of Allah say, "When you hear the muezzin make the call to prayer, repeat what he says and then pray for blessings upon me, for whosoever prays for blessings upon me [one time], Allah will send ten blessings upon him on account of it..."'[204]

Ibn Shāfiᶜ said:

> The Prophet's eminence is so vast that anyone who invokes blessings upon him receives this immense portion; for when would you otherwise receive Allah's blessings upon you? Had you spent your entire life performing every act of obedience, and had Allah then sent upon you a single blessing, that single blessing would outweigh all of the [acts of pious] obedience you performed throughout your entire life. The reason is that you pray for blessings [upon the Prophet (Allah bless him and give him peace)] according to your capacity, but Allah sends blessings upon him according to His Lordship. And that is speaking of a single blessing, so how will it be if Allah sends ten blessings upon you for every blessing that you invoke!

203 Narrated by Bazzār, Bayhaqī in *Shuᶜab al-īmān*, and Abū Nuᶜaym in *al-Ḥilya al-awliyāʾ*—but with a slightly different wording at the end: 'Instead, put me at the beginning and the middle of your supplication but do not put me at the end.'

204 Muslim.

The wording of the prayer that has been transmitted from the Prophet (Allah bless him and give him peace) in the rigorously authenticated reports is the following: 'O Allah, exalt Muḥammad and his wives and progeny, as You exalted Ibrāhīm; and bless Muḥammad and his wives and progeny, as You blessed the progeny of Ibrāhīm. Truly You are the All-Praiseworthy, the All-Glorious.'

This marks the completion of this blessed commentary upon the most auspicious ode. We ask Allah Most High to bring benefit through it just as He has brought benefit through the ode; and we ask Him to make it sincerely for His sake and to clothe it with the raiment of goodly acceptance. We ask Him to cause us to attain through it our greatest hope, for He Most Exalted is the Generous, and hopes that are placed in the Generous are never lost!

This work was completed in the late afternoon on Saturday, the sixth day of Shaʿbān in the year 1203 AH [2nd May 1789 CE] at the mausoleum of the famous saint and senior gnostic, Sīdī ʿAbd Allāh al-Fakhkhār, located below the trench of Tétouan, may Allah benefit us with his blessings and bless us with his fragrant breezes and resurrect us with the rest of the *Awliyāʾ* (saints) beneath the Standard of the Master of Emissaries and Leader of the God-fearing and Seal of the Prophets, our Master and Patron Muḥammad. May Allah bless him and give him peace, and ennoble him, honour, magnify and exalt him. Amen!

Bibliography

Ibn ʿAjība, Aḥmad. *al-ʿUmda fī Sharḥ al-Burda*. Beirut: Dār al-Kutub al-ʿIlmiyya, 1432/2011

Al-Talīdī, ʿAbdullāh. *Kashf al-kurba bi takhrīj al-ḥadīth sharḥ al-burda*. Tangiers: Maṭbaʿa Jarīda, 1430/2009.

Ibn ʿAjība, Aḥmad. *al-Fahrasa*. Cairo: Dār al-Ghad al-ʿArabī, 1411/1990.

Ibn ʿAjība, Aḥmad. *al-Baḥr al-madīd fī tafsīr al-Qurʾān al-Majīd*. Beirut: Dār al-Kutub al-ʿIlmiyya, 1431/2010.

Yusuf, Hamza. *The Burda of al-Busiri: The Poem of the Cloak* (London: Sandala Ltd., 2002)